THE STRATFORD-UPON-AVON LIBRARY 5

★

General Editors
JOHN RUSSELL BROWN
& BERNARD HARRIS

FOR L. J. LUDOVICI

κρεῖττον ἕνα φίλον ἔχειν πολλοῦ ἄξιον
ἢ πολλοὺς μηδενὸς ἀξίους

BENJAMIN WHICHCOTE

by Mary Beale (1682)

The Gallery, Emmanuel College, Cambridge; reproduced by permission of the Master and Fellows.

THE STRATFORD-UPON-AVON LIBRARY 5

★

THE CAMBRIDGE PLATONISTS

edited by
C. A. PATRIDES

Harvard University Press
Cambridge, Massachusetts
1970

© C. A. PATRIDES 1969

First published 1969
by Edward Arnold (Publishers) Ltd
41 Maddox Street, London W.1

SBN 674-09125-6

*Printed in Great Britain by
Butler & Tanner Ltd, Frome and London*

General Preface

THE Stratford Library has been formed for the student, teacher and general reader who is interested in Elizabethan and Jacobean life and literature. Further editions of Shakespeare's Works, or *The Faerie Queene*, or Jonson's Works will not be provided, nor will the Library duplicate readily available editions of any poet or dramatist. The editors hope to reprint what is generally unavailable outside the great libraries and microfilm and photostat collections, or available only in expensive and rare complete editions.

The first four publications in the Stratford Library are as follows: a selected works of Nashe (providing more than half his total writings and including four works in their entirety, *Pierce Penniless, Summer's Last Will and Testament, The Terrors of the Night* and *The Unfortunate Traveller*); an anthology entitled *The Elizabethans' America* (reprinting letters, reports and pamphlets about the New World); a collection of *Elizabethan Narrative Verse* (offering twelve examples in this kind from the anonymous 'Fable of Ovid treting of Narcissus' to Giles Fletcher's 'Christs Victorie and Triumph'); and a selected non-dramatic works of Dekker (including the first full version of *Lantern and Candlelight* and *Pound Wise and Penny Foolish*).

In preparation are volumes devoted to Sir Thomas Wilson's *Art of Rhetoric* with generous selections from Fraunce's *Arcadian Rhetoric* and other works, and to material illustrating Elizabethan and Jacobean concern with witchcraft and demonology.

It is the general policy of the series to present its texts in modernised form. Editors have been asked to reparagraph, repunctuate, substitute italic type for roman, or *vice versa*, wherever they consider that such changes will avoid unnecessary confusions or obscurities. However, this volume on the Cambridge Platonists retains the spelling, and the numerous Greek and Latin quotations (including some Hebrew phrases), for two important reasons. As a number of the reprinted texts were first published in the mid-seventeenth century, and the rest after the Restoration, the spelling and punctuation do not present the difficulties which a reader encounters with earlier-printed texts; had any changes been made they would have been limited and therefore pointless. The lengthy quotations from Greek and Latin were retained because they demonstrate, by their very presence on the page and the pattern they create, the nature of the mode of thinking which the Cambridge Platonists endeavoured to resuscitate.

Editors have provided annotations, a glossary or an index, whichever seems appropriate, and also textual notes, collating substantive changes to the copy-text and briefly discussing its special authority. Each volume has an introduction dealing with any topic that will enhance the reading of the texts. We have not aimed at minute consistency between each volume, or even between each item in a single volume; editors have been encouraged to present these texts in the clearest practicable manner and with due consideration of the fact that many of the works reprinted have hitherto been 'known about' rather than known, more honoured or dishonoured in scholarly works than read and enjoyed as substantial achievements and records of the late sixteenth and seventeenth centuries.

JOHN RUSSELL BROWN
BERNARD HARRIS

Contents

	page
Acknowledgements	viii
Abbreviations	xi
A Note on Method	xxv
Biographical Sketches	xxix
A Reading List	xxxi
'The High and Aiery Hills of Platonisme': An Introduction to the Cambridge Platonists	1
'The Use of Reason in Matters of Religion' BENJAMIN WHICHCOTE	42
'The Manifestation of Christ and the Deification of Man' BENJAMIN WHICHCOTE	62
'The Unity of the Church maintained by sincere Christians' BENJAMIN WHICHCOTE	77
'A Sermon preached before the House of Commons' RALPH CUDWORTH	90
'The True Way or Method of attaining to Divine Knowledge' JOHN SMITH	128
'The Excellency and Nobleness of True Religion' JOHN SMITH	145
'The Purification of a Christian Man's Soul' HENRY MORE	200
An Antidote against Atheism, Books I–II HENRY MORE	213
'The Digression concerning the Plastick Life of Nature, or an Artificial, Orderly and Methodical Nature' RALPH CUDWORTH	288
Appendix: Selections from Whichcote's *Moral and Religious Aphorisms*	326
Index	337

Acknowledgements

'He is not a *modest* man,' wrote Benjamin Whichcote, 'who thinks himself wise enough to find-out Truth by *Himself*: without submitting his Thoughts to *Examination* and Trial among *others*.' Not prepared to argue with Whichcote, I have sought and obtained the assistance of scholars on both sides of the Atlantic. I should like to express my gratitude to Professors William B. Hunter of the University of New Hampshire, Sears Jayne of Queens College of The City University of New York, and Ernest Tuveson of the University of California at Berkeley, for their indispensable suggestions on this edition in general and on my Introduction in particular; to Dr Dorothee Finkelstein of Yale University, Dr Jason P. Rosenblatt of the University of Pennsylvania, Dr Gordon Leff of the University of York, Dr Henry J. Blumenthal of the University of Liverpool, and my Greek friend Photios K. Litsas, for their assistance with the annotation of passages in Hebrew, medieval Latin, and Greek; to Mr C. B. L. Barr of the York Minster Library for shedding abundant light on several passages in Latin; and to Professors A. H. Armstrong of the University of Liverpool, Alvin B. Kernan of Yale University, W. K. Pritchett and Wayne Shumaker of the University of California at Berkeley, and R. C. Zaehner of All Souls College, Oxford, for various important recommendations. I am also grateful to Professor Marjorie H. Nicolson—herself a pioneer in our understanding of the Cambridge Platonists—who encouraged me to attempt this edition just as she has always lent me her indispensable support.

The frontispiece of Mary Beale's portrait of Whichcote is reproduced by permission of the Master and Fellows of Emmanuel College, Cambridge. I am particularly obliged to Dr F. H. Stubbings, the Librarian of Emmanuel, for providing me with details on Mary Beale (1632/3–1699), the reputable if prolific and variable painter whose best known work includes portraits of churchmen. Dr Stubbings also introduced me to Mr Richard Jeffree who is preparing with Miss Elizabeth Walsh a full-scale biography of Beale, scheduled for publication in the near future. Interested readers may in the meantime

Acknowledgements

consult the biographical details in Edward Croft-Murray and Paul Hulton, *Catalogue of British Drawings* (London, 1960), I, 198–9, with further references; and the accounts by Ida Procter in *Country Life* CXXVII (1960), 1242–3, with three plates; and especially by Elizabeth Walsh, 'Mrs Mary Beale, Paintress', *The Connoisseur*, CXXXI (1953), 3–8, with thirteen plates. Mr Jeffree informs me that Mary Beale was related by marriage to both Whichcote and Cudworth. An earlier version of the portrait reproduced here is available at Lambeth Palace.

Another portrait of Whichcote is in the Provost's Lodge, King's College, Cambridge. I am grateful to the Provost for arranging to have me inspect it and to Mr John Saltmarsh for providing the limited information available on it. The portrait is anonymous and its date of composition unknown.

The selections in this volume are reprinted from copies on deposit at the British Museum. I am grateful to the Trustees of the British Museum for permission to reprint, and to the staff of the Reading Room for assisting me in more ways than is possible to mention here.

Several works of reference have been extremely useful, notably the superb lexica of the Greek language by Henri Estienne, Θησαυρὸς τῆς ἑλληνικῆς γλώσσης, rev. ed. (Paris, 1831–65), 8 vols., and D. Demetrakos, Μέγα λεξικόν τῆς ἑλληνικῆς γλώσσης, ed. I. S. Zervos (Athens, 1936–50), 9 vols. I am also indebted to three past editors of the Cambridge Platonists: J. L. Mosheim, who annotated Cudworth's *True Intellectual System* in 1733; H. G. Williams, who edited Smith's *Discourses* in 1859; and F. I. Mackinnon, who edited More's *Philosophical Writings* in 1925. Finally, Professor Geoffrey Bullough's edition of More's poems (1931) has restored me to sanity more often than is perhaps wise to confess.

Gerald A. Cragg's edition of *The Cambridge Platonists* (New York: Oxford University Press, 1968) came to my attention when the present volume was already in the hands of the printer. Prefaced by a survey of the principal tenets of Cambridge Platonism, the edition provides readings in modernised spelling and arranged under distinct headings. Unlike Mr Cragg, I have not deleted classical quotations for the fundamental reason stated by the general editors (above, p. vi), and I have excluded Culverwell because he has not 'penetrated to the centre of Cambridge Platonism' (see below, p. xxvi). But I am gratified that Mr Cragg and I have independently contributed to the resuscitation of the Cambridge Platonists. It was indeed time that 'the school of Plato' in seventeenth-century England became known to a wider audience.

C. A. P.

Langwith College
University of York
16 November 1968

Abbreviations

I. *Primary Sources (A):* Works by the Cambridge Platonists and some related writers — xi
II. *Primary Sources (B):* The principal editions consulted in the preparation of the present edition — xiv
III. *Secondary Sources:* The principal commentaries on the Cambridge Platonists and related writers, with select editions of their works — xix

Sections I and III are also intended as a select bibliography of further readings in and about the Cambridge Platonists. For a more detailed bibliography see below, pp. xxxi–xxxii.

The place of publication is given only if it is other than London. Unless otherwise indicated the editions used are the first.

I.

PRIMARY SOURCES (A):

THE CAMBRIDGE PLATONISTS

Cudworth, *Freewill* — A Treatise of Freewill, ed. John Allen (1838).

Cudworth, *Imm. Morality* — A Treatise concerning Eternal and Immutable Morality (1731).

Cudworth, *Int. System* — The True Intellectual System of the Universe: the First Part; wherein, all the Reason and Philosophy of Atheism is Confuted; and its Impossibility Demonstrated (1678). [Also reproduced in facsimile (Stuttgart, 1964). Cf. JLM.]

Culverwell, *Discourse* — Nathanael Culverwell, An Elegant and Learned Discourse of the Light of Nature, ed. William Dillingham (1652). [Cf. Campagnac.]

More, *Antidote* — An Antidote against Atheisme, or an Appeal to the Natural Faculties of the Minde of Man, whether there be not a GOD (1653).

More, *Apology* — The Apology of Dr Henry More, appended to A Modest Enquiry into the Mystery of Iniquity (1664).

More, *Cabbala* — Conjectura Cabbalistica. Or, A Conjectural Essay of interpreting the Minde of Moses, according to

	a Threefold Cabbala: Viz. Literal, Philosophical, Mystical, or Divinely Moral (1653). Dedicated to Cudworth.
More, Dialogues	Divine Dialogues, containing sundry Disquisitions & Instructions concerning the Attributes of God and his Providence in the World (1688), 2 vols.
More, Discourses	Discourses on Several Texts of Scripture, ed. John Worthington (1692).
More, Ench. Eth.	Enchiridion ethicum, præcipua moralis philosophiæ rudimenta complectens (1666); tr. Edward Southwell, An Account of Virtue (1690). [Also reproduced in facsimile, with a Note by S. P. Lamprecht (New York, 1930).]
More, Ench. Met.	Enchiridion metaphysicum: sive, de rebus incorporeis succincta & luculenta dissertatio. Pars prima: de exsistentia & natura rerum incorporearum in genere (1671). [Ch. XXVII-XXVIII were translated in Joseph Glanvill's Saducismus Triumphatus (1681), pp. 99–179. Cf. FM.]
More, Enth. Tr.	Enthusiasmus Triumphatus, or, A Discourse of the Nature, Causes, Kinds, and Cure, of Enthusiasme (1656). Published under the pseudonym Philophilus Parresiastes. [Also reproduced in facsimile, with a Note by M. V. DePorte (Los Angeles, 1966).]
More, Godliness	An Explanation of the Grand Mystery of Godliness; or, A True and Faithfull Representation of the Everlasting Gospel of our Lord (1660).
More, 'Grounds of Faith'	'A Brief Discourse of the True Grounds of the Certainty of Faith in Points of Religion', in Dialogues (as above), II, 467–93.
More, Immortality	The Immortality of the Soul, so farre forth as it is demonstrable from the Knowledge of Nature, and the Light of Reason (1659).
More, Letters	Conway Letters: The Correspondence of Anne, Viscountess Conway, Henry More, and their Friends, 1642–1684, ed. Marjorie H. Nicolson (1930).
More, Poems	Philosophical Poems (Cambridge, 1647). Contains Psychozoia, Psychathanasia, Antipsychopannychia, Antimonopsychia (all initially published in 1642 as Ψυχωδία platonica), Demo-

Abbreviations

	critus platonissans (first published in 1646), *The Præexistency of the Soul;* etc. [Also edited by A. B. Grosart (1878; repr. 1967). Cf. Bullough.]
More, 'Preface'	'The Preface General' to *A Collection of Several Philosophical Writings*, 2nd rev. ed. (1662), pp. iv–xxvii.
More, *Reply*	*The Second Lash of Alazonomastix; conteining a solid and serious Reply to a very uncivill Answer to certain Observations* (Cambridge, 1651). Published under the pseudonym Alazonomastix Philalethes.
Norris	John Norris of Bremerton, *Christian Blessedness: or, Discourses upon the Beatitudes* (1690).
Smith, *Discourses*	*Select Discourses*, ed. John Worthington (1660), [Cf. HGW.]
Sterry, *Discourse*	Peter Sterry, *A Discourse of the Freedom of the Will* (1675).
Sterry, *Sermons*	Peter Sterry, *The Rise, Race, and Royalty of the Kingdom of God in the Soul of Man. Opened in several Sermons upon Matthew 18. 3. As also The Loveliness & Love of Christ set forth in several other Sermons upon Psal. 45. v. 1, 2* (1683).
Whichcote, *Aphorisms*	*Moral and Religious Aphorisms . . . published in MDCCIII, by Dr Jeffery. Now re-published, with very large additions, by Samuel Salter* (1753). [Also edited by W. R. Inge (1930).]
Whichcote, *Discourses*	*Several Discourses*, ed. John Jeffery (1701–1707), 4 vols.
Whichcote, *Dogmata*	Θεοφορούμενα Δόγματα: *or, Some Select Notions*, ed. 'Philantropus' (1685).
Whichcote, *Letters*	*Eight Letters of Dr. Antony Tuckney, and Dr. Benjamin Whichcote . . . written in September and October, MDCLI* (appended to Salter's edition of the *Aphorisms*, as above).
Whichcote, *Sermons*	*Select Sermons*, ed. Anthony, Third Earl of Shaftesbury (1698).
Worthington, *Discourses*	John Worthington, *Select Discourses* (1826; initially edited by the author's son in 1725).

II.

PRIMARY SOURCES (B):
EDITIONS CONSULTED

Aelian, *De nat. an.*	*De natura animalium*, ed. R. Hercher (*BT*: 1864), I.
Albinus	'Alcinous', Διδασκαλικὸς [*Didascalicus*], in *Platonis dialogi*, ed. C. F. Hermann (*BT*: 1884), VI, 153–89; tr. George Burges, in *The Works of Plato* (1854), VI, 241–314.
Alexander Aphrodisaeus	Φυσικαὶ καὶ ἠθικαὶ ἀπορίαι [*Quæstiones naturales et morales*], ed. L. Spengel (Munich, 1842).
ANCL	*Ante-Nicene Christian Library* (Buffalo, 1884 ff.).
Apollonius Rhodius	Ἀργοναυτικὰ [*Argonautica*], tr. R. C. Seaton (*LCL*: 1912); with the Greek text.
Aristophanes, *Nubes*	Νεφέλαι, tr. W. J. M. Starkie, *The Clouds* (1911); with the Greek text.
Aristotle	*Opera*, ed. E. Bekker (Berlin, 1831–70), 5 vols.; tr. W. D. Ross *et al.* (Oxford, 1908–52), 12 vols.
Athanasius, *De Inc.*	Περὶ τῆς ἐνανθρωπήσεως τοῦ Θεοῦ Λόγου [*De Incarnatione Dei Verbi*], tr. James Ridgway (Oxford, 1880); with the Greek text.
Augustine, *Conf.*	*Confessiones*, in *PL*, XXXII, 659–868; tr. A. C. Outler, in *LCC*, VII, 31–333.
Augustine, *De civ. Dei*	*De civitate Dei*, in *PL*, XLI; tr. John Healey (1610), rev. R. V. G. Tasker (1945), 2 vols.
Augustine, *Letters*	*The Letters of Saint Augustine*, tr. J. G. Cunningham, in *Works*, ed. Marcus Dodds (Edinburgh, 1872–75), vols. VI and XIII.
AV	The King James ('Authorised') Version of the Bible (1611).
Bacon	*Works*, ed. James Spedding, R. L. Ellis and D. D. Heath (1857–74), 14 vols.
Boethius	*De consolatione philosophiae*, tr. I. T. (1609), rev. H. F. Stewart (*LCL*: 1918); with the Latin text.
BT	*Bibliotheca scriptorum graecorum et romanorum Teubneriana* (Leipzig, 1849 ff.).
Chalcidius	*Platonis Timaeus interprete Chalcidio cum eiusdem commentario*, ed. J. Wrobel (*BT*: 1876).

	Abbreviations
Cicero, *De nat. deo.*	*De natura deorum*, ed. C. F. W. Mueller (*BT*: 1878); tr. Francis Brooks (1896).
Cicero, *De officiis*	*De officiis*, tr. Walter Miller (*LCL*: 1913); with the Latin text.
Cicero, *Disp.*	*Tusculanae disputationes*, tr. J. E. King (*LCL*: 1927); with the Latin text.
Clement of Alexandria	Λόγος προτρεπτικὸς πρὸς ῞Ελληνας [*Cohortatio ad gentes*], Παιδαγωγὸς [*Pædagogus*], and Στρώματα [*Stromata*], in *PG*, VIII–IX; tr. William Wilson, in *ANCL*, IV and XII.
Damascius	Περὶ τῶν πρώτων ἀρχῶν [*De primis principiis*], ed. J. Kopp (Frankfurt, 1826).
Descartes	*Philosophical Works*, tr. E. S. Haldane and G. R. T. Ross (Cambridge, 1911–12), 2 vols.
Diogenes Laertius	Βίοι καὶ γνῶμαι τῶν ἐν φιλοσόφοις εὐδοκιμησάντων [*De vita et moribus philosophorum*], tr. R. D. Hicks (*LCL*: 1925), 2 vols.; with the Greek text.
Empedocles	*The Fragments of Empedocles*, tr. W. E. Leonard (Chicago, 1908); with the Greek text.
Epictetus, *Ench.*	᾿Εγχειρίδιον [*Enchiridion*], ed. Anon. (Dublin, 1796); tr. P. E. Matheson (Oxford, 1916), II, 213–38.
Eusebius, *H.E.*	῾Εκκλησιαστικὴ ἱστορία [*Historia ecclesiastica*], tr. J. E. L. Oulton (*LCL*: 1926–32), 2 vols.; with the Greek text.
Ficino	Marsilio Ficino, *Opera* (Basle, 1576), 2 vols. (numbered consecutively). [The *Commentarium in convivium Platonis*, ed. & tr. Sears Jayne, University of Missouri Studies, XIX (1944), §1.]
Galen, *De usu partium*	Περὶ χρείας μορίων, ed. G. Helmreich (*BT*: 1907–9), 2 vols. [Also consulted: the Latin translation *De usu partium corporis humani*, ed. N. R. Calabrio (Paris, 1528).]
Hermes	'Hermes Trismegistus', *Hermetica*, tr. Walter Scott (Oxford, 1924–36), 4 vols.; with the Greek text.
Hierocles, *Aur. carm.*	Εἰς τὰ τῶν Πυθαγορείων χρυσᾶ ἔπη ὑπόμνημα [*In aurea Pythagorae carmina commentarius*], in *Fragmenta philosophorum græcorum*, ed. F. W. A. Mullach (Paris, 1860), I, 416–84; tr. William Rayner (Norwich, 1797).

Hippocrates, *Epid.*	Ἐπιδημιῶν βιβλία [*Epidemiorum libri*], in *Opera omnia. græce & latine*, ed. J. A. van der Linden (Leyden, 1665), vol. I.
Hobbes, *Leviathan*	*Leviathan, or the Matter, Forme & Power of a Common-wealth Ecclesiasticall and Civill* (Oxford, 1909; being a reprint of the 1651 ed.).
Homer, *Iliad*	Ἰλιάς, tr. A. T. Murray (*LCL:* 1924–5), 2 vols.; with the Greek text.
Homer, *Odyssey*	Ὀδύσσεια, tr. A. T. Murray (*LCL:* 1919), 2 vols.; with the Greek text.
Hyginus	*Fabulæ*, ed. B. Bunte (Leipzig, 1857).
Iamblichus, *De myst.*	Περὶ μυστηρίων [*De mystiriis*], ed. T. Gale (Oxford, 1678); tr. Thomas Taylor (2nd ed., 1895).
Iamblichus, *Vit. Pyth.*	Περὶ τοῦ Πυθαγορείου βίου [*De vita Pythagorica*], ed. L. Deubner (*BT:* 1937); tr. Thomas Taylor (new ed., 1926).
Julian	*The Works of the Emperor Julian*, tr. W. C. Wright (*LCL:* 1913–23), 3 vols.; with the Greek text.
LCC	*The Library of Christian Classics*, ed. John Baillie *et al.* (Philadelphia, 1953 ff.).
LCL	The Loeb Classical Library (Cambridge, Mass., 1912 ff.).
Longinus	Περὶ ὕψους [*De sublimitate*], tr. W. R. Roberts (2nd ed., Cambridge, 1907); with the Greek text.
Lucretius	*De rerum natura*, ed. J. Martin (*BT:* 1963); tr. Cyril Bailey (Oxford, 1910).
LXX	The Greek version of the OT: the Septuagint (third cent. B.C.?). [The Greek text edited by Alfred Rahlfs (8th ed., Stuttgart, 1965), 2 vols.]
Marcus Aurelius	M. Aurelius Antoninus, Τῶς εἰς ἑαυτόν [*Ad seipsum*], tr. C. R. Haines (*LCL:* 1916); with the Greek text.
NPNF	*Nicene and Post-Nicene Fathers* (Buffalo: 1st Series, 1886 ff.; 2nd Series, 1890 ff.).
NT	The New Testament [the Greek text edited by Kurt Aland *et al.* (New York etc., 1966)].
Origen, *De princ.*	Περὶ ἀρχῶν [*De principiis*], in *PG*, XI, 115–414; tr. G. W. Butterworth (1936).
Origen, *Cont. Cels.*	Κατὰ Κέλσου [*Contra Celsum*], in *PG*, XI, 641–1632; tr. Henry Chadwick (Cambridge, 1953).

Orpheus	'Orpheus', *Orphicorum fragmenta*, ed. Otto Kern (Berlin, 1922). [*The Hymns of Orpheus*, tr. Thomas Taylor (1792).]
OT	The Old Testament [the Hebrew text edited by R. Kittel (Stuttgart, 1945), 2 vols.].
Ovid, *Met.*	*Metamorphoses*, tr. F. J. Miller (*LCL:* 1916), 2 vols.; with the Latin text.
Pausanias	Ἑλλάδος περιήγησις [*Descriptio Graeciae*], tr. W. H. S. Jones (*LCL:* 1918–35), 5 vols.; with the Greek text.
PG	*Patrologia*, Series graeca, ed. J.-P. Migne (Paris, 1857 ff.).
Philo	*Philo*, tr. F. H. Colson and G. H. Whitaker (*LCL:* 1929–41), 9 vols.; with the Greek text.
Pico	Giovanni Pico della Mirandola, *Opera omnia* (Basle, 1572). [*De hominis dignitate, De ente et uno*, and *Heptaplus*, tr. C. G. Wallis. P. J. W. Miller, aud D. Carmichael (New York, 1965).]
Pirke Aboth	*Pirke Aboth—The Ethics of the Talmud: Sayings of the Fathers*, ed. & tr. R. Travers Herford (1945; repr. New York, 1962).
PL	*Patrologia*, Series latina, ed. J.-P. Migne (Paris, 1844 ff.).
Plato	*Platonis dialogi*, ed. C. F. Hermann and M. Wohlrab (*BT:* 1887–94), 6 vols.; tr. B. Jowett (4th rev. ed., Oxford, 1953), 4 vols.
Plotinus	Ἐννεάδες [*Enneades*], ed. R. Volkmann (*BT:* 1883–4), 2 vols.; tr. Stephen MacKenna, 3rd ed., rev. B. S. Page (1956). [The definitive edition of the Greek text is now in progress, ed. P. Henry and H.-R. Schwyzer (Paris, 1951 ff.), 3 vols.]
Plutarch	Τὰ ἠθικὰ [*Moralia*], in *Opera*, ed. F. Dübner (Paris, 1839–41), III–IV; tr. by several hands, ed. W. W. Goodwin (1870), 5 vols.
Porphyry, *Vit. Plot.*	Περὶ τοῦ Πλωτίνου βίου [*Vita Plotini*], in *Plotini opera*, ed. P. Henry and H.-R. Schwyzer (Paris, 1951), I, 1–41; tr. S. MacKenna (in the Plotinus edition cited above), pp. 1–20.
Porphyry, *Vit. Pyth.*	Πυθαγόρου βίος [*Vita Pythagorae*], in *Opuscula tria*, ed. A. Nauck (*BT:* 1860), pp. 14–39.
Proclus, *Inst. th.*	Στοιχείωσις Θεολογικὴ [*Institutio theologica*],

	Abbreviations
	tr. E. R. Dodds (Oxford, 1933); with the Greek text.
Proclus, *Primum Alc.*	Εἰς τὸν Πλάτωνος πρῶτον Ἀλκιβιάδην [*In Platonis primum Alcibiadem commentaria*], ed. L. G. Westerink (Amsterdam, 1954).
Proclus, *Primum Eucl.*	Εἰς τὸ πρῶτον τῶν Εὐκλείδους στοιχείων [*In primum Euclidis elementorum librum commentarii*], ed. G. Friedlein (*BT:* 1873); tr. Thomas Taylor (1788–9), 2 vols.
Proclus, *Tim.*	Εἰς τὸν Τιμαῖον Πλάτωνος [*In Platonis Timaeum commentaria*], ed. E. Diehl (*BT:* 1903–1906), 3 vols.; tr. Thomas Taylor (1820), 2 vols.
Pseudo-Dionysius	'Dionysius the Areopagite', Περὶ τῆς οὐρανίας ἱεραρχίας [*De coelesti hierarchia*], Περὶ θείων ὀνομάτων [*De divinis nominibus*], etc., in *PG*, III; tr. John Parker (1897–9), 2 vols.
Pythagoras	'Pythagoras', Χρυσᾶ ἔπη [*Carmina aurea*], in *Fragmenta philosophorum græcorum*, ed. F.W.A. Mullach (Paris, 1860), I, 193–9; tr. Anon. (1929).
Seneca, *Ep.*	*Ad Lucilium epistulae morales*, tr. R. M. Gummere (*LCL:* 1917–25), 3 vols.; with the Latin text.
Seneca, *Nat. quaest.*	*Naturales quaestiones*, ed. F. Haase (*BT:* 1862); tr. John Clarke (1910).
Simplicius, *Arist. Cael.*	Ὑπομνήματα εἰς τέσσερα βιβλία Ἀριστοτέλους περὶ οὐρανοῦ... *Commentarii in quatuor Aristotelis libros de cælo* (Venice, 1526).
Simplicius, *Arist. Phys.*	Ὑπομνήματα εἰς τὰ ὀκτὼ Ἀριστοτέλους φυσικῆς ἀκροάσεως βιβλία... *Commentarii in octo Aristotelis physicae auscultationis libros* (Venice, 1526).
Simplicius, *In Epict.*	Ἐξήγησις εἰς τὸ τοῦ Ἐπικτήτου Ἐγχειρίδιον [*Commentarius in Enchiridion Epicteti*], in the Wolfius–Salmasius ed. (Leyden, 1639–1640); tr. George Stanhope (5th ed., 1741).
SVF	*Stoicorum veterum fragmenta*, ed. Hans von Arnim (Leipzig, 1903–24), 4 vols.
Synesius	Περὶ Δίωνος [*De Dione*], etc., in *PG*, LXVI, 1053–1616; tr. Augustine FitzGerald (1930), 2 vols.
Talmud	*The Babylonian Talmud*, gen. ed. Isidore Epstein (1935–52), 35 vols.

Themistius	"Ἅπαντα, τουτέστι παραφράσεις, καὶ λόγοι ... Opera, hoc est paraphrases, et orationes, ed. V. Trincavellius (Venice, 1534).
Theophrastus, *Char.*	Χαρακτῆρες [*Characteres*], tr. J. M. Edmonds (*LCL:* 1929); with the Greek text.
Thomas Aquinas, *S. th.*	*Summa theologica*, in 4 vols. appended to *PL*; tr. by the English Dominican Fathers (1911–1925), 22 vols.
Virgil, *Aeneid*	*Aeneis*, ed. F. A. Hirtzel (Oxford, 1900); tr. J. W. Mackail (1908).
Vulgate	St Jerome's Latin version of the Bible (*c.* 384–404). [The text edited by A. C. Fillion (Paris, 1930).]

III.

SECONDARY SOURCES:

COMMENTARIES ON THE CAMBRIDGE PLATONISTS

Anderson	Paul R. Anderson, *Science in Defence of Liberal Religion: A Study of Henry More's Attempt to Link Seventeenth Century Religion with Science* (New York, 1933).
Arnold	Matthew Arnold, 'A Psychological Parallel', in *Last Essays on Church and Religion* (1877), Ch. I. On Smith, pp. 18–28.
Aspelin	Gunnar Aspelin, 'Ralph Cudworth's Interpretation of Greek Philosophy: A Study in the History of English Philosophical Ideas', *Göteborgs Högskolas Årsskrift*, XLIX (1943), § 1.
Baker	Herschel Baker, *The Wars of Truth: Studies in the Decay of Christian Humanism in the Earlier Seventeenth Century* (1952). On the Cambridge Platonists, Ch. III (v).
Baker, *S & T*	John Tull Baker, *An Historical and Critical Examination of English Space and Time Theories from Henry More to Bishop Berkeley* (Bronxville, N.Y., 1930). On More, Ch. II.
Bullough	*Philosophical Poems of Henry More*, ed. Geoffrey Bullough (Manchester, 1931). Reprints the *Psychozoia* and some minor poems.
Burtt	Edwin A. Burtt, *The Metaphysical Foundations*

	of *Modern Physical Science* (New York, 1924; 2nd rev. ed., 1932; repr. 1954). On More, Ch. V.
Bush	Douglas Bush, *English Literature in the Earlier Seventeenth Century*, 2nd rev. ed. (Oxford, 1962). On the Cambridge Platonists, Ch. X(7).
Campagnac	E. T. Campagnac, ed., *The Cambridge Platonists* (Oxford, 1901). Reprints three sermons and select aphorisms by Whichcote, four discourses by Smith, and an abridged version of 12 chapters from Culverwell's *Discourse*. See below, p. xxvi.
Cassirer	Ernst Cassirer, *The Platonic Renaissance in England*, tr. James P. Pettegrove (Austin, 1953).
Cohen	Leonora D. Cohen, 'Descartes and Henry More on the Beast-Machine—A Translation of their Correspondence pertaining to Animal Automation', *Annals of Science*, I (1936), 48–61.
Coleridge	*Coleridge on the Seventeenth Century*, ed. Roberta F. Brinkley (Durham, N.C., 1955). On More and Smith, pp. 316–21, 365–7.
Colie	Rosalie L. Colie, *Light and Enlightenment: A Study of the Cambridge Platonists and the Dutch Arminians* (Cambridge, 1957).
Cragg	G. R. Cragg, *From Puritanism to the Age of Reason: A Study of Changes in Religious Thought within the Church of England 1660 to 1700* (Cambridge, 1950). On the Cambridge Platonists, Ch. III.
Feibleman	James K. Feibleman, *Religious Platonism: The Influence of Religion on Plato and the Influence of Plato on Religion* (1959). On the Cambridge Platonists, Ch. XII (b).
FM	Flora I. Mackinnon, ed., *Philosophical Writings of Henry More* (New York, 1925).
Fowler	Edward Fowler, *The Principles and Practices, of certain Moderate Divines of the Church of England, (greatly mis-understood) Truly Represented and Defended* (1670).
George	Edward A. George, *Seventeenth Century Men of Latitude* (1909). On Whichcote, Smith and More, pp. 69–128.
Greene	Robert A. Greene, 'Henry More and Robert

	Boyle on the Spirit of Nature', *Journal of the History of Ideas*, XXIII (1962), 451–74.
Gregory	Joshua C. Gregory, 'Cudworth and Descartes', *Philosophy*, VIII (1933), 454–67.
Gysi	Lydia Gysi, *Platonism and Cartesianism in the Philosophy of Ralph Cudworth* (Bern, 1962).
HGW	Henry Griffin Williams, ed., *Select Discourses: by John Smith* (Cambridge, 1859).
Hoopes	Robert Hoopes, *Right Reason in the English Renaissance* (Cambridge, Mass., 1962). On the Cambridge Platonists, pp. 174–85.
Hunter	William B. Hunter, Jr., 'The Seventeenth Century Doctrine of Plastic Nature', *Harvard Theological Review*, XLIII (1950), 197–213.
Hutin	Serge Hutin, *Henry More: Essai sur les doctrines théosophiques chez les Platoniciens de Cambridge* (Hildesheim, 1966).
Jammer	Max Jammer, *Concepts of Space: The History of Theories of Space in Physics* (Cambridge, Mass, 1954). On More, pp. 38–46, 108–11.
JLM	J. L. Mosheim, ed. & tr., *Radulphi Cudworthi ... Systema intellectuale huius universi seu de veris baturae rerum originibus commentarii* (Jena, 1733), 2 vols. [Mosheim's notes are cited from their translation by John Harrison (1845), 3 vols.]
Jones	Rufus M. Jones, *Spiritual Reformers in the 16th and 17th Centuries* (New York, 1914; repr. Boston, 1959). On Whichcote and Smith, Ch. XV–XVI.
Jordan	Wilbur K. Jordan, *The Development of Religious Toleration in England* (1940), Vol. IV: *Attainment of the Theory and Accomodations in Thought and Institutions, 1640–1660*. On the Cambridge Platonists, pp. 94–137.
Koyré	Alexandre Koyré, *From the Closed World to the Infinite Universe* (Baltimore, 1957). On More, esp. Ch. V–VI.
Laird	John Laird, *Hobbes* (1934). On More and Cudworth, pp. 258–60, 273–5.
Lichtenstein	Aharon Lichtenstein, *Henry More: The Rational Theology of a Cambridge Platonist* (Cambridge, Mass., 1962).

Lovejoy	Arthur O. Lovejoy, *The Great Chain of Being: A Study of the History of an Idea* (Cambridge, Mass., 1936; repr. New York, 1960).
Lowrey	Charles E. Lowrey, *The Philosophy of Ralph Cudworth: A Study of the True Intellectual System of the Universe* (New York, 1884).
McAdoo	H. R. McAdoo, 'The Cambridge Platonists', in *The Spirit of Anglicanism: A Survey of Anglican Theological Method in the Seventeenth Century* (1965), Ch. III–IV.
Martineau	James Martineau, 'Dianoetic Ethics: Cudworth', in *Types of Ethical Theory* (Oxford, 1885), II, 396–424.
Mintz	Samuel I. Mintz, *The Hunting of Leviathan: Seventeenth-Century Reactions to the Materialism and Moral Philosophy of Thomas Hobbes* (Cambridge, 1962). On More and Cudworth, Ch. V–VI.
Mitchell	W. Fraser Mitchell, *English Pulpit Oratory from Andrewes to Tillotson: A Study of its Literary Aspects* (1932). On the Cambridge Platonists, Ch. VIII.
Muirhead	John H. Muirhead, *The Platonic Tradition in Anglo-Saxon Philosophy* (1931). On the Cambridge Platonists and esp. Cudworth, Pt. I, Ch. I–III.
Mullinger	James Bass Mullinger, *The University of Cambridge* (Cambridge, 1911), Vol. III. On the Cambridge Platonists, pp. 588–665.
Nicolson, *Aesthetics*	Marjorie H. Nicolson, *Mountain Gloom and Mountain Glory: The Development of the Aesthetics of the Infinite* (Ithaca, N.Y., 1959; repr. New York, 1963). On More, Ch. III.
Nicolson, 'Cartesianism'	Marjorie H. Nicolson, 'The Early Stages of Cartesianism in England', *Studies in Philology*, XXVI (1929), 356–74. Largely on More.
Nicolson, *Circle*	Marjorie H. Nicolson, *The Breaking of the Circle: Studies in the Effect of the 'New Science' upon Seventeenth-Century Poetry*, rev. ed. (New York, 1962). On More, pp. 158–65.
Passmore	J. A. Passmore, *Ralph Cudworth: An Interpretation* (Cambridge, 1951).

Pauley	W. C. de Pauley, *The Candle of the Lord: Studies in the Cambridge Platonists* (1937).
Pawson	G. P. H. Pawson, *The Cambridge Platonists and their Place in Religious Thought* (1930).
Pinto	Vivian de Sola Pinto, *Peter Sterry, Platonist and Puritan, 1613–1672: A Biographical and Critical Study with passages selected from his Writings* (Cambridge, 1934).
Powicke	Frederick J. Powicke, *The Cambridge Platonists: A Study* (1926).
Raven	Charles E. Raven, *Natural Religion and Christian Theology*, First Series: *Science and Religion* (Cambridge, 1953). On Cudworth, Ch. VI.
Shorey	Paul Shorey, *Platonism Ancient and Modern* (Berkeley, 1938). On Cudworth, pp. 198–201.
Snow	A. J. Snow, *Matter and Gravity in Newton's Physical Philosophy: A Study in the Natural Philosophy of Newton's Time* (1926). On More, Ch. I (2) and IV (3).
S.P., *Brief Account*	S.P. [Simon Patrick?], *A Brief Account of the new Sect of Latitude-Men together with some reflections upon the New Philosophy* (1662). [Also reproduced in facsimile, with a Note by T. A. Birrell (Los Angeles, 1963).]
Stewart	J. A. Stewart, 'Cambridge Platonists', *Encyclopaedia of Religion and Ethics*, ed. J. Hastings (Edinburgh, 1910), III, 167–73.
Tulloch	John Tulloch, *Rational Theology and Christian Philosophy in England in the Seventeenth Century*, 2nd ed. (1874; repr. 1968), Vol. II: *The Cambridge Platonists*.
Tuveson	Ernest L. Tuveson, *Millennium and Utopia: A Study in the Background of the Idea of Progress* (Berkeley and Los Angeles, 1949). On More, Ch. III (4).
Ward	Richard Ward, *The Life of the Learned and Pious Dr. Henry More . . . to which are annex'd divers of his useful and excellent letters* (1710). [Also edited, without the letters, by M. F. Howard (1911).]
Watkin	E. I. Watkin, 'John Smith the Cambridge Platonist', in *Poets and Mystics* (1953), Ch. X.

Willey	Basil Willey, *The Seventeenth Century Background: Studies in the Thought of the Age in Relation to Poetry and Religion* (1934). On the Cambridge Platonists, Ch. VIII.
Williamson	George Williamson, 'The Restoration Revolt against Enthusiasm', *Studies in Philology*, XXX (1933), 571–603. On More, pp. 585 ff.
Yates	Frances A. Yates, *Giordano Bruno and the Hermetic Tradition* (1964). On More and Cudworth, pp. 423–31.

A Note on Method

THE selections in this volume begin with three sermons by Whichcote, all published posthumously and thus much later (1685 ff.) than all but one of the discourses reprinted here. But Whichcote still deserves priority of place since he was the first publicly to utter the tenets characteristic of Cambridge Platonism (1636 ff.). He is also, by common consent, the group's acknowledged leader.

Whichcote's sermons are followed by Cudworth's sermon before the House of Commons (1647), the only exposition of Cambridge Platonism ever addressed to such an influential body. The sermon was published on the express 'desire' of Parliament.

John Smith is allotted the next place as the individual most directly in the line of descent from Whichcote and Cudworth. His *Discourses* first appeared posthumously in 1660 but were delivered for the most part sometime after 1644.

Henry More presented a number of problems. The selection of appropriate extracts from his works was repeatedly frustrated by his verbosity and repetitiveness, his fondness for digressions, and his frequent lapses into absurdities. In the end I decided to present him in as favourable a light as might be possible. The sermon which here introduces us to his thought (published posthumously in 1692) is representative not so much of his usual style as of his loyalty to Cambridge Platonism. The two books of *An Antidote against Atheism* (1653) flatter him even more, but then I have not reprinted either its later additions or its third book (I have given only its chapter headings, below, pp. 286 f.). His poetry was also excluded from these pages since More himself described it once—rather accurately I think —as 'A rude confused heap of ashes dead' (*Ad Paronem*, line 13). I have space only for his description of Dæmon, King of Autæsthesy ('Self-sensedness,' explained More helpfully):

> he himself is quite divided
> Down to the belly; there's some unity:
> But head, and tongue, and heart be quite discided:
> Two heads, two tongues, and eke two hearts there be.

> This head doth mischief plot, that head doth see
> Wrong fairly to o'reguild. One tongue doth pray,
> The other curse. The hearts do ne're agree
> But felly one another do upbray:
> An ugly cloven foot this monster doth upstay.
> (*Psychozoia*, II, 27)

More said once that his father had 'from childhood tuned mine ears to Spencers rhymes'. It does not seem to have helped.

The tendency toward 'philosophy' apparent in More's *Antidote* culminates in Cudworth's *True Intellectual System of the Universe* (1678) which provides the last selection in this volume. My choice of Cudworth's 'digression' on Plastic Nature was dictated by its central importance to the book itself, to Cudworth's development since he addressed the House of Commons in 1647, and to Cambridge Platonism considered as a philosophical system. But as Cambridge Platonism is not primarily a philosophical system, I decided that a reminder to that effect would not be out of place. Thus the present volume ends with an appendix which moves us beyond Cudworth's Plastic Nature to the quintessence of Cambridge Platonism inherent in Whichcote's *Moral and Religious Aphorisms* (1703; revised, 1753).

My failure to include a number of other writers often associated with the Cambridge Platonists may come as a surprise. There are in particular two candidates. One is Peter Sterry, extracts from whose work were edited by V. de S. Pinto under the title *Peter Sterry: Puritan and Platonist* (1934). The other is Nathanael Culverwell whose *Discourse of the Light of Nature* was abridged by E. T. Campagnac for his anthology *The Cambridge Platonists* (1901). I am however persuaded that neither Culverwell nor Sterry ever penetrated to the centre of Cambridge Platonism; both hovered on its circumference. Culverwell's loyalty to Calvinism and Sterry's denial of free will are sufficient of themselves to set both men in diametric opposition to Whichcote, Smith, Cudworth and More. Culverwell's *Discourse* is moreover quite different from what it appears to be in Campagnac's edition. Its careful abridgment there has improved its style considerably. Worse, its last two chapters were *not* reprinted, yet it is precisely in those two chapters that Culverwell (as his first editor in 1652 noted) forced reason to 'bow the head and worship, and then lay it self down quietly at the feet of Faith'. The Cambridge Platonists would have regarded such an abject surrender of Reason as treasonable.

A Note on Method

The annotation obliged me to spend many pleasant months amidst 'the ancient and wisest philosophers'. But there were some surprises. My most anxious moment came while reading the correspondence between Whichcote and Tuckney. 'I have bin apte to think,' Tuckney protested, 'that both in your sermons and privatt discourse you do often, as it were, quote your-selfe; in uttering latine sentences and axiomes, both in Logick Philosophie Law and Divinitie, which are of your owne making.' Whichcote's reply was not very reassuring. As he put it, 'By what rule you judge; that Hee, who useth a Latine or Greek phrase or sentence in an English discourse, must needs *quote*; I do not understand: much less, upon that account, be thought to quote himselfe.'

My annotation of Whichcote's sermons is understandably restrained.

Biographical Sketches

BENJAMIN WHICHCOTE (1609–1683)

Born 1609 at Stoke in Shropshire of 'an ancient and honourable family'. Admitted pensioner at Emmanuel College, Cambridge, 1626; initially tutored by Antony Tuckney. B.A. in 1629, M.A. in 1633, B.D. in 1640. Elected Fellow of Emmanuel, 1633. Ordained deacon and priest, and appointed Sunday Afternoon Lecturer in Trinity Church, 1636. Presented to the College living of North Cadbury in Somersetshire, and married to Rebecca the widow of Matthew Craddock, 1643 (there were no children). Parliamentary appointment as Provost of King's College, 1644. Created D.D. by mandate, 1649; Vice-Chancellor, 1650–51. Advised Cromwell on toleration of Jews. Did not subscribe to the Covenant yet in 1660 lost the provostship of King's by order of Charles II. Complied with the Act of Uniformity, and was appointed to the cure of St Anne's, Blackfriars, 1662. Brief retirement to Milton in Cambridgeshire; presented to the vicarage of St Lawrence Jewry, 1668. Died in Cudworth's house at Cambridge, May 1683. All his works were published posthumously (see above, p. xiii). On his portrait by Mary Beale, reproduced here as a frontispiece, see above, p. viii.

JOHN SMITH (1618–1652)

Born 1618 at Achurch near Oundle in Northamptonshire; his father was a farmer. Admitted pensioner at Emmanuel College, Cambridge, 1636; tutored by Whichcote, and may also have studied under Cudworth. B.A. in 1640, M.A. in 1644. Parliamentary appointment as Fellow of Queen's, 1644, where he delivered some of his discourses. Died of consumption, 7 August 1652. His *Select Discourses*—only ten —were published posthumously (see above, p. xiii).

HENRY MORE (1614–1687)

Born 1614 in Grantham in Lincolnshire; his father was 'a gentleman of fair estate and fortune'. Educated at Eton, 1628–31. Admitted at Christ's College, Cambridge, 1631. B.A. in 1635, M.A. in 1639. Elected Fellow of Christ's, 1639, a position he retained through the interregnum and the Restoration. Declined all ecclesiastical and academic preferments, including the mastership of his College which in 1654 passed to Cudworth. Left Cambridge infrequently, more often than not in order to visit his friend Lady Conway at Ragley in Warwickshire. Devoted to a life of study, he corresponded with numerous thinkers, notably Descartes (1649). Died 1 September 1687. His works include principally those listed above, pp. xi–xiii.

RALPH CUDWORTH (1617–1688)

Born 1617 at Aller in Somersetshire; his father was a clergyman and sometime Fellow of Emmanuel College, Cambridge. Admitted pensioner at Emmanuel, 1632. M.A., and Fellow of Emmanuel, 1639, B.D. in 1645. Parliamentary appointment as Master of Clare Hall, and election as Regius Professor of Hebrew, 1645. Held the College living of North Cadbury in succession to Whichcote, 1650. Created D.D. in 1651. Translated to the mastership of Christ's College, 1654, which he retained even after the Restoration. No details available on his marriage, but his daughter, Lady Masham, forms an important link between Cudworth, Locke and Newton. Presented to the vicarage of Ashwell in Hertfordshire, 1662; installed prebendary of Gloucester, 1678. Died at Cambridge, 26 June 1688. His works include principally those listed above, p. xi.

A Reading List

ON THE CAMBRIDGE PLATONISTS

Preliminary surveys include: Pawson; W. R. Inge, *Christian Mysticism*, 7th ed. (1933), pp. 285–96, and *The Platonic Tradition in English Religious Thought* (1926), Ch. II; and H. L. Stewart, 'Ralph Cudworth, the "Latitude Man"', *The Personalist*, XXXII (1951), 163–71. Highly-recommended introductions: Baker, Ch. III (v); Bush, pp. 358–67; Hoopes, pp. 174–85; McAdoo, Ch. III–IV; Muirhead, Pt. I, Ch. I; Mullinger, III, 588–665; Powicke; Stewart; Tulloch; Eugene M. Austin, *The Ethics of the Cambridge Platonists* (Philadelphia, 1935); Meyrick H. Carré, *Phases of Thought in England* (Oxford, 1949), Ch. VII (vi); Sterling P. Lamprecht, 'Innate Ideas in the Cambridge Platonists', *Philosophical Review*, XXXV (1926), 552–73; A. Nairne, 'The Cambridge Platonists', *Church Quarterly Review*, CI (1926), 209–29; Michael Roberts, *The Modern Mind* (1937), Ch. IV; Basil Willey, *The English Moralists* (1964), Ch. XI; and esp. Pauley. John J. de Boer's *The Theory of Knowledge of the Cambridge Platonists* (Madras, 1931) is relatively inaccessible and, in any case, superficial. Principal contributions: Cassirer; Colie; Cragg, Ch. III; Hunter; Jordan, pp. 94–137; Mitchell, Ch. VIII; and J. E. Saveson, 'Differing Reactions to Descartes among the Cambridge Platonists', *Journal of the History of Ideas*, XXI (1960), 560–7.

ON BENJAMIN WHICHCOTE

Preliminary surveys include: George, pp. 69–85; Pawson, Ch. II; Brooke F. Westcott, *Essays in the History of Religious Thought in the West* (1891), pp. 362–97, and *Masters in English Theology*, ed. Alfred Barry (1877), pp. 147–73. Highly-recommended introductions: Jones, Ch. XV; Pauley, Ch. I–II; Powicke, Ch. II; Tulloch, Ch. II; and Sarah Herndon, 'Benjamin Whichcote: Cambridge Platonist', *Florida State University Studies*, XI (1953), 1–18. Principal contributions: Jordan, pp. 99–116.

ON JOHN SMITH

Preliminary surveys include: George, pp. 89–106; and Powicke, Ch. III. Highly-recommended introductions: Jones, Ch. XVI; Pauley, Ch. III; Pawson, Ch. III; Tulloch, Ch. III; John K. Ryan, 'John Smith: Platonist and Mystic', *New Scholasticism*, XX (1946), 1–25; and esp. Watkin. Principal contributions: Willey, Ch. VIII (1); and J. E. Saveson, 'Descartes' Influence on John Smith', *Journal of the History of Ideas*, XX (1959), 258–63. See also Arnold, pp. 18–28, and Coleridge, pp. 365–7.

ON HENRY MORE

Preliminary surveys include: George, pp. 109–28; Pawson, Ch. IV; and Powicke, Ch. VI. Highly-recommended introductions: Pauley, Ch. V; Tulloch, Ch. V; Willey, pp. 160–9; and A. W. Harrison, 'Henry More, the Cambridge Platonist', *London Quarterly and Holborn Review*, CLVIII (1933), 485–92. Principal contributions: Anderson; Baker, *S&T*, Ch. II; Burtt, Ch. V; Cohen; Greene; Jammer, pp. 38–46, 108–11; Koyré, esp. Ch. V–VI; Lichtenstein (who also provides a full bibliography, pp. 217–44); Mintz, Ch. V; Nicolson, *Aesthetics*, Ch. III, *Circle*, pp. 158–65, and 'Cartesianism'; Snow, Ch. I (2) and IV (3); Tuveson, Ch. III (4); Williamson; Yates, pp. 423–7; C. A. Staudenbaur, 'Galileo, Filino, and Henry More's *Psychathanasia*', *Journal of the History of Ideas*, XXIX (1968), 567–78; and G. A. Panichas, 'The Greek Spirit and the Mysticism of Henry More', *Greek Orthodox Theological Review*, II (1956), No. 2, pp. 41–61. See also Coleridge, pp. 316–21.

ON RALPH CUDWORTH

Preliminary surveys include: Pawson, Ch. V; and Sir Herbert Grierson, *Cross Currents in English Literature of the XVIIth Century* (1929), pp. 221–31. Highly-recommended introductions: Lowrey; Pauley, Ch. IV; Powicke, Ch. IV; Tulloch, Ch. IV; Willey, pp. 154–60; and M. H. Carré, 'Ralph Cudworth', *Philosophical Quarterly*, III (1953), 342–51. Principal contributions: Aspelin; Colie, esp. Ch. VII; Gregory; Gysi; McAdoo, Ch. IV; Martineau; Mintz, Ch. V–VI; Muirhead, Pt. I, Ch. II–III; Passmore; Raven; Yates, pp. 427–31; Arthur N. Prior, *Logic and the Basis of Ethics* (Oxford, 1949), Ch. II; and Danton B. Sailor, 'Cudworth and Descartes', *Journal of the History of Ideas*, XXIII (1962), 133–40.

'The High and Aiery Hills of Platonisme':
An Introduction to the
Cambridge Platonists

ὁ δὴ θεὸς ἡμῖν πάντων χρημάτων μέτρον ἂν εἴη μάλιστα, καὶ πολὺ μᾶλλον ἤ
πού τις, ὥς φασιν, ἄνθρωπος

PLATO*

I

THE Emperor Julian, the 'apostate' who endeavoured to restore Hellenism in A.D. 361, once suggested the continuity of the Platonic tradition by listing in sequence the names of Plato, Plotinus, Porphyry and Iamblichus.[1] His failure to differentiate these philosophers need not concern us here since it was a failure shared by everyone else to the seventeenth century and beyond. Equally understandable is his omission of other formidable Platonists—Philo, Clement of Alexandria, the mighty Origen[2]—for Julian was too much of a partisan ever to

---

* 'Now God ought to be to us the measure of all things, and not man, as men commonly say' (*Leges*, 716c). The statement is made in express opposition to Protagoras (quoted below, p. 138, note).

[1] *Oration VII*, 222b. The chronological sequence is: Plato, 428/9–348/7 B.C.; Plotinus, A.D. 205–70; Porphyry, 233–c. 304; and Iamblichus, c. 250–c. 330. The succession passes to Proclus (410–85) and ends in the closing of the Academy at Athens by Justinian (529).

[2] All three are discussed in the excellent introductory study by Charles Bigg, *The Christian Platonists of Alexandria*, rev. ed. (Oxford, 1913). The definitive studies in English are, respectively, by H. A. Wolfson, *Philo* (Cambridge, Mass., 1947), 2 vols.; R. B. Tollington, *Clement of Alexandria* (1914), 2 vols.; and Jean Daniélou, *Origen*, tr. W. Mitchell (1955). The case for Philo as 'the chief founder of Neoplatonism' is aggressively stated by Feibleman, Ch. VII. The best general survey of Patristic Platonism is by R. Arnou, in *Dictionnaire de théologie catholique* (Paris, 1933), XII, 2258–392. Cf. R. P. Casey, 'Clement of Alexandria and the Beginnings of Christian Platonism', *Harvard Theological Review*, XVIII (1925), 39–101. The passages from Plato most often used by his divers disciples

consider seriously that a Jew and two 'Galileans' could possibly form part of the Platonic succession. Nevertheless his sequence from Plotinus to Porphyry and Iamblichus, with the further addition of Proclus who came later, focuses accurately enough on the revised edition of Platonism known for better or for worse as Neoplatonism.[1] A number of other editions have of course followed since, notably the one compiled by the less profound but equally influential Florentine Neoplatonists of the fifteenth century led by Marsilio Ficino and Pico della Mirandola.[2] An even more modest edition was published later, in seventeenth-century England, by the so-called Cambridge Platonists. Their inspiration came from their Plato, Benjamin Whichcote; their best writing issued from their Porphyry, John Smith; their perversities became most apparent with their Iamblichus, Henry More; while Ralph Cudworth as an acute and subtle philosopher was their Plotinus, and as a scholastic systematiser their Proclus.

Yet the achievement of the Cambridge Platonists can hardly be measured in terms of their loyalty to Plato, Plotinus, or any of the

---

will be found in Shorey, pp. 45–7, and Adam Fox, *Plato and the Christians* (1957). On the Platonism of the English Renaissance see Friedrich Dannenberg, *Das Erbe Platons in England bis zur Bildung Lylys* (Berlin, 1932), and Kurt Schroeder, *Platonismus in der englischen Renaissance vor und bei Thomas Elyot* (Berlin, 1920).

[1] The best survey of Neoplatonism is by Thomas Whittaker, *The Neo-Platonists*, 2nd ed. (Cambridge, 1918). The bibliography of Plotinus is extremely lengthy but I should recommend four excellent studies available in English: Émile Bréhier, *The Philosophy of Plotinus*, tr. J. Thomas (Chicago, 1958); W. R. Inge, *The Philosophy of Plotinus*, 3rd ed. (1929), 2 vols.; A. H. Armstrong, *The Architecture of the Intelligible Universe in the Philosophy of Plotinus* (Cambridge, 1940); and J. M. Rist, *Plotinus: The Road to Reality* (Cambridge, 1967). Continental studies include in particular: Maurice de Gandillac, *La Sagesse de Plotin* (Paris, 1952); Cleto Carbonara, *La filosofia di Plotino*, 3rd ed. (Naples, 1964), with full bibliography; and the multilingual *Entretiens sur l'antiquité classique*, V: *Les sources de Plotin*, by E. R. Dodds, W. Theiler, et al. (Geneva, 1960).

[2] On the relationship of the Cambridge Platonists to the Florentines (as also to Erasmus, Colet and Sir Thomas More), see esp. Cassirer, Ch. I and IV, whose account is here amended considerably. Cf. Sears Jayne, 'Ficino and the Platonism of the English Renaissance', *Comparative Literature*, IV (1952), 214–38. Hooker is not relevant (notwithstanding McAdoo, p. 124) for the reasons stated by Peter Munz, *The Place of Hooker in the History of Thought* (1952), pp. 171 ff. In any case, we may not merge Hooker, the Cambridge Platonists and all Latitudinarians into the single category—convenient but misleading—of 'Anglican rationalists', as Philip Harth has done in *Swift and Anglican Rationalism* (Chicago, 1961), pp. 20 ff.

Introduction 3

lesser luminaries in the Platonic succession. Suppose that a study of their antecedents were to persuade us that they were not 'Platonists' but (as Coleridge claimed) 'more truly Plotinists'.[1] What matter then? To be a Plotinist is not to negate the influence of Plato; it is to interpret Plato to suit one's particular sensibility, which I take it is the justification for that well-known generalisation which sees the entire European philosophical tradition as 'a series of footnotes to Plato'.[2] Certainly the ever-present tendency to regard Plato's Forms as thoughts in the Divine Mind[3] does not cancel the debt owed to Plato's original conception. Likewise, the testimony of Porphyry that in the writings of Plotinus 'both the Stoic and Peripatetic doctrines are sunk; Aristotle's Metaphysics, especially, is condensed in them, all but entire',[4] hardly

[1] Coleridge, p. 366. Cf. below, p. 41, note 1.
[2] Alfred North Whitehead, *Process and Reality* (Cambridge, 1929), p. 53. Etienne Gilson ventures a parallel affirmation in *History of Christian Philosophy in the Middle Ages* (1955), p. 542.
[3] Cf. Sterry: 'Philosophers and Divines call the first Images of things, as they rise up from the Fountain of eternity in the bosome of this universal and eternal Image, *Ideas*. The *Idea*, in this sense, is the first and distinct Image of each form of things in the Divine Mind' (*Discourse*, p. 49). Plato's conception is discussed by F. M. Cornford, *Plato's Theory of Knowledge* (1935), *passim*; Raphael Demos, *The Philosophy of Plato* (1939), Ch. X; Sir David Ross, *Plato's Theory of Ideas* (Oxford, 1951); *et al.* For subsequent developments consult H. A. Wolfson, *Philo* (Cambridge, Mass., 1947), I, 200 ff., and *The Philosophy of the Church Fathers* (Cambridge, Mass., 1956), I, Ch. XIII; Feibleman, pp. 109 ff., 153 ff., and *passim*; R. M. Jones, 'The Ideas as the Thoughts of God', *Classical Philology*, XXI (1926), 317–26; A. N. M. Rich, 'The Platonic Ideas as the Thoughts of God', *Mnemosyne*, 4th series, VII (1954), 123–33; and H. A. Wolfson, 'Extradeical and Intradeical Interpretations of Platonic Ideas', *Journal of the History of Ideas*, XXII (1961), 3–32. The most crucial utterances of the early Platonists (e.g. Philo, *De opificio mundi*, XX; Albinus, IX; Plotinus, V, i, 4) are repeatedly echoed in the seventeenth century, as by Donne (*Sermons*, ed. E. M. Simpson and G. R. Potter [Berkeley, 1962], X, 353 ff.), Cudworth (cf. Martineau, pp. 413 ff.), George Rust (*A Discourse of Truth* [1682], §§ 17–18), *et al.* The conception in *Paradise Lost*, VII, 557, is thoroughly traditional.
[4] Porphyry, *Vit. Plot.*, XIV. On the non-Hellenic elements in Plotinus' thought, see Émile Bréhier, *The Philosophy of Plotinus*, tr. J. Thomas (Chicago, 1958), Ch. VII; cf. Willy Theiler, *Die Vorbereitung des Neuplatonismus* (Berlin, 1930), esp. Ch. I. But it is also conceivable that Plotinus was influenced by Christian ideas, possibly through his teacher Ammonius who was once a Christian and had taught Origen. Cf. E. Zeller, 'Ammonius Sakkas und Plotinus', *Archiv für Geschichte der Philosophie*, VII (1894), 295–312; Heinrich Dörrie, 'Ammonios der Lehrer Plotins', *Hermes*, LXXXIII (1955), 439–77; and H. Langerbeck, 'The Philosophy of Ammonius Saccas', *Journal of Hellenic Studies* LXXVII (1957), 67–74.

affects the position of Plotinus as Plato's most important disciple. Even where the outlook is manifestly un-Platonic—as in Origen's firm commitment to an Incarnate God, or in Iamblichus' excessive attachment to theurgy, or in Pico's dazzling attempts to fuse mutually exclusive ideas —we may not conclude that Plato has been necessarily bypassed. To reach the appropriate conclusions wherever we observe individuals 'always consorting with Plato' (as Porphyry said of Origen)[1] we should indeed investigate the extent of their indebtedness to Plato but we must in particular examine the reasons for their predilection toward Plato in the first instance. To attempt the one without the other would be quite misleading, especially in the case of the Cambridge Platonists, who quote the minor Neoplatonists more often than Plotinus, and Plotinus more often than Plato. But to study their general attitude of mind as it emerges from their principal tenets is to see not only how far the spirit of Plato pervades their thought but also why they enrolled themselves among the 'platonicks', 'Those Eagle Eyed Philosophers', as Whichcote called them, 'the best and divinest of philosophers' according to More.[2]

The acceptance by the Cambridge Platonists of Plato and his disciples under the leadership of Plotinus—'Divine Plotinus!'[3]—went hand in hand with their bold rejection of the entire Western theological tradition from St Augustine through the medieval schoolmen to the classic Protestantism of Luther, Calvin, and their variegated followers in the seventeenth century. John Worthington's statement sometime after the Restoration that the Cambridge Platonists looked to 'the ancient and wisest philosophers, as also the primitive fathers, the Greek especially',[4] is an acknowledgement of a development staggering in its implications. Protestants had of course repeatedly pleaded for a return to 'the primitive fathers', but it was always understood that Origen should be on the whole avoided and that the other Greek Fathers should be studied in the light of Tertullian and especially St Augustine. The Cambridge Platonists inverted this procedure with almost mathematical precision. They tended to silence Tertullian altogether; they invoked Augustine only if he happened to agree with the eagle-eyed

[1] *Apud* Eusebius, *H. E.*, VI, xix, 7.

[2] Whichcote, *Discourses*, II, 400; More, Preface to *Philosophical Poems* (Bullough, p. 7).

[3] More, *The Oracle*, l. 17 (Bullough, p. 159). See also More's frequent references to Plotinus in the notes to his *Poems*, pp. 335 ff.

[4] Worthington, *Discourses*, p. 36. Cf. S.P., *Brief Account*, p. 9. Worthington himself remained loyal to the Augustinian tradition.

Introduction

philosophers;[1] and they granted primacy in theological matters to the Greek Fathers, all now led by Origen—'that Miracle of the Christian World'.[2] Among the major Western theologians only two found favour with the Cambridge Platonists: St Anselm, who provided the basis for their theory of the Atonement, and St Thomas Aquinas, who supplied them with the most advanced formulation of the Graeco-Roman theory of natural law.[3] Nearly all other exponents of the traditional modes of Western thought were mercilessly ostracised. St Jerome who is certainly the greatest humanist among the Latin Fathers was silently removed from his pedestal in recompense for his attacks on Origen as much as in reply to his frequent denigrations of classical literature ('Quid facit cum psalterio Horatius? cum evangeliis Maro? cum apostolo Cicero?').[4] Even Western 'platonicks' such as Macrobius and Chalcidius were unceremoniously dismissed. Above all, Aristotle—once so highly favoured by the medieval schoolmen and lately no less admired by the Protestant scholastics—was obliged to surrender his traditional designation as 'the Philosopher' to Plato or Plotinus or even (the unkindest cut of all!) to Epictetus, Hierocles or Simplicius.[5] Lastly, Luther

---

[1] The Cambridge Platonists thought that Augustine had altogether subordinated Platonism to Augustinianism. They knew that he acknowledged the extensive influence of the 'platonicks' in *Conf.*, VII, 9–21; that he endorsed Platonism in *De civ. Dei*, VIII, 4 ff.; and that he praised Plato and Plotinus in most extravagant terms in *Contra academicos*, III, 18 (*PL*, XXXII, 956). But they also knew that in *Retractationes*, I, he qualified his earlier pronouncements rather drastically.

[2] More, 'Preface', pp. xxi–xxiii; see further his *Antidote*, sig. A4, and *Democritus platonissans*, st. 75. I am inclined to think that the course of Platonism in the West can be read in terms of Origen's fluctuating fortunes. The road leads from his censure by St Jerome, through many years in the medieval wilderness, to his acceptance by the Florentine Neoplatonists and esp. by Erasmus, Colet and Sir Thomas More.

[3] I am now investigating the extent of Anselm's influence. On St Thomas' formulation of natural law, see below, pp. 149, 150. R. J. Henle's *Saint Thomas and Platonism* (The Hague, 1956) is a thorough study but not in the least relevant. It is also very dull.

[4] *Epistula* XXII, 29: 'What has Horace to do with the Psalter? Virgil with the Gospels? Cicero with St Paul?' (*Corpvs scriptorvm ecclesiasticorvm latinorvm* [Vienna, 1910], LIV, 189.)

[5] Their dates: Epictetus, late 1st cent. A.D.; Hierocles, 5th cent. A.D.; and Simplicius, 6th cent. A.D. Yet Aristotle's influence was as extensive on all the Cambridge Platonists as it had been on Plotinus. He is indeed repeatedly invoked: More cites him throughout his formal treatises *Ench. Eth.* and *Ench. Met.*; Cudworth commends the 'Aristotelical System of Philosophy' even as he bends

and Calvin and the entire array of Protestant theologians were greeted with the worst possible form of disapprobation: a stony silence.¹

The return of the Cambridge Platonists to 'the ancient and wisest philosophers, as also the primitive fathers, the Greek especially', was a return to a tradition which included many more philosophers besides Plato, the Neoplatonists, the Greek Fathers, and the thinkers of fifteenth-century Florence. This tradition was rooted in 'the primitive theology of the Gentiles' which according to Ficino had begun with Zoroaster or perhaps with the mythical Hermes Trismegistus, had passed thence to Orpheus and Pythagoras and several others, and had at last found its way 'entire' into the books of 'our Plato'.² None of the Cambridge Platonists formulated this imaginative scheme with such precision, but a variant of it appears to be implicit in Cudworth's *True Intellectual System* and it was once outlined by More in lines which he mistook for poetry:

> Plato's school
> ... well agrees with learned Pythagore,
> Egyptian Trismegist, and th' antique roll
> Of Chaldee wisdome, all which time hath tore
> But Plato and deep Plotin do restore.³

One is conscious of an irony as the Cambridge Platonists are here observed challenging one tradition only to confine themselves to another. Perhaps the most regrettable result of this development was their

---

it to demonstrate his belief that Aristotle 'trode in *Plato's* footsteps'; and Whichcote on occasion even alludes to him as 'the Philosopher' (*Discourses*, II, 95; III, 164; etc.). He was nevertheless 'out of request with them' (as 'S.P.' reports in his *Brief Account*, p. 14) because he was thought to have been 'not over-zealous of Religion' (Smith, *Discourses*, p. 48).

¹ The best study of the decline of Calvinism is by Cragg, esp. Ch. II. It has been argued that the Cambridge Platonists did not discard Calvin (Pauley, App. I), but while they do agree in some details, their spirit is utterly dissimilar.

² Ficino, p. 25 (*De christiana religione*, Ch. XXII): 'Prisca Gentilium Theologia, in qua Zoroaster, Mercurius, Orpheus, Aglaophemus, Pythagoras consenserunt, tota in Platonis nostri uoluminibus continetur.' This important formulation—also quoted by Shorey, p. 124, and Feibleman, pp. 209 ff.—is discussed by Aspelin, pp. 33 ff. and P. O. Kristeller, *The Philosophy of Marsilio Ficino*, tr. V. Conant (New York, 1943), pp. 25 ff. See also D. P. Walker, 'Orpheus the Theologian and Renaissance Platonists', *Journal of the Warburg and Courtauld Institutes*, XVI (1953), 100–20, and Charles B. Schmitt, 'Perennial Philosophy: From Agostino Steuco to Leibniz', *Journal of the History of Ideas*, XXVII (1966), 505–32.

³ *Psychozoia*, I, 4 (Bullough, p. 12).

Introduction

uncritical acceptance of the legend that 'the primitive theology of the Gentiles' had been profoundly influenced by Pythagoras who as a contemporary of Moses (!) had read the Hebrew Scriptures, had grafted their principal ideas to his own philosophy, and so had altered the character of the tradition which he bequeathed to Plato. The implications were neatly summed up in the oft-quoted rhetorical question ventured by Numenius of Apamea in the second century A.D.: τί γάρ ἐστι Πλάτων ἢ Μωϋσῆς ἀττικίζων; ('What is *Plato* but *Moses Atticus?*').[1] Cudworth saw the point without much difficulty. So did More, who in fact assures us

> that *Pythagoras* drew his Knowledg from the *Hebrew* Fountains, is what all Writers, Sacred and Prophane, do testifie and aver. That *Plato* took from him the principal part of that Knowledg, touching *God*, the *Soul's Immortality*, and *the Conduct of Life and Good Manners*, has been doubted by no Man. And that it went from him, into the Schools of *Aristotle*, and so deriv'd and diffus'd, almost into the whole World, is in like manner attested by all.[2]

Yet the Cambridge Platonists were not nearly so uncritical as might appear at first glance. Smith, for example, never committed himself to the legend of the Attic Moses, while Whichcote expressly said that the Greek philosophers attained their conclusions not through plagiarism from the Hebrews but 'by Natural Light'.[3] We need not doubt that More and Cudworth would also have discounted their theories if facts tended to dispute them. Never the slaves of any tradition, not even of the Platonic, we find that they lent their ears to Casaubon's thesis (1614) that the writings attributed to Hermes Trismegistus were actually written after the advent of Christianity, and on being convinced, adjusted their attitude toward the Hermetic corpus accordingly.[4] Their reluctance to avail themselves of the writings of that other 'platonick',

---

[1] Numenius, *apud* Clement of Alexandria, *Stromata*, I, 22, 150; the (imprecise) translation quoted is by More, *Cabbala*, sig. B1 and p. 188. The debt of the Greek philosophers to the Scriptures had been argued by Tatian, *Oratio adversus graecos*, XL., but esp. by Clement, *Stromata*, V, 14; cf. Augustine, *De civ. Dei*, VIII, 11. Consult further the references in Henry Chadwick, *Early Christian Thought and the Classical Tradition* (Oxford, 1966), pp. 13-15. For one of the fullest seventeenth-century expositions, see Theophilus Gale, *The Court of the Gentiles* (Oxford, 1671), Pt. II, Bk. II, Ch. II *et seq.*
[2] *Ench. Eth.*, p. 2 67; but see also his *Cabbala*, sig. B1, and 'Preface', pp. xvi-xviii. Cudworth's agreement is recorded in *Int. System*, pp. 12 ff. (I, i, 10).
[3] *Discourses*, II, 407.
[4] See the account by Yates, Ch. XXI, esp. pp. 423 ff.

Dionysius the Areopagite, was similarly affected by the discovery that his claim to have been the disciple of St Paul was altogether fraudulent.[1]
But it is time to take a closer look. I propose to start with Bunyan.

II

In 1671 Bunyan was still in prison, and incensed. Edward Fowler's *Design of Christianity* had just subordinated theology to mere ethics and Bunyan felt that the world should have the benefit of his views as well. He therefore launched into *A Defence of the Doctrine of Iustification* (1672) in which he sneered at the 'BRAVE Phylosophers' invoked by Fowler, denounced all their 'Moral Natural Principles', and at last uncovered (as he told Fowler) 'the rotteness of your heart'. Fowler rose to the occasion at once. Where earlier he had insisted on the importance of being 'unbyassed' and had earnestly sought to promote 'Genuine acts of Righteousness and true Holiness', he now called Bunyan a 'wretch', 'a most Black-mouth'd Calumniator', indeed a *'naughty* man', and denounced his treatise as 'hideous non-sense', 'lamentable stuff', *'deadly* poison'. The pamphlet containing these sentiments was entitled *Dirt wipt off: or a manifest discovery of the Gross Ignorance, Erroneousness and Most Unchristian and Wicked Spirit of one John Bunyan* (1672).

Fowler's conduct is by no means an isolated phenomenon in the seventeenth century: nearly everyone involved in a controversy would likewise wipe off the dirt flung at him, and return it promptly to its source. But as Fowler is often mentioned in connexion with the Cambridge Platonists, it is imperative to realise at the outset that the discrepancy between his theories and his practice stands in diametric opposition to the manner in which More or Whichcote engaged in controversies. Thus when Thomas Vaughan—the brother of the poet—published in 1650 two wildly speculative treatises, the *Anthroposophia theomagica* and the *Anima magica abscondita*, Henry More replied in an ambitious effort to curtail the ever-present tendency 'to bee filled with high-swoln words of vanity, rather then to feed on sober truth, and to heat and warm our selves rather by preposterous and fortuitous imagin-

[1] See my account in 'Renaissance Thought on the Celestial Hierarchy: The Decline of a Tradition', *Journal of the History of Ideas*, XX (1959), 155–66. Another evidence of constructive criticism is More's rejection of Josephus' celebrated 'testimony' on Christ as a forgery (*Godliness*, p. 318; cf. Josephus, *Antiquitates judaicae*, XVIII, iii, 3, and the account of F. H. Schoedel, *Flavivs Iosephvs de Iesv Christo testatvs* [Leipzig, 1840]).

ations, then to move cautiously in the light of a purified minde and improved reason'.[1] He therefore attempted to tabulate Vaughan's errors but managed only to become the recipient of an abusive counter-attack in *The Man-Mouse taken in a Trap* (1650). But he persisted, issuing next his bitingly satiric *Second Lash*, whereupon Vaughan responded with *The Second Wash: or the Moore scour'd once more* (1651). A badly-shaken More decided at last to sound retreat, aware now that the appeal to reason could not possibly influence a narrow-minded fanatic. But the principle was not compromised. Convinced even before his encounter with Vaughan of the destructive nature of fanaticism in any form—be it secular or religious 'enthusiasm'—he generalised his recent experience in a work issued in 1656, the *Enthusiasmus triumphatus*, voicing in it the concern he was to express on many occasions, that 'if ever *Christianity* be exterminated, it will be by *Enthusiasme*'.[2]

The conviction that the most serious threat to Christianity is posed by the irrational, not the rational, underlies also the views set out in 1651 by Whichcote in reply to the strictures of Anthony Tuckney. Whichcote was at the time Provost of King's College, Cambridge, as well as the University's Vice-Chancellor; Tuckney was Master of Emmanuel, and would in a few years be appointed Master of St John's and then Regius Professor of Divinity. Tuckney had been distressed ever since Whichcote first began to deliver his 'discourses' in Trinity Church (1636), and now decided that the constant emphasis on 'reason' had reached a point where his intervention was a matter of the utmost necessity. In the first of the six letters the two men were to exchange,[3] Tuckney asserted the supremacy of faith over reason in what at first sight appears to be the uncompromising position of a Calvinist. But classic Protestantism had been just as uncompromising, whether in asserting with Richard Sibbes in 1638 that 'it is the greatest reason, to yeeld reason to Faith', or in urging with Francis Quarles in 1640 that

> In the Meditation of divine Mysteries, keep thy heart humble, and thy thoughts holy: Let Phylosophy not be asham'd to be confuted, nor Logick blush to be confounded; What thou canst not compre-

---

[1] *Observations* (1650), Preface. On the More–Vaughan controversy see Bullough, pp. lxviii ff., but esp. Nicolson, 'Cartesianism', pp. 364 ff., and Greene, pp. 456 ff.
[2] *Godliness*, p. vi. See further below, pp. 24 f.
[3] See Whichcote, *Letters*. Brief accounts of this correspondence are provided by Tulloch, pp. 59 ff., and Jones, pp. 292 ff. Tuckney's position should be studied in the light of his *Forty Sermons*, ed. Jonathan Tuckney (1676).

hend, beleeve; and what thou canst beleeve, admire; So shall thy Ignorance be satisfied in thy Faith, and thy doubts swallowed up with wonders; The best way to see day-light is to put out thy Candle.[1]

'Sir,' replied Whichcote to a parallel assertion by Tuckney, 'I oppose not rational to spiritual; for spiritual is most rational.'[2]

It requires no profound knowledge of the intellectual developments in the seventeenth century to recognise that here if anywhere we have one of the boldest challenges to the mode of thought characteristic of traditional Protestantism. All that the Cambridge Platonists ever uttered reverts in the end to Whichcote's refusal to oppose the spiritual to the rational, the supernatural to the natural, Grace to Nature. John Smith was merely echoing his master when he proclaimed that 'Truth' —the truth of divine revelation—'needs not any time flie from Reason, there being an Eternal amitie between them'. Could it be otherwise so long as all the Cambridge Platonists shared More's belief that Reason connects man to God, that it is 'so far from being any contemptible Principle in man, that it must be acknowledged in some sort to be in God himself'?[3] Such an acknowledgement does not of course terminate in itself. It leads inevitably to the persuasion that the Primal Reason has imparted to the created order a religion at once 'rational, accountable, and intelligible'. It involves the conviction that every 'motion of Religion doth begin with Reason', that indeed Reason is 'awakened, excited, employed, directed, and improved' by religion. It assents to the proposition that there is divine sanction for any endeavour 'to satisfie a Man's self, in the Reason of things; to look to the Grounds and Assurance that Man hath for his Thoughts, Apprehensions, and Perswasions'. Most importantly, it regards as 'greatly Mistaken' anyone who thinks that in religion 'we are not to know, but only to believe'.[4] No man should ever be invited to say with Anselm, *credo ut*

---

[1] Sibbes, *The Fovntaine Opened* (1638), I, 22, and Quarles, *Enchyridion* (1640), III, 91. Cf. Pascal: 'There is nothing that so conforms with reason as this renunciation of reason' (*Pensées*, § 465; tr. J. M. Cohen [1961]).

[2] *Letters*, p. 108; cf. *Aphorisms*, § 1183: 'what is most Spiritual is most Rational'.

[3] Smith, *Discourses*, p. 14, and More, *Cabbala*, sigs. A7ᵛ–A8. Cf. S.P., *Brief Account*, p. 11. Here as elsewhere one is reminded of Hooker. Yet his influence remains nominal, not actual. See Munz (above, p. 2, note 2).

[4] Whichcote, *seriatim: Sermons*, p. 75 (also in *Aphorisms*, § 220; but see esp. § 889 [below, p. 334]); *Discourses*, I, 54, and IV, 253 (also in *Sermons*, p. 298); *Sermons*, p. 58; and *Discourses*, III, 34.

intelligam, much less be demanded to silence his reason with that odd resolution of Tertullian's, *certum est quia impossibile*.¹

The precise nature of the challenge posed by the Cambridge Platonists may best be understood by glancing at the divers uses of the metaphor of the candle, ultimately deriving from *Proverbs* 20. 27 ('the spirit of man is the candle of the Lord'). Protestants normally deployed the metaphor in order to emphasise the inadequacy of natural knowledge, to assert in particular that the Greek and Roman philosophers were immersed in darkness because they had only 'the dimme Candle-light of Nature', a light 'as a small candle: yea rather as little sparks, or as a glimmering', 'no more than the Glow-worme to the Sun'.² This belief was shared even by individuals often associated with the Cambridge Platonists, for example Nathanael Culverwell and Peter Sterry. 'Though the *candle* of *Reason* excell in light the Glow-worms of sense,' declared Sterry, 'Yet it is but a *candle*, not the *Sun* it self; it makes no day; only shines in the darknesse of the night.' Culverwell should have been somewhat more permissive since he composed a paean to reason based on Proverbs 20. 27. But in the end even he circumscribed Reason in no uncertain terms:

> A Candle has no such goodly light, as that it should pride and glory in it. 'Tis but a brief and compendious flame, shut up, and imprison'd in a narrow compasse. How farre distant is it from the beauty of a Starre? How farre from the brightnesse of a Sun? This Candle of the Lord when it was first lighted up, before there was any thief in it, even then it had but a limited and restrained light. God said unto it, Thus farre shall thy Light go. Hither shalt thou shine, and no further. *Adam* in innocency was not to crown himself with his own sparks. God never intended that a creature should rest satisfied with its own candle-light, but that it should run to the fountain of light, and sunne it self in the presence of its God.³

¹ Anselm: 'I believe in order to understand' (*Proslogion*, I; in *PL*, CLVIII, 227); Tertullian: 'it is certain because impossible' (*De carne Christi*, V; in *PL*, II, 761).

² *Seriatim:* Joseph Hall, *Meditations* (1606), I, 195; George Gifford, *A Treatise of True Fortitude* (1594), sig. C4ᵛ; and George Hall, *Two Sermons* (1641), p. 24. Cf. Charles Odingsells, *The Pearle of Perfection* (1637), p. 10: 'the Philosophers of *Greece* . . . walked in the owle-light of naturall knowledge onely' etc.

³ Sterry, *The Spirit convincing of Sinne* (1645), p. 10, and Culverwell, p. 122 [the dedication of whose treatise to Tuckney would have caused less surprise than many scholars are inclined to believe]. Cf. above, p. xxvi, and Sterry, *Sermons*, p. 48. See also George Rust's sermon on *Proverbs* 20. 27, in *Remains* (1686), pp. 21–43 [incorporating his entire *Discourse of Truth* (1682)].

Culverwell's view differs substantially from Quarles' uncompromising command, 'put out thy Candle'. Yet the difference hardly justifies the enrolment of Culverwell among the Cambridge Platonists.

The Cambridge Platonists also invoked Proverbs 20. 27 frequently —'over-frequentlie', complained Tuckney[1]—but they interpreted 'the candle of the Lord' differently. The usual designation of Reason as intellection, the reasoning faculty, the sum of the mental processes, was not rejected. It was acuminated by reference to mathematics. How? In the sense that mathematics, as Proclus had long since pointed out,

> especially refers to the contemplation of nature, since it discloses the order of those reasons by which the universe is fabricated, and that proportion which binds, as Timaeus says, whatever the world contains, in union and consent; besides, it conciliates in amity things mutually opposing each other, and gives convenience and consent to things mutually disagreeing, and exhibits to our view simple and primary elements, from which the universe is composed, on every side comprehended by commensurability and equality, because it receives convenient figures in its proportions, and numbers proper to every production, and finds out their revolutions and renovations, by which we are enabled to reason concerning the best origin, and the contrary dissolution of particulars.[2]

The centre of gravity in Proclus' statement was also located by Hierocles when he said that mathematics 'purify a rational soul'.[3] As Whichcote explained,

---

[1] In Whichcote, *Letters*, p. 20. *Proverbs* 20. 27 is quoted below, pp. 50 and 334; but see also Whichcote, *Dogmata*, pp. 9, 55, 85; *Sermons*, p. 67; *Letters*, p. 112; *Discourses*, I, 264; II, 151, 342; III, 330; IV, 9; etc.

[2] *Primum Eucl.*, I, 8. Kepler, one of the many 'platonicks' to admire Proclus' statement (cf. Max Caspar, *Kepler*, tr. C. D. Hellman [1959], pp. 92 ff.), considered that God is 'the very source of geometry and, as Plato wrote, "practices eternal geometry"' (*Gesammelte Werke*, ed. M. Caspar [Munich, 1940], IV, 299; tr. C. G. Wallis, in *Great Books of the Western World*, ed. R. M. Hutchins [Chicago, 1952], XVI, 1017). On the importance of mathematics within the Platonic tradition, consult Burtt, Ch. I–III; Thomas Whittaker, *The Neo-Platonists*, 2nd ed. (Cambridge, 1918), App. III; J. H. Randall, Jr., *The Making of the Modern Mind* (Boston, 1940), Ch. X; and Alexandre Koyré, 'Galileo and Plato', *Journal of the History of Ideas*, IV (1943), 400–28. See further P. H. Kocher, *Science and Religion in Elizabethan England* (San Marino, Calif., 1953), pp. 150 ff., and my paper on 'The Numerological Approach to Cosmic Order during the English Renaissance', *Isis*, XLIX (1958), 391–7.

[3] *Aur. carm.*, XXVI. See also the illuminating letter by Nicholas of Cusa, quoted by E. F. Jacob, 'Cusanus the Theologian', *Bulletin of the John Rylands Library*, XXI (1937), 411.

Introduction

in that study, Men Abstract from matter, they never concern themselves either with *meum* or *tuum*, but in all their common Enquiries, they separate from matter; for they do only Contemplate and Speculate upon the Idea's, and Forms of Things: Thus they propose to take Men off from Matter, and to subtilize Men's parts, and to raise them to more Noble and Generous Apprehensions.[1]

Man's ability to elevate himself to 'Noble and Generous Apprehensions' led the Cambridge Platonists to think of 'the candle of the Lord' as a spiritual faculty, as that power of mind which the Areopagite termed 'the union above mind' (τὴν ὑπὲρ νοῦν ἕνωσιν) and which Plotinus described as 'something greater than reason, reason's Prior, as far above reason as the very object of that thought must be'.[2] Henry More's term for this faculty was 'Divine Sagacity', said to be 'ever antecedaneous to that Reason which in Theories of the greatest importance approves it self afterwards'. Its province is the universe and therefore may not be limited in any way. It is indeed Reason as

> a Power of Facultie of the Soul, whereby either from her Innate Ideas or Common Notions, or else from the assurance of her own Senses, or upon the Relation or Tradition of another, she unravels a further clew of Knowledge, enlarging her sphere of Intellectual light, by laying open to her self the close connexion and cohesion of the Conceptions she has of things, whereby inferring one thing from another she is able to deduce multifarious Conclusions as well for the pleasure of Speculation as the necessity of Practice.[3]

Reason's ever-expanding circumference is moreover centred about man's moral conduct, persistently defined as the *practice* of the highest ethical principles. The Cambridge Platonists agreed with Clement of Alexandria that the transcendently clear vision of the Divine is 'the privilege of intensely loving souls'. They also agreed with that ex-

---

[1] *Discourses*, II, 400. Cf. *Aphorisms*, § 298 (below, p. 330). See further Lichtenstein, pp. 28 f.

[2] Pseudo-Dionysius, *De divinis nominibus*, VII, 3, and Plotinus, VI, ix, 10. The same idea was often suggested through the Platonic metaphor of 'the eye within us' (Synesius, *De Dione*, VII; cf. *Republic*, 508d).

[3] More, 'Preface', pp. vii–ix, and *Godliness*, p. 51, respectively. On Divine Sagacity see esp. Lichtenstein, pp. 63 ff. For various accounts of the Cambridge Platonists' idea of Reason, see S.P., *Brief Account*, p. 10; Fowler, pp. 42 ff.; Bullough, p. xx; Cragg, pp. 42 ff.; Hoopes, p. 177; McAdoo, pp. 84 ff.; Pauley, pp. 10 f.; Powicke, p. 47; and Basil Willey, *The English Moralists* (1964), p. 183. Cf. Mintz, p. 83.

quisite sentiment of Plotinus, 'Never did eye see the sun unless it had first become sunlike, and never can the Soul have vision of the First Beauty unless itself be beautiful.'[1] The tradition was explicitly clear. So was the response. Henry More upheld the indivisible relationship between morality and man's highest philosophical aspirations by insisting that 'the onely safe Entrance into Divine Knowledge' is 'true Holiness', that 'the Oracle of God is not to be heard but in his Holy Temple, that is to say, in a good and holy man, throughly sanctified in Spirit, Soul and body'. Smith's concurrent affirmation ('the powerful energy of Divine knowledge displaies it self in purified Souls') led him to his significant proclamation that theology is rather 'a *Divine life* then a *Divine science*'—in itself an extension of Whichcote's breathtaking generalisation that *'the State of Religion* lyes, in short, in this; *A good Mind, and a good Life.* All else is *about* Religion.'[2]

The 'orthodox' Protestants were not amused. John Donne did not live to hear the actual formulations of the Cambridge Platonists but he was sufficiently aware of parallel speculations in his own time to venture a protest:

> He that undervalues *outward things*, in the religious service of God, ... will come quickly to call *Sacraments* but outward things, and *Sermons,* and *public prayers,* but outward things ... As some *Platonique* Philosophers, did so over-refine Religion, and devotion, as to say, that nothing but the *first thoughts* and *ebullitions* of a devout heart, were fit to serve God in. If it came to any *outward action* of the body, *kneeling,* or lifting up of *hands,* if it came to be but invested in our *words,* and so made a *Prayer,* nay if it passed but a revolving, a turning in our inward thoughts, and thereby mingled with our *affections,* though *pious affections,* yet, say they, it is not pure enough for a service to God ... Beloved, outward things apparrell God; and since God was content to take *a body,* let us not leave him naked, or ragged.[3]

Donne's protest is applicable to the Cambridge Platonists at least so

---

[1] Clement, *Stromata*, VII, 3, and Plotinus, I, vi, 9 (adapted by Smith, below, p. 129).

[2] *Seriatim:* More, *Godliness*, p. v, and 'Preface', p. viii; below, p. 128; Whichcote, *Discourses*, III, 164 (also below, p. 334). Significantly, Whichcote bypassed the traditional cardinal virtues (prudence, justice, temperance, fortitude) in favour of the three virtues in Titus 2. 12 (sobriety, righteousness, godliness). See the discussion by Pauley, pp. 13–18, but also Fowler, pp. 75 ff. Cf. Whichcote, *Discourses*, II, 116 ff., on 'the great Things in Religion'.

[3] *Sermons,* ed. G. R. Potter and E. M. Simpson (Berkeley, 1957), III, 368.

far as it anticipates their explicit castigation of 'notions'—doctrinal assertions generally—and their implicit disapproval of every form of institutionalised religion. But they would have justified their 'ethical inwardness' with reference to the most basic aspect of Christ's ministry, that 'this is the most proper and formal *Difference* between the *Law* and *Gospel*, that the one is considered only as an *External* administration, and the other as an *Internal*'.[1] They would have supported their denunciation of religious conventions by invoking the precedent of the great prophets whose voices are heard in Whichcote's sombre warning that 'God who is of purer Eyes than to behold Iniquity, cannot be pleas'd with any thing that may pretend, by way of recompense, for any impure, filthy, immoral Acts'.[2] They would have argued that a man's moral behaviour is not an isolated activity but partakes of the 'Universal Righteousness' that has existed 'at *all* times', even as it reflects the 'Eternal and Immutable Morality' that has always emanated from Heaven.[3] They would have insisted on the utter importance of action, convinced that man is acknowledged by God only when he is 'in motion', 'upon Action', so that the Cartesian *cogito ergo sum* should be revised to read 'I act, therefore I am'.[4] They would have urged in particular that a Christian's application of moral principles to life is an imitation of Christ, now proclaimed by Smith to be our 'first Copy & Pattern' as he was once averred by Ficino to be 'a living book of moral, nay of divine philosophy, and the very divine idea of virtue manifest to human eyes'.[5] Other exponents of this tradition of *imitatio Christi*

---

[1] Smith, *Discourses*, p. 311. Cf. Whichcote, *Aphorisms*, § 586 (below, p. 332).

[2] *Sermons*, p. 126. The prophets' denunciations extend from I Samuel 15. 22 through Amos 5. 21–23, Hosea 6. 6, and Isaiah 1. 10–17, to the summary statement in Micah 6. 6–8. Cf. Whichcote's sermon on Micah 6. 8 (*Discourses*, II, 241 ff.).

[3] See Whichcote, *Aphorisms*, § 957 (below, p. 334). The other phrase is cited from More, *Apology*, p. 528, but it was also the title of a treatise by Cudworth (see his *Imm. Morality* and its exposition by Passmore, Ch. IV, and Martineau). Cf. More's treatise on ethics, *Ench. Eth.*, and the discussion by Pauley, pp. 132–44.

[4] Whichcote, *Discourses*, II, 135, and III, 328 (cf. Descartes, *Discourse*, IV; *Principles*, I, 7).

[5] Smith, *Discourses*, p. 341, and Ficino, p. 24 (tr. Nesca Robb, *Neoplatonism of the Italian Renaissance* [1935], p. 64, from *De christiana religione*, XXIII: 'Christus est idea, & exemplar uirtutum'). Cf. Jeremy Taylor, *The Great Exemplar of Sanctity and Holy Life* (1649; 4th ed., 1667). On More's view, consult Tuveson, pp. 97, 230 ff. Cf. Whichcote, *Aphorisms*, § 1104 (below, p. 336), and *Sermons*, pp. 331 ff.

had perhaps failed to translate theory into practice. The Cambridge Platonists did not. Whichcote's belief that 'the sum of all Religion is *Divine Imitation*' was a principle which all demonstrated in their lives. Each shared in what we are told was the distinguishing characteristic of Whichcote, his 'universal charity and goodness, which he did continually preach and practise'. Each strove to attain More's 'Extraordinary Pitch of *Sanctity* and *Purity*'. Each was like Smith 'incomparable as well for the loveliness of his Disposition and Temper, the inward ornament and beauty of a meek and humble Spirit, as for the extraordinary amiableness of his outward person'.[1]

Tuckney's position during his exchanges with Whichcote was hardly enviable. He might have had the better of the argument with a theologian or a philosopher or a moralist. But he was at a loss when confronted by Whichcote's 'God-like Disposition'.[2] Overwhelmed, he lapsed into silence and passed into oblivion.

III

The emphasis of the Cambridge Platonists on 'reason' may well be thought to have led in time to Locke's assertion of *The Reasonableness of Christianity* (1695) and even to John Toland's controversial thesis in *Christianity not Mysterious* (1696). There is of course no doubt that the general developments which these works represent were profoundly influenced by the reiterated proclamation of the Cambridge Platonists concerning 'the Reasonableness of our Religion';[3] but they were developments which failed to take into account the importance attached

---

[1] *Seriatim:* Whichcote, *Discourses*, III, 332 (also in *Sermons*, p. 284); John Tillotson, *A sermon preached at the Funeral of the Reverend Benjamin Whichcote* (1683), p. 31; Ward, p. 90; and John Worthington, 'To the Reader', in Smith, *Discourses*, p. vii. See also Gilbert Burnet, *History of his own Time* (1724), I, 186, and Fowler, pp. 22, 37, etc.

[2] From Shaftesbury's Preface, in Whichcote, *Sermons*, sig. A8ᵛ. The Cambridge Platonists abandoned their normally irenic temper only during their denunciations of 'the *Epicurean* herd of Brutish men' who are drowned in 'the Muck of this World', 'the filthy puddle of fleshly Pleasures' (Smith, below, p. 140; More, *Discourses*, p. 256; Cudworth, below, p. 114). Once, however, More and Cudworth crossed swords themselves. See *The Diary and Correspondence of Dr. John Worthington*, ed. James Crossley (Chetham Society, XXXVI [1855]), II (i), pp. 157 ff., 164 ff., 172 ff.

[3] More, 'Preface', p. iv. More's disconcerting habit of referring to his own work is at least helpful in finding one's way through his manifold volumes. Of

by Whichcote and his disciples to the 'mystery' at the heart of the Christian faith. Even when we find Whichcote himself asserting that Christianity is not 'Mystical, Symbolical, Ænigmatical, Emblematical; but uncloathed, unbodied, intellectual, rational, spiritual',[1] it behooves us to observe that his sequence of terms culminates in the word which as we have seen confirms the connexion between the mundane and the celestial, the visible and the transcendental, Nature and Grace. The 'mystery' is not denied; it is in fact accentuated. It is accentuated because the candle of the Lord was said to enable man to attain an almost mystical awareness of God at the point where the rational and the spiritual merge.

The mysticism of the Cambridge Platonists must be carefully differentiated from the mysticism of other traditions. The shadow of St Theresa or St John of the Cross never fell upon them so as to divert their reason into paroxysms of love. They were never stifled by any 'clouds of unknowing', they were never tempted to traverse the 'negative way', and while they borrowed some of the Areopagite's phrases they were never affected by his paradoxical ejaculations or his incandescent language. Their mysticism is perhaps closer to the mysticism of the *Theologia Germanica*, that favourite of Luther's which had impressed More in his greener days. It also has a nominal share in that mysticism which in Pico is joined to a refusal to betray the speculative faculty.[2] But when all is said we must revert once more to Plotinus.[3]

Plotinus is certainly crucial. The Cambridge Platonists manifest the same rational mysticism so characteristic of him, and endorse in particular his experimental knowledge that the vision of God is attained

---

the matter on hand he says (in 'Grounds of Faith', II, 480): 'See also Dr More's *Mystery of Godliness*, where the Reasonableness of our Christian Faith is more fully represented, and plainly demonstrated.'

[1] *Aphorisms*, § 889 (below, p. 334). On the extent to which the Cambridge Platonists contributed to the decline of 'mystery', see Lichtenstein, pp. 177 ff.

[2] Cf. Ernst Cassirer, 'Giovanni Pico della Mirandola', *Journal of the History of Ideas*, III (1942), 138 f.

[3] Cf. G. A. Panichas' discussion of Plotinus and More in 'The Greek Spirit and the Mysticism of Henry More', *Greek Orthodox Theological Review*, II (1956), § 2, pp. 41–61. I am personally tempted by the possibility that the Cambridge Platonists were most directly inspired by St Gregory of Nyssa. This might be explored by way of Jean Daniélou's *Platonisme et théologie mystique: Doctrine spirituelle de Saint Grégoire de Nyssa* (Paris, 1944).

νοερᾷ ἐπαφῇ, 'by *an Intellectual touch*'.[1] But there are important differences even here. Plotinus as a pagan could assert that man achieves union with the Divine unaided, but the Cambridge Platonists as Christians regarded the candle of the Lord as a God-directing gift of God, as 'A Candle lighted by God, and serving to this Purpose; to discern and discover God'.[2] Moreover Plotinus' reiterated counsel that a man should withdraw into himself is indeed echoed in many a statement by the Cambridge Platonists,[3] but his further insistence on the necessity of man's total isolation from the world ('Cut away everything')[4] was resisted at every turn. Smith quoted on occasion the celebrated phrase that concludes the *Enneads*—'the flight of the alone to the alone'[5]—but he was never prepared to maintain that such a flight involves man's translation into another region. It involves rather a transmutation into another *state*, the state wherein the soul is 'inebriated as it were, with the delicious sense of the Divine life'.[6] At no time is the soul 'out of Nature', swallowed up and lost in the wide womb of the Divine. Always aware of its responsibilities within the arena of this world, it utilises the insight gained by 'ecstasy' to propel man from contemplation into action. Simplicius, who is often quoted by the Cambridge Platonists, had phrased the point admirably: 'our knowledge is intended only to qualify us for action, and lead us to it; and therefore the practice of virtue and a good life is the ultimate design of all study'.[7] Once this goal is attained, the Cambridge Platonists would have added, man is at last able to act in imitation of his 'first Copy & Pattern'. Already 'deiform'—'As Plato's school doth phrase it'[8]—he has now become deified.

---

[1] Plotinus, I, ii, 6 (quoted by Smith, below, p. 129). On the sanity that marks the mysticism of the Cambridge Platonists, see esp. Cragg, pp. 52 ff.

[2] Whichcote, *Sermons*, p. 449. Cf. *Aphorisms*, § 916 (below, p. 334).

[3] Plotinus, I, vi, 9; IV, viii, 1; etc. Cf. Whichcote, *Sermons*, p. 69: 'the Minds Substraction from the World is necessary, by way of Preparation . . .' etc. See also Smith, below, p. 139.

[4] Plotinus, V, iii, 17. Émile Bréhier correctly observes that the solitude of the sage is 'the Plotinian theme par excellence' (*The Philosophy of Plotinus*, tr. J. Thomas [Chicago, 1962], p. 5). But this is not true of the Cambridge Platonists—despite Muirhead, p. 29. See esp. Smith, below, p. 177.

[5] Plotinus, VI, ix, 11 (translated by MacKenna as 'the passing of Solitary to solitary'); quoted by Smith, below, p. 180.

[6] More, *Antidote*, sig. A5. On the important word 'sense', cf. Smith's comment, below, p. 140, 'When *Reason* once is raised . . .' etc.

[7] *In Epict.*, LXXVI.

[8] More, *Antimonopsychia*, XXV (*Poems*, p. 291). The word 'deiform' is used

IV

The deification of man is one of the most thoroughly Greek ideas espoused by the Cambridge Platonists. Its infrequent appearances in the West never managed to overcome the opposition of St Augustine, and it was in time stamped to death by Calvin. The exception is of course to be found among the Florentine Neoplatonists, especially in Pico's exuberant celebration of the dignity of man.[1] But these philosophers had drunk from the same fountains that were to allay the thirst of the Cambridge Platonists: the unqualified conviction of Plato that man has the capacity 'to become like God'; the ambitious aspiration of Plotinus to merge with The One, 'to be God'; and above all the triumphant proclamation of the Greek Fathers that man *has* become God through the Incarnation of the Logos. Origen had thought it self-evident that the Godhead assumed manhood so that 'by fellowship with divinity human nature might become divine'. St Athanasius, in agreement, contended that 'the Son of God was made man so that we might be made gods'. St Gregory of Nyssa had declared as much even while he had added that man partakes with the Godhead 'both in rank and name' through the divine image in him. Gregory Palamas, in a far more spectacular utterance, had maintained that 'man, by virtue of the body created in the likeness of God, is higher than the angels'.[2] Is it not obvious that these voices constitute the original choir later to be joined by Pico and in turn by the Cambridge Platonists? In the selections made available here the 'sobersense' according to which we are said to be

---

repeatedly: see for example Whichcote, *Discourses*, II, 227, and *passim*; More, *Reply*, pp. 43 ff., and *Psychathanasia*, I, ii, 47; III, i, 30; etc. Consult also Lichtenstein, pp. 45 ff.

[1] Note also John Colet, in *De corpore Christi mystico:* 'God, made man, was the means whereby men were to be made gods' (*Coleti opuscula quædam theologia*, ed. & tr. J. H. Lupton [1876], pp. 40, 190). This is a restatement of the Athanasian view quoted below.

[2] *Seriatim:* Plato, *Theaetetus*, 176b; Plotinus, I, ii, 6; Origen, *Cont. Cels.*, III, 28; Athanasius, *De Inc.*, LIV; Gregory of Nyssa, *Oratio catechetica*, XXV, and *De hominis opificio*, IV, 136; and Gregory Palamas, *apud* Robert Payne, *The Holy Fire* (1958), p. 306 [Payne also relevantly quotes St Macarius *et al.*, pp. 171, 174, 306]. See also Hierocles, *Aur. carm.*, XXVII, and further: W. R. Inge, *Christian Mysticism*, 7th ed. (1933), App. C, 'The Doctrine of Deification', but esp. the thorough survey by M. Lot-Borodine, 'La doctrine de la "déification" dans l'Église grecque jusqu'au XIe siècle', *Revue de l'histoire des religions*, CVI–CVII (1932), 5–43, 525–74, and CVII (1933), 8–55.

deified is made repeatedly clear,[1] and the appeal in each case is directly to the rational mystics of 'Plato's school'.

Expositions by the Cambridge Platonists of the deification of man often unfold in terms of the metaphor of the 'seed' implicit in the concept of man's 'deiformity'. This 'seed' was most frequently said to be the Word of God implanted in the soul of man.[2] But the Cambridge Platonists, in line with their usual stress on the primacy of the literal sense,[3] also connected their metaphor to the prophecy of the Seed of Woman (*Gen.* 3. 15) traditionally identified with Christ.[4] In sum, the 'seed' appears to be that aspect of man's 'deiform' nature which upon its deification through the God-man is empowered to win the battle with 'the Seed of the Evil Spirit which is perpetually at enmity with the Seed of God'.[5]

The God-man is of central importance to the thought of the Cambridge Platonists. He was not regarded merely as man's 'assistant' in the battle with the Evil Spirit, much less simply as man's 'first Copy & Pattern'. He was said to occupy the most crucial position in the history of the world, 'that large voluminous Period of Providence, which, beginning with the first *Fiat lux* in *Genesis*, ends not till the last *Thunder-clap* intimated in *Revelation*'.[6] Yet Christ is not just a reality within history; he is also a reality in the innermost recesses of each individual soul. This double manifestation—'*Christ within* and *Christ without*'[7]— was seen as the clearest possible testimony that God has bestowed on man, two gifts in particular. The first is Grace; the second is free will.

Tuckney in one of his letters to Whichcote complained that the re-

---

[1] See below, pp. 70 ff., 101, 167.

[2] See esp. More's account, below, pp. 208 ff. Thus also Smith: 'Religion is ... *the Seed of God* in the Spirits of men' (below, p. 000), and further: Whichcote, *Sermons*, pp. 131 f., and *Discourses*, II, 182, etc.; More, in Ward, p. 14; Sterry, *Sermons*, p. 36, and indeed *passim*; etc.

[3] Cf. More, 'Grounds of Faith', II, 482: 'the true and primarie Sense of Holy Scripture is *Literal* or *Historicall*'. The Cambridge Platonists diverge here from all the allegorising 'platonicks' (Philo, Origen, Proclus, *et al.*).

[4] See my account in *Milton and the Christian Tradition* (Oxford, 1966), pp. 123 ff.

[5] Smith, below, p. 162. But see also his comments on p. 193 and esp. Whichcote's sermon on pp. 62 ff.

[6] More, *Dialogues*, II, 287. The Cambridge Platonists accepted the traditional interpretation of history which I have outlined in *The Phoenix and the Ladder: The Rise and Decline of the Christian View of History* (Berkeley, 1964). But only More believed that the Last Judgement was imminent (*Apology*, p. 482). Cf. p. 90.

[7] More, *Godliness*, p. ix.

peated emphasis on Reason was all too often at the expense of Grace. As he put it, 'to say that the ground of God's reconciliation is from any thing in Us; and not from his free grace, freely justifying the ungodly; is to deny one of the fundamental truths of the Gospel.'[1] Tuckney had a point, but it was the point of the suspicious Calvinist who equates the assertion of Reason with a denial of Grace. Whichcote and his fellow Platonists could not possibly accept an equation which reduces religious experience to an either/or proposition. They believed that man possesses free will even as his life unfolds under the ever-present influence of Grace. Grace does not overpower man; it liberates him to perform the tasks which God has always intended him to perform. In More's words,

> the Theatre of the world is an exercise of Mans wit, not a lazy *Polyanthea* or book of Common places. And therefore all things are in some measure obscure and intricate, that the sedulity of that divine Spark the Soul of Man, may have matter of conquest and triumph when he had done bravely by the superadvenient assistance of his God.

Belief in God's 'superadvenient assistance' also informs Whichcote's claim that 'God expects, Man should *Do*; as He makes him capable'. In Whichcote's fuller statement,

> The Grace of God, to which we owe our Salvation, it doth not only give assistance, recovery, and furtherance to all the Principles of real Righteousness and true Goodness; which do very much need a help for their Recovery, because of Man's Fall; but the Grace of God doth its own work besides; it empties the Mind of fond Persuasion, foolish Self-conceit and presumption, and so makes room, gives a Man Capacity to receive from God, both the grace of Assistance, and also makes him capable of Forgiveness.[2]

The operative word here, as always with the Cambridge Platonists, is 'both'. It links God's Grace and man's free will. It links the spiritual and the rational, in further confirmation of Whichcote's statement to Tuckney that 'spiritual is most rational'.

---

[1] In Whichcote, *Letters*, p. 4.

[2] *Seriatim:* More, below, p. 262; Whichcote, *Aphorisms*, § 927 (below, p. 334); *idem*, *Discourses*, III, 195 ff. See also Whichcote's assertion of 'prevenient' Grace (*Sermons*, p. 427) and esp. his sermon on man's dependence on Christ (*Dogmata*, pp. 13–51). Cudworth (below, pp. 124 f.) makes the important point that God's law frees even as it enslaves.

William Hull in 1612 described fallen man in terms acceptable to the majority of his contemporaries. He said that man is 'laden with sinne, darkened with ignorance, itching with lusts, subiect to passions, repleat with illusions, prone to euill, fraught with shame and basenesse'.[1] Whichcote's view was somewhat different. He saw man as 'the Masterpiece of God's workmanship', 'the glory of God's creation', 'fit for Attendance upon God, and converse with Angels'.[2] We are of course reminded of Pico and the other Florentine Neoplatonists, perhaps also of Erasmus, Colet and Sir Thomas More. But Whichcote, I should think, was again invoking 'the ancient and wisest philosophers, as also the primitive fathers, the Greek especially'. As they had been the first to assert the dignity of man, so they were the first to instil in the Cambridge Platonists the conviction that 'God hath left us, in the Christian Religion, as *Free* as we may be'.[3] They also provide the basis for Whichcote's triumphant proclamation, 'we are mightily for *Liberty*'. They bolster Smith's view that the 'right knowledge of God' begets 'a *freedome* & *Liberty* of soul within us, and not *servility*'. They support More's belief that God is 'the Author of the necessary and fatal Sequels and Concatenations of things; but we our selves are the cause of our being illaqueated by them'. They vindicate the inability of all the Cambridge Platonists to 'swallow down that hard Doctrine concerning *Fate . . . or Calvinistick Predestination*'. And they sustain Cudworth's thesis in *The True Intellectual System of the Universe*, which is 'A Discourse concerning *Liberty* and *Necessity*, or to speak out more plainly, *Against the Fatall Necessity* of all *Actions* and *Events*'.[4]

When the Cambridge Platonists fused Grace and free will into one unified experience they severed themselves not only from Calvinism but also from Plato and Plotinus. Calvinism was acceptable so far as it maintained Grace, but unacceptable so far as it denied free will; Plato

[1] *Repentance not to be Repented of* (1612), fol. 29v. Hull's view is not specifically Calvinistic. It was also shared by, say, Donne. See my *Milton and the Christian Tradition* (Oxford, 1966), pp. 101 ff.

[2] *Discourses*, II, 25–50 *passim*.

[3] Whichcote, *Sermons*, p. 342. We have here the reason for the rejection of astrology by all the Cambridge Platonists. Whichcote's occasional comments (e.g. *Sermons*, pp. 407 ff.) led to More's full argument (*Godliness*, Bk. VII, Ch. XIV–XVII; also reprinted separately as *Tetractys anti-astrologica* [1681]).

[4] *Seriatim:* Whichcote, below, p. 69; Smith, *Discourses*, p. 28; More, *Apology*, p. 529 (cf. his *Ench. Eth.*, Bk. III); More, in Ward, p. 6 (cf. his letter to Limborch on the 'horrible' decree of predestination, in Powicke, p. 111); and Cudworth, *Int. System*, sig. A3. On the important association between the Cambridge Platonists and the Dutch Arminians, see the definitive study by Colie.

and Plotinus were acceptable so far as they maintained free will, but unacceptable so far as they denied Grace. The Cambridge Platonists sought a more balanced view and found it, readily, in the writings of 'the primitive fathers, the Greek especially'. But it is of some moment that they did not hesitate to reject both Plato and Plotinus when these were discovered to be in opposition to an essential point of the Christian faith. '*Vitals* in religion', said Whichcote, 'are *Few*'.[1] Grace was deemed to be one of them, and the Cambridge Platonists were not prepared to surrender it for the sake of any philosopher, however 'platonick', however eagle-eyed.

v

'I am persuaded', wrote Whichcote in one of his letters to Tuckney,

> that Christian love and affection, among all partakers of the Gospell-grace is a point of such importance, and certain foundation; so pressed upon us by our Saviour, and his Apostles; that itt is not to be prejudiced, by *supposals* of differences, in points of religion anie wayes disputable; though thought weightie, as determined by the parties on eyther side: nor yett by the *trulie* different persuasions of those; who cannot bee satisfied, eyther in our conceited formes of expression; or particular determinations beyond scripture: which, as some have observed, have indeed enlarged Divinitie; but have lessened Charitie, and multiplied Divisions.[2]

We expect Whichcote's irenic spirit to have appealed to most of his contemporaries, yet it managed only to stimulate their anger, even to harden their hearts. This is not surprising. The Cambridge Platonists understood by '*supposals* of differences' nothing less than the sum total of beliefs that distinguished one religious sect from another, and demanded that all should be set aside as mere 'notions'. Whichcote in particular never made a secret of his utter distaste for '*Divinity methodized*', nor wavered in his belief that it is a mistake to 'think that Religion lies in a *System* of Propositions; for a Man may have all the Doctrines of Religion, as Notions in his Mind, and yet never have his Spirit mended by them.'[3] We think this the reasonable conclusion of a

---

[1] *Aphorisms*, § 1008.
[2] *Letters*, p. 118. Cf. *Aphorisms*, § 981 (below, p. 335).
[3] *Sermons*, p. 233, and *Discourses*, III, 161; respectively. The censure of 'notions' was constant: see for example, below, pp. 96 ff., 110, 128, 330. See further Sterry, in Pinto, pp. 201 ff.

reasonable man—and so it is. But it is also a sweeping criticism of all organised religion which was not likely to impress his contemporaries favourably.

Yet the Cambridge Platonists wished not to dispense with organised religion but to reform it. To this end their primary endeavour became the formulation of principles—what Whichcote terms 'the reasons of things'—for the guidance of human behaviour at its best. While the Tuckneys of the world continued to assert the primacy of individuals in relation to ecclesiastical pronouncements ('we should look rather to their doctrines, than their persons'),[1] the Cambridge Platonists insisted on the subordination of the individual to principles. 'Believe *Things*, rather than *Men*', counselled Whichcote, for 'we shall be judged by things, as they be; not by our own presumptuous Imaginations'.[2]

The Cambridge Platonists felt that men's presumptuous imaginations had already yielded two ills, superstition and 'enthusiasm', respectively represented (so 'S.P.' reported excitedly in 1662) by 'the meretricious gaudiness of the Church of *Rome*, and the squalid sluttery of Fanatick conventricles'.[3] The opposition of the Cambridge Platonists to enthusiasts and Catholics alike was not in itself a novel development;[4] the novelty lay rather in the reasons they now offered for such an opposition. Whichcote best suggests the approach of his fellow Platonists by an appeal to their ultimate authority. '*Socrates*', he said, 'overthrew Enthusiasm and Superstition; when he taught men to receive *no* Doctrine, against or without reason'.[5] In other words, whereas most people who opposed enthusiasts objected to them on the grounds of the divisive tendencies inherent in their private beliefs, the Cambridge Platonists censured them for displacing reason by 'any hot, wild Imagination or forcible and unaccountable suggestion'. In like manner, whereas the Catholic Church was usually denounced in emotional terms as the whore of Babylon or the guardian of the Antichrist, the Cambridge Platonists elected to emphasise one familiar argument in

[1] In Whichcote, *Letters*, p. 27.
[2] *Aphorisms*, §§ 39 and 116 (below, pp. 326 and 328). On the common desire to achieve a 'true Reformation' see Cudworth, below, pp. 114 ff.
[3] S.P., *Brief Account*, p. 7.
[4] On the common Protestant animosity toward Catholics see my *Milton and the Christian Tradition* (Oxford, 1966), *passim*. On the frequent censure of enthusiasts see Umphrey Lee, *The Historical Backgrounds of Early Methodist Enthusiasm* (New York, 1931), and Williamson, both of whom place More's *Enth. Tr.* within its historical context (see respectively pp. 84 ff. and 585 ff.).
[5] *Aphorisms*, § 1085.

particular, that Catholicism has ever attempted to '*Adulterate* what is true in Religion, and *Superadd* what is False'.[1] It were of course a remarkable achievement had these views been set forth with a consistent regard to 'the reasons of things'. But More in particular slid repeatedly into 'enthusiasm'[2] even as he indulged in anti-Catholic outbursts of astonishing bigotry. To read him in the light of John Smith[3] is to understand why he so often irritates where Smith constantly enchants by his infinite good will displayed to all men alike. Henry More can be loved at a distance but never, I think, at close quarters.

'Enthusiasm' and superstition were regarded as serious dangers but not nearly so serious as was 'atheism'. The term 'atheism' should be approached with some caution since today it does not carry the implications it had during the Renaissance.[4] A convenient starting point is supplied by Cudworth whose colossal treatise *The True Intellectual Systeme of the Universe* was written expressly in order to confound 'atheism'. He distinguished between theists and atheists as follows:

> these are they who are strictly and properly called *Theists*, who affirm that a Perfectly *Conscious Vnderstanding Being*, or *Mind*, existing of it self from Eternity, was the Cause of all other things; and they on the contrary who derive all things from *Senseless Matter*, as the First Original, and deny that there is any *Conscious Vnderstanding* Being *Self-existent* or *Vnmade*, are those that are properly called *Atheists*.[5]

The basic generalisation here appears more explicitly in Cudworth's

---

[1] More, *Godliness*, pp. 408 ff., and Whichcote, *Aphorisms*, § 698; respectively. On their anti-'enthusiasm' see further Whichcote, *Aphorisms*, §§ 114, 349, 499, 1182 (all given in the present Appendix), though it should be understood that Smith and Cudworth held qualified views (see Smith, *Discourses*, VI: 'Of Prophesie', and Cudworth, in Passmore, pp. 69 ff.). On their anti-Catholicism see Whichcote's sermon on 'The Malignity of Popery' in *Discourses*, I, 247–78, and several works by More: *Dialogues*, II, 124 ff.; *Apocalypsis Apocalypseos* (1680), *passim*; and esp. *A Modest Inquiry into the Mystery of Iniquity* (1664). Cf. Anderson, pp. 44 ff.

[2] 'His response was frequently emotional rather than logical. He was touched by the "enthusiasm" against which he warned his generation' (Nicolson, *Aesthetics*, p. 115). Consult More's works cited in the previous note.

[3] See either of the two discourses printed below, but esp. the one on superstition (*Discourses*, II) where Smith (as Watkin rightly says, p. 250) is 'too charitable, too deeply absorbed in communion with God' even to allude to Catholicism.

[4] Cf. Ernest A. Strathmann, *Sir Walter Ralegh* (New York, 1951), Ch. III.

[5] *Int. System*, p. 195 (I, iv, 4).

further statement that 'all *Atheists* are mere *Corporealists*, that is, acknowledge no other *Substance* besides *Body* or *Matter*', indeed '*Madly dote* upon *Matter*, and *Devoutly worship* it, as the only *Numen*'.¹ Whichcote agreed. 'It is the Foundation of Atheism', he said, 'that all Being is Body.' In contrast, Cambridge Platonism was based on the kind of 'confession of faith' ventured by Cudworth:

> we acknowledge, that *God* and *Nature* do things every where, in the most *Frugal* and *Compendious way*, and with the least *Operoseness*, and therefore that the *Mechanick Powers* are not rejected, but taken in, so far as they could comply serviceably with the *Intellectual Model and Platform*. But still so, as that all is supervised by One *Understanding* and *Intending Cause*, and nothing passes, without His *Approbation*; who when either those *Mechanick Powers* fall short, or the *Stubborn Necessity* of *Matter* proves uncompliant, does over-rule the same, and supply the Defects thereof, by that which is *Vital*; and that without setting his own Hands immediately to every work too; there being *a Subservient Minister* under him, an *Artificial Nature*, which is an *Archeus* of the whole world, governs the *Fluctuating Mechanism* thereof, and does all things faithfully, for Ends and Purposes, Intended by its Director.²

Cudworth's central allusion here is to his concept of Plastic Nature (see below, pp. 288 ff.), a close relative of More's Spirit of Nature and, like it, a direct descendant of the tradition of the *logoi spermatikoi* or *rationes seminales* introduced by the Stoics, qualified by the Neoplatonists, and adapted finally by any number of thinkers during the Renaissance.³ The common origin of the Cudworth–More concepts is suggested in More's statement that the Spirit of Nature is 'a substance incorporeal'

> in every part *naturally* appointed to doe all the best services that Matter is capable of, according to such or such modifications, and according to that *Platform* of which it is the *Transcript*, I mean according to the Comprehension and Purpose of those *Idea's* of things which are in the eternal Intellect of God. Whence it is plain,

---

[1] *Int. System*, p. 135 (I, iii, 30). Cudworth supplied the necessary qualification: 'though all *Corporealists* [are not] of necessity *Atheists*; yet *Atheists* universally have been *Corporealists*' (*ibid.*, p. 768 [V, iii]).

[2] Whichcote, *Discourses*, IV, 337, and Cudworth, *Int. System*, p. 672 (V, i); respectively. See also Smith, *Discourses*, III: 'Of Atheism'.

[3] The tradition is outlined by W. C. Curry, *Shakespeare's Philosophical Patterns* (Baton Rouge, 1937), Ch. II, and by Hunter. See also W. R. Inge, *The Philosophy of Plotinus*, 3rd ed. (1929), I, 155 ff.

That there need be no other λόγοι σπερματικοὶ [*logoi spermatikoi*], or *Seminal Forms*, then this one, which virtually contains all every where, and is therefore rightly styled *The Universal Spirit of Nature*.[1]

If the Cambridge Platonists could appeal to a distinct tradition, so could the 'atheists'. Henry More thought that atheism was 'first nourished up in the stie of *Epicurus*'.[2] Cudworth traced it to the emergence of what he called 'Democritick Fate' and went to such pains to expound its lineage that his zeal began to be regarded with suspicion.[3] But his intention was first of all to demonstrate that the seemingly novel ideas current in his time had been uttered before, secondly to indicate the extent to which they had been overthrown already, and lastly to assert the 'intellectual' (that is to say the rational, the 'spiritual') order pervading the universe. The Herculean labours of Cudworth as of the other Cambridge Platonists were in fact a concerted effort to stem the rising tide of materialism, presently reinforced by the advent of the mechanical theory of the universe. It was an effort directed generally against 'corporealists' but specifically against Hobbes.

VI

Hobbes in the following passage of his *Leviathan* appears bent on placing himself within Whichcote's definition of atheism as belief that 'all Being is Body':

> The World, (I mean not the Earth onely . . . but the *Universe*, that is, the whole masse of all things that are) is Corporeall, that is to say, Body; and hath the dimensions of Magnitude, namely, Length, Bredth, and Depth: also every part of Body, is likewise Body, and

[1] 'Preface', p. xv. More's concept is set forth in his *Immortality*, Bk. I, Ch. III, and discussed by Burtt, pp. 140 ff., but esp. Greene, pp. 453 ff. On Cudworth's concept see Aspelin, pp. 12 ff.; Gregory, pp. 458 ff.; Mintz, pp. 96 ff.; and Raven, pp. 114 ff. (who also indicates its 'explicit approval' in John Ray's *Wisdom of God in the Works of Creation* [1691]). The influence of both theories is traced by J. W. Beach, *The Concept of Nature in Nineteenth-Century English Poetry* (New York, 1936), Ch. III.

[2] *Godliness*, p. vii. The third of Smith's *Discourses* ('Of Atheism') deals largely with Epicureanism.

[3] Dryden reported in 1697 that Cudworth 'has raised such strong objections against the being of a God, and Providence, that many think he has not answered them' (*Dedication of the Æneis*, in *Essays*, ed. W. P. Ker [Oxford, 1900], II, 187). William Warburton has a similar report in *The Divine Legation of Moses* (1741), II, p. xi.

hath the like dimensions; and consequently every part of the Universe is Body; and that which is not Body, is no part of the Universe; And because the Universe is All, that which is no part of it, is *Nothing*; and consequently *no where*. Nor does it follow from hence, that Spirits are *nothing*: for they have dimensions, and are therefore really Bodies.[1]

Fate had driven iron wedges betwixt Hobbes and the Cambridge Platonists. He was a naturalist, they were idealists. He posited a universe permeated by matter, they believed in a world palpitating with spirit. He postulated determinism in a mechanical universe obedient to inflexible laws, they asserted man to be a free agent within a vital, dynamic, 'plastic' nature. He was never conscious of the transcendental, they were never without 'the delicious sense of the Divine'. He implicitly denied the divine origin of man, they explicitly upheld it. He located the ultimate authority in the sovereign, they placed it in the mind of man, 'the candle of the Lord'. He claimed that man is motivated by fear, they asserted that man is instinct of love. It is I think apparent that the Cambridge Platonists did not look on Hobbes quite the way that Cowley did, as the 'great *Columbus* of the *Golden Lands* of new *Philosophies*'.[2]

Whichcote remarked on the philosophy of Hobbes only rarely, and Smith not at all. The burden of its refutation was carried by Cudworth and to a lesser extent by More.[3] More's limited participation is understandable not because he was a modest writer—he wrote, alas, *too much*, and promptly translated everything into Latin—but because he felt

---

[1] *Leviathan*, XLVI (one of the passages quoted by More in his attack on Hobbes' denial of spirits [*Immortality*, pp. 55 ff.]). The most relevant study is by Frithiof Brandt, *Thomas Hobbes' Mechanical Conception of Nature* (Copenhagen, 1928). It is I suppose no longer fashionable to think of Hobbes as an 'atheist' (cf. W. B. Glover, 'God and Thomas Hobbes', in *Hobbes Studies*, ed. K. C. Brown [Oxford, 1965], Ch. VIII) but we should not go so far as to draw him within the circle of Christian orthodoxy (cf. F. C. Hood, *The Divine Politics of Thomas Hobbes* [Oxford, 1964]).

[2] *Pindarique Odes:* 'To Mr. Hobs', l. 56. According to a legend often taken seriously, Hobbes had said '*That if his own Philosophy was not True, he knew of none that he should sooner like* than MORE'S' (Ward, p. 80). But I think that Ward's biography trespasses the limits permissible even in hagiographies!

[3] The best account of the Cudworth–More refutations of Hobbes is by Mintz, Ch. V–VI. Cf. Passmore, Ch. I, and Hutin, pp. 90 ff. The brilliant expression of Hobbes' limitations in Cudworth's *Imm. Morality* (first publ. 1731) is most ably discussed by Muirhead, pp. 60 ff.

obliged to fight on another front against a warrior far more subtle than Hobbes. I mean, of course, Descartes.

The war was preceded—as all wars are—by a period of friendship. Cartesianism seemed on the face of it to be the one modern philosophy most likely to accomplish the marriage between the theistic demands of the Cambridge Platonists and the mechanical view of nature upheld by the 'new philosophy'. Descartes—'that admirable Master of Mechanicks'—had said that philosophy must be concerned to demonstrate 'the two questions respecting God and the Soul', which are precisely the 'two grand Pillars' of Cambridge Platonism.[1] Might it not be that he alone could prevent the ever-threatening disespousal between mind and body, matter and spirit? Impressed, More in December 1648 addressed the first of his four letters to Descartes. The letter begins with More's gracious rejection of all other philosophers as mere pygmies next to Descartes[2] and proceeds in the same generous manner to differ with the theory set out in the *Discours de la méthode* (5ᵉ partie) pertaining to the mechanical motions of animals. The transition from the initial compliment to the criticism is so smooth that we could easily fail to sense More's uneasiness over the implications of Cartesianism. Yet More persisted in the hope that his differences with Descartes might prove minimal. 'That which enravishes me most', he wrote,

is, that we both setting out from the same *Lists*, though taking several wayes, the one travailing in the lower Rode of *Democritisme*, amidst the thick dust of Atoms and flying particles of *Matter*, the other tracing it over the high and aiery Hills of *Platonisme*, in that more thin and subtil Region of *Immateriality*, meet together

[1] *Seriatim:* More, *Immortality,* sig. b6ᵛ; Descartes, *Meditations,* Dedication (cf. his *Discourse,* IV); and More, 'Preface', p. iv. Smith also observes that God's existence and the soul's immortality have been 'most insisted upon by the *Platonists*' (*Discourses,* p. 60). Hence Smith's discourse and More's treatise on the immortality of the soul, in obvious continuation of the tradition extending from Plato (*Phaedo,* 70c ff.) through Plotinus (IV, vii) to Ficino (*Theologia platonica,* in Ficino, pp. 78 ff.). See esp. Giovanni di Napoli, *L'immortalità dell' anima nel Rinascimento* (Turin, 1963).

[2] 'Omnes quotquot exstiterunt, aut etiamnum existunt, Arcanorum Naturæ Antistites, si ad Magnificam tuam indolem comparentur, Pumilos planè videri ac Pygmæos...' (*Epistolæ quatuor ad Renatum Des-Cartes,* in *A Collection of Several Philosophical Writings* [1662], II, 61; also available in *Descartes: Correspondance avec Arnaud et Morus,* ed. Geneviève Lewis [Paris, 1953], pp. 93 ff.). The More–Descartes discussion of animal mechanism (see Cohen, pp. 50 ff.) should be read in the light of the broader developments outlined by Leonora C. Rosenfield, *From Beast–Machine to Man–Machine* (New York, 1941).

notwithstanding at last (and certainly not without a Providence) at the same *Goale*, namely at the Entrance of the holy Bible.[1]

In 1653 a persistently optimistic More hailed Descartes as 'a man more truly inspired in the knowledge of Nature, then any that have professed themselves so this sixteen hundred years', and again confessed himself 'ravished with admiration of his transcendent *Mechanical* inventions, for the salving the *Phænomena* in the world'.[2] But in the end he discovered that Cartesianism was more '*Mechanical*' than 'transcendent'. In 1665 he wrote to Boyle 'that the phænomena of the world cannot be solved merely mechanically, but that there is the necessity of the assistance of a substance distinct from matter, that is, of a spirit, or being incorporeal'.[3] In 1668 he said as much publicly and gave notice of divorce by branding the philosophy of Descartes 'pure Mechanism'.[4] At last, in the *Enchiridion metaphysicum* of 1671, More severed himself from the 'upstart Method of *Des Cartes*' altogether.[5]

Pascal once remarked that Descartes 'would gladly have left God out of his whole philosophy. But he could not help making Him give one flip to set the world in motion. After that he had no more use for God.'[6] If More reached the same conclusion rather late, he was at least always suspicious that Cartesianism pointed unfailingly in the direction of

---

[1] 'Preface', p. xii. But the shape of things to come is apparent even here (p. xi) as More attempts to clear Descartes from 'that giddy and groundless suspicion of Atheism'.

[2] *Cabbala*, p. 189. Similar comments will be found in his *Poems*, p. 189; *Reply*, pp. 41 ff., etc. See esp. Nicolson, 'Cartesianism'; Hutin, pp. 97 ff.; and Anderson, Ch. V.

[3] Letter of 4 December 1665; in *The Works of the Honourable Robert Boyle* (1772), VI, 515. See also More's letter to Limborch, in Colie, p. 53.

[4] Preface to *Dialogues*, where Cartesianism is attacked repeatedly (I, 31 ff., 94 ff., etc.). Cudworth also censured Descartes for his 'mere *Fortuitous Mechanism*' and further found that 'some of the ancient Religious Atomists, were also too much infected with this *Mechanizing Humour*; but *Renatus Cartesius* hath not only outdone them all herein, but even the very Atheists themselves also' (*Int. System*, p. 175 [I, iii, 38]). On Cudworth and Descartes see Passmore, Ch. I; Pauley, pp. 96 ff.; but esp. Colie, Ch. VII. Cf. Sailor *et al.* in the note following.

[5] But Descartes decisively influenced More and the other Cambridge Platonists. See Gregory; Pauley, pp. 4 ff.; John Laird, 'L'Influence de Descartes sur la philosophie anglaise du XVIIe siècle', *Revue Philosophique*, CXXIII (1937), § 2, 226–56; J. E. Saveson, 'Descartes' Influence on John Smith', and 'Differing Reactions to Descartes among the Cambridge Platonists', *Journal of the History of Ideas*, XX (1959), 258–63, and XXI (1960), 560–7; and D. B. Sailor, 'Cudworth and Descartes', *Journal of the History of Ideas*, XXIII (1962), 133–40.

[6] *Pensées*, § 194; tr. J. M. Cohen (1961).

dualism, toward an absolute dichotomy between matter (body) and spirit (mind or soul). Descartes' attribution of 'extension' only to matter[1] confirmed More's worst suspicions. To confine extension to matter and further to regard spirit as unextended was clearly to divide the universe into two separate entities. If matter is extended and therefore everywhere and infinite, how can God be immanent in the universe? If spirit is without extension and therefore to all intents and purposes an abstraction which 'is' nowhere, are we not in effect denying the existence of spirit? But this were to revert to materialism, to 'corporealism', to 'atheism'. We must therefore understand, claimed More, that matter and spirit are alike endowed with extension. Matter is extended but finite, 'impenetrable'; spirit is extended and infinite, 'penetrable', so unlike matter that it is best to think of it as a fourth dimension which More elected to call 'essential spissitude'.[2] Spirit is like space. Infinite spirit and infinite space are indeed interchangeable, and so—at least in terms of attributes—are space and God.[3]

VII

More's assertion of the infinitisation of space entitles him to be ranked as a philosopher.[4] His concept influenced many other serious thinkers,

[1] *Principles*, I, 53; II, 4, 10; etc. See Snow, pp. 37 ff., and Norman K. Smith, *New Studies in the Philosophy of Descartes* (1952), pp. 109 ff., 191 ff., 324 ff. Cf. A. B. Gibson, *The Philosophy of Descartes* (1932), pp. 193 ff., 264 ff., 300 ff.

[2] 'I mean nothing else by *Spissitude*, but the redoubling or contracting of Substance into less space then it does sometimes occupy' (*Immortality*, p. 13). The idea is pursued in *Ench. Met.*, tr. in Glanvill's *Saducismus triumphatus* (1681), pp. 151 ff. (also in FM, pp. 213 ff.).

[3] See his 'Preface', pp. xii–xv; *Dialogues*, I, 94 ff.; but particularly *Ench. Met.*, esp. p. 69 (where More lists twenty attributes shared by God and space) and Ch. XXVII–XXVIII (which in Glanvill [*op. cit.*: previous note] are entitled 'The Easie, True and Genuine Notion and Consistent Explication of the Nature of a Spirit'). See FM, pp. 281 ff.; Baker, *S&T*, Ch. II; Burtt, pp. 143 ff.; Koyré, Ch. V; and Willey, pp. 163 ff. Cudworth's views on extension are in *Int. System*, pp. 769 ff. (V, iii). His Plastic Nature is (according to Mitchell, p. 279) a direct refutation of Cartesianism.

[4] See Koyré, Ch. VI. More's concept of space and its influence are also discussed by Baker and Burtt (as in the previous note); Greene, pp. 466 ff.; Jammer, pp. 38 ff.; Nicolson, *Aesthetics*, pp. 134 ff.; Snow, pp. 194 ff.; Ernest Tuveson, 'Space, Deity, and the "Natural Sublime" ', *Modern Language Quarterly*, XII (1951), 20–38; and Robert Zimmerman, 'Henry More und die vierte Dimension des Raumes', *Sitzungsberichte der Philosophisch-Historischen Classe der Kaiserlichen Akademie der Wissenschaften*, XCVIII (1881), 403–48.

most notably Newton. It is however necessary to remember that even as More was rising to the apex of his philosophical endeavours, he was also falling into belief in spiritualism, occultism, witchcraft. His indulgence in these perversities sets him quite apart from the other Cambridge Platonists, in a manner distressingly reminiscent of Iamblichus' deviation from Neoplatonism through his practice of theurgy. Admittedly More made an effort to explain his uncritical fondness for the occult. He wished to awaken all 'benummed and lethargic Mindes' to an awareness that 'there are other intelligent Beings besides those that are clad in heavy Earth or Clay'.[1] But he also thought that such an effort was doomed to failure unless one first established the existence of witches. Is not the denial of witches tantamount to a denial of spirits, which is bound to lead to a denial of God? *'No Spirit,'* said More, *'no God.'*[2] We are reminded of Sir Thomas Browne:

> I have ever beleeved, and doe now know, that there are Witches; they that doubt of these, doe not onely deny them, but Spirits; and are obliquely and upon consequence a sort not of Infidels, but Atheists.[3]

More's actual demonstration of this thesis is certainly unnerving. In both the entire third book of *An Antidote against Atheism* (1653) and throughout *The Immortality of the Soul* (1659) he introduced whatever might be comprehended under the 'one generall terme of *Apparitions*', including for example such 'extraordinary effects' as 'speakings, knockings, opening of doores when they were fast shut, sudden lights in the midst of a room floating in the aire, and then passing and vanishing...'[4] Henry More, I fear, could not always tell a hawk from a handsaw.

Yet More is not the only Cambridge Platonist who offends. Cud-

---

[1] From a letter prefixed to Glanvill's *Saducismus triumphatus* (1681), I, 16 Glanvill was More's fellow-spiritualist: see Jackson I. Cope, *Joseph Glanvil* (St Louis, 1956), Ch. IV, 'Glanvill, More, and a World of Spirits in an Age of Reason'. Glanvill's *Lux orientalis* (1662) upholds the pre-existence of souls in imitation of 'the great Dr H. More'—not to mention Origen (*De princ.*, I, viii, 4; III, i, 22; etc.). [2] From the concluding line of his *Antidote*.

[3] *Religio Medici*, I, 30; ed. J.-J. Denonain (Cambridge, 1955), p. 40. One is shocked to learn that Browne testified in the trial of two 'witches' who were later hanged (see F. L. Huntley, *Sir Thomas Browne* [Ann Arbor, 1962], pp. 241 ff.).

[4] *Immortality*, pp. 90 ff. This nonsense should be compared with Smith's superb discourse on witchcraft (*Discourses*, X). On this see the comments by Arnold.

Introduction 33

worth also offends, not indeed because his reason was ever eclipsed[1] but because his style failed him at the very moment when he needed it most. One can hardly believe that the same person was responsible for both the magnificent sermon before the House of Commons in 1647 (see below, pp. 90 ff.) and the colossal *Intellectual System of the Universe* (cf. pp. 288 ff.). Readers of the *System* have repeatedly attacked its 'diffuse repetitions and enormous digressions', its 'vast and unwieldy' size, its lack of 'any graces of style'. It has even been called 'monstrously obese'[2]—and who can demur? The pity is that the style of the Cambridge Platonists was initially very promising. Smith is certainly an excellent writer, not only the best of the four but also one of the very best in seventeenth-century literature. His sentences undulate within a lovely pattern that constantly merges style and thought:

> There is nothing that so *embases* and *enthralls* the Souls of men, as the dismall and dreadfull thoughts of their own *Mortality*, which will not suffer them to look beyond this short span of Time, to see an houres length before them, or to look higher then these materiall Heavens; which though they could be stretch'd forth to infinity, yet would the space be too narrow for an enlightened mind, that will not be confined within the compass of corporeal dimensions. These black Opinions of Death and the Non-entity of Souls (darker then Hell it self) shrink up the free born Spirit which is within us, which would otherwise be dilating and spreading it self boundlesly beyond all Finite Being: and when these sorry pinching mists are once blown away, it finds this narrow sphear of Being to give way before it; and having once seen beyond Time and Matter, it finds then no more ends nor bounds to stop its swift and restless motion. It may then fly upwards from one heaven to another, till it be beyond all orbe of Finite Being, swallowed up in the boundless Abyss of Divinity,

---

[1] Though it *was* eclipsed in the *Int. System*, pp. 546–632 (I, iv, 36), where Cudworth (like More in *Psychoʒoia*, Canto I) attempted to relate 'the famous Platonicall Triad' of The One, Mind, and Soul, to the Christian Trinity (see further Gysi, pp. 105 ff.). A modern scholar believes that there is 'hardly any disagreement' between the Platonic and the Christian Trinities (P. V. Pistorius, *Plotinus and Neoplatonism* [Cambridge, 1952], pp. 58–66), yet the history of dogma demonstrates that any attempt to relate the two is bound to lead to heresy or at least to subordinationism. Origen is a case in point; so is Cudworth, who was violently attacked for his views esp. by John Turner in *A Discourse concerning the Messias* (1685). Tendencies similar to Cudworth's are also obvious in Milton (see William B. Hunter, 'Milton's Arianism Reconsidered', *Harvard Theological Review*, LII [1959], 9–35).

[2] *Seriatim:* Martineau, p. 400; Cragg, p. 49; Tulloch, p. 241; and Laird, p. 260.

ὑπεράνω τῆς οὐσίας, beyond all that which darker thoughts are wont to represent under the Idea of Essence. This is that θεῖον σκότος[1] which the Areopagite speaks of, which the higher our Minds soare into, the more incomprehensible they find it. Those dismall apprehensions which pinion the Souls of men to mortality, churlishly check and starve that noble life thereof, which would alwaies be rising upwards, and spread it self in a free heaven: and when once the Soul hath shaken off these, when it is once able to look through a grave, and see beyond death, it finds a vast Immensity of Being opening it self more and more before it, and the ineffable light and beauty thereof shining more and more unto it; when it can rest and bear up itself upon an Immaterial centre of Immortality within, it will then find it self able to bear it self away by a self-reflexion into the contemplation of an Eternall Deity.[2]

Whichcote's style is quite different from Smith's yet no less impressive. Whichcote is consistently 'plain'. His ideas are communicated in a way that anticipates Sprat's description of the 'manner of Discourse' appropriate to those harbingers of the new era, the members of the Royal Society:

> They have ... a constant Resolution, to reject all the amplifications, digressions, and swellings of style: to return back to the primitive purity, and shortness, when men deliver'd so many *things*, almost in an equal number of *words*. They have exacted from all their members, a close, naked, natural way of speaking; positive expressions; clear senses; a native easiness; bringing all things as near the Mathematical plainness as they can: and preferring the language of Artizans, Countrymen, and Merchants, before that, of Wits, or Scholars.[3]

This 'constant Resolution' was violated, oddly enough, by the only Cambridge Platonists to become members of the Royal Society, More and Cudworth. Their stylistic tactics can of course be justified. It is possible to claim that the immense learning displayed by Cudworth in the *System* and by More in works such as *The Grand Mystery of Godliness* is used not for its own sake but 'by way of illustration and to support particular arguments'; it represents also 'an honest attempt to make available the evidence of Greek and Roman philosophy'.[4] But

---

[1] 'divine darkness'.

[2] *Discourses*, pp. 124–5. Smith's emphasis on the immensity of God—a distinctly Platonic idea—is echoed repeatedly by his fellow Platonists. See the passages collected by Pauley, pp. 82–8.

[3] Thomas Sprat, *The History of the Royal-Society* (1667), p. 113 (Pt. I, § 20).

[4] Mitchell, p. 359, and Cragg, p. 43; respectively.

the result is unfortunate none the less. The decision of More and Cudworth to construct vast edifices reminiscent of the medieval 'cathedrals of the mind' was utterly misguided so long as their opponents erected modern structures which were plain and well-executed. Cudworth and More might have imitated the style of their favourite Plotinus—'concise', as Porphyry describes it, 'dense with thought, terse, more lavish of ideas than of words'[1]—but in the event this was the style of Hobbes, of Descartes, of the 'atheists' generally.

And the 'atheists' won.

VIII

Cudworth's *True Intellectual System* was designed both as a refutation of 'atheism' and as an affirmation of the order pervading the universe. The order was upheld in terms of the sacrosanct concept of the Scale of Nature so popular during the Middle Ages and the Renaissance.[2] Here the Neoplatonists had again been instrumental since they had maintained that 'all things are for ever linked', that the several parts of the universe are 'limbs of one entire body'.[3] The Cambridge Platonists, in full agreement, asserted with Whichcote 'the Scale of the Creatures', with More the arrangement of all beings in 'distinct degree', and with Cudworth 'a *Scale* or *Ladder of Perfections* in Nature, one above the other, as of *Living* and *Animate Things*, above *Senseless* and *Inanimate*; of *Rational* things above *Sensitive*'.[4] In a further concession to this tradition they also described the universal order in terms of music, as when More fancifully posited an 'ogdoas' or eightfold hierarchy in these alarming verses:

> Upon this universal Ogdoas
> Is found every particularment:
> From this same universall Diapase
> Each harmony is fram'd and sweet concent.[5]

---

[1] *Vit. Plot.*, XIV.

[2] See esp. Lovejoy, but also my discussion and further references in *Milton and the Christian Tradition* (Oxford, 1966), Ch. III.

[3] Plotinus, IV, viii, 6, and Synesius, *De insomniis*, II; respectively. But see esp. Plotinus, V, ii, 1 ff., and the important commentary by Lovejoy, pp. 61 ff.

[4] Whichcote, *Discourses*, III, 26; More, *Psychathanasia*, I, iii, 25 (*Poems*, p. 101); and Cudworth, *Int. System*, p. 648 (V, i).

[5] *Psychozoia*, II, 15. Note also Cudworth's use of music, below, pp. 95, 117 f., but see esp. Sterry's *Discourse*, *passim*. On the background consult Leo Spitzer, *Classical and Christian Ideas of World Harmony*, ed. A. G. Hatcher

Still another traditional idea was often deployed in connexion with God's providential control of the universe. As More phrased it, 'the Ancients' —specifically Hermes Trismegistus and his disciples—'have defined Him to be a Circle whose Centre is every where and Circumference no where'.[1]

But the Cambridge Platonists did not expound the order pervading the universe in terms of mere commonplaces. The burden of their emphasis was constantly on the principle that God is Love.

We are once more at the crossroads which separate the Cambridge Platonists from their fellow-Protestants. Classic Protestantism had stressed Divine Justice but the Cambridge Platonists stressed Divine Love. Tradition had it that the wrath of the Almighty had been kindled by man's sin and demanded 'rigid satisfaction', but they calmly maintained that 'a mild and gentle Spirit governs the World', 'a lover of Souls' whose '*Justice* is the *Justice of Goodness*, and so cannot delight to punish'.[2] Other Protestants also shared Cudworth's belief that God is 'an Infinite overflowing Fulness and Fecundity' dispensed to all 'Uninvidiously', but none had proclaimed it as often before, much less thought of God as distinguished by 'Gayety and Festivity'.[3] The dis-

---

(Baltimore, 1963); John Hollander, *The Untuning of the Sky* (Princeton, 1961); G. L. Finney, *Musical Backgrounds for English Literature* (New Brunswick, N.J., 1962); and James Hutton, 'Some English Poems in Praise of Music', *English Miscellany*, II (1951), 1–63.

[1] *Poems*, pp. 409 f. This famous affirmation has been traced (by E. Gilson [as above, p. 3, n. 2], pp. 174, 636) to an anonymous work of the twelfth century, generally known as *Liber XXIV philosophorum* and attributed to 'Hermes' by Alan of Lille and others. The work has been studied and edited by Clemens Baeumker, in *Studien und Charakteristiken zur Geschichte der Philosophie insbesondere des Mittelalters* (Münster i.W., 1927), pp. 194–214; the relevant passage ('Deus est sphaera infinita, cuius centrum est ubique, circumferentia nusquam') is on p. 208. Other Cambridge Platonists who use it include Cudworth, *Imm. Morality*, pp. 36 ff. (I, iii, 8); More, *Poems*, p. 193, and *Immortality*, p. 23; Sterry, in Pinto, p. 146; *et al.* Cf. Plotinus' view of God as 'the centre of all centres' (VI, ix, 8). The most relevant discussion is by Nicolson, *Circle*, esp. Ch. II.

[2] 'Rigid satisfaction' is Milton's term (*Paradise Lost*, III, 212) which I discuss within context of the Protestant theory of the Atonement in *Milton and the Christian Tradition* (Oxford, 1966), pp. 130–42. The other statements are, *seriatim*, from: Whichcote, *Sermons*, p. 120; *idem, Discourses*, IV, 374; and Smith, *Discourses*, p. 153. Numerous similar pronouncements were finally gathered up in George Rust's sermon on I *John* 4. 16 ('God is love'), in *Remains* (1686), pp. 1–20.

[3] Cudworth, *Int. System*, p. 117 (I, iii, 28), and More, *Dialogues*, I, 180. More's view of God's 'gaiety' is a resuscitation of the basically Platonic tradition outlined by Hugo Rahner, *Man at Play* (1965).

Introduction

tance travelled by the Cambridge Platonists can be measured even in terms of the drastic reconsideration of a celebrated comment by St Augustine. John Norris—himself deeply influenced by the Cambridge Platonists—reports:

> The *Doctors* of the *Talmud* speaking concerning the Employment of God before the making of the World, say, not as St. *Austin*, that he was preparing an Hell for the Inquisitive, but that he was contriving how to be *merciful* to Mankind.[1]

An inordinate emphasis on Divine Love was bound to lead sooner or later to the 'heresy' most often associated with Origen, that God shall eventually forgive even Satan. Smith and Cudworth suggested as much implicity but it was left to George Rust to argue it explicitly and with More's enthusiastic approval.[2]

The Cambridge Platonists would not have endorsed any attempt to distinguish between *agape* and *eros*.[3] They regarded Love as a single entity 'which issuing forth from God centres it self within us, and is the Protoplastick virtue of our Beings'. This basic assumption led them to several conclusions. They believed that religion is a 'bond of Union between God and Man, and between Man and Man', and therefore imposes on all human beings responsibilities toward each other which must be carried out. They believed at the same time that God has instilled in man 'a secret *Genius* to humanity; a *Bias* that inclines him to a Regard of all his own Kind', which of itself obliges us to 'detest and

---

[1] Norris, p. 130. Augustine's view is stated in *Conf.*, XI, 12.

[2] See Smith and Cudworth, below, pp. 107, 195; Rust, *A Letter of Resolution concerning Origen* (1661), esp. pp. 71 ff., 130 ff.; and More, *Letters*, p. 194. I have traced the development of this distinctly Greek 'heresy' in 'The Salvation of Satan', *Journal of the History of Ideas*, XXVIII (1967), 467–78. See also D. P. Walker, *The Decline of Hell* (1964), Ch. VII–X.

[3] See esp. Anders Nygren, *Agape and Eros*, tr. A. G. Hebert (1932–9), 3 vols. The Cambridge Platonists would have endorsed the several censures of Nygren's thesis (as by John Burnaby, *Amor Dei* [1938], and M. C. D'Arcy, *The Mind and Heart of Love* [1945]) since they always regarded the Neoplatonic *eros* as a variant of Christian *agape* (cf. A. H. Armstrong, 'Salvation, Plotinian and Christian', *Downside Review*, LXXV [1957], 126–39). Note for example Porphyry's concurrent mention of truth, faith, hope and *eros* (*Epistola ad Marcellam*, XXIV, in *Opuscula tria*, ed. A. Nauck [Leipzig, 1860], p. 206) as well as Proclus' projection of *eros* to the universe at large (*Primum Alc.*, XXX, 5 ff.; cf. Plato, *Symposium*, 202e, and Plotinus, III, v). Hence the acceptance by Worthington (*Discourses*, p. 215) of the celebrated statement by Ignatius, 'My Love [*eros*] was crucified' (*Epistola ad Romanos*, VII, ii; *apud* Dionysius the Areopagite, *De divinis nominibus*, IV, 12).

reject that Doctrine [of Hobbes] which saith, that God made Man *in a State of War*'. They believed above all that man should never 'center himself in himself' but should seek to 'put off himself', to attain what Smith termed '*Self-nothingness*'.¹

Love was for the Cambridge Platonists so much the sum total of reality that they almost overlooked evil. They provide us indeed with further restatements of the thesis already popular among the Greek Fathers and Plotinus when St Augustine adopted it, that evil is εἶδός τι τοῦ μὴ ὄντος, 'a kind of *Non-Entity*', 'not *true* Existence', 'no *positive being*'.² But even more striking is their unwillingness so much as to mention 'original sin'. The exception is perhaps More who wrote that 'Original Sin [is] that over-proportionated Proneness and almost irresistible Proclivity to what is evil'.³ But tradition-bound Protestants, we can be certain, would have been scandalised by More's 'almost'. They would have been even more shocked to hear Whichcote aver that 'We are not born with *Habits*; but born only with *Faculties*'.⁴ What then of the 'habitual' nature of original sin? What of the corruption of all our faculties through Adam's Fall? Was it being suggested that sin is reversible?

Whichcote never hesitated. Sin, he said, is 'the Act or Defect of a *Fallible Creature*, and so Reversible'.⁵ Sin is reversible because man possesses the candle of the Lord which kindles 'a secret *Sympathy* in

---

¹ *Seriatim:* Smith, *Discourses*, p. 157; Whichcote, *Discourses*, IV, 400; *idem, Sermons*, pp. 381, 382 (cf. Hobbes, *Leviathan*, Ch. XIII); *idem, Sermons*, p. 213; *idem, Discourses*, II, 117; and Smith, *Discourses*, p. 156. See also below, pp. 113, 165, 328; and the comments by Pauley, pp. 13 ff. (on Whichcote), and Passmore, pp. 76 ff. (on Cudworth).

² The Greek is from Plotinus (see I, viii, 1 ff., and L. Sweeney's commentary in *Gregorianum*, XXXVIII [1951], 521 f.). The other statements are, *seriatim*, from More, 'Preface', p. xvii (who is describing 'hyle'); Whichcote, *Sermons*, p. 229; and Sterry, *Discourse*, pp. 141 ff. Cf. Origen, *Commentaria in Evangelium Joannis*, II, 7 (*PG*, XIV, 136); Athanasius, *De Inc.*, IV; John of Damascus, *De fide orthodoxa*, II, 4 (*PG*, XCIV, 876); and among others esp. Augustine, *Conf.*, VII, 18–22, and *Enchiridion*, XI (see also the references in *LCC*, VII, 343n, and in Bruno de Jesus-Marie, ed., *Satan* [1951], pp. 79–81). More's 'hyle' (*Poems*, pp. 103 ff., 421, etc.) should be compared with Plotinus' ὕλη (W. R. Inge, *The Philosophy of Plotinus*, 2nd ed. [1923], I, 128 ff.) and with Cudworth's lengthy exposition of 'hylozoick atheism' (*Int. System*, pp. 104 ff. [I, iii, 1 ff.]).

³ 'Preface', p. xxv. ⁴ *Sermons*, p. 174.

⁵ *Discourses*, I, 364. Whichcote also stated that 'our Nature [was] vitiated by the Fall' (*ibid.*, III, 128) but the strategy of all the Cambridge Platonists—esp. Smith's—was to assert an accepted dogma and promptly to place it within a larger context, in this case sin's reversibility.

Human Nature, with Vertue and Honesty; with Fairness and good Behaviour'. Sin is also reversible because of Christ's obedience-in-love, in itself 'enough to *thaw* all the *iciness* of mens hearts which *Self-love* had quite frozen up'. But sin is then most reversible when man's innate tendency toward goodness is shaped by Christ's example into a thoroughly *rational* awareness of the wisdom inherent in the practice of universal love. Here, I believe, we have reached the high point of the ethical teaching of all the Cambridge Platonists. It was best summarised by Whichcote. '*Universal Charity*', he said, 'is a Thing *final* in Religion'.[1]

IX

The ideas of the Cambridge Platonists were not, I think, 'tepid speculations'.[2] They affected a number of divers thinkers, among them Barrow and Boyle, Tillotson and Locke, Ray and Shaftesbury, Leibniz and Newton, Berkeley and even Kant.[3] Their indirect influence was even more important. The Cambridge Plantonists allowed (as Burnet said) 'a great freedom both in philosophy and in divinity'.[4] 'Philosophy'—that is to say science, the 'new philosophy'—benefited from their enthusiastic response which cleared the air of the vestiges of suspicion still clinging to any scientific endeavour.[5] 'Philosophy' (in our sense of

[1] *Seriatim:* Whichcote, *Sermons*, p. 381; Smith, *Discourses*, p. 344; and Whichcote, *Sermons*, p. 289. Cf. *Aphorisms*, § 679 (below, p. 333).
[2] Evelyn Underhill, *Mysticism*, 12th rev. ed. (1960), p. 72.
[3] See Cassirer, Ch. VI; Jammer, pp. 108 ff.; Koyré, Ch. VII; Pauley, pp. 127 ff., and *passim*; Powicke, pp. 197 ff.; Snow, Ch. IV (3); R. L. Brett, *The Third Earl of Shaftesbury* (1951), esp. Ch. I; Walter Feilchenfeld, 'Leibniz und Henry More', *Kant-Studien*, XXVIII (1923), 323–4; Georg F. von Hertling, *John Locke und die Schule von Cambridge* (Freiburg i.B., 1892); A. O. Lovejoy, 'Kant and the English Platonists', in *Essays... in Honor of William James* (New York, 1908), Ch. IX [cf. Martineau, pp. 410 f.]; Charles E. Raven, *John Ray* (Cambridge, 1942), pp. 37, 376, 458–61; Ernest Tuveson, 'The Importance of Shaftesbury', *Journal of English Literary History*, XX (1953), 267–99 *passim*; Basil Willey, *The Eighteenth Century Background* (1940), pp. 58 ff.; G. I. Wade, *Thomas Traherne* (Princeton, 1944), Ch. XX; C. L. Marks, 'Thomas Traherne and Cambridge Platonism', *PMLA*, LXXXI (1966), 521–34; *et al.*
[4] Gilbert Burnet, *History of his own Time* (1724), I, 188. Burnet adds: 'From whence they were called men of Latitude'. The term is most fully explored by Marjorie H. Nicolson, 'Christ's College and the Latitude Men', *Modern Philology*, XXVII (1929–30), 35–53. See also S.P., *Brief Account*. Cf. Fowler.
[5] See esp. the account by Raven. The Cambridge Platonists accepted Copernicanism (e.g. More, *Apology*, p. 483), responded enthusiastically to the unfolding infinite universe (see esp. Nicolson, *Circle*, pp. 158–65), rejected all superstitions

the term now) had its character determined as the Cambridge Platonists asserted the primacy of liberal rationalism, pointed in the direction of deism, and introduced that strain of idealism which was never thereafter permitted to vanish altogether. Theology was altered so dramatically that we might even claim that in Cambridge Platonism we have 'the highest expression of Christian theology in England'.[1] 'Enthusiasm' was curbed. Protestant scholasticism was discarded. The progress of Calvinism was arrested. Fixed points of view—'that highly-esteemed Knowledge called *Orthodoxness* or *Rightness of Opinion*'[2]—collapsed under the impact of new ideas forged from old. Above all, perhaps, the repeated pleas for toleration which had already emanated from several quarters were now joined to a remarkable latitude in thought. 'Everie Christian must think and beleeve', said Whichcote, 'as hee findes cause.' He added:

> I dare not blaspheme free and noble spirits in religion, who search after truth with indifference and ingenuity: lest in so doing I should degenerate into a spirit of *Persecution*, in the reallitie of the thing; though in another guise: For a mistaken spirit may conceit itt self to bee acted by the zeal of God.

Variations on this theme abound. One is More's argument that liberty of conscience is a *'natural and common Right'*. Another is Cudworth's entire sermon before the House of Commons. A third is Smith's ever-present desire to impart his love to men everywhere.[3] One thing, how-

---

concerning earthquakes and comets (e.g. Smith, *Discourses*, pp. 31 ff.), etc. The 'new philosophy' affected even More's apocalyptic thought (see esp. Tuveson, pp. 93 ff.). On the background to their views cf. Cassirer, pp. 44 ff., but also P. H. Kocher, *Science and Religion in Elizabethan England* (San Marino, Calif., 1953), *passim*, and M. H. Carré, 'The New Philosophy and the Divines', *Church Quarterly Review*, CLVI (1955), 33–44.

[1] Muirhead, p. 28.
[2] More, *Godliness*, p. 494.
[3] *Seriatim:* Whichcote, *Letters*, pp. 56 and 115 f.; and More, *Apology*, p. 544. More's thesis (stated with important qualifications by Lichtenstein, pp. 118–20) is most fully argued in *Godliness*, Bk. X, Ch. X et seq., and in *Apology*, pp. 540 ff. (which prompted Joseph Beaumont's violent reaction in *Some Observations upon the Apologie of Dr Henry More* [Cambridge, 1665], pp. 143 ff.). Cudworth's sermon was one of many similar pleas for toleration in the mid-1640s (see William Haller, *Liberty and Reformation in the Puritan Revolution* [New York, 1955], pp. 248 ff.), but the contribution of the Cambridge Platonists to the advancement of toleration should never be underestimated (as it used to be, e.g. by A. A. Seaton, *The Theory of Toleration under the Later Stuarts* [1911], pp. 66 f.). See the definitive study by Jordan, pp. 94–137.

Introduction

ever, always remained constant: the common appeal to the Platonic tradition.

The Cambridge Platonists shared More's conviction that Plato's philosophy is 'the most consistent and coherent Metaphysicall *Hypothesis*, that has yet been found out by the wit of man'.[1] We may well protest that Plato never cared to be 'consistent' and that he was only incidentally 'Metaphysicall'. But no matter. The Cambridge Platonists interpreted Plato in such a way that his spirit still informs the better part of their work. If they diverge in detail as when they seek to subordinate all 'the transactions of Time to the Subsistencies of Eternity', they revert to Platonism the moment they commence urging all men to be 'Naturalized to Heaven' in order to 'relish and savour Divine Things', those originals behind the copies in this world.[2] But perhaps the best single manifestation of their diffuse indebtedness to 'Plato's school' is supplied by Cudworth. He quoted on the title page of *The True Intellectual System* from Origen: Γυμνάσιον τῆς ψυχῆς ἡ ἀνθρωπίνη σοφία, τέλος δὲ ἡ θεία ('human wisdom is a means of education for the soul, divine wisdom being the ultimate end').[3] We recall Whichcote's point that the rational is not opposed to the spiritual. They are aspects of that one reality which is always poured forth into the mind of the good man so as to transport him 'from strength to strength', as John Smith said, 'from glory to glory'.[4]

---

[1] *Reply*, p. 85. Plotinus did not think that Plato was all that 'consistent' (IV, viii, 1) and Cudworth once complained that Plato often speaks 'Cloudily' (*Int. System*, p. 205 [I, iv, 9]). But Cudworth also appreciated Plato's tendency to 'play and toy sometimes' (*ibid.*, p. 53 [I, i, 44]).

[2] Whichcote, *Aphorisms*, § 992, and *Discourses*, I, 90 (cf. *Aphorisms*, § 290, below, p. 330).

[3] Origen, *Cont. Cels.*, VI, 13. The statement looks back to Clement of Alexandria (*Stromata*, I, 5; VII, 3) and thence to Pico (*De hominis dignitate*; in Pico, p. 316, tr. in *The Renaissance Philosophy of Man*, ed. E. Cassirer *et al.* [Chicago, 1948], p. 229).

[4] Below, pp. 191 and 193.

BENJAMIN WHICHCOTE

The Use of Reason in Matters of Religion*

Romans 1. 18

For the Wrath of God is revealed from Heaven against all Ungodliness, and Unrighteousness of Men, who hold the Truth in Unrighteousness.

To proceed to the Declaration of this great and horrid *Sin*, which gives God that high Offence; alienates us from him; exposes us to his Displeasure; *and* against which he doth thus declare; This *holding Truth in Unrighteousness*; it doth admit of several degrees.

1*st. Where Knowledge doth not go forth into Act:* Where *it* doth not attain the Effect of Goodness. For, *bare* Knowledge doth not sanctifie. No Man is renew'd by his Knowledge only. It is said of the degenerate Spirits, the Devils, *that they know and tremble.* The Effect is Fear, and Astonishment: because there is not the Product of Goodness.

2*dly. Not attaining due Growth.* For there will be *Growth*, where there is not Violence, or some ill Accident. Where Nature begins, it goes on, towards Perfection; and it is in the State of Increase, till it come to the State of Consistency. *Growth* in Bulk or Maturity; as *in Nature*, so *in Grace*. The Apostle tells us of the *Measure of the Stature of the Fulness of Christ*.[1]

3*dly. Eluding one's own Judgment.* By an Evasion, unsound Distinction; pretending to Difference, when there is none; doing *that* under one notion, which a Man's own Judgment will not let him do, under

---

* From *Select Sermons*, ed. Anthony, Third Earl of Shaftesbury (1698), Part I, Sermon III [pp. 79–117]. Some italicised words, indicating Shaftesbury's additions to improve the sense, are not shown here. The title of the sermon is by the present editor.

[1] *Ephesians* 4. 13.

another, when the Case is much the same.—Thus when things are under a disguise: when *Intemperance* is called *Good-fellowship*; or when any Man is *Conceited*, or of a *Turbulent Spirit in Religion*, for him to please himself with a notion of *Zeal for Truth*.[2]—We should be very careful and exact to observe the Difference of Moral Good and Evil. Herein we should be severe and impartial; not giving our selves leave to comply with our own Humours; for, as to the great *Notices* of Reason and Nature; the Measures of Vertue and Vice; the Grand Instances of Morality; there can be no Allowance, no Variation; because they are Matters unalterable, unchangeable, indispensible; *Laws of themselves*; without Sanction *by Will*; but by the Reason of the thing.[3] In the great Matters of Righteousness, there is no Variation; but in *Positives* and *Institutes* there is a Latitude of Sense, Interpretation, Time, and Observance. Institutes were never intended to be in Compensation or Recompence for Failure in *Morals*: but for *their* better Security.

4*thly. Not following Truth fully:* but, as *Herod. He heard* John *gladly*, &c.[4] Our Saviour doth mightily accuse the Pharises, because they did pick and chuse; singling out *one* Precept, and in the Observance of *that*, being exact: and this, to make a Compensation for *the rest*: Zealous in *one* thing; loose in *others*: they are charg'd, therefore, with Hypocrisie. Not following Truth fully, is, when all Worldly things do not vail to Religion; but Worldly Conveniences are unduly consider'd: for Truth is so noble and generous a thing, that it will not submit to a Compromise with its opposite.

5*thly. The high degree of Sin:* To go against a Man's own Judgment and Conscience; by violent and unnatural Practice, to contract Reprobacy of Mind, Seardness of Conscience, Hardness of Heart. This, Men will do, when Lust is strong and high. Persons of unsubdu'd and unmortified Affections, they are exposed to such horrid and unnatural use of themselves, and so come to be prodigiously naught. For no Man is suddenly most desperately wicked: but no Man knows, when he is a going; how far he shall go. For the breaking in of Sin

---

[2] Whichcote's frequent censures of zeal (see below, pp. 79 ff., 327 f., and esp. 86; cf. Powicke, pp. 76 ff.) should be compared with Cudworth's discussion, below, pp. 118 ff.

[3] Cudworth similarly argued that morality is eternal and immutable, insisting that 'every thing is what it is by Nature, and not by Will' (*Imm. Morality*, p. 17 [I, ii, 3]).

[4] *Mark* 6. 20.

is as the Inundation of Water.—This by way of Explication.—Two Observations from these words, *the Wrath of God is reveal'd*:

(1.) Men have wrong and injurious Apprehensions of God.

(2.) All those that are condemn'd for Sinners, are first *self-condemn'd*. For every one that in Scripture-Sense is *a Sinner*, is *self-condemn'd*.

1*st*. The wrong Apprehensions that Men have of God *that Sinners have no Warning; that they are surprized by God's Judgments, and taken unawares*. This is without all ground: since *the Wrath of God is declared*; by his *Word*, and by his *Works*; besides the Sense of Mens Minds, the Guilt of their Consciences, and their own Heart misgiving them: for no Man is true to himself, if he be ill employ'd: for he that is employ'd in an Evil Work, is always possess'd with Fear, and he is not certain that he shall be true to himself. Wherefore let the Declaration of God in Scripture be acknowledg'd as true; *Thy Destruction is of thy self. Why will ye die, O ye Sinners? Righteous art thou, O Lord, and true are all thy Judgments.*[5] For God, of his great Goodness and Compassion to Men, doth graciously begin: but we often find Men wilful, obstinate, and rebellious. God is ready to pursue his Good Beginning; and, if they answer his Call, further to carry them on: for you have an express Promise, *To him that hath shall be given*.[6] All Grace is help; and where God is, there is Strength. Therefore cannot any one say, his Miscarriage is of God. It is not want on God's part: but failure on ours. It is not that God fails in what is becoming him, in the relation he stands to us, as Creatures; but we are wanting to our selves. What is all the Misery that befalls Sinners, in their most forlorn Condition, but the Fruit of their own Sins? Not any thing, that proceeds from God's Arbitrary Will and Power: But they contract Guiltiness of Conscience, Impenitence of Mind, Hardness of Heart, and an Incapacity to act God-ward, or to receive from God.

2*dly*. The Scripture doth suppose, that ungodly Men are *self-condemn'd*.[7] For this super-addition, *Who hold the Truth in unrighteousness*, is, as rendring an Account; not making a Distinction: As rendring an Account how it comes to pass, notwithstanding all God's Endeavours and Declarations, that Men continue ungodly Persons: The Reason is; *Because they offer Violence to Truth, go contrary to their*

[5] *Hosea*, 13. 9, *Ezekiel* 18. 31, *Psalms* 19. 9.   [6] *Matthew* 13. 12.

[7] One of Whichcote's most seminal ideas. Cf. *Aphorisms*, § 232 (below, p. 329).

The Use of Reason in Matters of Religion 45

Light, and neglect the Declarations of God: Not, as if it distinguish'd between *ungodly* and *unrighteous* Persons.—All that in any Scripture are branded for Sinners, they are Men that sin against their Knowledge, imprison the Truth of God, and hold it in Unrighteousness. In the Language of Scripture, none are nominated Sinners, but such as *now* we are representing. The Scripture doth never fasten the Title or Denomination upon them that mean well, but are in something mistaken; who now and then are under an Error, having Failings, Imperfections, and Shortnesses; that miscarry upon a violent Temptation, or sudden surprizal. You never find these Men are call'd *Sinners*. Neither are the Infirmities of the Regenerate, call'd *Sin*: Tho' these are Sins that require God's Forgiveness, and are a true Cause for us to be Humble, and Modest, and to depend upon God: But they do not break our Peace with God; neither do they havock Conscience, or denominate a Person *a Sinner*. The Scripture tells us. That *those that are born of God do not commit Sin*;[8] that is, in this Sence; no one that is regenerate, doth pass into the contrary Nature: It is unnatural: They may have Shortnesses, Failings, Imperfections: But voluntarily to consent to known Iniquity; or wilfully to controul the settled Laws of Heaven, of Piety to God, Justice to Men, and Sobriety to our selves; this is unnatural. These Persons have the Guilt of evil Practice lying upon their Minds. They have their own internal Sence reproving them, challenging them, condemning them. For the Cause of all Creatures Misery is *rational*, and *accountable*; and Men do dishonour God, and misrepresent him, when they say that any Creature falls into Misery *by the Use of God's Sovereignty*: It doth really arise *from within us*:[9] And there is no Danger in respect of God, (notwithstanding his great Priviledge,) if Men be innocent, and not self-condemn'd.—Misery and Harm do not proceed from *abroad*; but do arise from *within*. If Omnipotence it self should load me with all Burthens; If I am innocent within, I shall be able to bear it: But if I am guilty, I have a Wound *within*; and have nothing within me true to my self.—All Misery arises

---

[8] 1 *John* 5. 18. As this is our first encounter of a Johannine verse, it is perhaps needful to observe that while other seventeenth-century thinkers normally favoured the epistles of Paul, the Cambridge Platonists were partial to the Fourth Gospel and the three epistles of John—the most distinctly Hellenic works in the entire New Testament. Such favouritism is also displayed by other Neoplatonists, for instance John Scotus Erigena.

[9] Whichcote's most frequently reiterated idea: cf. *Aphorisms*, § 926 (below, p. 334), and *passim* in the three sermons reprinted here.

out of our selves. It is a most gross Mistake; and Men are of dull and stupid Spirits, who think that that State which we call *Hell*, is *an incommodious place*, only; and that God, by his Sovereignty, throws Men therein. For Hell arises *out of a Man's self*: And Hell's Fewel is *the Guilt of a Man's Conscience*.¹⁰ And it is impossible that any should be *so* miserable as Hell makes a Man, and as there a Man is miserable, but by his own condemning himself: And on the other side, when they think that Heaven arises from any *Place*, or any nearness to God, or Angels: This is not principally so; but it lies in a *refin'd Temper*, in *an internal Reconciliation to the Nature of God, and to the Rule of Righteousness*. So that both Hell, and Heaven, have their Foundation *within* Men. Evil knowingly admitted, is our Burthen: For all Evil is forcible, violent, and unnatural:¹¹ And a Sinner wrongs his own Principles.— This might be made appear in respect of God; in respect of one another; in respect of our selves.

1st, *In respect of God.* For, consider him as the Father of our Beings, and that we are derivatively from him; or that our State is Dependency; or that we are sinful; or that we are under his Love; or that he is to be our Judge; all these, will cause Acts of Piety. So that all Acts of Impiety are contrary to the Light of our Reason: And whosoever is impious in any Degree or Particular whatsoever, he doth *hold the Truth in Unrighteousness*; he confounds his Principles, acts contrary to his Nature, and contradicts the Principle of God within him. For this is Fundamental to all Religion; that Man in the Use of his Reason,¹² by Force of Mind and Understanding, may as well know, that there is a God that governs the World, as he may know, by the Use of his

---

[10] A tenet asserted by all the Cambridge Platonists with indefatigable energy (cf. below, pp. 50 f., 122, 182 ff., 192 f., 196, 329 f., etc.). See further: Whichcote, *Sermons*, pp. 77, 144, 153, 180, 406, 441, 447, and esp. 417; *Discourses*, I, 370; II, 354, 378, 432 ff.; III, 197 ff., etc.; cf. Worthington, *Discourses*, pp. 48, etc. I have discussed this idea in relation to changing patterns of thought in 'Renaissance and Modern Views on Hell', *Harvard Theological Review*, LVII (1964), 217–36.

[11] Cf. Whichcote, *Sermons*, p. 156: 'Vice is contrary to the Nature of Man; because contrary to the Order of Reason, which is Man's highest Perfection.' See also his *Discourses*, I, 194 (cf. pp. 206 ff.); *Aphorisms*, § 42 (below, p. 326); and the similar views of Norris, p. 24, and Sterry, *Sermons*, pp. 74, etc.

[12] Here begins Whichcote's exposition of natural law, to be developed later (pp. 52 ff.). Cf. Smith's discourse, below, pp. 149 ff.

Eyes, there is a Sun. For are we not *made* to know there is a God? If we were not *made* to know that he is; we could never know. For this we can never be taught: For upon whose Credit shall we believe it? It is not *Divine Faith*, unless it be grounded on Divine Authority: All else, is either *Reason*, or *Human Perswasion, Credulity*, or *Experience*. We are not capable of *Faith*, unless we know there is a God: For if there be Faith in God; we must suppose, that He is. For Faith is *a receiving something upon Divine Authority*. And if there be not a Natural Knowledge, that God *is*; there is no Possibility of any Faith. Men know by the Use of their Reason, that there is a God: And then when a Man receives any Proposition from God's Authority; *that*, is *Faith*. Natural Knowledge, you see, is anticedent and Fundamental to Faith.—It is as natural and proper for Mind and Understanding to tend towards God, as for heavy Things to tend towards their Center: For God is the Center of immortal Souls. All Understandings seek after God, and have a Sense and Feeling of God. If Reason did not apprehend God; Religion could not be learn'd: For there would be nothing in Nature to graft it on. Besides, we know in Reason, that first Principles are self-evident, must be seen in their own Light, and are perceived by an inward Power of Nature. For, as we say, *out of nothing comes nothing*; so, grant nothing; and nothing can be proved. Wherefore it must be within the Reach of Reason, to find that there is a God: For upon God's Authority, supposing his Being and Veracity, we admit and receive all the Results of his Will.—If God had not *made* Man to know there is a God; there is nothing that God could have demanded of him; nothing wherein he might have challenged him; nor nothing that he could have expected, Man should have received from him. Therefore the Make of Man, the natural Use of Mind and Understanding, this is enough to satisfie any one concerning the Being of God, and his essential Perfections: And if so; whosoever is impious to God, whosoever is not subject to all his Commands, this Man doth certainly sin against his Conscience, and doth practise against his Light, and is guilty of *holding the Truth in Unrighteousness*.—Thus, every one that is Impious, Ungodly, Prophane, or a Despiser of Deity, is self-condemn'd; sins against his Light, and goes against his Conscience; goes against his very Make; and doth that which is violent, horrid, and unnatural.

The second Species of Sin, is *Unrighteousness*. Now Righteousness refers to the Duties we mutually owe one another: *To do as we would be done by. To do equally and justly; not arbitrarily.*—How doth Violence and Fraud perplex and interrupt Humane Affairs? How settledly do Men live, where Love and Justice do take place; in comparison of Places Arbitrary, and Lawless.—There is a secret Harmony in the Soul, with the Rule of Righteousness; there is no Displacency, Offence, or Reluctancy: And there is an Antipathy arising at the Appearance of Evil, as unnatural to it: But a Complacency in Good, as the eldest and first Acquaintance. So *Gen.* 39. 9. *How can I do this Wickedness?* We see that the Mind of a good Man takes Offence at Evil, is grieved at it, not at all fitted to it? There arises a Displacency, as in all Force and *Contra-natural* Impression.—Iniquity and Sin in the Conscience, are of the most mischievous Nature and Quality. Should all the World agree and concur to sink a Man into a State of Lowness, Beggary, and Misery; it would not be brought about so effectually by any other Means, as by Sin and Guilt. Where there is a pure Mind, and an upright Conscience, Innocency, and Integrity; there, consequently, are internal Peace, Satisfaction, Composure. But on the other side; if a Man have Sence of Guilt on his Mind; where a Man knows himself faulty; he fears uncertainly, infinitely: He fears every thing that appears, yea, that which doth not appear; as the Poet expresses it; for Guilt is always Prophetical of what is mischievous. A Man may better apply, here, in this Case, the Words of *Ahab* (*Kings* 22. *ver.* 8.) than he did to the Prophet; *He always prophesies Evil concerning me.*[13]

3*dly, In respect of our selves.* As we consist of *two* Parts; of Spirit, and of Body; so we shall fall under a double Obligation, as to our selves. And if we do our selves right, we are under Obligation to our Minds *doubly*: To inform our Understandings, and to refine our Spirits by moral Principles. The Mind is to be inform'd with Knowledge, and refin'd with moral Vertue. Ignorance and Improbity are mental Diseases. And it is worse for a Man to have an ill affected Mind, than an ill dispos'd Body. It is so much the worse, as, the Mind of Man is better than his Body. We find that Nature hath given Faculties: And Industry and Study acquires Habits. A neglected Mind is, according to *Solomon's* Observation, *A Sluggard's Field grown over with Thistles and Thorns.*[14] We may say of such a Man, that he hath his Mind only for Salt: But can any Man that is rational, or sober, think that God gave him an immortal Spirit, but as *Salt*, to keep his Body from Stench and Putrifaction. The Mind being Superiour, is not to be subjected

[13] 2 *Corinthians* 18. 7.   [14] Cf. *Proverbs* 15. 19, 24. 30–1.

to the Body, nor to the things of the Body; neither ought there to be an unequal Distribution of Attendance; but according to the Proportion of the Worth and Value. We ought to improve our Minds so far, as much over and above, as our Minds do transcend the Body.

Whosoever is proud and conceited, whosoever is intemperate, lascivious, or wanton, he doth *hold the Truth in Unrighteousness.* For these things have Foundation, and are grounded in Man, viz. Sobriety, Modesty, and an humble Sense. The Desires of Nature are moderate, and do keep within bounds: So that in whatsoever miscarriages Men do fall, in all these they do go against their Light, and *hold the Truth in Unrighteousness.*

Therefore *Vertue,* in every kind, is according to the Sense of Humane Nature, the Dictates of Reason and Understanding, and the Sense of Man's Mind. And *Vice,* in every kind, is grievous, monstrous, and unnatural. A Man forces himself, when he is vicious; and a Man kindly uses himself, when he acts according to the Rules of Vertue. And this is so true, that all but those that have abused themselves, all but habituated Sinners, understand *that Vertue is conservative to the Nature of Man*; and that all Evil Practices *destroy it.*—Vertue is conservative to the Reason of Man's Mind by Sobriety and Modesty; for these keep Men in their Wits. And then it preserves the Health, and the Strength of our Bodies, by Chastity, and by Temperance.

Thus have I shewn you the *three* Fundamentals of Religion; the three great Materials of Conscience, which are immutable, unalterable, and indispensible; that are settled in the very Foundation of God's Creation. I have also shew'd you that Vertue is connatural, and well-founded: and that Vice is unnatural and destructive to the Nature of Man. So that there is no Man hath internal Peace, that is either neglective of his Duty to God; or that is unrighteous; or that is intemperate, as to the use of the things *of the Body*; or intoxicated by fond Conceits *in the Sense of his Mind.* For as it is requisite and comely that *Sobriety* be the Mind's Temper; so it is, that there be a moderate and sober use of the things of the Body. For Nature is content with a few things. That which is violent, is unnatural. That Excess which is unhealthy for the Body, doth also stupifie the Mind. So that upon this account also, Vice is unnatural.—What is contrary to the Order of Reason, is contrary to the State of Nature, in Intellectuals.

Those that are ungodly or unrighteous in these *three* great Instances: that bear no Reverence to God; that do not act towards their fellow-Creatures according to the Rules of Justice; that abuse their Bodies, do not govern their Minds, neither improve them in Knowledge, nor refine them by Vertue: All these, do controul their Natural Light, and are *self-condemn'd*.

Now if the Unrighteous and Ungodly are *self-condemn'd*; can it be imputed to God, as Severity, to condemn them? That Judge will be excused from all Severity, who passes Sentence of Execution upon a Malefactor, whom his own Conscience accuses. This will be the World's Condemnation: that where Men either *did* know, or *might* know, they go against their Light: that Men put out the Candle of God in them,[15] that they may do Evil without Check or Controul; that Men take upon them to controul the settled and immutable Laws of Everlasting Righteousness, Goodness, and Truth; which is the Law of Heaven; that Men are bold to confound Order and Government in God's Family, (for *so* the World is;) that Men do Evil, *knowingly*, in the use of their Liberty and Freedom: whereas God himself, in whom there is the Fulness of all Liberty, doth declare of himself, that all his Ways *are Ways of Goodness, Righteousness and Truth*. And can God by Power or Priviledge, do that which is not just? Is there any Unrighteousness in God? God forbid. Yet those that have Liberty but by Participation; pretending the Use of Liberty; do *that* which is not fit to be done. This will be the World's Condemnation. In the case of Sin, there is internal Guilt: a Man doth wrong the Principles of his Mind: he breaks his Internal Peace; and will rue it to Eternity. The Judgment of God at the last day will be easie: for there will be none to be condemn'd, but what were condemn'd before. For Man's Misery arises *out of himself*; and is not by *Positive Infliction*. Men run upon Mistakes, the Wicked and Prophane think, that if God *would*, they may please themselves, and no harm done: and that it is *the Will* of God only, that limits, and restrains them: and they think, that they were out of Danger; if God would forbear a Positive Infliction. This is the Grand Mistake. Hell is not *a Positive Infliction*: but the Fewel of it, is the Guiltiness of Mens Consciences, and God's withdrawing, because the Person is uncapable of his Communication. Sin is an Act of Violence in it self. The Sinner doth force himself: and stirs up Strife within himself; and in a Sinner, there is that *within*, which doth reluctate, and condemn him in the inward Court of his own Conscience. For if our Hearts did not condemn us,[16] all *without*, might

---

[15] On this basic metaphor of the Cambridge Platonists, see the Introduction (above, p. 12) and the statements by Smith and Whichcote (below, pp. 197 and 334). [16] Cf. 1 *John* 3. 20.

be avoided: all else would fail, if this Internal Guilt, and Self-Condemnation, might be removed. But this Naughtiness of Disposition, and Incapacity of Repentance, is *that* which continues the Subject in Misery. Hell therefore is not a Positive Infliction, but doth naturally follow upon Guiltiness, and a spightful, devilish, naughty Disposition unto God and Goodness.

There is something in every Man, upon which we may work, to which we may apply; to wit, *the Light of Reason and Conscience*; to which the Difference of Good and Evil may be made appear. If we, therefore, declare Godliness, Righteousness, and Truth; Men have a *Voice* to give Testimony; and *Conscience* in Men, will yield; notwithstanding the power Lust hath over them. If Reason may not *command*; it will *condemn*.

Lastly; *Here* you may have an account, what it is that gives a Check and a Stop to the Motion of the Divine Spirit. There is an Error in the first Concoction, which is hardly remedied: which is want of Advertency, and Consideration. Men do not awaken their Principles, but give themselves leave to do what they cannot justifie themselves in. Now there is no place for the further Motion of the Divine Grace, where the *former* Grace is neglected, and render'd ineffectual. It is *self-neglect*, and *voluntary allowing of our selves in Evil*, which brings us to Misery. For there is no *Invincible Ignorance*, in respect of things good in themselves, and necessary. No Ignorance excuses *Immorality*, in any Instance whatsoever: but, invincible Ignorance doth excuse *Infidelity*, in the chiefest Point. The Reason is, because the high Points of Sobriety, Righteousness, and Temperance, God hath *made* every Man to know: but, for the Resolutions of his Will, Man must be perswaded of God; and if God do not make Application to him; where he doth not *give*, he doth not *require*.

Take notice, then, of the Boldness and Presumption of these obstinate, rebellious, and contumacious Sinners; who having this Proclamation from the Majesty of Heaven, that the *Wrath of God*, &c. yet will dare to continue in Practices of Unrighteousness, and assume to themselves power to controul the establish'd Laws of everlasting Goodness, Righteousness, and Truth; and to vary from the Reason of things, to gratifie their own Sence, and to please their own Humours, and to serve their own Ends, and take upon them to over-rule all things that are holy, settled, and established from Eternity. What shall a Man say to such Persons? Yet the Atheistical and Prophane are guilty of this Contumacy. But as the Apostle says, *Their Condemnation is just*, *and their Judgment lingers not.*¹⁷ We seem agriev'd at God's Plagues and Judgments, which do so much disturb our Peace and Settlement in the World: but we do greater Acts of Violence. For we imprison Truth, and give God true cause of Offence, and take upon us to controul the Establish'd Laws of Heaven, and to do other things than the reason of things dictates to us, and directs us to do. For the Text tells us, that those that are obnoxious to God's Wrath, *are Persons of ungodly Practice; so that they are, of themselves, condemn'd*: They cannot give an account to the reason of their own Minds, nor satisfie their own Consciences; but are hurried on, and transported by furious and violent Lusts; *holding the Truth in Unrighteousness; they are self-condemn'd before they be condemn'd of God*: BECAUSE THAT WHICH MAY BE KNOWN OF GOD, IS MANIFEST IN THEM, FOR GOD HATH SHEWED IT UNTO THEM.¹⁸

The Apostle doth *here* take upon him, and thinks fit, in this great Affair of Life and Death, to shew, and *prove* by Reason. From hence we may learn *three* things.

(1*st.*) That here is a Check and Controul to the forward and presumptuous Imposers, that take upon them, to dectate, and determine; and are angry with all Persons that are not concluded by *their* Sence. These Persons take upon them, more than the Apostle did.

(2*dly.*) That Religion stands upon the Grounds of *truest Reason*: for the Apostle, here, after he hath asserted, *proves by Reason.*

(3*dly.*) God's Ways and Dealings with his Creatures, are accountable in a way of Reason. But some think that God uses *Arbitrary Power*; and that they might escape without Punishment, if he *would*: and that it is nothing but his Will and Pleasure.—In the 17th Verse he hath declared *the way of Life and Salvation*: and in the 18th. *the way of Misery and Death*. Therefore the Ways of God are accountable, in Reason.

If this were not the Way of God; a Way worthy of Truth; we might ask, why this Apostle may not refer us to his publick Authority; who might, if any one, because of his extraordinary Conversion and Commission from Heaven? but he declines *that*: and *proves by Reason*. But this great Truth is hereby hinted; *that the way of Reason, is the way most accomodate to Humane Nature*. Therefore let us lay aside imposing one upon another; or to use any canting in Religion. Let us

---

¹⁷ 2 *Peter* 2. 3.

¹⁸ *Romans* 1. 19. Cf. Whichcote's two sermons on *Romans* 1. 19–20, in *Discourses*, III, 272–96.

The Use of Reason in Matters of Religion 53

talk Sense, and Reason: for the Apostle doth here shew, and prove *by Reason*. And God himself, who hath all Priviledge; he says, he will draw them *with the Cords of Men*: and what is that, but *Arguments* satisfactory to the Mind of Men? and in the Evangelical Prophet, *Isaiah*; *shew your selves to be Men*:[19] that is, awaken your rational and intellectual Faculties; and take things into serious, and impartial Consideration; and I will convince you.—It is an Apology for any finite, fallible Creature, when he is mistaken; *if he had some Reason for his Mistake*: and if he can but *shew why he did so think*, you have him excused.—'Tis a high Advantage, and Double Security to any Teacher, or Instructor, to have in readiness to shew, that what he saith, is not his *private Imagination*; but is *in Conjunction with the Reason of Things*, or *the Principles of God's Creation*; and of *Divine Revelation*, if it be a Matter of *Faith*.

This, but by way of Observation: Because the Apostle doth decline his Commission of *Apostleship*, and doth prove by *common Reason*.

That which is the Apostle's Argument, is, that all those who in the Language of Scripture are Sinners, all that are ungodly, impious towards God, and unrighteous in his Family, they sin against their Light, go against the Principles of natural Conscience, imprison Truth, and sin against their Knowledge. The argument is, because God *made* Men to know, that he himself IS, and his natural Perfections.

This is here plainly attested in this Verse. It is shortly spoken to. But, because it is a Matter of great Weight; it is spoken more fully in the next Verse. THE INVISIBLE THINGS OF GOD FROM THE CREATION, ARE NOW CLEARLY SEEN [*by the Light of Reason and Understanding*,] BEING UNDERSTOOD BY THE THINGS THAT ARE MADE; EVEN HIS ETERNAL POWER AND GODHEAD:[20] That is: *That there is a God, and his Natural Perfections*. For, whereas here is exprest only his POWER; it is a usual *Synecdoche*; instancing in *one* and understanding *all*: Because there is the same Reason for one, as another.—Now since this Scripture, and other Scriptures, use no other Arguments to prove there is a God (for Revelation cannot prove it, Revelation supposes it;) therefore I shall forbear all other Reasons. For tho' I might produce many *Metaphysical* Things; yet, because they are abstract from Sence, they shall not be nam'd. Therefore I shall, as in the Text, only name

---

[19] *Isaiah* 46. 8.   [20] *Romans* 1. 20.

THE EFFECTS OF GOD. And this is *the best Demonstration*; the demonstrating an *antecedent Cause*, by *subsequent Effects*.

There are *Effects* in the World natural; of Inanimates, of Vegetables, and Sensitives; and in the World moral, of spiritual Substances, and intelligent Agents, that shew there is a God. For they do far transcend Mind and Understanding in Man: Therefore they must be the Product of some higher Being. And if we bring a Man to acknowledge a Being that is abler and wiser than himself, he acknowledges *Deity*.

This *natural Knowledge of God* is wrapt up in the Inward of Man's Mind and Soul; that Men, whether they will or no, whether they be pleased or disaffected, whensoever they look into themselves, and consult with their own Principles, and answer their very Make, so oft are they satisfy'd in this Knowledge, *that there is a God*: And if they are averse; they are self-confounded. So that we may conclude that if any Creature on Earth, that is born in the Species of Man, and that is Partaker of Human Nature, be devoid of *Sence of Deity*; it is one of these *Three* Cases.

(1*st*,) It is where there is not one serious Thought; nothing becoming Man's Principles; no Product of Reason, Mind, and Understanding; but where a Man is sunk below his Nature; nay, where he ceases to be in his Kind, and is worse than a *Gibeonite*.[21]—This is Atheism, *by gross self neglect*. Such a Man may be without God in the World, who only hath Reason and Understanding to live according to Sence, or to pursue his Animal Desires. And this Man lives every Day to his Loss; he doth not act according to the Excellency of the Principles of his Kind.

(2*dly*,) It is where there is Affectation and Choice to be an Atheist: And then he would have it so; struggles with himself; doth what he can to keep all Thoughts of Deity out of his Mind.—*He* is one that hath an ill Affectation of being Lawless and Arbitrary, and gratifying his Senses: And so, he doth *affect being an atheist*; that he may be free from Controul.—*Or*,

(3*dly*,) It is where there is contracted Reprobacy of Mind, by violent and unnatural Practice. And this Case is often represented in Scripture, as by the Prophet *Isaiah*; where it is said, *Make the Heart of this People fat*, &c.[22] which place is referr'd to, *six* times in the New Testament, and speaks to his Purpose; that *Man, by gross abuse of himself, may*

---

[21] The inhabitants of Gibeon were noted for their guile (*Joshua* 9. 3 ff.).
[22] *Isaiah* 6. 10.

choak the Principles of his Nature.—These Men have confounded their Principles, and transform'd themselves into a monstrous State: And we must not produce any thing from what is true of a Monster, to prove a Natural State: For, by Wickedness, Mens Minds come to be blinded. *Aristotle* doth well tell us, that the Wickedness of Mens Lives, and Practices, viciates and corrupts the Judgment of Mind and Understanding.[23]

To conclude with *Tully's* Argument, (who is a better *Divine* than some who pretend to be Christians; and yet seem to deny Reason.) 'Man, himself, being a rational and intelligent Agent; so an Agent of highest Order, Ability, and Perfection, in this visible World; finding his highest Principle, *his Understanding*, transcended by sundry Effects of Wisdom and Power, where to he well knows he can make no Pretence; he cannot avoid acknowledging a higher Agent than himself: Upon whose Power, and will, these surpassing Effects depend.'[24] A Man, in the Use of his Reason, surveys the Things that are about him; he sees *Causes* and *Effects*; he sees things depending one upon another; he sees things done with the greatest Skill and Exactness: He doth very well know, he did not order these things: How came they to pass, then?—We our selves are intelligent Agents: We can do many things: We can disarm the Creation below us, and turn them to our own defence; but for the Sun, Moon, and Stars, *&c.* We cannot produce these things. But, we, that are intelligent Agents, do many strange Effects in Comparison of what the Beasts below, do: *They* cannot take Cognizance of *our* Actions. But there are Operations beyond our Understandings, and which surpass our Wisdom: Therefore, because we (who are able to do such things our selves,) are Intelligent, and have Understanding; we must assert, that there must be an intelligent Agent that is higher and nobler than our selves; upon whose Power and Skill these surpassing Effects depend. This is a true Knowledge of God, and where more is not reveal'd, God will not require more. This is *Tully's* Argument: And this comes home to the Apostle in the Text, for the Apostle says, his BEING, his POWER (*one,* for *all* his Perfections) they are understood in a Way of Reason, *by the Effects of God in the World.* The Height and Excellency of Man, in the Use of his Reason, is over-born and transcended

---

[23] The idea is of course not merely Aristotelian. Whichcote's statement, in any case, defines the limits of his interest in Aristotle.
[24] Cf. Cicero, *De nat. deo.*, Bk. II, *passim*, but esp. II, 16 ff.

by the *Effects* in Nature. Therefore they are the Effects of an Agent more perfect and more skilful, more knowing and more powerful; and he is abundantly good.

Hitherto, I have only shewn, that it is knowable, by the Use of Reason and Understanding, that there is a God; ALL THINGS BEING MADE IN SUCH PROPORTION AND SUCH FITNESS, ONE TO ANOTHER: And Man's Reason is transcended: For we going after God, are at a Loss; there is so much of Wisdom, and Knowledge, and Curiosity, in the Things that are made. We cannot therefore but Reverence an Agent that is higher than we *are*. For, an Account is not be given of them, in way of Human Understanding.— Now I will give *Four* Arguments, that it is more knowable there is a God, and what God is, in some measure, than any thing else.

(1*st*,) God is more knowable, *in respect of the Amplitude and Fulness, of his Being*; because of that Ocean of *Entity*, that Fulness of Being, that is in him. This is as the Sea in Comparison to a small Rivulet. Every Creature is *a Line* leading to God. God is every-where, in every thing. So we cannot miss of him. For *the Heavens declare the Glory of God*,[25] and every Grass in the Field declares God. Man's Understanding is every-where transcended. He cannot give an Account how several Varieties of Colours are in a Flower; how the same Juice or Glebe of Earth should produce such Variety of Colours. We say in Natural Philosophy, we know not the *Modes* of any thing. No Man knoweth the *Mode* how his Soul and Body are united: How the several Particles of Matter meet. We are puzzled to know what Motion is: We can give no Account of these Things. Now there being an *Amplitude*, and *Fulness of Being* in God, he is the more intelligible. He hath all *Being* perfectly in him. He is therefore more knowable than Creatures, that are of limited, confin'd, narrow Beings. The divided, separated, scatter'd Perfections of the whole Creation, are united in God; and, with that Advance, and Improvement, extended to infinite Perfection.

(2*dly*,) The *Ways of our knowing*, do more truly hold of God, than of any thing else.

There are two Ways of coming to the Knowledge of Things: The Way of *Perfection*, and the Way of *Negation*: By these *two* Ways we come to a more full Knowledge.—(1.) In the Way of *Perfection*; we cannot exceed; we need not fear to add to much. If you speak of Man's

---

[25] *Psalms* 19. 1.

Soul; you may say too much: But speaking of God, you cannot transcend Divine Existence, in the Enumeration of any Perfections. If we would express a Notion of our Maker, we should employ our Mind and Understanding, to find out what is best, and what is most perfect; and, then, attribute and ascribe it to God. And this is the best Way to come to the Knowledge of God.—(2.) In the Way of *Negation,* we are also certain: For we cannot remove Imperfection, Contraction, Limitation, far enough from him. Therefore we say, that Words and Phrases are all to be purg'd and purified from their Contraction, and Limitation, before we can ascribe them to God. Therefore, where, in Scripture, God is represented by the Eyes, or other Parts of our Body; we must not understand these things formally, but in a Way of Perfection. So that our *Ways of knowing*, do more truly hold *of God* than *of anything else*. For in the Way of *adding Perfection*, we cannot do too much: And in the Way of *Limitation*, we cannot take away too much.

(3*dly*,) *Our Relation to God.*—We stand nearer related to God, than we do to any thing in the World. Our *Souls* and *Bodies* are not nearer related, than our *Souls* to *God.* God is more inward to us than our very Souls. In him we live, move, and have our Being.[26] God is nearer to us than what is most our selves.—Also it is the natural and proper Employment of Mind and Understanding, to make Search and Enquiry after God. The wise Man says, God is known *by the Fitness and Proportion of one thing to another*,[27] Mind and Understanding in Man, is given on purpose, that Man should search after God, and acknowledge him. So that there is a greater Propriety of Man's *Rational Faculties* to *God*, than there is of his *Eye* to *Light*, or his *Ear* to *Sound*. And it is of greater Deformity for a Man to be *void of Sence of Deity*, than for any Man to be *blind*, so as not to see.

(4*thly,*) *Our Dependance upon God*; his Conservation of us; and his Co-operation with us; this leads us to know him.—Universal and general *Causes* have ready Acknowledgment: Because to them so many things are beholding. *Aristotle* well observes, the Sun which is the universal Cause, doth concur with every particular Cause to every Production,[28] So the *Psalmist, Nothing is hid from the Heat of it.*[29] For, tho' the Earth be not perceptive of the Light of the Sun, because

---

[26] *Acts* 17. 28—a favourite verse of the Cambridge Platonists. Cf. Smith, below, p. 156.
[27] Cf. *Job* 41. 12.   [28] *Physica*, II, 3; *De generatione et corruptione*, II, 10.
[29] *Psalms* 19. 6.

of its Grossness and Opacity; yet it hath the Vertue of it. So God is acknowledg'd. God's concerning himself in our Affairs, and our Dependance upon him, hath a kind of *Universal Acknowledgment*. Take any Man of any Sobriety of Mind, if he relate any thing that befals him; he will interpose, *as God would have it*: If he escape any Danger; he will say, *as God put it into my Mind*, and give God the chief Place. Thus in several Cases: As in Distress, *O God!* our Undertakings, *in the Name of God*: Our Protestations, *in the Presence of God*. Tho', these in the Mouths of many, be but Words of course, spoken without inward Sence of God in the Mind; yet the Custom of them proceeds from a good Original. They carry Reason in them, and shew Nature's Sence. What is without Ground, is not of any long Continuance: But *these* meet with no Reproof; gain Credit, give Assurance, find Acceptance, and become Religious Persons, when us'd in weighty Cases, and with serious Minds and due Intention. Since, therefore, there is such a Dependance of our Souls upon God; it is impossible but that we should know him. They who are in any degree Spiritual, or Intelectual, and are not altogether sunk down into a brutish Spirit and sensual Affection; find, and *feel*, within themselves, Divine Suggestions, Motions and Inspirations. Any Man that hath obtain'd any Degree of the Perfection of Reason; that doth follow the Divine Governour of Man's Life, *Reason*; he doth find that there are *Suggestions* and *Inspirations*; and that, many times, when he was resolv'd another way, there comes *a Light* into his Mind, a *still Voice*;[30] he hears, and he is better directed. Except the Atheistical, and Prophane, and those that are Diabolical, all others, *feel* God, in his Motions and Suggestions.—Thus, is God most knowable of any thing in the World.

Here, you have an Account of the Use of Reason, in Matters of Religion: The Natural Knowledge of God: And the Knowledge of the Revelation of his Will.—The *Natural Knowledge* of God, *that*, is the very Issue, Effect, and Product of Reason. *Revelation* is the other part of Religion: And Reason is the Recipient. What doth God give his Commands to, or his Councels, but to the intelligent Agent, and the Reason of Man? So that *Reason* hath great place in Religion. For Reason is the *Recipient* of whatsoever God declares. And those things that are according to the Nature of God, the Reason of Man can

---

[30] Cf. the 'still small voice' heard by Elijah atop Mount Horeb (1 *Kings* 19. 12).

discover. It is either the *Efficient*, or the *Recipient* of all that is call'd Religion, of all that is communicated from God to Man. The Natural Knowledge of God is the Product *of Reason*: The Resolutions of his Will, for our further Direction, are proposed and communicated *to Reason*: and, in both these ways, we are *taught of God*.[31] In the former, we are *made* to know: And in the latter, we are call'd to be made Partakers of God's Councel. By *the former*, we know what God is, his Nature, that he is: By *the latter*, what God would have us to do. So here you see the Use of Mind and Understanding in the Way of Religion. God teaches us in his Creation, in giving us such Faculties; he teaches us further, in the Resolution of his Will; because he satisfies us in what he doth impose upon us. Therefore *the Use of Reason in Matters of Religion*, is so far from doing any Harm to Religion; that it is the proper *Preparatory* for Men to look out to God. Reason may say, *I did expect it, I did believe such a thing, from the first and chiefest Good*: Now, *I am told it is so.* Man in the true Use of sober and impartial Reason, knowing that he hath not perform'd his Duty to God; is put upon laying out, for God's Pardon, in the Way of the Grace of the Gospel. Man knows he is of limited Perfection, he is not good enough to his own Satisfaction: And therefore knowing that he hath fail'd, his Reason leads him to look abroad, to look out, for every good Word that comes from the Mouth of God: And when he reads in the Bible, *that God will pardon Sin*;[32] that which he expected in the Use of Reason, he may be satisfied is true.

Thus Scripture represents the State of Man's Creation; that it is the proper Imployment of Mind and Understanding, to seek after God, to act our Faculties, *to feel God*.[33] Therefore it is the Depth of Degeneracy, to be without God in the World; to have God far from our Remembrance. There is a natural and indelible Sence of Deity, and consequently of Religion, in the Mind of Man. Neither is there any Plea or Apology for the want of this. For there is no invinsible Difficulty; no Ignorance: We are not *taught*, but *made* to know. There is no Impotency: For every one can use the Parts of Nature; at least, when at Age. There is no Impediment: For it is transacted *within ones self*: Not subject to the Controul of any Usurper. For, an internal *Elicit* Act is exempt from all the World: And may be done by the

---

[31] θεοδίδακτος—a popular idea among the Cambridge Platonists. Cf. below, pp. 92, etc.

[32] Cf. *Matthew* 12. 31; *Romans* 5. 20; etc.   [33] *Acts* 17. 27.

Mind, which is at liberty; when the Person is under restraint. For, unless you can keep him perpetually from himself; you cannot keep him from Reflection upon God, or from other internal Acts.

God's Communications awaken to this. Now all we have are such (viz. Communications from God.) What have we that we receive not?

Man's Principles incline: For, all Understanding tends to God. God is the Center of reasonable Souls, and Spirits.

Things about us, contribute objectively: *The Heavens declare the Glory of God.* Man cannot look abroad; but something of God offers it self; something sounds in his Ear. No Voice in Nature so loud: No Language so easie to be understood.

To the Christian World, there is God's superadded Instrument, *the Scripture*; which contains Matters of Revelation from God; whereby, also, the natural *Notices* of God, are awaken'd, and inliven'd.

To Sum up all. The Language of our Souls *within*; the Impressions of the Divine Wisdom throughout the Creation; the objective Acclamations of all Creatures, carry us on, strongly, to Application to God. *All thy Works praise thee, O Lord.*[34] Holy Scripture comes in pursuance of these, to repeat and reinforce them. So that *He* must of Necessity be very dissolute, and profligate, in respect of his Manners; of a havock'd Conscience, and confounded Understanding; who being Partaker of intelectual Nature; intelligent, by Vertue of his Faculties; living in the midst of *Speaking Arguments* (for Things *speak*,) doth not spell God out, in the Variety or Curiosity of his Creatures; nor understand the Language of Heaven and Earth.

I must needs tell the loose, prophane World; those who being harden'd by Custom and Practice, do controul Grounds and Principles of sober Reason and Judgment; thinking all to be lawful that others do, and the Guise of the World an account of Action; pretending the Doubtfulness and Uncertainty of Reason, from the several Opinions of incompetent Persons (which is the only Defence and Apology, for exorbitant living, such credulous Persons have;) willing to believe what their Lusts lead them to, and what they would fain have to be true; I must tell them, that if ever they come to be awaken'd; to have serious Thoughts; to reflect upon themselves; comparing what they have done, with Principles of severe and impartial Reason, not born to gratifie Sence, or to comply with Humour; they will prove burthensome to their Conscience, and to the Sence of Nature; so that they

[34] *Psalms* 145. 10.

will be confounded in themselves; ready to call on Mountains and Hills to fall upon them, and cover them from the Face of their Judge; and will be found Speechless. Man cannot be at ease, till all he hath sinfully done, be undone; till *right Judgment*, which hath been violently forc'd, be renew'd; and regular Life and Conversation restor'd. All this must be done by mental Illumination, Conviction, and Satisfaction.

The Scripture-way of Dealing with Men, in Matters of Religion, is always by Evidence of Reason and Argument. In Conversion, there must be a Transformation of the whole inward Man. The Sence of the Soul must incline to God: The *Reason of the Mind*, must be the same with the *Reason of Things*.[35]

Religion, indeed, is openly contradicted, by the licentious Practices of such who take to themselves Power and Priviledge to do as they list: But it is mis-represented, scandalized, made ridiculous, and contemptible, by the fond Imaginations, nauseous, fulsome Principles, of the Superstitious: And I reckon that *what* hath not Reason in it, or for it; if held out for Religion, is, *Man's Superstition*.[36] Some things of this Nature may be well meant, by those who are weak: but it is not Religion *of God's making*. But we make our selves Slaves, to be under the Power of it.

It is the Excellency of Religion, that it is highly reasonable; gives an account of it self to Man's Mind; and satisfies.—*Truth* clears it self, and discloses its contrary, *Error*.

[35] Cf. below, pp. 68, 326, 328, etc.

[36] On superstition see further below, pp. 66 f. It is also the subject of one of Smith's *Discourses* (pp. 23 ff.).

BENJAMIN WHICHCOTE

The Manifestation of Christ and the Deification of Man*

Acts 13. 23.

Of this Man's Seed hath God, according to his Promise, raised unto Israel a Saviour Jesus.

THE Promise of the *Messias* doth bear the most ancient Date. No sooner was there place for it, but he was promis'd, and declar'd: Which was upon the Fall of *Adam*. And it was not reasonable to think, that God should declare himself for the Pardon of Sin, before Sin was committed: For, that would have been, to indulge, invite, or encourage Man to Sin: But, no sooner is Man become guilty; but the Promise is made, *That the Seed of the Woman shall break the Serpent's Head.*[1] Which St. *John* comments upon, in these Words, *For this Cause the Son of God was manifested, to destroy the Works of the Devil.*[2]

And this Promise is often repeated to the Patriarchs successively one after another; to *Abraham*, to *Isaac*, to *Jacob*: As also in the Types and Shadows that were under the Mosaical Dispensation;[3] as the Apostle tells us (*Heb.* 1. 1.) *God who at sundry Times, and divers Manners, spake*

---

* From *Select Sermons*, ed. Anthony, Third Earl of Shaftesbury (1698), Part II, Sermon III [pp. 331–60]. Some italicised words, indicating Shaftesbury's additions to improve the sense, are not shown here. The title of the sermon is by the present editor.

[1] *Genesis* 3. 15—often referred to as 'the first gospel'. Whichcote's sermon might be read against the background of ideas I have outlined in 'The "Protevangelium" in Renaissance Theology and *Paradise Lost*', *Studies in English Literature*, III (1963), 19–30.

[2] 1 *John* 3. 8.

[3] Cf. the 'types and shadows' which in *Paradise Lost* (XII, 232–3) are said to be preparatory to the advent of the Messiah. Whichcote supplied a detailed survey of the major 'types' of Christ in his *Discourses*, III, 81 ff. Cf. More, *Dialogues*, II, 94 ff.

The Manifestation of Christ 63

unto our Fathers by the Prophets, hath in these last Days spoken unto us by his Son, &c. That which is now plainly declar'd unto us by the *Messias,* was darkly represented by the Prophets. But, in *the Fulness of Time* (*that is,* the Time that God had appointed and resolv'd upon) he sent forth his Son, and exhibited his *Messias* unto the World. Now this is a Point of the greatest Import to Mankind that could be, after the Fall of *Adam*: For, Remission of Sin depended upon it. And this is a Matter of so great Concernment, that we are undone without it. For, unless we can get discharg'd of our Sin and Guilt, we must sink under it. See therefore how punctual and particular the Scripture is, in this Matter! As is plainly shown in *the Text*: In which you have *Six* Things very remarkable.

1st, It is declar'd here, *WHO He was,* by his *Name JESUS*; by which *He* was as well known among Men, as other Persons are known by *their* Names.

2*dly,* The Text tells you of his FAMILY. He was of the Seed of *David,* as the very Verse before says.[4] And this is done upon a double Account: *For Distinction*; and *for better Satisfaction*; because the former Predictions and Promises that were concerning *Messias,* declar'd that he should be of the House and Lineage of *David,* that *so* Men might be more assur'd that this was *He.*

3*dly,* You have in the Words; *Who* appointed him. *Of this Man's Seed hath GOD rais'd up to Israel a Saviour.*

4*thly,* You have *the Moving Principle*: And that is *God's Faithfulness.* 'Tis *according to his PROMISE, that he hath rais'd up to Israel a Saviour Jesus.*

5*thly,* You have to what *Purpose* God rais'd him up: Namely, to be *a Saviour*; which is more fully explain'd a little before, *Chap.* 5. *Ver.* 31. *He rais'd him up to be a Prince, and Saviour, to give Repentance unto Israel, and Forgiveness of Sins.* Where you have the *Two* great Gospel-Benefits, *Repentance* and *Remission of Sin*: And the *one* in order unto the *other.* You have *an extraordinary Person* rais'd up, to an eminent Purpose; to give Repentance, and Remission of Sins. You have heard of others that were Saviours in Measure, and Degree; as *Moses* sav'd the People from the *Egyptians*; and *the Judges* that God rais'd up successively, that deliver'd the People of *Israel* from their Enemies; but, *never* a Saviour in this kind, before: For *the Redemption of the Soul is precious*; and *no Man can redeem his brother,* in this respect.[5] It must be

[4] *Acts* 13. 22.   [5] *Psalms* 49. 7–8.

such a Person, as is *a Prince*, and *a Saviour*, made so of God, that must appear in this Business; to save Men from their Sins. And this *Jesus* it is, that God sent to bless us, in turning away every one of us from his Iniquity.

6thly, You have *Them* to whom He is thus given to be a Saviour; *the Nation of the Jews*. To *Israel* in the first place, as the Scripture speaks, (*Acts* 3. 26.) *to you first, and then to all Nations*, (*Acts* 13. 47.) *I have set thee for a Light to all Nations, and for Salvation to the Ends of the Earth*.

You see that all these great Things which concern the *Messias*, and are Matter of our Faith, you have them *all* in these Words: But, in other Institutions of God, you have either *all*, or *most* of the Circumstances left out; and many Things left to our Christian Prudence, Liberty, and good Affection. And this I shall observe in one or two Cases.

And first I will instance in the Institution of *the Lord's Supper*, which you have in these few Words, *Do this in Remembrance of me*:[6] Where you have only the Action, and the Explication of the Action. But, *now*, there is abundance of Questions mov'd about it. As for instance; *In what Company? What Preparation? At what Time? How often? In what Posture?* Whereas, all these are left undetermin'd. So that as to these, I dare undertake that we are not liable and obnoxious to God; provided we do with Reason; and observe that which is comely; and retain Christian Charity. And because this is a matter of Consequence, and worth taking notice of; I will make it evident, *that there is no Appointment of God, in any of these Matters*.

First, We are not appointed, *in what Company*. And yet, how many lay this for a Foundation? Yet, at our Saviour's first Institution, there was no Curiosity at all, in respect of the Company: For, he did admit *Judas*, whose internal malign Disposition he did very well know: And yet he was present at the first Sacrament. And you know that all Laws are most rigorously and punctually observ'd at their first making. For, if a Law-giver do not insist upon a punctual Observation of his Laws, at their first Constitution; he doth tacitly consent to the laying of them aside.

Secondly, Nor any Appointment *at what time*: No set Season for the doing of it, commanded by our Saviour. For, they were met upon another Occasion; not for this Business.

Thirdly, Nor any *particular Disposition* that we find requir'd by our

---

[6] *Luke* 22. 19; 1 *Corinthians* 11. 24.

Saviour, as *peculiar* to that Business. It is true, they were taken in a Passover-preparation: but they had no antecedent Warning, nor knew what our Saviour was about to do; till he did the Thing. At the *Passover* there were *Four* Eatings; and *Two* Drinkings: And our Saviour puts a new Notion upon one of the Cups; and one of the Breads. It was *a Religious Exercise* they came about; and so were in *a Religious Disposition*; wherein Approach was to be made to God: Which doth intimate *this Notion*; that *they who lead Christian Lives, and follow the Rule of our Saviour's Doctrine, may freely and indifferently make Application to God, in one holy Exercise, as well as another*. Whosoever lives according to the Difference of Good and Evil, and governs himself so that he may make Application to God, either by Prayer, Reading, Meditation, or Christian Conference, or any other Christian Duty, is in a Preparation and Disposition, wherein he may come safely to the Table of the Lord. I know there are many Men that think not of any Preparation for *Prayer*, or *other Christian Duties*; yet pretend to some Curiosity in their Preparation, when they are to come to *the Sacrament*. Not that I would discourage Mens Preparation for this Duty: But, is not the Object of Worship the same? It may be, their Apprehensions of Danger are grounded on these Words which tell us, That *they eat and drink Damnation to themselves*.[7] But, is it not also said, *The Sacrifice of the Wicked is an Abomination to the Lord?* And, that *he will not hear them, when they pray unto him?*[8] By which it appears, that it is not safe for Men to lay all the Weight upon *one* Piece of Religion; and to be trifling and neglective *in others*.

Fourthly, Neither is it said *how often* Men must communicate in this Sacrament; but, *as oft as you do it*, &c. 1 *Cor.* 11. 25. Now the Nature of the Thing doth sufficiently secure *Frequency*. For, it is a Thing grateful in the Matter, and *beneficial*; so, quite another thing than many of the Mosaical Rites and Ceremonies were; of which it is said, that many of them were *grievous* and *burthensome*: But this is highly grateful and beneficial. What can be more pleasing, than to remember so great a Benefactor as our Saviour? One that did undertake and engage on our behalf? They that are rightly apprehensive of the Reason of the Thing, will be induc'd to Frequency, and careful Attendance upon it.

Fifthly, Neither is it set down *in what Posture* they should communicate: For, our Saviour takes them, as he finds them. But we are apt to be

---

[7] 1 *Corinthians* 11. 29.
[8] *Proverbs* 15. 8 and *Psalms* 66. 18, respectively.

Superstitious; and to make our selves Rules; and to form such Notions[9] by which we create Difference in Religion, and Trouble to our selves and others. And it is greatly to be fear'd, that so much of Curiosity as a Man bestows about any Piece of Religion and Devotion that is *of his own Formation*, so much he will abate in his Conscientious Observance of that which is *of God's Institution*.

I might also shew you the very same Thing in *the other Institution*.[10] For, there you have only *the material Action*, and the *Acknowledgement*. *BAPTIZING them in the Name of the Father, and of the Son, and of the Holy Ghost*.[11] Now, how hath the World been troubl'd about the Circumstance of *Time*, and several other Things about this Sacrament? And *all* without Foundation. But, there is no warrant for this, from the Institution. And Charity hath been wanting, when Men have gone about to make out Scripture further than what hath been plainly declar'd. So that I resolve with my self, that GOD having invested Man with *Intelectual Nature*; and given him that high Priviledge, and Prerogative of *Reason* and *Understanding*; doth expect that he should act according to those Principles: And, where HE doth not constitute and appoint, limit and determine; that *there* He doth refer himself to the rational Determination of *that first Principle*, the Principle *of his Creation*. So that, whatsoever is done throughout the Life of Man, that *there is Reason for*; it is warranted by *God*: Provided, still, that a Man doth not vary from any particular and express Institution of God, in Scripture. And, if this were understood; we should have the very Foundation of Differences in the Church of God taken away. It is but a vain Pretence of *Zeal for GOD*, and *doing him service*; for US to limit, appoint, constitute, and determine, beyond what *HE himself* hath done.

'Tis a good Notion, universally; *Let us be as FREE under God, as we can*; and resolve, with St. *Paul, Not to be brought under the Power of any Thing*.[12] So far as God doth declare, we must follow his Direction. But it is best for us, where he doth not limit and determine, to follow the Reason of our own Minds, in the free Use of our Liberty. God doth so far acknowledge his own *Workmanship*, as to refer himself to the Principles of Creation in Man, so far forth as he doth not limit and determine. For, *do* but with Reason, and you *do* well. There is no

[9] Whichcote rarely foregoes an opportunity to castigate the multitude of irrelevant 'notions' in religion. See esp. below, pp. 71, 96 ff., 330, etc.

[10] Whichcote limits himself to the two sacraments normally recognised by Protestants, baptism and the Eucharist.

[11] *Matthew* 28. 19.   [12] 1 *Corinthians* 6. 12.

Superstition in using Things *not commanded of God*: But, in using them *as necessary Pieces of Religion*, they are *Superstition*, and offensive to God. I say there is no Superstition in using Things not commanded by God, *even in the Worship of God*; if they be Comely, and such as Reason doth allow of. But, there is Superstition in assuming to our selves *Authority to use them*, as *necessary Peices of Religion*, and as *santified* by Divine Institution; when they are not of God's Appointment.

You see now, that in Matters of Weight, wherein the Honour of God, and the Safety of Mens Souls are concerned, Scripture is punctual, clear, full, and particular:[13] That our Faith may be better directed, and we our selves preserved against Cheats and Impostures. But as to other Matters, they are left to Christian Prudence, Discretion, and Fidelity. And God's Love and Goodness appears to us exceedingly, in *Both* these *Cases*:—Both that *He is clear, full, and particular, where 'tis for our Advantage and Security*.—And, also, *that He doth not unnecessarily resolve or determine us, where the Things themselves do not require it*:—In *the Former*; because if we should mistake *there*, it would be to our Loss and great Disadvantage, because of the Importance of the Matter; whether it relate either to Matter of Faith, or Practice: In *the Latter*, where the Matter is not so *necessary in it self*; nor our Obligation *to the Thing it self*; nor any intrinsick Value in it; *here*, it is God's Goodness to us, that he will not *limit* and *determine*. For, it is hazardous to a Man, in *Minute Things* to be obliged in Point of Conscience. If the Thing be good in it self; I am admonished daily how to act, by *the Rectitude of my Temper*; because the Thing is good, in its own Nature, and Quality: But, in the other Case, I have nothing but *the Security of my Memory*. This is a great Point of Divinity; that God hath left us, in the Christian Religion, as *Free* as we may be, without Loss or Prejudice *to our selves*: We being only determin'd to Things of Weight, and to such Things wherein if we should fail, we should greatly hurt our selves. For, it is a great Priviledge, not to be oblig'd without Necessity; not to be under Restraint *through the Necessity of the Precept*; where there is no Necessity *in the Matter*. And this I account one of the great Priviledges that we have by the Gospel. And here, as the Apostle adviseth, (*Gal.* 5. 1.) we should *stand fast in that Liberty, wherewith Christ hath made us free*. And that this is a great Priviledge, is clear, from *Acts* 15. 10. where the Apostle calls *the Ceremonies*, and *Observances*, commanded under the Law, *a Yoak which neither They nor their Fathers were able to bear*. In

---

[13] Cf. *Aphorisms*, § 1188 (below, p. 336).

this Dispensation, there was every Thing punctually determined, both for Substance, and Circumstance: So that they had need of very good *Memories*, to bear them all in Mind. Whereas, it is a great Security for my Observance of God, that I have *the Security of the Goodness of my Temper*, as well as *my Memory*. And thus it is, in all Matters of Weight, and Moment. But, if it be a *positive Command*; and *that*, of a Thing wholly *Arbitrary*; and which (if God had pleased) might have been omitted; then, I have only *the Security of my Memory*. And this is a choice Notion in *Divinity*: But, prepossest Minds will not bear it; tho' it be never so much for their Ease and Advantage. But, let him *that hath Ears to hear*, hear.[14] I will say it again. There is not, in Christian Religion, any Obligation upon us, but it is either one or other of these *Two*:

Either, *First*, the Reason of the Thing doth require it: And then it is necessary *in it self*; as is *Observance of God*; *Reverence of Diety*; *and regardful Apprehensions of him*;—*Righteousness and Justice between Man and Man*; *fair and equal Consideration*; *Doing as we would be done unto*;—or, *Sobriety and Temperance, Purity and Chastity, in the Government of our selves*: I say; either they are such great Things as *These*; Or else,

Secondly, The Things commanded, are *Medicinal*, and *Supplemental*, in Case of Guilt, and contracted Impotency by Reason of Sin; as *going to God, by Jesus Christ*; and *the Application of the Benefits that are by our blessed Lord and Saviour; the Vertue of his Blood, for Pardon of Sin*; and *what he hath done, engaging in our behalf*. And we shall see great Cause thankfully to acknowledge God for this great Benefit, if we do but consider the Occasion of *Adam's* Fall; who did not fall upon a Transgression of *a Moral Point*; but, in Variation from a *positive Institution*. And, for ought I, or any Body else, know; if God had not prohibited him *the Tree of Life*; he might as well have eaten of *that*, as of any *other Tree* in the Garden: For, *She saw it was lovely to the Eye, and fit for Food: And therefore she took of the Fruit of that Tree, and did eat, and gave unto her Husband*.[15] Here, they had only *the Security of their Memories*; and, not of any *internal Disposition*. So it is said of *Nadab* and *Abihu*, that they were struck dead *for offering strange Fire before the Lord*.[16] *One Fire*, to Reason, seemed as good as *another*, to offer Sacrifice with: But, because there was an Institution to the contrary; whether they did it wilfully, or carelesly; they perished *by Fire*. Also, let us remember the *Bethshemites*, who being transported with Joy and

---

[14] *Matthew* 11. 15.   [15] *Genesis* 3. 6.   [16] *Numbers* 3. 4.

The Manifestation of Christ

Affection, *looked into the Ark* (a Thing contrary to God's Appointment) to the Hazard of their Lives.[17] Likewise *Uzza* in his Zeal, when he found *the Ark* ready to fall, as he thought; put to his Hand to keep it up, and was slain for his Labour:[18] it being contrary to God's Institution. When we think of these things seriously; we shall find cause in abundance, thankfully to acknowledge God's Goodness, that we are *engaged* only where *the Nature of the thing doth engage*; and that we are not made liable, and obnoxious to God, in things that are not *Evil in themselves, and hurtful for us*.

It is greatly hazardous, for a Finite and Fallible Creature, to be limited and confined by *Will* and *Pleasure*, where there is no Reason, that the Mind of Man can discern, why he should be restrained. For, we are mightily for *Liberty*: And, unless we be satisfied in the Reason of the thing; we have a great Desire to look into that which we are prohibited. 'Tis hard to be subject to *Will*; as it is Natural to yield to Reason. Therefore, it is not a thing that we should affect, to come into Bondage, or be determined more than God hath determined us.—Let these things be weighed by those Men who love to multiply *Positive Institutions*, and to determine the Liberty of our Minds, in Circumstances and Punctilio's; in things where God hath not limited or determined us. For my part, I will not part with that *Liberty wherewith Christ hath made us free*. And, this is one Part of our *Liberty*: I must confess the greatest of all, is, *to free us from Guilt and Power of our Sins*: but, the next, is this; *to put us out of Danger, and free us from the Obligation of Conscience, where Reason, and the Matter it self, doth not oblige us*.

The *Moral Part* of Religion is indispensably necessary; because every piece of It doth sanctifie by its Presence; As for instance, *Humility, Modesty, Righteousness, Temperance, Reverence of Deity*, and the like: *These Things* cannot be in any Man's Mind but they make him Holy: Whereas *the Instrumental Part of Religion* doth not sanctifie by Presence. For, you may *pray*, and *hear the Word*, and *receive the Sacrament*, and *be wicked* still: But every thing of *the Moral Part* of Religion, doth sanctifie by Presence, just as a Remedy, or Cordial, or Diet, doth do a Man good, by receiving it.

But to speak, now, of the great Benefits that accrue to us, by our Saviour's being in our Nature. He doth acquire the Right of Redeeming us; and makes Satisfaction in that Nature that had trangressed: And, he

---

[17] 1 *Samuel* 6. 19.   [18] 2 *Samuel* 6. 7.

doth repair the ruined Nature of Man; by dwelling in it, and by working Righteousness in it: by which means he hath wrought out, *all Malignity*, and *naughty Habits*, by contrary Acts; *the Acts of Sin and Vice*, by Acts of Vertue and Goodness; *the Acts of Intemperance*, by Acts of Sobriety and Temperance.

Now, let us look for the Explication of this, *in our selves*; in our *Nativity from above*; in *Mental Transformation*, and DEIFICATION. Do not stumble at the use of *the Word*. For, we have Authority for the use of it, in Scripture. 2 *Pet.* 1. 4. *Being made Partakers of the Divine Nature*; which is in effect our *Deification*.[19] Also, let it appear *in our Reconciliation to God*, to *Goodness, Righteousness*, and *Truth*; in our *being created after God, in Righteousness, and true Holiness*.[20] It was a signal Evidence of a Divine Power in the Disciples of Christ, at the first Publication of the Gospel, that it wrought so great an Alteration in all those that did receive it. The Envious, Debauched, and Disobedient; It made Temperate, Sober, and Religious, Humble, and *Good-natured*. It converted the Embracers of it, to a Life more suitable to Reason, and Nature, and Moral Vertue.

We may observe from this, that nothing of the Natural State is *base* or *vile*. Whatsoever hath Foundation in God's Creation, or whatsoever the Providence of God calls any Man unto, it is not *base*. For, our Saviour himself *took Flesh* and *Blood*: and *that* is the meaner Part of Humane Nature. Whatsoever is *Natural*, hath nothing of Disparagement in it; nothing that exposeth a Man to Contempt, and Scorn. And this may satisfie those that are in the meanest Offices and Employments; that there is nothing base, that hath place in God's Creation. That which is Vile, Base, and Filthy, is *unnatural*, and depends upon *unnatural Use*, and *degenerate Practice*.

Also, observe here, the great Honour put upon Humane Nature; when *the Son of God* came into it; when Divine Goodness did take into Consideration the Rise and Advance of Created Nature; and to recover and raise It to all possible Perfection: *He did take to himself a peculiar relation to Humane Nature.*—Then, let us take Consolation in this. For, it cannot be thought, that God did so great a thing, and of so deep a Consideration, as to unite Humane Nature to his own Existence, and to set it at his own Right hand, to the Admiration of Angels, (for he saith, *let all the Angels of God worship him*;)[21] that he did such a thing as this is,

---

[19] Cf. Cudworth, below, p. 101.   [20] *Ephesians* 4. 24.
[21] *Hebrews* 1. 6.

to beget a Notion, or to raise a Talk, and make a Wonder in the World, and put the Creation into a Gaze and Astonishment. God doth nothing, for so light an end; and especially not his great things, such as these, which call for Fear and Reverence on our part. This we may say, is one of the greatest Works of God. This, if possible, doth transcend the very Creation of God, at first:[22] for, there was nothing there to resist him: but, in the Restoration, there was Malignity and Sin. God did this, therefore, for the great and unconceivable Good of that *Nature* that he hath so highly honoured. Therefore, what Consolation should we have from it! what Declaration should we make of it! what Thanksgiving for it! Having this Knowledge; how should we rejoyce in God, and be above the World! how should we depress the immoderate Motions of Sense, and savour Spiritual things! that so we may the better understand this great *Mystery*, by which we are so highly honoured. And this is the proper use of this High and Noble Argument.

Therefore, let this be explicated, verified, and fulfilled in us. For, *this* you must understand; that *Religion* is not satisfied in Notions; but doth indeed, and in reality, come to nothing, unless it be in us not only Matter of Knowledge and Speculation; but doth establish in us a Frame and Temper of Mind, and is productive of a holy and vertuous Life. Therefore, let these things take effect in us; in our *Spirituality*, and *Heavenly-mindedness*; in our *Conformity to the Divine Nature*, and *Nativity from above*. For, whosoever professes that he believes the Truth of these things; and wants the Operation of them upon his Spirit, and Life; he doth, in fact, make void, and frustrate what he doth declare as his Belief: and so he doth *receive the Grace of God in vain*;[23] unless this Principle, and Belief doth descend into his Heart, and establish a good Frame and Temper of Mind; and govern in all the Actions of his Life and Conversation.

RELIGION is not a *particular Good* only; as Meat against Hunger; or Drink against Thirst; or Cloaths against Cold; but it is *Universally Good*; a Good, *without Limitation or Restraint*. For *Holiness* and *Purity of Mind*, is the self same thing to the Mind, that *Health* and *Strength* is to the Body.—It is good also in point of *Satisfaction to the Judgment*. For, no Man that useth Reason, can otherwise sit down contented,

---

[22] The superiority of the redemption of man over the creation of the world is a commonplace of Western thought; but the emphasis Whichcote places on the honour extended to human *flesh and blood* is not. It is Greek. (Cf. the Introduction, above, pp. 19 ff.)

[23] 2 *Corinthians* 6. 1.

unless he be in Reconciliation with God; unless there be fair Terms between God and him.—It is good also upon the account of *Peace and Settlement of Conscience*; upon which, the greatest Good of Man doth depend; for want of which, nothing *without him*, can make any Compensation.

Now, to shew it in Particulars. RELIGION (which is, in substance, *our Imitation of God in his Moral Perfections, and Excellency of Goodness, Righteousness, and Truth*) is that wherein our Happiness doth consist: And we *then* relish the truest Pleasure and Satisfaction, *when* we find our selves reconciled to God, by *Participation of his Nature*. They who have not this Sence of God, may have a Religion to talk of, and profess; a *Religion*, to give them a Denomination: but, they are not at all in the true State and Spirit of Religion: nor, have they any real Benefit by it: nor, are they any whit enabled by it: nor have they the more Peace and Satisfaction from it. But, when our Minds are transformed by Religion; then, we feel (at least, *at times*) strong and vigorous Inclinations towards God. And, with these Motions our Minds are best pleas'd and satisfied: because these are most suitable to Nature, and the highest Use and Employment that Humane Nature is capable of. Upon this account it is, that there is more Pleasure and Satisfaction in *Contemplation*, than in any of the Pleasures of Sense; and that those Men that live a-part from the World, and are taken up in Meditation, and Contemplation, their Pleasures are more intense and solid, than those of the Licentious, and of such as please themselves in all the Gratifications of Sense. There is no Heart's-ease like to that which riseth from Sence of Reconciliation to God, and walking in Ways of Righteousness. For, in these Ways, Mens Hearts never check them, nor occasion them any Disquiet. For, let the World say what they will, to be challenged by the Reason of a Man's Mind, goes nearer to a Man's Heart than the Censure of all the World besides. To act contrary to the Reason of one's own Mind, is to do a thing most *unnatural* and *cruel*: it is *to offer Violence to a Man's self*; and to act against a Man's truest *Use* and *Interest*. For, all manner of Wickedness is *a Burthen* to the Mind: and every Man that doth amiss, doth *abuse himself*. For, it is not possible for any Man to run away from himself, or to forget what he hath done. He must stand to the Bargain that he hath made; and abide by the Choice that he hath taken: And, in the whole World, there is nothing so grievous for a Man to think of, as that, when he did amiss, and made a mad Choice, he went against the Sense of his own Mind: For, in this Case, he is not Heart-whole. There is no Man who *knows himself*, but knows what I now speak is *true*. Tho'

The Manifestation of Christ

I know it is common in the World, for Men to do against Reason, and *to live by Chance*; and not to pursue any true Intention, or follow any worthy Design: But, as it happens; and, as Company and Occasion leads them; so they act; be it better or worse: Not considering that *what*, Matter of Disease, is *to the Body* (which many times is very grievous, and so indisposes a Man, as to put him quite out of Self-enjoyment) the same Is, Malignancy *in the Mind*, Guilt in the Conscience. Nay, I may say, that *These* are much more troublesome and grievous to be born, than any malignant Matter of Disease can be to the Body.

They make not true Judgment of Religion, that take it to be *a Limitation*, and *Restraint* upon Man's Liberty. Yet, some are so foolish as to think, that, if God would, we might have lived as we list, and have been released from those many Obligations that Religion seems to lay upon us. Whereas, this is as great *a Lye* as ever *the Father of Lyes* could invent. For, Religion is not a burthensome and troublesome Thing; which, if God had not commanded, might have been forborn, and all Things have been as well. No: There is nothing in *real* and *true* Religion, that is of that Nature. And, this I dare defend against the whole World; that there is no one thing in all that Religion which is *of God's making*, that any sober Man, in the true Use of his Reason, would be released from; tho' he might have it under the Seal of Heaven. For, such a Dispensation would be greatly to his Loss, and Prejudice: As much as if the Physician, instead of giving wholsome Physick to his Patient, should give Poyson. For, all Things in *real Religion* tend either to *conserve*, or *restore* the Soundness and Perfection of our Minds; and to continue God's Creation in the true State of Liberty and Freedom. So that if a Man did understand himself, and were put to his Choice; he would rather choose to part with the Health and Soundness *of his Body*, than with the Purity and Integrity *of his Mind*. For as much as the one is his far greater Concern: And he had much better live with a distempered crazy Body, than with a troubled disquiet Mind, and guilty Conscience.—But, on this Subject, I have many Things to say; and therefore will digest them into Five Heads.

First, Man by his Nature and Constitution, as God made him at first, being an intelligent Agent, hath *Sense of Good and Evil, upon a Moral account*. All inferior Beings have *Sense of Convenience or Inconvenience, in a natural Way*: And, accordingly, all inferior Creatures do chuse, or refuse. For, you cannot get a meer Animal, either to eat or drink that which is not good and agreeable to its Nature. And, whereas we call this *Instinct*; it is most certain that, in intelligent Agents, this other is INSTINCT, at least. And, for this Reason, Man is faulty, when either he is found in a naughty Temper, or any bad Practice. For, he hath Judgment and Power of Discerning: He is *made* to know the Difference of Things: And he acts as a mad Man, that knowing what is *better*, chuseth *the worse*. This is the Ground and Foundation of Man's being truly *miserable*: For, to be happy, or miserable: is mainly in his intelectual Nature. Inferior Natures may suffer Wrong: But they are not capable of Happiness or Misery, as intelectual Agents are; because they are not acquitted or condemned *from within*; nor have any thing to challenge or reprove them.

Secondly, Man being *made* to know God; hath Sense of his own Privation, in the Loss of so great and universal *a Good* as GOD is. For, he is made happy in the Enjoyment, and miserable in the Loss of Him.[24] And, tho' Diversion, and other Enjoyments, may give some Entertainment, for a while; yet when a Man strays at Home, or returns to himself by Consideration, he feels inward Perplexity in himself; because some necessary Good is wanting to him. His own Knowledge makes him capable of Good and Evil; and sensible of being miserable if he be depriv'd of that Good which God made him capable of. Such is the Nature of our Souls, that they cannot be happy, but in this way, and by the Use of their intelectual Faculty. Otherwise, the Soul will be sensible of its own Privation and Loss.—VERTUE, and VICE, are the Foundations of *Peace and Happiness*; or *Sorrow and Misery*. *There* is inherent Punishment belonging to all Naughtiness: And no *Power* can divide or separate them; but they will follow one another. For, tho' God should not, in a *positive Way*, inflict Punishment; or any Instrument of God punish a Sinner; yet he would punish *himself*: Because he cannot be satisfied in what he doth contrary to Reason, and the Sense of his own Mind. There is no Security to a Sinner: The least that will attend him, is *Fear*, and *Suspicion* of *Danger*. Diversion (which is the Way that many Men take,) going to some Pleasure, or into Company; is but a *Put-off*, for a while; and when they retire, it will return upon them, with greater Force and Violence. For, all *Moral Evil* is against the Nature of Man; and condemned by the Reason of the Mind: And can no other way be prevented but by the Motion of Repentance, and Application to God.

---

[24] The torments of Hell were traditionally said to be two-fold: the pain of sense and the pain of loss. The Cambridge Platonists invariably emphasised the latter. (Cf. above, p. 46, note.)

Thirdly, Our Souls acting upon God, discover their Vertues; and display their Powers; and show their Mettle and Sprightfulness. Whereas, if a Man be diverted from God; the *Reason of his Mind* is as much without Employment, as the *Eye* which is *in the Dark*: For, it is the Presence of the Object, that puts the Faculty upon acting. So, if *God* be withdrawn; our Minds cannot be drawn forth; for, they are without their *proper Object*: For, other-where, save only *in God,* our Souls are not matched, so as to make Proof of themselves. We know not our Powers and Faculties, but by their *Acts*: And we cannot act, but in the Presence of the *Object*. If a Man be separated from God; his Mind and Understanding are without their proper Object; and, so, are as little to him, as his Sight is to him, when he is in the Dark. I am apt to think, that in the Heavenly State hereafter, when God shall otherwise declare himself to us, than now he doth; thoses Latent Powers which *now* we have, may open, and unfold themselves; and thereby we may be made able to act in a far higher Way, than we are at present. *Now,* we have many Avocations and Diversions: But, *when* we shall come to have nearer Approaches to God; we shall have more *Use of our selves;* and shall find our selves more *able,* than we are at present, in this limited and contracted State. For, this we have present Experience of; that if we give our selves up, to Meditation upon God; and employ our Minds in sincere Intention of Him, and his Service; we do thereby ennoble, and enlarge our Faculties; which otherwise would shrivel up, and grow every Day less and less. I am very confident, that by Religious Motion Men are a Thousand times more improved, than by any Worldly Drudgery whatsoever.

Fourthly, Because of the vast Desires that are in Man, there is great Dissatisfaction in all Things *below a Man's self*: And *that,* all Worldly Things are. The Mind of Man is greater and larger than to be satisfied with any Thing in this World. So that when Application is made to him by *Riches, Honour, Pleasure,* and the like; it is but all in vain; For, *they* will all, say, *Content is not in me*: And, that they are not able to do what Men expect. And from hence will arise great Dissatisfaction and Discontent, because of *Frustration* and *Disapprovement*: For, here, a Man must call himself a Fool; to doat upon any Thing, without Grounds; and for making an ill Choice; and conceiting as a Fool. This will make him uneasie and ashamed of himself.

Lastly, Every State, and Temper, according to its Quality, whether Good or Evil, is to have a suitable Portion of Happiness or Misery. Now the State of Sin, is the worst State in the World; and therefore it is meet that it should fare the worst: And the State of Goodness, is the best State; and it is meet that it should fare accordingly.—As I said before: If God should let a Sinner alone, his Misery and Unhappiness would arise *from himself*. And should a good Man fall into never so many Troubles and Afflictions; yet he would have *Satisfaction in himself*, and Peace in his own Soul; because he was not Conscious to himself of any Evil, nor had contracted Guilt in his Mind.

BENJAMIN WHICHCOTE

The Unity of the Church maintained by sincere Christians*

Phil. 3. 15, 16

Let as many of us therefore as be perfect, be thus minded: and if in any thing ye be otherwise minded, God shall reveal even this unto you. Nevertheless, whereto ye have already attained, let us walk by the same Rule, let us mind the same things.

THE Substance of these Words may be gathered up in these four Propositions.

I. There is *that* in Religion, which is necessary and determined; fixt and immutable, clear and perspicuous; about which Good Men, they who are of growth and proficiency in Religion, do not differ. *As many as are perfect are thus minded.*

II. There is also in Religion *that* which is not so necessary, and immutable, clear, and plain; in which Good-men may happen to be otherwise minded one than another; or otherwise than ought to be. *If any be otherwise minded.*

III. There is Reason to think that God will bring out of particular mistake him that is right in the main. *God shall reveal even this unto you.*

IV. They who agree in the main, but differ in other particulars, ought nevertheless to hold together, as if they were in all things agreed. *To walk by the same Rule, to mind the same things.*

I am come to the last of these Propositions.[1]

---

* From *Several Discourses*, ed. John Jeffery (1703), Sermon XXX [vol. III, pp. 437–53]. The full title of the sermon is, 'That the Unity of the Church is carefully maintained by all those who are sincere Christians'. Most of the Biblical references, originally inserted in the text, have been transferred to the notes.

[1] The present sermon is the last in a series of three (*Discourses*, II, 155–91; III, 419–53).

Nevertheless, though God hath not cleared up all things to several Understandings; though in all things concerning Religion, we are not agreed, as understanding alike. God hath not yet declared in particular, the Truth of that wherein we differ, which in time it may be hoped he will: *Nevertheless whereunto ye have already attained*; as being come to a State of Religion; as having made some Progress and Proficiency; being arrived towards Perfection: *Walk by the same Rule* of Faith and good Life, wherein they who are sincere and honest understand themselves alike; which is in it self certain and determinate: Things of Reason and Scripture, given out by the Spirit, and attested by the Spirit. *Mind the same things.* Live according to the Rule of Faith and Holiness; in hearty Love and Good-will. *Be like-minded, having the same Love, being of one accord, of one mind.*[2] There is Harmony, Concord, and Agreement; notwithstanding difference in some Apprehensions, in all degrees of Perfection.

1. This is a Representation of the *Heavenly State*, a true Resemblance of it: It speaks the Motion of the Lower World, proportionable to the Motion of the higher World: The two States Symmetral, of like measures; Concentrical, meeting in one point. 'Tis his *New Jerusalem come down from Heaven*: Devout Souls ascending in a Cloud, upon a Call from Heaven, *Come up hither.*[3] For they are come into one Spirit; are become as one and the same Inhabitants; all Enmity subdued and vanquished.[4] In Heaven it is *God all in all.* So it will be in the Consummation of all things; when *all things shall be subdued unto him, that God may be all in all;*[5] This is the Communication of God to the World, Heaven's Blessing and Influence; *On Earth Peace, Good-will among Men.* There is no Discord in Heaven; no cause of Offence there. The Selfish and Froward, who are the Disturbers and Incendiaries, are in a worldly State, are not naturalized to Heaven.[6] But 'tis rational, and to be expected, that there should be Accord here upon Earth among Men, τὸ πολίτευμα ἐν οὐρανοῖς,[7] who are *Citizens of Heaven*, account their Names registered there; who look up-themselves as now belonging to that place, and in due time to come thither. Fellow-Travellers and Countrymen, when abroad, are glad one of another; are faithful and kind each to other.

2. 'Tis the *Cause* of *Religion*, and natural to the Regenerate State.

---

[2] *Philippians* 2. 2.
[3] *Revelation* 11. 12.
[4] Cf. 1 *Corinthians* 15. 25.
[5] 1 *Corinthians* 15. 28.
[6] Cf. *Aphorisms*, §§ 290 and 750 (below, pp. 330 and 333).
[7] *Philippians* 3. 20.

The Unity of the Church

The Wisdom which is from above, is first pure, and then peaceable, gentle, and easie to be entreated, full of Mercy and good Fruits.[8] If Religion attains not this Effect, it is barren and ineffectual; it is not in Truth, but only pretended: There must be inward Composure, and outward good Behaviour. The *Psalmist* makes a good Explication of Religion in the Subject. *My Heart is not haughty, nor mine Eyes lofty; neither do I exercise my self in great Matters, or in things too high for me. I behave and quiet my self as a Child.*[9] Religion doth bridle *Evil Desires*: Doth subdue and moderate the Exorbitances and Unruliness of Mens Spirits. The Profane and Irreligious are boisterous, tempestuous within themselves, are stormy and clamorous; are in Darkness, Disorder and Confusion; through Passion, Inordinacy of Appetite, are ground between contrary Affections, as Corn between Mill-stones: Whereas the Work of Religion is to calm and quiet, to content and satisfie, to make gentle, and to compose the rolling tumbling Mind of Man.

If a Man be not far better-natur'd towards God and all the World; more kind and loving to Men; more at Peace within himself after his Regeneration than before; there hath been Motion, without a Form introduced; which in Nature is monstrous and Abortive.

'Tis a scandal to the World, where Professors of Religion do not agree: Either it makes strangers to it call the thing in question, as *Pilate* did, *What is Truth?*[10] who will let all alone till they be agreed: Or else they think that they are all *Mala fidei possessores*,[11] no Natural Parents, because they are for Division: No Rightful Owners, all Thieves, because of their several Interests and Shares. Truth being single, if Men did meet in Truth they would be united. 'Tis a Sign the Cause is not Right and undoubted, when the Maintainers of it do so interfere, go such gross ways to work. This hath tired out the best of Men, wearied them out of the World. Good-tempered *Melancton*'s Satisfaction, when he came to die was, that he should be freed from the Temptations to Sin: From the Troubles of the World; and from the Fury of Theologues; from quarelsom Persons in Matters of Religion; as vexatious and troublesom as either of the former.[12] 'Twas *Origen*'s

---

[8] *James* 3. 17.   [9] *Psalms* 131. 1–2.
[10] *John* 18. 38.
[11] 'possessed of bad faith'. In annotating Whichcote's 'quotations'—here as well as below, pp. 82, 83, 84 and 85—I had to bear in mind his own attitude (quoted above, p. xxvii).
[12] Philipp Melanchthon (1497–1560), the greatest humanist among the Reformers, is the only leading Protestant whom the Cambridge Platonists

Argument against *Celsus*, that through the Virtue and Efficacy of the Christian Religion, the State of the *Church* was calm and quiet; whereas other States were turbulent.[13] *Lest when I come, I should not find you such as I would: Lest there be Debates, Envyings, Wraths, Strifes, Backbitings, Whisperings, Swellings, Tumults. The Works of the Flesh are, Hatred, Variance, Emulations, Wrath, Strife, Seditions, Heresies, Envyings, Murder.*[14] *But the Fruits of the Spirit are, Love, Peace, Long-suffering, Gentleness, Meekness, Goodness.*[15]

3. 'Tis the Conversation of Christians each with other for *mutual Gain and Advantage.* (1.) For Spiritual *Edification*. Whereas if Variance and Contests obtain, there will be Alienation of Hearts and Affections, a Suspension of all Christian Acts; there will be neither Prayer nor Discourse: Whereas they who are Religious, they that *fear the Lord, should speak often to one another.*[16] (2.) This is for their better *Subsistence* in an evil World. Foreign Opposition and Force cannot do the Mischief that internal Feuds and Treachery may. (3.) There is more Hearts-ease and Quiet of Mind. 'Tis burdensome to live out of Love and Good-will: The Mind is still contriving Defence or Offence: And so not vacant towards the highest and noblest Objects.

4. This prevents all *Mischiefs* which infest Humane Society. Such as, (1.) Sideings one against another; Part-takings, and Factions. (2.) False Suspicions, Jealousies, Heart-burnings. (3.) Plottings, Contrivings, Underminings of each other. (4.) Competitions of Parties, envious Comparisons. There should be but one division, the *Church* and the *World: Born after the Flesh, and born after the Spirit.* Those who are united by Religion, should be one in Heart and Affection, to all Issues, Intents, Purposes of Succour and Supply.

The *Objections* against this are,

1. *Obj.* But we do *not think alike*, are not of the same Opinion.

Answ. No more are we in *other Matters.* All *Artists* differ in their Notions: there are different Opinions in several Points of *Philosophy*: the several Constellations in the Heavens have different Influence: What is one Man's Meat, is another's Medicine, and another's Poison. We differ in Age, in Stature, in Feature, in Gate, in Complexion,

---

normally deign to mention. On the story related by Whichcote, cf. the Wittenberg *Brevis narratio* (1560), in *Philipp Melanchthons letzte Lebenstage, Heimgang und Bestattung,* ed. Nikolaus Müller (Leipzig, 1910).

[13] *Cont. Cels.*, III, *passim.*   [14] *2 Corinthians* 12. 20.
[15] *Galatians* 5. 20.   [16] Cf. *Malachi* 3. 16.

in Institution of *Life*, in Profession. These Varieties and Differences, as well as Harmonies and Proportions, explicate the infinite Wisdom of the Creator. Yet all, agreeing in Humane Nature, are fit Companions one for another, can take delight in each others Company. Why should not they, who meet in the Regenerate Nature, who agree in the great Articles of Faith, and Principles of good Life; over-look subordinate Differences? If there be Love and Good-will, we come to be more Rational, better grounded in our Resolutions, from our different Apprehensions. Discourse is as soon ended as begun, where all say the same: whereas he that speaks after, and says a new thing, searcheth the former;[17] so no Truth will be lost for want of being offered to consideration.

'Tis a *Salvo* amongst the *Romanists*; they may be *Catholicks* who differ, because they submit their Sense to the Authority of the Church. Our *Salvo* may be, Implicit Faith in God; that we believe in such Sense as the Holy Ghost meant: So we may meet in the Rule of Truth, though we differ in the particular Explication. If there were no Contradiction in the several Apprehensions of Men, we might never be awakened to search into things; and so, if we were once in a mistake, we should never come out of it. Those who are Credulous, Presumptious, Confident, and light of Faith; are taken with all Shews and Appearances, and are never prepared to withstand Gainsayers.

Obj. 2. But their Errour is *dangerous*.

Answ. That is *not thy Charge*, but *his*. Thy Work is to propose what thou believest to be true; together with the Reason and Ground of it. To say what is fit to perswade, is the utmost thou canst do: And when thou hast done all thou canst do, there will remain *that* which must be left to God.

2. Since all things that are *necessary* to Salvation are delivered plainly in the Holy Scriptures; we may resolve, that none but those who are gross Neglecters, do err *dangerously*. There is no need of Curiosity since the Appearance of Christ; no need of Inquisition since the writings of the Gospel: For now we readily believe, that there is nothing beyond believing. The Points of Christian Faith are as clearly intelligible to all Capacities, as they are clearly necessary to be believed by all Men. God accepts alike the Faith that results from the dark Mists of the Ignorant, and from the clearest Intelligence of the Learned.

[17] Cf. *Proverbs* 18. 17.

The Holy Scriptures are so written, that they are sooner understood by an unlearned Man that is pious and modest, than by a Philosopher who is arrogant and proud.

Obj. 3. But where is then the *Zeal of God*, and for Truth[?]

Answ. Zeal for Truth hath its principal Operation on *One's self* in pursuit of Judgment; when, after care of right Information we hold *our selves* in Practice exactly to our Judgment; so as to *Hold no Truth in Unrighteousness*; nor to *turn the Grace of God into Wantonness*:[18] to be, and do, according to what we know.

Towards *Others* it shews it self in strength of *Argument*; seasonable and renewed *Proposals*; attractive Recommendation by the effect of a well governed Spirit, Candour and Christian Patience toward those, who are not yet satisfied. To be transported with irregular and disproportioned Zeal, is a greater Miscarriage on thy part, than a simple Error in smaller Matters is on thy Brother's part.

I subjoin two things.

1. That a high Respect is due to *Governours*, *Superiors*, and the *Church* of God.

2. That 'tis of the two safer; To err, *Errare communi quam proprio*: To err with the generality, than to err alone. In Modesty and Humility, we should rather Question our own Opinion; than in self-confidence, be wilful and peremptory.

The *Suggestions* following I offer, for Accord, or mutualy Forbearance at least.

1. Why should not *Consent* in the main be more available to Concord, and Union, than *Difference* in less Principal matters, prevail to distance and separation? All that are right in the main, are virtually informed by the same Spirit. The things they are agreed in, are far more for number: more weighty for importance: The things they differ in are fewer, and of less consequence.

2. Why should Men *Differ* from occasion of Religion, which is the greatest Bond of Union? Religion hath two things *Final* in it, Reconciliation with God: Harmony, Concord, Suitableness, Agreement to run through the whole Creation. Religion obliges us to God, and to one another.

3. Why should we be aggrieved, where every one useth but his own *Right*? There is none more inherent Right than to worship God with our Understanding. Every one hath a Right of *Judging*, if he be

---

[18] *Romans* 1. 18 (as above, p. 42) and *Jude* 4, respectively.

capable: Yea, can a Man, ought a Man to believe otherwise than he sees cause? Is it in a Man's Power to believe as he would, or only as the Reason of the thing appears to him? If a Man could believe as he hath a Mind, the Sinner would never be self-condemned; which is the worst of this World, and of the other.

4. Why dost thou lay so much stress upon Difference in such points, wherein thou thy self (if Temperate and Sober) art *afraid* peremptorily to *assert*. In the sense of thy own Fallibility, shortsightedness, and the obscurity of Things, 'tis more becoming, neither to undervalue anothers sense nor to over-value thine own.

5. Why do I not make like *Favourable Interpretation* in behalf of *another*, which ere-while I made for my *self* in like case? I erred and expected good Mens Patience. If I am Ignorant, or Mistaken in any point, I hope God will not impute it to me. 'Twas never more than Finite and Fallible. Why may not that pass for Weakness in another which I account Infirmity in my self, or not worse?

6. May I not hope to *Asswage*, and *Lessen* that Difference, by fair Debate, which will Increase if I keep at a distance, giving way to Jealousy and Suspicion? There may be some Misapprehensions in Discourse; but there is more danger of false Reports. There is *Gratia Vultus*: The Light of ones Countenance: Presence is winning; the Persons of Men Concitiate[19] favour and acceptance: by Discourse Men Accommodate things; in Conference they render a Reason. When Persons at difference talk together, they often find, that they stand not at that Distance they did Imagine. Distance gives Talebearers opportunity and advantage.

7. Is it safe to *Reject* him as to Christian Converse, whom we cannot conclude God hath cast off from Interest in himself by Christ? At least we cannot ground such an Opinion on *that* wherein we Differ.

8. Why should I think that so necessary to *another to know*, upon the Belief whereof I dare not lay the stress of my acceptance with God, nor build my future hopes upon? *Ignorance of that will not destroy him, the Knowledge whereof will not save me.*

9. Why, since I my self came *leisurely* to Knowledge, do I not hope another may see and acknowledge that to Morrow which he sticks at to

---

[19] Possibly 'concitate', which an authoritative seventeenth-century dictionary defines as 'to provoke, to stir up, or prick forward' (Thomas Blount, *Glossographia* [1656], sig. K4v).

Day? We know not what a Day may bring forth. *Days teach Wisdom and Experience.* Wherefore they who Understand not alike to day, may agree to morrow. Therefore the Philosophers Rule is Rational, *Hate now, as one who may love afterward.* Part to Day upon such Terms, as you may come together to Morrow.

Again. Why think I not, that *I was taught* of God to teach him? *When thou art Converted strengthen thy Brethren.*[20] A Candle is not lighted to be put under a Bushel. *Two are better than one, for they have a good reward for their Labour. If they fall, the one will lift up his Fellow, but wo unto him that is alone, when he falleth; for he hath not another to help him up. Again, if two lye together then they have heat; but how can one be warm alone. And if one prevail against him, two shall withstand him: and a threefold Cord is not easily broken.*[21] *Two are better for Help, for Warmth and for Strength.*

Again. Why do I imagine that *he* should *always* know, what I *my self,* knew but *lately?* There were several Hours of hiring the Labourers. He may err long, and yet make as happy an escape from his Error and mistake, as I my self have done.

Again, It may be he hath a *lower plate* in the Mystical Body of *Christ.* If he has any, he is not despicable, because he is useful. *The Body is not one Member, but many. If the Foot shall say, because I am not the Hand, I am not of the Body, is it therefore not of the Body? And if the Ear shall say, because I am not the Eye, I am not of the Body; is it therefore not of the Body?*[22] *He gave some Apostles, and some Prophets, and some Evangelists, and some Pastors and Teachers; For the perfecting of the Saints, for the Work of the Ministry, for the edifying of the Body of Christ.*[23]

Again. Shall I *disown* that which is *good* in him, because he is not such as I would have him? Who is this that despiseth the day of small things? Shall I reject him for as little, as God Pardons to me?

Again. May there not be as great a difference in the *make* of his Apprehensions and Faculties, and *mine,* as is betwixt us, in the point wherein we think not altogether alike? If so, neither he, nor I can keep it. 'Tis neither of our fault, that our Understandings are not cast into the same Mould: or that our Organs or Bodily Constitutions, which occasion Variety, are not alike. It may be also, our Apprehensions are *nearer* than our Expressions. Two think they say not the same, may

[20] *Luke* 22. 32.
[21] *Ecclesiastes* 4. 9–12.
[22] 1 *Corinthians* 12. 14–16.
[23] *Ephesians* 4. 11–12.

think the same as to God. Our Apprehensions are unavoidably short, and unworthy in respect of God: yet God doth not reject our Devotion. God receives of all sorts and sizes; Rejects none for weakness of Parts, and shallowness of Understanding. Love and Good-will have Power of assimilation; work things into a suitable Proportion. An abatement and allowance must be made for Constitution, Complexion, Age, Temper, Education, Temptation, different Natural Inclination. So much at least by a Common Law Rule. Two Men speak together cannot hit it, when a third hearing both, shews them, that they mean the same thing.

Again. Why so ventrous to censure, and refuse, where *ones self,* by the same reason, is so much in danger? Our own case will not bear much severity. Who knows whereinsoever he hath been, is, or may be mistaken? Who hath *new* experience of all the Temptations he may come to be in? One may happen to condemn himself in another Person, as *David* did.[24] If we determine the *minimum ut sic salutis,* what is the least that is necessary to Salvation, we take upon us to make a Law for Heaven.

Again. Since I vary so much from *my self,* at times, and in cases; why do I severely examine others by my sense, and hold them to that? *I would do good, but evil is present with me.*[25] I will first lay out my pains upon my self, to subdue all within my self to right Reason.

Again. Circumstances of cases are to be *stated* and setled, before a determination for Parting; as, (1.) That some Revelation from God in Scripture, or Reason of things, *require* it, (2.) Upon what *Terms* we are again to be reconciled, and the Party readmitted, (3.) While we are at a distance, *how far* we shall go, and no further, (4.) A *reconcileable Disposition* must be maintained all the while.

Again. Why *part* from them on *Earth,* whom we may *meet* with all in *Heaven?* What is perfected hereafter, must be begun here. Things *here,* are both admitted and preferred upon this account, as most subservient and conducive to the affairs of our *future State.* Would it not be strange that two should meet there as one, who could never agree here? Twould prove that both, or one of them was grievously mistaken. God, who will not lose any thing that is Good, will finally save what is Capable of Salvation: Will only reject Malign Dispositions which will not be altered, and subdued to the Temper of

---

[24] 2 *Samuel* 12. 5–6. The sentence immediately following has been emended to improve its sense.   [25] *Romans* 7. 21.

Heaven. *Jerom* and *Rufinus* charged one another with Heresie: *Chrysostom* and *Epiphanius* refused to join in Prayer; the former wishing the latter might not return alive, the latter that the former might not dye a Bishop; both which came to pass.

'Tis a great mistake in *Zeal for Truth*, to let it run out in some smaller matters, which have scarce been Thought of by the whole Series of Christians of all Ages, but only of late. Some alledge the *Severity* of some of the Ancient Prophets; as *Elijah*, *Elisha*, and the *Baptist*. But the Dispensation wherein such Carriage and Practice was not unusual from extraordinary Persons, is now changed into a new one, whose distinguishing Character is Charity. We are carefully to bridle all Motions of distempered Heat, the effects whereof are as unjustifiable, as it self. *Christ* hath made it the Cognisance of his Disciples, to *love one another*.[26]

What havock did *Paul* make in his Judaism, among *Christians*, upon the account of Zeal? Whereof he found cause to be ashamed all Days of his Life. *Concerning Zeal, persecuting the Church.*[27] *Saul breathing out Threatenings and Slaughter against the Disciples of the Lord.*[28] *I was zealous towards God, and I persecuted this way unto the Death.*[29] *Being exceeding mad against them, I persecuted them even unto a strong City.*[30] *I am not worthy to be called an Apostle, because I persecuted the Church of God.*[31] How refractory was St. *Peter* against a Vision to send him to *Cornelius, a just Man, who feared God, and was of good Report among the Jews?*[32] Archbishop *Laud* says, The Church of *England* is not such a Shrew to her Children, as to deny her Blessing, or to denounce Anathema against them, if some peaceably dissent in some Particulars remoter from the Foundation.[33] If the Church of *Rome*, since she grew to her Greatness, had not been so fierce, had not been so particular in determining too many things; and making matters of necessary belief, which had gone for many hundred of Years before, only for things of pious Opinion, I persuade my self, that Christendom had been at happier Peace at this Day, than I doubt we shall ever live to see it. They have rashly augmented the materials

---

[26] *John* 13. 35; etc.
[27] *Philippians* 3. 6.
[28] *Acts* 9. 1.
[29] *Acts* 22. 3, 4.
[30] *Acts* 26. 11, which reads '... even unto *strange* cities'.
[31] 1 *Corinthians* 15. 9.
[32] Cf. *Acts* 10. 1 ff.
[33] Quoted *verbatim* from *A Relation of the Conference betweene William Lawd, ... Arch-Bishop of Canterbury, and Mr Fisher the Jesuite* (1639), p. 50 [§ 14].

of Faith; and thereby have weakned, and diminished Charity. This is contrary to the Apostolical Practice. *Why Tempt ye God to put a Yoke upon the Neck of the Disciples? My sentence is, that we trouble them not. It seemed good to the Holy Ghost, and to us, to lay upon them no greater Burden than these necessary things.*[34] *Not that I would cast a snare upon you.*[35]

Two things are *final* in Religion, (1.) To be in Reconciliation with God: And (2.) To be in Reconciliation one with another: And by St. *John's* Argument they are not one without the other. *If a Man say I love God, and hateth his Brother, he is a Liar.*[36]

In matters of *Philosophy* there are different Opinions: *Aristotelians*, and *Platonists*. *Copernicus* for the Earth's Motion against the generality. Of late the New Philosophy. Formerly *Scotists*, and *Thomists*; in matters of *Divinity*. In our Saviour's time, *Pharisees*, *Sadduces*, and *Esseners* [sic]. Our Saviour was not severe, save against the *Hypocrisy* of the *Pharisees*.

There are no less different Capacities of *Mind*, than Constitutions of *Body*: and no less difference in Mens outward Circumstances, than in either of the former.

I intend not by this the *Patronage* of the Refractory and Presumptuous; but Apology for those who are *Honest* in their way, but of weaker parts, and slower Apprehensions; who are therefore of modest and teachable Spirits; of whom it may be verified, *Errare possum, Hæreticus esse nolo.* I may be mistaken, but I will not be Heretical. Two things a Man may easily perceive, whether he be an *Hypocrite*, whether an *Heretick*. Not the former, if he means well; not the latter if he be wilful, but patient to be informed. In all Reason it may be safest for such as have little leisure to examine; or are less competent to judge, through want of Education, to give the more advantage to their *Guides*. I therefore caution *four* things.

1. Great *Reverence* is to be given to *Superiors*. Government is not to be disturbed upon Pretence of *private Judgment*: that is to be confined to the Direction of the inferior Man.

2. No *Disturbance* must thence arise to the *Church of God. If any seem to be contentious, we have no such Custom, nor the Churches of God.*[37]

3. Suppose the worst; 'tis safer to *Err* in an Error that is *Common*, than in an Error that is Personal.

---

[34] *Acts* 15. 10, 19, 28.
[36] 1 *John* 4. 20.
[35] 1 *Corinthians* 7. 35.
[37] 1 *Corinthians* 11. 16.

4. It becomes the *Modesty* of Particular Persons, where their Sentiments are singular, to bethink themselves better: to ask themselves this sober Question. How went the Spirit of God from the generality of his Worshippers, and determined it self to me? Which being done, these good things will find place; *Caution* and Wariness: more *Diligence* in Enquiry: Expectation of being further informed. *These* instead of conceitedness, fondness of our own Opinions, self-confidence and peremptoriness.

If we would do what becomes us, in sense of our liableness to be mistaken; if what is due to the discerning of Truth; we should not run away with an Opinion, before we have submitted it to severe and impartial Examination by others, and Persons most Competent; and have well weighed what others can say: Not till after we our selves have thought it again and again; day after day. *We should doubt and deliberate, before we resolve and determine.* Nothing are we so sure of, as of that which we are sure of after doubting. Where this is not done, there are easie Perswasions, Credulity, Rightness of Faith: whence it comes to pass, that Men are greatly possessed, strangely persuaded in matters where there is very good assurance that things are otherwise. Let therefore the *Modesty* always becoming a Christian Spirit, accompany *private Judgments*: and if you would give *Credit* to it, let good Life and unblamable Conversation attend upon it: Think that thou mayest be mistaken, as well as others.

I have my *Cautions*, bound up *private Judgment* in particular Persons to its *good Behaviour*; so that it neither extend, nor enlarge it self, to the disturbance of Government, or confusion of Order, or other act of Unruliness in God's Family; which things are in the first place to be resolved on, and secured: For rather a particular Mischief, than a general Inconvenience.

But I wish more were *capable* of the Use of *private Judgment* than there are. 'Tis a Fundamental Right belonging to Intellectual Natures: But to the Exercise of it more is requisite than most Men have to shew: Preparation thereto, by Education, Consideration, and Conference: For we are born only with Powers and Faculties; and so with possibilities of Acts and Habits: We are no-bodies where we have not thought. 'Tis the lamentable Condition of lapsed Mortals, that, of the generality of Men it may be said (through non-use, misuse and abuse of themselves) what God said of the great City of *Nineveh*, wherein are more than an hundred and twenty thousand Persons who cannot discern between the Right Hand and the

Left:[38] I say, who, in matters of Reason, Religion, and Conscience, have no Judgment of Right or Wrong, True and False, Good and Evil. And *Man that hath no Understanding may be compared with the Beasts that perish.*[39] He hath not *Honour and Pre-eminence* above Beasts.

Now, I say, having secured publick Settlement and Peace, those *Suggestions* for Accord, Harmony, and Charity, notwithstanding difference of Apprehensions in certain Matters, may take place: But I have here no consideration of *Four* sorts of Persons.

1. Not of *Atheists*, whose Sentiments are forced, and unnatural.

2. Not of *Enthusiasts*, who know not to day what they shall think to morrow.

3. Not of *Self-flatterers*, who are fondly perswaded concerning themselves; and will hardly admit *that* for Evil in themselves, which passes for such otherwhere.

4. Not of *Hypocrites*, who do not mean what they pretend. Truth with them is not an End, but a Means.

But all *fair Allowance* for the *Humble, Modest, Meek* and *Ingenuous*; with great Abatement for their many Disadvantages, weaknesses of Parts, want of Leisure, probable Ignorance: For all which, their honest Simplicity, and sincere meaning make Compensation. Some think, that if they agree not in all things about Religion, they must stand at distance from one another. But this is a great mistake: The Text saith, *Whereunto we have already attained, let us walk by the same Rule.*[40] And *Charity never faileth, doth not behave it self unseemly; beareth all things; endureth all things; hopeth all things.*[41] *Charity covereth a multitude of Sins:*[42] Both of the Object and of the Subject; of him we have to do with, and also of our selves: For to the Compassionate, God shews Compassion: And it shall be measured to us according to our own Measures.[43]

---

[38] *Jonah* 4. 11. On the parenthetical remark, cf. *Aphorisms*, § 184 (below, p. 328).
[39] Cf. *Psalms* 49. 12.
[40] Above, p. 77.
[41] 1 *Corinthians* 13. 7–8.
[42] 1 *Peter* 4. 8.
[43] Cf. *Matthew* 7. 2.

RALPH CUDWORTH

A Sermon
Preached before the House of Commons.
March 31, 1647*

I John ii. 3, 4

And hereby we do know that we know him, if we keep his Commandments. He that saith, I know him, and keepeth not his Commandments, is a liar, and the truth is not in him.

WE have much enquiry concerning knowledge in these latter times.[1] The sonnes of Adam are now as busie as ever himself was, about the *Tree of Knowledge* of good and evil, shaking the boughs of it, and scrambling for the fruit: whilest, I fear, many are too unmindful of the *Tree of Life*. And though there be now no Cherubims with their flaming swords, to fright men off from it; yet the way that leads to it seems to be solitary and untrodden, as if there were but few that had any mind to tast of the Fruit of it. There be many that speak of new glimpses, and discoveries of Truth, of dawnings of Gospel-light; and no question, but God hath reserved much of this for the very Evening and Sun-set of the World, for *in the latter dayes knowledge shall be increased*:[2] but I wish we could in the mean time see that *day* to *dawn*, which the Apostle speaks of, and that *day-starre to arise in mens hearts*.[3] I wish whilest we talk of light, and dispute about truth, we could walk

---

* *A Sermon preached before the Honourable House of Commons, at Westminster, March 31, 1647* (Cambridge, 1647). Reprinted here in its entirety but without the prefatory address to the House of Commons.

[1] Cudworth appears to have subscribed to the age's widespread conviction that the Last Judgement was imminent. But only More continued to believe that he lived in 'the last *Semi-time* of those seven that comprehend the ὕστεροι καιροί properly so called' (*Apology*, p. 482; but see further Tuveson, Ch. III).

[2] Cf. *Daniel* 12. 4.   [3] Cf. 2 *Peter* 1. 19.

A Sermon Preached before the House of Commons 91

more as *children of the light*. Whereas if S. Johns rule be good here in the Text, that no man truly knows Christ, but he that keepeth his Commandments; it is much to be suspected, that many of us which pretend to light, have a thick and gloomy darknesse within overspreading our souls. There be now many large Volumes and Discourses written concerning Christ, thousands of controversies discussed, infinite problems determined concerning his Divinity, Humanity, Union of both together; and what not? So that our bookish Christians, that have all their religion in writings and papers, think they are now compleatly furnished with all kind of knowledge concerning Christ; and when they see all their leaves lying about them, they think they have a goodly stock of knowledge and truth, and cannot possibly misse of the way to heaven; as if Religion were nothing but a little *Book-craft*, a mere *paper-skill*. But if S. Johns rule here be good, we must not judge of our knowing of Christ, by our skill in Books and Papers, but by our keeping of his Commandments. And that I fear will discover many of us (notwithstanding all this light which we boast of round about us) to have nothing but Egyptian darknesse within upon our hearts.[4] The vulgar sort think that they know Christ enough, out of their Creeds and Catechismes, and Confessions of Faith: and if they have but a little acquainted themselves with these, and like Parrets conned the words of them, they doubt not but that they are sufficiently instructed in all the mysteries of the Kingdome of Heaven. Many of the more learned, if they can but wrangle and dispute about Christ, imagine themselves to be grown great proficients in the School of Christ. The greatest part of the world, whether learned or unlearned, think that there is no need of purging and purifying of their hearts, for the right knowledge of Christ and his Gospel; but though their lives be never so wicked, their hearts never so foul within, yet they may know Christ sufficiently out of their Treatises and Discourses, out of their mere Systems and Bodies of Divinity; which I deny not to be usefull in a subordinate way: although our Saviour prescribeth his Disciples another method, to come to the right knowledge of Divine truths, by doing of Gods will; *he that will do my Fathers will* (saith he) *shall know of the doctrine*

---

[4] A recurrent metaphor, strikingly appropriate when addressed to men who regarded themselves as latter-day Israelites. By contrast, More's reference to those who are 'grown *Æthiopians* in wickedness' (*Apology*, p. 529) merely capitalises on a popular prejudice.

whether it be of God.[5] He is a true Christian indeed, not *he* that is onely *book-taught*, but he that is *God-taught*;[6] he that hath an *Unction from the holy one* (as our Apostle calleth it)[7] *that teacheth him all things;* he that hath the Spirit of Christ within him, that *searcheth* out the *deep things of God*: *For as no man knoweth the things of a man, save the spirit of man which is in him, even so the things of God knoweth no man but the Spirit of God.*[8] Inke and Paper can never make us Christians, can never beget a new nature, a living principle in us; can never form Christ, or any true notions of spirituall things in our hearts. The Gospel, that new Law which Christ delivered to the world, it is not merely a *Letter* without us, but a *quickning Spirit* within us. Cold Theorems and Maximes, dry and jejune Disputes, lean syllogisticall reasonings, could never yet of themselves beget the least glympse of true heavenly light, the least sap of saving knowledge in any heart. All this is but the groping of the poore dark spirit of man after truth, to find it out with his own endeavours, and feel it with his own cold and benummed hands. Words and syllables which are but dead things, cannot possibly convey the living notions of heavenly truths to us. The secret mysteries of a Divine Life, of a New Nature, of Christ formed in our hearts; they cannot be written or spoken, language and expressions cannot reach them; neither can they ever be truly understood, except the soul it self be kindled from within, and awakened into the life of them. A Painter that would draw a Rose, though he may flourish some likenesse of it in figure and colour, yet he can never paint the sent and fragrancy; or if he would draw a Flame he cannot put a constant heat into his colours; he cannot make his pensil drop a Sound, as the Echo in the Epigramme mocks at him—*si vis similem pingere, pinge sonum.*[9] All the skill of cunning Artizans and Mechanicks, cannot put a principle of Life into a statue of their own making. Neither are we able to inclose in words and letters, the Life, Soul, and Essence of any Spirituall truths; & as it were to incorporate it in them. Some Philosophers have determined, that ἀρετή is not διδακτόν, vertue cannot be taught by any certain rules or precepts.[10] Men and books may propound some directions to us, that may set us in such a way of life and practice, as in which we shall at last find it within our selves, and be experimentally

[5] *John* 7. 17.   [6] θεοδίδακτος—as above, p. 59, note.
[7] 1 *John* 2. 20.   [8] 1 *Corinthians* 2. 10–11.
[9] 'If you wish to paint a likeness, paint a sound'.
[10] Cf. Plato, *Euthydemus*, 274e; etc. Διδακτόν should read διδακτή.

A Sermon Preached before the House of Commons

acquainted with it: but they cannot teach it us like a Mechanick Art or Trade. No surely, *there is a spirit in man*: and *the inspiration of the Almighty giveth this understanding.*[11] But we shall not meet with this spirit any where, but in the way of Obedience: the knowledge of Christ, and the keeping of his Commandments, must alwayes go together, and be mutuall causes of one another.

Hereby we know that we know him, if we keep his Commandments. He that saith, I know him, and keepeth not his Commandments, is a liar, and the truth is not in him.

I come now unto these words themselves, which are so pregnant, that I shall not need to force out any thing at all from them: I shall therefore onely take notice of some few observations, which drop from them of their own accord, and then conclude with some Application of them to our selves.

First then, If this be the right way and methode of discovering our *knowledge of Christ*, by our *keeping of his Commandments*; Then *we may safely draw conclusions concerning our state and condition, from the conformity of our lives to the will of Christ.* Would we know whether we know Christ aright, let us consider whether the life of Christ be in us. *Qui non habet vitam Christi, Christum non habet;*[12] He that hath not the life of Christ in him, he hath nothing but the name, nothing but a phansie of Christ, he hath not the substance of him. He that builds his house upon this foundation; not an airy notion of Christ swimming in his brain, but Christ really dwelling and living in his heart, as our Saviour himself witnesseth, he *buildeth his house upon a Rock;*[13] and when the flouds come, and the winds blow, and the rain descends, and beats upon it, it shall stand impregnably. But he that builds all his comfort upon an ungrounded perswasion, that God from all eternity hath loved him, and absolutely decreed him to life and happinesse, and seeketh not for God really dwelling in his soul; he builds his house upon a Quicksand, and it shall suddenly sink and be swallowed up: *his hope shall be cut off, & his trust shall be a spiders web; he shall lean upon his house, but it shall not stand, he shall hold it fast but it shall not endure.*[14] We are no where commanded to pry into these secrets, but the wholesome counsell and advise given us, is this;

---

[11] *Job* 32. 8.
[12] An adaptation of the Vulgate's reading of 1 *John* 5. 12 ('Qui habet Filium, habet vitam; qui non habet Filium, vitam non habet').
[13] *Matthew* 7. 24.   [14] *Job* 8. 14–15.

to *make our calling and election sure.*[15] We have no warrant in Scripture, to peep into these hidden Rolls and Volumes of Eternity, and to make it our first thing that we do when we come to Christ, to spell out our names in the starres, and to perswade our selves that we are certainly elected to everlasting happiness: before we see the *image of God*, in righteousnesse and true holinesse, shaped in our hearts. Gods everlasting decree, is too dazeling and bright an object for us at first to set our eye upon: it is far easier and safer for us to look upon the raies of his goodnesse and holinesse as they are reflected in our own hearts; and there to read the mild and gentle Characters of Gods love to us, in our love to him, and our hearty compliance with his heavenly will: as it is safer for us if we would see the Sunne, to look upon it here below in a pale of water; then to cast up our daring eyes upon the body of the Sun it self, which is too radiant and scorching for us. The best assurance that any one can have of his interest in God, is doubtlesse the conformity of his soul to him. Those divine purposes, whatsoever they be are altogether unsearchable and unknowable by us, they lie wrapt up in everlasting darknesse, and covered in a deep Abysse; who is able to fathom the bottome of them? Let us not therefore make this our first attempt towards God and Religion, to perswade our selves strongly of these everlasting Decrees: for if at our first flight we aime so high, we shall happily but scorch our wings, and be struck back with lightning, as those *Giants* of old were, that would needs attempt to invade and assault heaven.[16] And it is indeed a most *Giganticall* Essay, to thrust ourselves so boldly into the lap of heaven; it is the pranck of a *Nimrod*, of a *mighty Hunter* thus rudely to deal with God, and to force heaven and happinesse before his face whether he will or no.[17] The way to obtain a good assurance indeed of our title to heaven, is not to clamber up to it, by a ladder of our own ungrounded perswasions; but to dig as low as hell by humility and self-denyall in our own hearts: and though this may seem to be the furthest way about; yet it is indeed the neerest, and safest way to it. We must $\dot{\alpha}\nu\alpha\beta\alpha\acute{\iota}\nu\varepsilon\iota\nu\ \varkappa\acute{\alpha}\tau\omega$ and $\varkappa\alpha\tau\alpha\beta\alpha\acute{\iota}\nu\varepsilon\iota\nu\ \mathring{\alpha}\nu\omega$, as the Greek Epigramme speaks, *ascend downward, & descend upward*; if we would indeed come to heaven, or get any true perswasion of our title to it. The most gallant and triumphant confidence of a Christian,

---

[15] 2 *Peter* 1. 10.   [16] *Genesis* 6. 4 ff.
[17] *Genesis* 10. 8–9. Cf. Milton's commonplace conception of Nimrod in *Paradise Lost*, XII, 24 ff.

riseth safely and surely upon this low foundation, that lies deep under ground; and there stands firmely and stedfastly. When our heart is once tuned into a conformity with the word of God, when we feel our will, perfectly to concurre with his will, we shal then presently perceive a *Spirit of adoption* within our selves, teaching us to cry *Abba. Father*.[18] We shall not then care for peeping into those hidden Records of Eternity, to see whether our names be written there in golden characters: no, we shall find a copy of Gods thoughts concerning us, written in our own breasts. There we may read the characters of his favour to us, there we may feel an inward sense of his love to us, flowing out of our hearty and unfained love to him. And we shall be more undoubtedly perswaded of it, then if any of those winged *Watchmen* above, that are privie to heavens secrets, should come & tel us; that they saw our names enrolled in those *volumes of eternity*. Whereas on the contrary; though we strive to perswade our selves never so confidently, that God from all eternity hath loved us, and elected us to life and happinesse if we do yet in the mean time entertain any iniquity within our hearts, and willingly close with any lust; do what we can, we shall find many a cold qualme ever now and then seizing upon us at approaching dangers; and when death it self shall grimly look us in the face, we shall feel our hearts even to die within us, and our spirits quite faint away, though we strive to raise them and recover them never so much, with the *Strong Waters* and *Aqua vitæ* of our own ungrounded presumptions. The least inward lust willingly continued in, will be like a *worme*, fretting the *Gourd* of our jolly confidence, and presumptuous perswasion of Gods love, and always gnawing at the root of it: and though we strive to keep it alive, and continually besprinkle it with some dews of our own; yet it will alwayes be dying and withering in our bosomes. But a good Conscience within, will be always better to a Christian, then *health to his navell, and marrow to his bones*;[19] it will be an everlasting cordiall to his heart: it will be softer to him then a bed of doune, and he may sleep securely upon it, in the midst of raging and temptuous seas; when the winds bluster, and the waves beat round about him. A good conscience, is the best looking-glasse of heaven; in which the soul may see God's thoughts and purposes concerning it, as so many shining starres reflected to it. *Hereby we know that we know Christ, hereby we know that Christ loves us, if we keep his Commandments.*

[18] *Romans* 8. 15. [19] *Proverbs* 3. 8.

Secondly, If hereby onely we know that we know Christ, by our keeping his Commandments; *Then the knowledge of Christ doth not consist merely in a few barren Notions, in a form of certain dry and saplesse Opinions.*[20] Christ came not into the world to fil our heads with mere Speculations; to kindle a fire of wrangling and contentious dispute amongst us, and to warm our spirits against one another with nothing but angry & peevish debates, whilst in the mean time our hearts remain all ice within towards God, and have not the least spark of true heavenly fire to melt and thaw them. Christ came not to possesse our brains onely with some cold opinions, that send down nothing but a freezing and benumming influence upon our hearts. Christ was *Vitæ Magister*, not *Scholæ*: and he is the best Christian, whose heart beats with the truest pulse towards heaven; not he whose head spinneth out the finest cobwebs. He that endeavours really to mortifie his lusts, and to comply with that truth in his life, which his Conscience is convinced of; is neerer a Christian, though he never heard of Christ; then he that believes all the vulgar Articles of the Christian faith, and plainly denyeth Christ in his life.[21] Surely, the way to heaven that Christ hath taught us, is plain and easie, if we have but honest hearts: we need not many Criticismes, many School-distinctions, to come to a right understanding of it. Surely, Christ came not to ensnare us and intangle us with captious niceties, or to pulse our heads with deep speculations, and lead us through hard and craggie notions into the Kingdome of heaven. I perswade my self, that no man shall ever be kept out of heaven, for not comprehending mysteries that were beyond the reach of his shallow understanding; if he had but an honest and good heart, that was ready to comply with Christs Commandments. *Say not in thine heart, Who shall ascend into heaven?* that is, with high speculations to bring down Christ from thence: or, *Who shall descend into the abysse beneath?* that is with deep searching thoughts to fetch up Christ from thence: but loe, *the word is nigh thee, even in thy mouth, and in thy heart.*[22] But I wish, it were not

---

[20] Cf. Whichcote's censure of 'notions', above, p. 66.

[21] Frequently reiterated, this view was hardly calculated to endear the Cambridge Platonists to their contemporaries. The commonly accepted view was set forth by William Dell, Master of Gonville and Caius College, Cambridge, when he consigned Plato and all 'Wretched Heathens' to Hell for not knowing Christ (*The Stumbling-Stone* [1651], in *Several Sermons* [1709], p. 407). Cf. Whichcote on Cicero, above, p. 55.

[22] *Romans* 10. 6–8.

the distemper of our times, to scare and fright men onely with *opinions*, and make them onely solicitous about the entertaining of this and that speculation, which will not render them any thing the better in their lives, or the liker unto God; whilst in the mean time there is no such care taken about *keeping of Christs* Commandments, and being renewed in our minds according to the image of God, in righteousnesse and true holinesse. We say, *Loe, here is Christ*; and *Loe, there is Christ*, in these and these *opinions*; whereas in truth, Christ is neither here, nor there, nor any where; but where the Spirit of Christ, where the life of Christ is. Do we not nowadayes open and lock up heaven, with the private key of this and that opinion of our own according to our severall fancies as we please? And if any one observe Christs Commandments never so sincerely, and serve God, with faith and a pure conscience, that yet happely skils not of some contended for *opinions*, some darling *notions*; he hath not the right Shibboleth, he hath not the true Watch-word; he must not passe the Guards into heaven. Do we not make this and that *opinion*, this and that outward *form*, to be the *Wedding-garment*, and boldly sentence those to outer darknesse, that are not invested therewith? Whereas every true Christian, finds the least dram of hearty affection towards God, to be more cordiall and sovereign to his soul; then all the *speculative notions*, and *opinions* in the world: and though he study also to inform his understanding aright, and free his mind from all errour and misapprehensions; yet it is nothing but the *life of Christ* deeply rooted in his heart which is the Chymicall Elixer that he feeds upon. Had he *all faith that he could remove mountains* (as S. Paul speaks) had he *all knowledge, all tongues and languages*;[23] yet he prizeth one dram of love beyond them all. He accounteth him that feeds upon mere *notions* in Religion, to be but an aiery and Chamelion like Christian. He findeth himself now otherwise rooted and centred in God, then when he did before merely contemplate and gaze upon him: he tasteth and relisheth God within himself, he hath *quendam saporem Dei*, a *certain savour of him*; whereas before he did but rove and guesse at random at him. He feeleth himself safely anchored in God, and will not be disswaded from it; though perhaps he skill not many of those *subtleties*, which others make the Alpha and Omega of their Religion. Neither is he scared with those childish affrightments, with which some would force their private conceits upon him; he is above the superstitious dreading, of mere

---

[23] Cf. 1 *Corinthians* 13. 1–2.

speculative opinions; as well as the superstitious reverence of outward ceremonies: he cares not so much for subtlety, as for soundnesse and health of mind. And indeed, as it was well spoken by a noble Philosopher, ἄνευ ἀρετῆς Θεὸς ὄνομα μόνον, that *without purity and virtue God is nothing but an empty name*;[24] so it is as true here, that without obedience to Christs Commandments, without the *life of Christ* dwelling in us, whatsoever *opinions* we entertain of him, Christ is but onely named by us, he is not *known*. I speak not here against a free and ingenuous enquiry into all Truth, according to our severall abilities and opportunities, I plead not for the captivating and enthralling of our judgements to the Dictates of men, I do not disparage the naturall improvement of our understanding faculties by true Knowledge, which is so noble and gallant a perfection of the mind: but the thing which I aime against is, the dispiriting of the life and vigour of our Religion, by dry speculations, and making it nothing but a mere dead skeleton of *opinions*, a few dry bones without any flesh and sinews tyed up together: and the misplacing of all our zeal upon an eager prosecution of these, which should be spent to better purpose upon other objects. Knowledge indeed is a thing farre more excellent than riches, outward pleasures, worldly dignities, or any thing else in the world besides Holinesse, and the Conformity of our wills to the will of God: but yet our happinesse consisteth not in it, but in a certain Divine Temper & Constitution of soul which is farre above it. But it is a piece of that corruption that runneth through humane nature, that we naturally prize Truth, more than Goodnesse; Knowledge, more than Holinesse. We think it a gallant thing to be fluttering up to Heaven with our wings of Knowledge and Speculation: whereas the highest mystery of a Divine Life here, and of perfect Happinesse hereafter, consisteth in nothing but mere Obedience to the Divine Will. Happinesse is nothing but that inward sweet delight, that will arise from the Harmonious agreement between our wills and Gods will. There is nothing contrary to God in the whole world, nothing that fights against him but *Self will*.[25] This is the strong Castle, that we all keep garrison'd against heaven in every one of our hearts, which God continually layeth siege unto: and it must be conquered and demolished before we can conquer heaven. It was by reason of this *Self-will*, that

[24] Plotinus, II, ix, 15—one of the *loci classici* for all the Cambridge Platonists, quoted by Smith (below, p. 134), More (*Discourses*, p. 172), etc.

[25] Cudworth's prolonged castigation of self-will (to p. 102) should be compared with Smith's (below, pp. 161 ff.).

Adam fell in Paradise; that those glorious Angels, those *Morning-starres*, kept not their first station, but dropt down from heaven like Falling Starres, and sunk into this condition of bitterneffe, anxiety, and wretchednesse in which now they are. They all intangled themselves with the length of their own wings, they would needs will more and otherwise then God would will in them: and going about to make their wills wider, and to enlarge them into greater amplitude; the more they strugled, they found themselves the faster pinioned, & crowded up into narrownesse and servility; insomuch that now they are not able to use any wings at all, but inheriting the *serpents* curse, can onely creep with their *bellies* upon the earth. Now our onely way to recover God & happiness again, is not to soar up with our Understandings, but to destroy this *Self-will* of ours: and then we shall find our wings to grow again, our plumes fairly spread, & our selves raised aloft into the free Aire of perfect Liberty, which is perfect Happinesse. There is nothing in the whole world able to do us good or hurt, but *God* and our own *Will*; neither riches nor poverty, nor disgrace nor honour, nor life nor death, nor Angels nor Divels; but Willing or Not-willing as we ought to do. Should Hell it self cast all its fiery darts against us, if our *Will* be right, if it be informed by the Divine Will; they can do us no hurt; we have then, (if I may so speak,) an inchanted Shield that is impenetrable, and will beare off all. God will not hurt us, and Hell cannot hurt us, if we vvill nothing but vvhat God wills. Nay, then we are acted by God himself, and the whole Divinity floweth in upon us; and when we have cashiered this *Self-will* of ours, which did but shackle and confine our soules, our wills shall then become truly free, being widened and enlarged to the extent of Gods own will. *Hereby we know that we know Christ indeed*, not by our *Speculative Opinions* concerning him, *but by our keeping of his Commandments*.

Thirdly, if hereby we are to judge whether we truly *know Christ*, by our *keeping of his Commandments*; so that *he that saith he knoweth him, and keepeth not his Commandments, is a lyar*; Then, *This was not the Plot and designe of the Gospel, to give the world an indulgence to sin, upon what pretence soever*. Though we are too prone, to make such misconstructions of it: as if God had intended nothing else in it, but to *dandle* our corrupt nature, and contrive a smooth and easie way for us to come to happinesse, without the toilsome labour of subduing our lusts and sinfull affections. Or, As if the Gospel were nothing else but a Declaration to the World, of Gods ingaging his affections from all eternity, on some particular persons, in such a manner, as that he would resolve to love them, and dearly embrace them, though he never made them partakers of his Image in righteousnesse and true holinesse: and though they should remain under the power of all their lusts, yet they should still continue his *beloved ones*, and he would not withstanding at last bring them undoubtedly into heaven. Which is nothing else, but to make the God that we worship, the God of the new Testament, a προσωπολήπτης, *an accepter of persons:*[26] and one that should encourage that in the world which is diametrally opposite to Gods own Life and Being. And indeed nothing is more ordinary, then for us to shape out such monstrous and deformed Notions of God unto our selves, by looking upon him through the *coloured Medium* of our own corrupt hearts, and having the *eye* of our soul *tinctured* by the suffusions of our own lusts. And therefore, because we mortals can *fondly* love and hate, and sometimes, hug the very Vices, of those to whom our affections are engaged, and kisse their very Deformities; we are so ready to shape out a Deity like unto our selves, and to fashion out such a *God*, as will in Christ at least, hug the very wickednesse of the world: and in those that be once his own, by I know not what, *fond* affection, appropriated to himself, connive at their very sinnes, so that they shall not make the least breach betwixt himself and them. Truly, I know not whether of the two, be the worse Idolatry, and of the deeper stain; for a man to make a god out of a *piece of wood*, and *fall down unto it and worship it, and say, Deliver me, for thou art my God*, as it is expressed in the Prophet *Isaiah*;[27] or to set up such an Idol-god of our own Imagination as this is, fashioned out according to the similitude of our own *fondnesse* and wickednesse: and when we should paint out God with the liveliest Colours, that we can possibly borrow from any created being, with the purest Perfections that we can abstract from them; to draw him out thus with the blackest Coal of our own corrupt hearts; and to make the very blots and blurs of our own souls, to be the Letters, which we spell out his name by. Thus do we that are Children of the Night, make black and ugly representations of God unto our selves, as the *Ethiopians* were wont to do, copying him out according to our own likenesse; and setting up that unto our selves for a God, which we love most dearly in our selves, that is, our Lusts. But there is no such *God* as this any

---

[26] Cf. *Acts* 10. 34: 'God is no respecter of persons.'
[27] *Isaiah* 44. 15–17.

A Sermon Preached before the House of Commons

where in the world, but onely in some mens false imaginations, who know not all this while, that they look upon themselves instead of God, and make an Idol of themselves, which they worship and adore for him; being so full of themselves, that whatsoever they see round about them, even God himself, they colour with their own Tincture: like him that *Aristotle* speaks of, that wheresoever he went, and whatsoever he looked upon, he saw still his own face, as in a glass, represented to him. And therefore it is no wonder if men seem naturally more devoutly affected tovvard such an Imaginary God, as we have now described, then to the True Reall God, clothed with his own proper Attributes; since it is nothing but an Image of themselves, which *Narcissus-like* they fall in love with: no wonder if they kisse and dandle such a *Baby-god* as this, which like little children, they have dressed up out of the clouts of their own fond Phancies, according to their own liknesse, of purpose that they might play and sport with it. But God will ever *dwell* in spotlesse *light*, howsoever we paint him and disfigure him here below: he will still be circled about, with his own raies of unstained and immaculate glory. And though the Gospel be not God, as he is in his own *Brightnesse*, but God *Vailed* and *Masked* to us, God in a state of Humiliation, and Condescent, as the Sun in a Rainbow; yet it is nothing else but a clear and unspotted Mirrour of Divine Holinesse, Goodnesse, Purity; in which Attributes lies the very Life and Essence of God himself. The Gospel is nothing else, but God descending into the World in *Our Form*, and conversing with us in our likenesse; that he might allure, and draw us up to God, and make us partakers of his *Divine Form*. Θεὸς γέγονεν ἄνθρωπος (as *Athanasius* speaks) ἵνα ἡμᾶς ἐν ἑαυτῷ θεοποιήσῃ, *God was therefore incarnated and made man, that he might Deifie us*,[28] that is, (as S. *Peter* expresseth it) make us *partakers of the Divine nature*.[29] Now, I say, the very proper Character, and Essentiall Tincture of God himself, is nothing else but *Goodnesse*. Nay, I may be bold to adde, That God is therefore God, because he is the highest and most perfect Good: and Good is not therefore Good, because God out of an arbitrary will of his, would have it so. Whatsoever God doth in the World,

---

[28] *De Inc.*, LIV, actually reads ὁ τοῦ Θεοῦ Λόγος ... ἐνηνθρώπησεν, ἵνα ἡμεῖς θεοποιηθῶμεν ('the Word of God ... was made man, that we might be made gods'). A favourite of the Cambridge Platonists, this affirmation is rarely quoted by other seventeenth-century Protestants. See also above, pp. 19 ff.

[29] 2 *Peter* 1. 4.

he doth it as it is suitable to the highest Goodnesse; the first Idea, and fairest Copy of which is his own Essence. Vertue and Holinesse in creatures, as *Plato* well discourseth in his *Euthyphro*, are not *therefore Good, because God loveth them*, and will have them be accounted such; but rather, *God therefore loveth them because they are in themselves simply good.*[30] Some of our own Authors, go a little further yet, and tell us; that God doth not fondly love himself, because he is *himself*, but therefore he loveth himself because he is the highest and most absolute *Goodnesse*: so that if there could be any thing in the world better then God, God would love that better then himself: but because he is Essentially the most perfect *Good*; therefore he cannot but love his own *goodnesse*, infinitely above all other things. And it is another mistake which sometimes we have of God by shaping him out according to the Model of our selves, when we make him nothing but a *blind, dark, impetuous Self will*, running through the world; such as we our selves are furiously acted with, that have not the Ballast of *absolute goodnesse* to poize and settle us. That I may therefore come nearer to the thing in hand: God who is *absolute goodnesse*, cannot love any of his Creatures & take pleasure in them, without bestowing a communication of his Goodnesse and Likenesse upon them. God cannot make a Gospel, to promise men Life & Happinesse hereafter, without being *regenerated*, & made partakers of his *holinesse*. As soon may Heaven and Hell, be reconciled together, and lovingly shake hands with one another; as God can be fondly indulgent to any sinne, in whomsoever it be. As soon may Light and Darknesse be espoused together, and Mid-night be married to the Noon-day; as God can be joyned in a league of friendship, to any wicked Soul.

 The great Designe of God in the Gospel, is to clear up this Mist of Sin and Corruption, which we are here surrounded with: and to bring up his creatures, out of the *shadow of death*, to the *Region of Light* above, the Land of Truth and Holinesse. The great Mystery of the Gospel, is to establish a *Godlike* frame and disposition of spirit, which consists in Righteousnesse and true Holinesse, in the hearts of men. And Christ, who is the great and mighty Saviour, he came on purpose into the World; not onely to save us from *Fire and Brimstone*, but also to save us from our *Sins*. Christ hath therefore made an Expiation

---

[30] Plato, *Euthyphro*, 10d–e; slightly adjusted in order to coincide with 1 *John* 4. 10 ('Herein is love, not that we loved God, but that he loved us'). Shorey, p. 201, argues that this Platonic principle is reaffirmed throughout Cudworth's *Imm. Morality*.

A Sermon Preached before the House of Commons 103

of our sins, by his death upon the Crosse, that we being thus *delivered out of the hands of* these our greatest *enemies, might serve God without fear, in holinesse and righteousnesse before him, all the dayes of our life.*[31] This *grace of God that bringeth salvation,* hath therefore *appeared to all men,* in the Gospel, that it might *teach us to deny ungodlinesse and worldly lusts, and that we should live soberly, righteously, and godlily in this present world: looking for that blessed hope, and glorious appearing of the great God, and our Saviour Jesus Christ; who gave himself for us, that he might redeem us from all iniquity, and purifie unto himself a peculiar people, Zealous of good works.*[32] *These things I write unto* you (saith our *Apostle* a little before my text) *that you sinne not:*[33] therein expressing the end of the whole Gospel, which is, not onely to *cover sinne,* by spreading the Purple Robe of Christs death and sufferings over it, whilst it still remaineth in us, with all its filth and noisomnesse unremoved; but also, to convey a powerfull and mighty spirit of holinesse, to *cleanse* us, and *free* us from it. And this is a greater grace of Gods to us, then the former, which still go both together in the Gospel; besides the free remission and pardon of sinne in the *bloud of Christ,* the delivering of us from the power of sinne, by the *Spirit of Christ* dwelling in our hearts. Christ came not into the world onely, to cast a Mantle over us, and hide all our filthy sores, from Gods avenging eye, with his merits and righteousnesse; but he came likewise, to be a Chirurgeon, and Physitian of souls, to free us from the filth and corruption of them; which is more grievous and burdensome, more noysome to a true Christian, then the guilt of sinne it self. Should a poore wretched, and diseased creature, that is full of sores and ulcers, be covered all over with Purple, or clothed with Scarlet; he would take but little contentment in it whilest his sores and wounds, remain upon him: and he had much rather be arraied in rags, so he might obtain but soundnesse and health within. The Gospel is a true *Bethesda,*[34] *a pool of Grace,* where such poore, lame, and infirme creatures, as we are, upon the moving of Gods spirit in it, may descend down, not onely to wash our skin and outside, but also to be cured of our diseases within. And what ever the world thinks, there is a powerfull Spirit that *moves* upon these *waters,* the waters of the Gospel, for this new Creation, the Regeneration of souls; the very same Spirit, that once *moved* upon *the waters* of the universe at the first Creation,

---

[31] *Luke* 1. 74–5.   [32] *Titus* 2. 11–14.
[33] 1 *John* 2. 1.   [34] Cf. *John* 5. 2 ff.

and spreading its mighty wings over them, did hatch the new-born World into this perfection: I say, the same *Almighty* spirit of Christ, still worketh in the Gospel, spreading its gentle, healing, quickening wings, over our souls. The Gospel, is not like *Abana* and *Pharphar*, those common Rivers of *Damascus*, that could onely cleanse the outside; but it is a true *Jordan*, in which such leprouse *Naamans*, as we all are, may *Wash and be clean*.[35] *Blessed* indeed *are they, whose iniquities are forgiven, and whose sinnes are covered: Blessed is the man to whom the Lord will not impute sinne*: but yet, rather Blessed are they, whose sinnes are removed like a *Morning-cloud*, and quite taken away from them: *Blessed*, thrice blessed, *are they, that hunger and thirst after righteousnesse, for they shall be satisfied: Blessed are the pure in heart for they shall see God*.[36] Our Saviour Christ came (as *John* the *Baptist* tell us) *with a Fan in his hand, that he might throughly purge his floore and gather his wheat into his garner: but the chaff he will burn up, with unquenchable fire*.[37] He came (as the Prophet *Malachy* speaks) *like a Refiners fire, and like Fullers sope; to sit as a Refiner and Purifier of silver, and to purifie all the sonnes of Levi, and purge them as gold and silver, that they may offer unto the Lord an offering in righteousnesse*.[38] Christ came not onely, to write *Holinesse to the Lord* upon *Aarons* forehead, and to put his *Urim* and *Thummim* upon his Breast-plate, but *This is the Covenant, saith the Lord, that I will make with them in those dayes; I will put my Law into their inward parts, and write it in their hearts, and* then *I will be their God, and they shall be my people: they shall be all Kings and Priests unto me. God sent his own sonne* (saith St. *Paul*) *in the likenesse of sinfull flesh, and by a sacrifice for sinne, condemned sinne in the flesh: that the righteousnesse of the Law might be fulfilled in us, who walk not after the flesh, but after the Spirit*.[39] The *first Adam*, as the Scripture tells us, brought in a reall defilement, which like a noisome Leprosie, hath overspread all mankind: and therefore *the second Adam* must not onely fill the World with a *conceit*, of Holinesse, and meer Imaginary Righteousnesse; but he must really convey, such an *immortall seed* of Grace into the hearts of true Believers, as may prevaile still more and more in them, till it have at last, quite wrought out that *poison* of the *Serpent*. Christ, that was nothing, but *Divinity dwelling in a Tabernacle of flesh*, and God himself immediately acting a humane nature; he came

[35] Cf. 2 *Kings* 5.   [36] Cf. *Matthew* 5. 3 ff.
[37] *Matthew* 3. 12, *Luke* 3. 17.   [38] *Malachi* 3. 2–3.
[39] The allusions here progress from *Exodus* 28. 30, through the celebrated 'New Covenant' proclaimed in *Jeremiah* 31. 31 ff., to *Romans* 8. 3–4.

into the World to kindle here that *Divine life* amongst men, which is certainly dearer unto God, then any thing else whatsoever in the World; and to propagate this Celestiall fire, from one heart still unto another, untill the end of the World. Neither is he, or was he ever absent from this Spark of his Divinity, kindled amongst men, wheresoever it be, though he seem bodily to be withdrawn from us. He is the standing, constant, inexhausted Fountain, of this divine Light and Heat; that still toucheth every soul that is enlivened by it, with an outstretched Ray, and freely lends his Beams, and disperseth his *influence* to all, from the beginning of the World to the end of it. *We all receive of his fulnesse, grace for grace*,[40] as all the Starres in heaven, are said to light their Candles at the Suns flame. For though his body be withdrawn from us, yet by the lively and *virtuall Contact* of his Spirit, he is always kindling, cheering, quickening, warming, enlivening hearts. Nay, this *Divine life* begun and kindled in any heart, wheresoever it be, is *something of God in flesh*; and, in a sober and qualified sence, *Divinity incarnate*; and all particular Christians, that are really possessed of it, so many *Mysticall Christs*. And God forbid, that *Gods own Life* and *Nature* here in the World, should be forlorn, forsaken, and abandoned of God himself. Certainly, where-ever it is, though never so little, like a sweet, young, tender *Babe*, once born in any heart; when it crieth unto God the *father* of it, with pitifull and bemoning looks imploring his compassion; it cannot chuse but move his *fatherly bowels*, and make them *yerne*, and turn toward it, and by strong sympathy, draw his compassionate arm to help and relieve it. Never was any tender Infant, so dear to those Bowels that begat it as an *Infant new-born Christ, formed in the heart* of any true believer, to God the *father* of it. Shall the *children of this World*, the *sonnes of darknesse*, be moved with such tender affection, and compassion, towards the fruit of their bodies, their own Naturall offspring; and shall God who is the *Father of lights*, the fountain of all goodnesse, be moved with no compassion towards his true Spiritual Offspring, and have no regard to those sweet *Babes of Light*, ingendered by his own beams in mens hearts, that in their lovely countenances, bear the resemblance of his own face, and call him their *father?* Shall he see them lie fainting, and gasping, and dying here in the World, for want of nothing to preserve and keep them, but an *Influence* from him, who first gave them life and breath? No; hear the language of Gods heart, heare *the sounding of his bowels* towards

---

[40] *John* 1. 16.

them: *Is it Ephraim my dear sonne? Is it that pleasant child? since I spake of him I do earnestly remember him, my bowels, my bowels are troubled for him; I will surely have mercy upon him, saith the Lord.*[41] If those expressions of goodnesse and tender affection here amongst creatures, be but drops of that full Ocean that is in God; how can we then imagine, that this *Father* of our *spirits*, should have so little regard to his own dear Offspring, I do not say our souls, but that which is the very Life and Soul of our souls, the *Life of God* in us; which is nothing else but Gods own Self communicated to us, his own Sonne born in our hearts; as that he should suffer it to be cruelly murdered in its *Infancy* by our Sinnes, and like young *Hercules* in its very *cradle*, to be strangled by those filthy *vipers*;[42] that he should see him to be crucified by wicked *Lusts*, nailed fast to the crosse by invincible *Corruptions*; pierced and gored on every side with the poisoned spears of the Devils *temptations*, and at last to give up the Ghost; and yet his tender heart not at all relent, nor be all this while impassionated with so sad a spectacle? Surely, we cannot think he hath such an *adamantine* breast, such a *flinty* nature as this is. What then? must we say that though indeed he be willing, yet he is not able, to rescue his crucified and tormented *Sonne*, now bleeding upon the crosse;[43] to *take him down* from thence *and save him*? Then must Sinne be more powerfull then God: that weak, crasie, and sickly thing, more strong then the *Rock of ages*: and the Devil the Prince of Darknesse, more mighty, then the God of Light. No surely, there is a weaknesse and impotency in all Evil, a masculine strength and vigour in all Goodnesse: and therefore doubtlesse the *Highest Good*, the πρῶτον ἀγαθὸν as the Philosophers call it, is the strongest thing in the World. *Nil potentius Summo Bono.*[44] Gods *Power* displaied in the World, is nothing

---

[41] *Jeremiah* 31. 20.

[42] On the traditional idea that 'Our blessed Saviour is the true *Hercules*' (Alexander Ross, *Mystagogus poeticus*, 2nd rev. ed. [1648], p. 169), see D. C. Allen, in *Journal of English and Germanic Philology*, LX (1961), 620 ff.; J. M. Steadman, in *University of Toronto Quarterly*, XXXI (1962), 417 ff., 428; and E. M. Waith, *The Herculean Hero* (1962), esp. Ch. II.

[43] This allusion to the Passion should be noted if only in order to remind ourselves how infrequently the Cambridge Platonists dwelt on the sufferings of Christ.

[44] 'Nothing is more powerful than the Highest Good.' Neoplatonists have always tended to regard the Idea of Good—so memorably discussed in Plato's *Respublica*, VI, 506 ff.—as another name for God.

but his *Goodnesse* strongly reaching all things,⁴⁵ from heighth to depth, from the highest Heaven, to the lowest Hell: and irresistibly imparting it self to every thing, according to those severall degrees in which it is capable of it. Have the Fiends of Darknesse then, those poore forlorn spirits, that are fettered and locked up in the Chaines of their own wickednesse, any strength to withstand the force of infinite *Goodnesse*, which is infinite *Power*? or do they not rather skulk in holes of darknesse, and flie like Bats and Owls, before the approaching beams of this Sun of Righteousnesse? Is God powerfull to kill and to destroy, to damne and to torment, and is he not powerfull to save? Nay, it is the sweetest Flower in all the Garland of his Attributes, it is the richest Diamond in his Crown of Glory, that he is *Mighty to save*: and this is farre more magnificent for him, then to be stiled *Mighty to destroy*. For that, except it be in the way of Justice; speaks no Power at all, but mere Impotency, for the Root of all Power, is Goodnesse. Or must we say lastly, that God indeed is able to rescue us out of the Power of sinne & Satan, when we sigh and grone towards him, but yet sometimes to exercise his absolute Authority, his uncontrollable Dominion, he delights rather in plunging wretched souls down into infernal Night, & everlasting Darknesse? What shall we then make the God of the whole World? Nothing but a cruell and dreadfull *Erynnis*, with *curled fiery Snakes* about his head, and *Firebrands* in his hands, thus governing the World? Surely this will make us either secretly to think, that there is no God at all in the World, if he must needs be such, or else to wish heartily, there were none. But doubtlesse, God will at last, confute all these our *Misapprehensions* of him, he will unmask our *Hypocriticall pretences*, and clearly cast the shame of all our sinfull Deficiencies, upon our selves, and vindicate his own Glory from receiving the least stain or blemish by them. In the mean time, let us know, that the Gospel now requireth, far more of us, than ever the Law did; for it requireth a *New Creature*, a *Divine Nature*, *Christ formed in us*: but yet withall, it bestoweth a *quickening Spirit*, an *enlivening Power* to inable us, to express that, which is required of us. Whosoever therefore truly *knows Christ*, the same also *keepeth Christs Commandments*. But, he *that saith, I know him, and keepeth not his Commandments, he is a liar, and the truth is not in him*.

    I have now done with the *First part* of my Discourse, concerning

⁴⁵ Cf. Cudworth, *Int. System*, p. 886: 'God did not make the World meerly to Ostentate his *Skill* and *Power*; but to communicate his Goodness.' Thus also Smith, *Discourses*, p. 142 and below, p. 169.

those *Observations*, which arise naturally from the Words, and offer themselves to us: I shall in the next place, proceed to make some generall *Application* of them, all together.

Now therefore, I beseech you, Let us consider, whether or no we know *Christ* indeed: Not by our acquaintance with *Systems and Modells* of Divinity; not by our skill in *Books and Papers*; but by our *keeping of Christs Commandments*. All the Books and writings which we converse with, they can but represent spirituall Objects to our understandings; which yet we can never see in their own true Figure, Colour, and Proportion, untill we have a *Divine light* within, to irradiate, and shine upon them. Though there be never such excellent truths, concerning Christ, and his Gospel, set down in words and letters; yet they will be but unknown Characters to us, untill we have a *Living spirit* within us, that can decypher them: untill the same Spirit, by secret Whispers in our hearts, do comment upon them, which did at first endite them. There be many that understand the Greek and Hebrew of the *Scripture*, the Originall Languages in which the Text was written, that never understood the *Language of the spirit*. There is a *Caro* and a *Spiritus*, a *Flesh* and a *Spirit*, a *Bodie* and a *Soul*, in all the writings of the Scriptures: it is but the *Flesh*, and *Body*, of Divine Truths, that is printed upon Paper; which many Moths of Books and Libraries, do onely feed upon; many Walking Scheletons of knowledge, that bury and entombe Truths, in the Living Sepulchres of their souls, do onely converse with: such as never did any thing else, but pick at the mere Bark and Rind of Truths, and crack the Shels of them. But there is a *Soul*, and *Spirit* of divine Truths, that could never yet be congealed into Inke, that could never be blotted upon Paper, which by a secret traduction and conveiance, passeth from one Soul unto another; being able to dwell and lodge no where, but in a Spirituall being, in a Living thing; because it self is nothing but *Life* and *Spirit*. Neither can it, where indeed it is, expresse it self sufficiently in Words and Sounds, but it will best declare and speak it self in Actions: as the old manner of *writing* among the Egyptians was, not by Words, but Things. The *Life* of divine Truths, is better expressed in Actions then in Words, because Actions are more *Living* things, then words; Words, are nothing but the dead Resemblances, and Pictures of those Truths, which *live* and *berath* in Actions: and the *Kingdome of* God (as the Apostle speaketh) *consisteth not in Word*, but in Life, and *Power*.[46] Τὰ πρόβατα, οὐ χορτὸν φέροντα τοῖς ποιμέσιν

[46] 1 *Corinthians* 4. 20.

ἐπιδεικνύει πόσον ἔφαγεν· (saith the Morall Philosopher) ἀλλὰ τὴν νομὴν ἔσω πέψαντα, ἔριον ἔξω φέρει καὶ γάλα· *Sheep do not come, and bring their Fodder to their Shepheard, and shew him how much they eat, but inwardly concocting and digesting it, they make it appear, by the Fleece which they wear upon their backs, and by the Milke which they give.*⁴⁷ And let not us Christians affect onely to talk and dispute of Christ, and so measure our knowledge of him by our words; but let us shew ἀπὸ τῶν θεωρημάτων πεφθέντων τὰ ἔργα, our *knowledge concocted* into our lives and actions; and then let us really manifest that we are Christs *Sheep* indeed, that we are his *Disciples*, by that *Fleece* of Holinesse, which we wear, and by the *Fruits* that we dayly yield in our lives and conversations: for *herein* (saith Christ) *is my Father glorified, that ye bear much fruit; so shall ye be my Disciples.*⁴⁸ Let us not (I beseech you) judge of our *knowing Christ*, by our ungrounded *Perswasions* that Christ from all Eternity hath loved us, and given himself particularly for Us, without the Conformity of our lives to *Christs Commandments*, without the reall partaking of the Image of Christ in our hearts. The great Mysterie of the Gospel, it doth not lie onely in *Christ without us*, (though we must know also what he hath done for us) but the very Pith and Kernel of it, consists in *Christ inwardly formed* in our hearts. Nothing is truly Ours, but what lives in our Spirits. *Salvation* it self cannot *save* us, as long as it is onely without us; no more then *Health* can cure us, and make us sound, when it is not within us, but somewhere at distance from us; no more than *Arts and Sciences*, whilst they lie onely in Books and Papers without us; can make us learned. The Gospel, though it be a Sovereigne and Medicinall thing in it self, yet the mere knowing and believing of the history of it, will do us no good: we can receive no vertue from it, till it be inwardly digested & concocted into our souls; till it be made *Ours*, and become a *living thing* in our hearts. The Gospel, if it be onely without us, cannot save us; no more then that Physitians Bill, could cure the ignorant Patient of his disease, who, when it was commended to him, took the Paper onely, and put it up in his pocket, but never drunk the Potion that was prescribed in it. All that Christ did for us in the flesh, when he was here upon earth; From his lying in a *Manger*, when he was born in *Bethlehem*, to his bleeding upon the *Crosse* on *Golgotha*; it will not save us from our sinnes, unlesse Christ by his Spirit dwell in us. It will not avail us, to believe that he was born of a *Virgin*, unlesse the *power of the most*

---

⁴⁷ Epictetus, *Ench.*, XLVI.   ⁴⁸ *John* 15. 8.

High overshadow our hearts, and beget him there likewise. It will not profit us, to believe that he died upon the *Crosse* for us; unlesse we be *baptized into his death*, by the Mortification of all our lusts; unlesse *the old man of sinne be crucified* in our hearts.⁴⁹ Christ indeed hath made an Expiation for our sinnes upon his Crosse; and the Bloud of Christ is the onely sovereign Balsame to free us from the guilt of them: but yet besides the *sprinkling* of the *bloud* of Christ upon us, we must be made partakers also of his *spirit*. Christ came into the World, as well to redeem us from the power and bondage of our sinnes, as to free us from the guilt of them. *You know* (saith S. *John*) *that he was manifested, to take away our sinnes; whosoever therefore abideth in him, sinneth not, whosoever sinneth, hath not seen nor known him.*⁵⁰ Loe the end of Christs coming into the World, Loe a designe worthy of *God manifested in the flesh*. Christ did not take all those paines; to lay aside his Robes of Glory, and come down hither into the World; to enter into a Virgins wombe; to be born in our humane shape, and be laid a poore crying infant in a Manger; & having no *form nor comlinesse* at all upon him, to take upon him the *Form of a servant*;⁵¹ to undergo a reprochfull and ignominious life, and at last to be abandoned to a shamefull death, a death upon the Crosse; I say, he did not do all this, merely to bring in a *Notion* into the World, without producing any reall and substantial effect at all, without the changing, mending, and reforming of the World: so that men should still be as wicked as they were before, and as much under the power of the Prince of Darknesse; onely, they should not be *thought so*: they should still remain as full of all the filthy sores, of sinne & corruption as before; onely, they should be *accounted whole*. Shall God come down from heaven, & pitch a *Tabernacle* amongst men? Shall he undertake such a huge Designe, and make so great a noise of doing something, which, when it is all summed up, shall not at last amount to a *Reality*? Surely, Christ did not undergo all this to so little purpose; he would not take all this paines for us, that he might be able at last, to put into our hands, nothing but a Blanck. He *was with child*, he *was in pain and travel*, and hath *he brought forth nothing but wind*, hath he been delivered *of the Eastwind*?⁵² Is that great designe that was so long carried in the Wombe of Eternity, now proved abortive, or else nothing but a mere windy birth? No surely, The end of the Gospel is *Life* and *Perfection*, 'tis a

---

⁴⁹ Cf. *Romans* 6. 6.
⁵¹ Cf. the Suffering Servant in *Isaiah*, esp. 53. 2.
⁵⁰ 1 *John* 3. 5–6.
⁵² Cf. *Isaiah* 26. 18.

Divine nature, 'tis a *Godlike* frame and disposition of spirit; 'tis to make us partakers of the *Image of God* in Righteousnesse and true Holinesse, without which, Salvation itself were but a Notion. Christ came indeed into the World, to make an Expiation and Atonement for our sinnes, but the end of this was, that we might eschew sinne, that we might forsake *all ungodlinesse and wordly lusts*. The Gospel declares pardon of sinne to those, that are *heavy laden* with it, and willing to be disburdened, to this end, that it might quicken and enliven us to new obedience. Whereas otherwise, the *Guilt* of sinne might have detained us in horrour and despair, and so have kept us still more strongly under the *Power* of it, in sad and dismall apprehensions of Gods wrath provoked against us, and inevitably falling on us. But Christ hath now appeared, like a *Day-starre* with most cheerfull beames; nay, he is the *Sun of Righteousnesse himself*; which hath risen upon the World with his *healing wings*, with his exhilarating light, that he might chase away all those black despairing thoughts from us. But Christ did not rise, that we should play, and sport, and wantonize with his light; but that we should do *the works of the day* in it: that we should walk εὐσχημόνως (as the Apostle speaketh)[53] not in our *Night-clothes* of sinfull Deformity, but clad all over with the comely *Garments of Light*. The Gospel is not big with child of a *Phancie*, of a mere *Conceit* of righteousnesse without us, hanging at distance over us; whilst our hearts within, are nothing but Cages of *unclean birds*, and like Houses continually haunted with Devils, nay the very Rendezvous of those Fiends of Darknesse. Holinesse, is the best thing, that God himself can bestow upon us, either in this World, or the World to come. True Evangelicall Holinesse, that is *Christ formed* in the hearts of believers, is the very Cream, and Quintessence of the *Gospel*. And were our hearts sound within, were there not many thick and dark fumes, that did arise from thence, and cloud our understandings, we could not easily conceive the substance of Heaven it self, to be any thing else but *Holinesse*, free from those encumbrances, that did ever clog it, and accloy it here; neither should we wish for any other Heaven, besides this.[54] But many of us are like those Children, whose Stomacks

[53] *Romans* 13. 13: 'becomingly' (according to the Revised Standard Version; where the AV reads 'honestly'). Cf. Whichcote's sermon on this text, in *Discourses*, III, 168 ff.

[54] This exposition of Heaven and Hell (to p. 113), typical of many similar pronouncements by the Cambridge Platonists, is further elaborated later (pp. 122 f.). See Whichcote, above, p. 46 and note.

are so vitiated by some disease, that they think, Ashes, Coal, Mudwall, or any such trash, to be more pleasant, then the most wholesome food: such sickly and distempered Appetites have we about these spirituall things, that hanker after I know not what vain shews of happinesse, whilst in the mean time we neglect that which is the onely true food of our souls, that is able solidly to nourish them up to *everlasting life*. Grace is *Holinesse Militant*, Holinesse encumbered with many enemies and difficulties, which it still fights against, and manfully quits it self of: and Glory is nothing else, but *Holinesse Triumphant*; Holinesse with a Palme of Victorie in her hand, and a Crown upon her head. *Deus ipse, cum omni sua bonitate, quatenus extra me est, non facit me beatum; sed quatenus in me est: God himself cannot make me happy, if he be onely without me; and unlesse he give in a participation of himself, and his own likenesse into my soul.* Happinesse is nothing, but the releasing and unfettering of our souls, from all these narrow, scant, and particular good things; and the espousing of them to the Highest and most Universall Good, which is not *this* or *that* particular good, but *goodnesse* it self: and this is the same thing that we call Holinesse. Which, because we our selves are so little acquainted with; being for the most part ever courting a mere Shadow of it; therefore we have such low, abject, and beggerly conceits thereof; whereas it is in it self, the most noble, heroicall, and generous thing in the World. For I mean by Holinesse, nothing else but *God stamped*, & *printed* upon the Soul. And we may please our selves, with what conceits we will; but so long as we are void of this, we do but *dream* of heaven, and, I know not what, fond *Paradise*; we do but blow up and down an *airy Bubble* of our own Phancies, which riseth out of the froth of our vain hearts; we do but court a *painted Heaven*; and woo happinesse in a *Picture*: whilst in the mean time, a *true* and *reall* Hell will suck in our souls into it, and soon make us sensible of a *solid woe*, and *substantiall misery*. Divine wisdome, hath so ordered the frame of the whole Universe, as that every thing should have a certain proper Place, that should be a Receptacle for it. Hell is the Sinke of all sinne and wickednesse. The strong *Magick* of Nature, pulls and draws every thing continually, to that place which is suitable to it, and to which it doth belong; so all these heavy bodies presse downwards, towards the Centre of our earth, being drawn in by it: In like manner Hell wheresoever it is, will by strong *Sympathy* pull in all sinne, and *Magnetically* draw it to it self: as true Holinesse, is always breathing upwards, and fluttering towards Heaven, striving to embosome it self with God: and it will at last undoubtedly be conjoyned with him, no *dismall shades* of darknesse, can possibly stop it in its course, or beat it back;

Ὥς αἰεὶ τὸ ὅμοιον ἄγει θεὸς ὡς τὸ ὅμοιον.[55]

Nay, we do but deceive our selves with names; Hell is nothing but the Orbe of Sinne and Wickednesse, or else that Hemisphear of Darknesse, in which all Evil moves: and Heaven, is the opposite Hemisphear of Light, or else, if you please, the Bright Orbe of Truth, Holinesse, and Goodnesse: and we do actually in this life, instate our selves in the possession of one or other of them. Take Sinne and Disobedience out of Hell, and it will presently clear up, into Light, Tranquillity, Serenity, and shine out into a Heaven. Every true Saint, carrieth his Heaven about with him, in his own heart; and Hell that is without him, can have no power over him. He might safely wade through Hell it self, and like the *Three children*, passe through the midst of that *fiery Furnace*, and yet not at all be scorched with the flames of it: he might walk through the *Valley of the shadow of death*, and yet *fear no evil*.[56] Sinne, is the onely thing in the World, that is contrary to God: God is Light, and that is Darknesse: God is Beauty, and that is Uglinesse and Deformity. All sinne is direct Rebellion against God; and with what Notions soever, we may sugar it, and sweeten it, yet God can never smile upon it, he will never make a truce with it. God declares open warre against sinne, and bids defiance to it; for it is a professed enemy to Gods own Life and Being. God which is infinite Goodnesse, cannot but hate sinne, which is purely Evil. And though sinne be in it self, but a poore, impotent, and crazy thing, nothing but Straitnesse, Poverty, and Non-entity;[57] so that of it self it is the most wretched and miserable thing in the world, and needeth no further punishment besides it self; yet Divine Vengeance, beats it off still further and further from God, and wheresoever it is, will be sure to scourge it, and lash it continually. God and Sinne can never agree together.

[55] *Odyssey*, XVII, 218: 'As ever, the god is bringing like and like together.'
[56] Cf. *Daniel* 3. 19 ff., and *Psalms* 23. 4
[57] The 'nothingness' of sin is one of the great commonplaces of Christian theology (see the Introduction, above, p. 38 and note). The idea persisted through the Renaissance. Formulations include a lengthy one by Donne (*Sermons*, ed. E. M. Simpson and G. R. Potter [Berkeley, 1953], VI, 238–40) and this assertion by John Robinson, the pastor of the Pilgrim Fathers: 'sinne is nothing that hath being in nature, but an *absence* of, and *crossenesse* to that which should bee; as *darknesse* is of, and unto *light*' (*Essayes*, 2nd ed. [1638], p. 39).

That, I may therefore come, yet nearer to our selves. *This is the Message, that I have now to declare unto you, That God is Light, and in him is no darknesse at all: if we say that we have Fellowship with him, and walke in Darknesse, we lie, and do not the truth.*[58] *Christ*, and the *Gospel* are light, and there is no darknesse at all in them; if you *say that you know Christ* and his Gospel, & yet *keep not Christs Commandments*, but dearly hug, your private darling corruptions; *you are liars, and the truth is not in you*; you have no acquaintance with the God of Light, nor the Gospel of Light. If any of you say, that you *know Christ*, and have an interest in him, and yet (as I fear, too many do) still nourish Ambition, Pride, Vainglory within your brests; harbour Malice, Revengfulnesse, & cruell Hatred to your neighbours in your hearts; eagerly scramble after this worldly Pelfe, and make the strength of your parts and endeavours serve that blind *Mammon*, the God of this World; If you wallow and tumble in the filthy puddle of fleshly Pleasures; or if you aime onely at your selves in your lives, and make your *Self* the Compasse by which you fail, and the Starre by which you steer your Course, looking at nothing higher, and more noble then *your selves*; deceive not your selves, *you have neither seen Christ, nor known him*; you are deeply incorporated, (if I may so speak) with the *Spirit of this World*, and have no true *Sympathy* with God and Christ, no *fellowship* at all with them. And (I beseech you) let us consider; Be there not many of us, that pretend much to Christ; that are plainly in our lives, as Proud, Ambitious, Vainglorious as any others? Be there not many of us, that are as much under the power of unruly Passions; as Cruell, Revengefull, Malicious, Censorious as others? that have our minds as deeply engaged in the World, & as much envassalled to Riches, Gain, Profit, those great admired Deities of the sonnes of men, and their souls as much overwhelmed, and sunke with the cares of this life? Do not many of us, as much give our selves to the Pleasures of the flesh, and though not without regrets of Conscience, yet ever now and then secretly soke our selves in them? Be there not many of us that have as deep a share likewise, in Injustice & Oppression, in *vexing the fatherlesse and the widows?*[59] I wish, it may not prove some of our Cases, at that last day, to use such pleas as these unto Christ in our behalfe; *Lord, I have prophecied in thy name;*[60] I have preached many a zealous Sermon for thee; I have kept many a long

---

[58] 1 *John* 1. 5–6.   [59] Cf. *Ezekiel* 22. 7, *Zechariah* 7. 10, etc.
[60] Thus *Isaiah, Ezekiel,* et al.—*passim.*

A Sermon Preached before the House of Commons

Fast; I have been very active for thy cause in Church, in State; nay, I never made any question, but that my name was written in thy book of Life; when yet alas, we shall receive no other return from Christ, but this, *I know you not; Depart from me ye Workers of Iniquity*.[61] I am sure, there be too many of us, that have long pretended to Christ, which make little or no progresse in *true Christianity*, that is, Holinesse of life: that ever hang hovering in a *Twilight of Grace*, and never seriously put our selves forwards into clear *Day-light*, but esteem that glimmering *Crepusculum* which we are in, and like that faint *Twilight* better then broad open Day: whereas, *The Path of the just* (as the *Wiseman* speaketh) *is as the shining light, that shineth more and more unto the perfect day*.[62] I am sure, there be many of us, that are perpetuall *Dwarfs* in our spiritual Stature; like those *silly women* (that S. *Paul* speaks of) *laden with sinnes, and led away with divers lusts, that are ever learning, and never able to come to the knowledge of the truth*:[63] that are not now one jot taller in Christianity, then we were many years ago; but have still as sickly, crazy, and unsound a temper of soul, as we had long before. Indeed we seem to do something, we are always moving and lifting at the stone of Corruption, that lies upon our hearts, but yet we never stirre it notwithstanding, or at least, never roll it off from us. We are sometimes a little troubled with the guilt of our sinnes, and then we think we must thrust our lusts out of our hearts, but afterwards we sprinkle our selves over, with I know not what *Holy-water*, and so are contented to let them still abide, quietly within us. We do every day truly confesse the same sinnes, and pray against them, and yet still commit them as much as ever, and lie as deeply under the power of them. We have the same Water to pump out in every prayer, and still we let the same, leake in again upon us. We make a great deal of noise, and raise a great deal of dust with our feet; but we do not move from off the ground on which we stood, we do not go forward at all: or if we do sometimes make a little progresse, we quickly loose again, the ground which we had gained: like those upper *Planets* in the Heaven, which (as the *Astronomers* tell us) sometimes move forwards, sometimes quite backwards, and sometimes perfectly stand still; have their *Stations* and *Retrogradations*, as well as their *Direct Motions*.[64] As if Religion were nothing else, but a *Dancing*

---

[61] *Luke* 13. 27.   [62] *Proverbs* 4. 18.   [63] 2 *Timothy* 3. 6–7.

[64] On the movement of the planets as understood before and during the Renaissance, consult Francis R. Johnson, *Astronomical Thought in Renaissance England* (Baltimore, 1937), pp. 21 ff., 100 ff., etc.,

up and down, upon the same piece of ground and making severall Motions and Friskings on it; and not a sober Journying, and Travelling onwards toward some certain place. We Doe and Undoe; we do *Penelopes telam texere*,⁶⁵ we weave sometimes a *Web of Holinesse*, but then we let our lusts come, and undoe, and unravell all again. Like *Sisyphus* in the Fable,⁶⁶ we roll up a mighty Stone with much ado, sweating and tugging up the Hill; and then we let it go, and tumble down again unto the bottome: and this is our constant work. Like those *Danaides*, which the *Poets* speak of,⁶⁷ we are always filling water into a Sive, by our Prayers, Duties, and Performances; which still runs out as fast as we poure it in. What is it that thus cheats us and gulls us of our Religion? That makes us, thus constantly to tread the same Ring, and Circle of Duties, where we make no progresse at all forwards; and the further we go, are still never the nearer to our journeys end? What is it that thus starves our Religion; and makes it look like those *Kine* in *Pharaohs* Dream, *illfavoured and lean fleshed*;⁶⁸ that it hath no Colour in its face, no Bloud in its veines, no Life nor Heat at all, in its members? What is it that doth thus *bedwarfe* us in our Christianity? What low, sordid, and unworthy Principles do we act by, that thus hinder our growth, and make us stand at a stay, and keep us always in the very Porch and Entrance, where we first began? Is it a sleepy, sluggish Conceit, That it is enough for us, if we be but once in a *State of Grace*, if we have but once stepped over the threshold, we need not take so great paines to travel any further? Or is it another damping, choaking, stifling Opinion, That Christ hath done all for us already *without* us, and nothing need more to be done *within* us? No matter, how wicked we be in our selves, for we have holinesse *without us*; no matter, how sickly and diseased our souls be within, for they have health *without them*. Why may we not as well be satisfied, and contented, to have Happinesse without us too to all Eternity, and so our selves forever continue miserable? *Little Children, let no man deceive you: he that doth righteousnesse, is righteous, even as he is righteous*: but, *he that committeth sinne is of the Devil*.⁶⁹ I shall therefore exhort you in the wholesome words of S. *Peter; Give all diligence, to adde to your faith, vertue; and to vertue, knowledge; to knowledge, temperance; and to temperance, patience; to patience, godlinesse; and to godlinesse,*

---

⁶⁵ The allusion is to Penelope's web, woven by day only to be unwoven by night (*Odyssey*, II, 89 ff.; XIX, 137 ff.).
⁶⁶ Cf. *Odyssey*, XI, 593–600.   ⁶⁷ Cf. Horace, *Carmina*, III, xi, 30 ff.
⁶⁸ Genesis 41. 4.   ⁶⁹ 1 *John* 3. 7–8.

brotherly kindnesse; and to brotherly kindnesse, charity; For if these things be in you, and abound, they make you that ye shall neither be barren, nor unfruitfull in the knowledge of our Lord Jesus Christ. The Apostle still goes on, and I cannot leave him yet; *But he that lacketh these things is blind, and cannot see far off, and hath forgotten that he was once purged from his old sinnes. Wherefore the rather Brethren, give diligence to make your calling and election sure: for if ye do these things, ye shall never fall.*[70] Let us not onely talk and dispute of Christ, but let us indeed *put on the Lord Jesus Christ.* Having those *great and precious promises,* which he hath given us, let us strive to be made *partakers of the Divine Nature, escaping the corruption that is in the world through lust*: and being begotten again to a *lively hope* of enjoying Christ hereafter, *let us purifie our selves as he is pure.* Let us really declare, that we *know Christ,* that we are his Disciples, by our *keeping of his Commandments:* and amongst the rest, that *Commandment* especially which our Saviour Christ himself commendeth to his Disciples in a peculiar manner; *This is my commandment, That ye love one another, as I have loved you:* and again; *These things I command you, that you love one another. Let us follow peace with all men, and holinesse, without which, no man shall see God. Let us put on as the Elect of God, holy, and beloved, bowels of mercies, kindnesse, humblenesse of mind, meeknesse, longsuffering, forbearing one another, and forgiving one another, if any man have a quarel against any, even as Christ forgave us: And above all these things let us put on Charity, which is the bond of perfectnesse. Let us in meeknesse, instrust those that oppose themselves, if God peradventure will give them repentance, to the acknowledging of the truth, that they may recover themselves out of the snares of the Devil, that are taken captive by him at his will. Beloved, Let us love another, for Love is of God, and whosoever loveth is born of God and knoweth God.* O Divine Love! the sweet Harmony of souls! the Musick of Angels! The Joy of Gods own Heart, the very Darling of his Bosome! the Sourse of true Happinesse! the pure Quintessence of Heaven! that which reconciles the jarring Principles of the World, and makes them all chime together! That which melts mens Hearts into one another! see how S. *Paul* describes it, and it cannot choose but enamour your affections towards it: *Love envieth not, it is not puffed up, it doth no behave it self unseemly, seeketh not her own, is not easily provoked, thinketh no evil,*

---

[70] 2 *Peter* 1. 6–10. Hereafter (to p. 118) Cudworth offers a catena of Pauline and Johannine verses, esp. 1 *Corinthians* 13 and 2 *John* 4.

rejoyceth not in iniquity; beareth all things, believeth all things, hopeth all things, endureth all things: I may adde in a word, it is the best natur'd thing, the best complexioned thing, in the World. Let us expresse this sweet harmonious Affection, in these jarring times: that so if it be possible, we may tune the World at last, into better Musick. Especially, in matters of Religion, let us strive with all meeknesse to instruct and convince one another. Let us endeavour to promote the *Gospel of Peace*, the *Dove-like Gospel* with a *Dove-like Spirit*. This was the way by which the Gospel at first, was propagated in the world: *Christ did not cry, nor lift up his voice in the streets, a bruised reed he did not break, and the smoking flax he did not quench and yet he brought forth judgement into victory.*[71] He whispered the Gospel to us from Mount Sion, in a still voice, and yet the sound thereof went out quickly throughout all the earth. The Gospel at first came down upon the world gently and softly, like the *Dew* upon *Gideons fleece*, and yet it quickly soaked quite through it: and doubtlesse this is still the most effectuall way to promote it further. Sweetnesse, and Ingenuity, will more powerfully command mens minds, then Passion, Sowrenesse, and Severity: as the soft Pillow sooner breaks the Flint, then the hardest Marble. Let us ἀληθεύειν ἐν ἀγάπῃ, *follow truth in love*:[72] and of the two indeed, be contented rather, to misse of the conveying of a Speculative Truth, then to part with Love. When we would convince men of any errour by the strength of *Truth*, let us withall poure the sweet Balme of Love upon their heads. *Truth and Love*, are two the most powerfull things in the world, and when they both go together, they cannot easily be withstood. The Golden Beams of Truth, and the Silken Cords of Love, twisted together, will draw men on with a sweet violence, whether they will or no.[73] Let us take heed we do not sometimes call that Zeal for God, and his Gospel, which is nothing else, but our own tempestuous and stormy Passion.[74] True Zeal is a sweet, heavenly and gentle Flame, which maketh us active for God, but always within the Sphear of Love. It never calls for *Fire from*

---

[71] Cf. *Isaiah* 42. 2–3. There follow two allusions to 1 *Kings* 19. 12 and *Judges* 6. 36–40.

[72] *Ephesians* 4. 15.

[73] Sterry, *Discourse*, sig. c4v, sets out the same idea by way of the common misunderstanding of the 'golden chain' in *Iliad*, VIII, 19–27. See further my survey of 'Renaissance Interpretations of Jacob's Ladder', *Theologische Zeitschrift*, XVIII (1962), 411–18.

[74] Cf. Whichcote, above, p. 43.

A Sermon Preached before the House of Commons 119

Heaven, to consume those that differ a little from us in their Apprehensions. It is like that kind of Lightning, (which the Philosophers speak of) that melts the sword within, but singeth not the Scabbard:[75] it strives to save the Soul, but hurteth not the Body. True Zeal is a loving thing, and makes us always active to *Edification*, and not to *Destruction*. If we keep the Fire of Zeal within the Chimney, in its own proper place, it never doth any hurt; it onely warmeth, quickeneth, and enliveneth us: but if once we let it break out, and catch hold of the Thatch of our Flesh, and kindle our corrupt Nature, and set the House of our Body on fire, it is no longer Zeal, it is no heavenly Fire, it is a most destructive and devouring thing. True Zeal is an *Ignis lambens*, a soft and gentle Flame, that will not scorch ones hand;[76] it is no predatory or voracious thing: but *Carnall and fleshly Zeal*, is like the Spirit of Gunpowder set on fire, that tears and blows up all that stands before it. True Zeal is like the *Vitall heat* in us, that we live upon, which we never feel to be angry or troublesome; but though it gently feed upon the *Radicall Oyl* within us, that sweet Balsame of our *Natural Moisture*; yet it lives lovingly with it, and maintains that by which it is fed: but that other furious & distempered Zeal, is nothing but a *Feaver* in the Soul. To conclude, we may learn what kind of Zeal it is, that we should make use of in promoting the Gospel, by an Emblem of Gods own, given us in the Scripture, those *Fiery Tongues* that upon the Day of *Pentecost*, sate upon the Apostles; which sure were harmlesse Flames, for we cannot reade that they did any hurt, or that they did so much as singe an haire of their heads. I will therefore shut up this, with that of the *Apostle: Let us keep the unity of the Spirit in the bond of peace.*[77] Let this soft and silken Knot of *Love*, tie our Hearts together; though our Heads and Apprehensions cannot meet, as indeed they never will, but alwayes stand at

---

[75] Simon Harward, in *A Discourse . . . of Lightnings* (1607), sigs. B2ᵛ–B3, reports that one kind of lightning is commonly termed '*a pearcing lightening*, because by the puritie of the flame, it pearceth thorough such outward parts as haue powers of passage, & worketh his forces inwardly . . . So it killeth the child in the mothers wombe, leauing the mother safe: and it melteth the siluer in the purse, the purse sustaining no damage' etc.

[76] John Swan, in *Speculum mundi* (Cambridge, 1635), p. 97, reports that '*Ignis lambens* is a cleaving and licking fire or light; and is so called because it useth to cleave and stick to the hairs of men or beasts, not hurting them, but rather (as it were) gently licking them' etc.

[77] *Ephesians* 4. 3.

some distance off from one another. Our Zeal if it be heavenly, if it be true *Vestall Fire* kindled from above, it will not delight to tarry here below, burning up Straw and Stubble, and such combustible things, and sending up nothing but grosse earthy fumes to heaven; but it will rise up, and return back, pure as it came down, and will be ever striving to carry up mens hearts to God along with it. It will be onely occupied, about the promoting of those things, which are *unquestionably good*; and when it moves in the irascible way, it will quarrel with nothing but *sinne*. Here let our zeal busie and exercise it self, every one of us beginning first at our own hearts. Let us be more Zealous than ever we have yet been, in fighting against our lusts, in pulling down those *strong holds of Sinne and Satan* in our hearts. Here let us exercise all our Courage and Resolution, our Manhood and Magnanimitie. Let us trust in the *Almighty Arme* of our God, and doubt not, but he will as well deliver us, from the *Power of Sinne* in our hearts, as preserve us from the *wrath to come*. Let us go out against these *uncircumcised Philistines*, I mean our Lusts, not with *Shield or Spear*, not in any confidence of our own strength, but in the name of the *Lord of Hosts*, and we shall prevail: we shall overcome our Lusts, *for greater is he that is in us, then he that is in them. The Eternal God is our refuge, and underneath are the everlasting arms: He shall thrust out these enemies from before us, and he shall say, Destroy them.*[78] We shall enter the *true Canaan*, the good Land of Promise, *that floweth with milk and honey*, the Land of Truth and Holinesse. *Wherefore take unto you the whole armour of God, that you may be able to withstand: let your loines be girt about with truth; have on the brestplate of righteousnesse; and let your feet be shod with the preparation of the Gospel of peace. Above all take the shield of faith, whereby you shall be able to quench all the fiery darts of the Wicked, and take the helmet of salvation, and the sword of the spirit, which is the word of God.* And lastly, be sure of this, That *ye be strong onely in the Lord*, and *in the power of his might*.[79] There be some that dishearten us in this spirituall warfare, and would make us let our weapons fall out of our hands, by working in us a despair of Victory. There be some *evil Spies*,[80] that *weaken* the hands and the hearts of the *children* of *Israel*: and bring an ill report upon that land that we are to conquer, telling of nothing but strange *Gyants*, the *sonnes of Anak* there, that we shall never be able to overcome. *The*

---

[78] *Deuteronomy* 33. 27.
[79] *Ephesians* 6. 13–17, 10.
[80] Cf. *Numbers* 13–14.

Amalekites, (say they) *dwell in the South, the Hittites, Jebusites, Amorites in the Mountains, and the Canaanites by the Sea-coast:* huge armies of tall invincible *Lusts: we shall never be able to go against this people,* we shall never be able to prevail against our *Corruptions.* Hearken not unto them (I beseech you) but hear what *Caleb* and *Joshuah* say; *Let us go up at once, and possess it, for we are able to overcome them:* not by our own strength, but by the power of the *Lord of Hosts.* There are indeed *Sonnes of Anak* there, there are mighty *Gyantlike Lusts,* that we are to graple with; nay there are, *Principalities,* and *Powers* too, that we are to oppose: but the great *Michael, the Captain of the Lords Host* is with us; he commands in chief for us, and we need not be dismayed. *Understand therefore this day, That the Lord thy God is he, which goeth before thee, as a consuming fire, he shall destroy* these *enemies, and bring them down before thy face.* If thou wilt be faithfull to him, and put thy trust in him; *as the fire consumeth the stubble, and as the flame burneth up the chaff,* so will he destroy thy *Lusts* in thee: *their root shall be rottennesse, and their blossome shall go up as dust.*[81] But let us take heed that we be not discouraged, and before we begin to fight, despair of Victorie: but to believe and hope well in the power of our God and his strength, will be half a Conquest. Let us not think, Holinesse in the hearts of men here in the World, is a forlorn, forsaken, and outcast thing from God; that he hath no regard of. Holinesse where-ever it is, though never so small, if it be but hearty and sincere, it can no more be cut off, and discontinued from God; then a *Sun-beam* here upon Earth can be broken off, from its entercourse with the *Sun,* and be left alone amidst the mire and dirt of this World. The Sun may as well discard its own *Rayes,* and banish them from it self, into some Region of darknesse, far remote from it, where they shall have no dependence at all upon it, as God can forsake and abandon Holinesse in the World, and leave it a poore Orphane thing, that shall have no influence at all from him to preserve and keep it. Holinesse is something of God, where-ever it is; it is an *Efflux* from him, that always hangs upon him, and lives in him: as the *Sun-beams* though they guild this lower World, and spread their golden wings over us; yet they are not so much here, where they shine, as in the Sun, from whence they flow. God cannot draw a Curtain betwixt himself and Holinesse, which is nothing, but the *Splendor* and *Shining* of himself: He cannot hide his face from it, he cannot desert

---

[81] *Deuteronomy* 9. 3 and *Isaiah* 5. 24.

it, in the World. He that is once *born of God, shall overcome the World*, and the Prince of this World too, by the Power of God in him. Holinesse is no solitary neglected thing; it hath stronger Confederacies, greater Alliances than Sinne and Wickednesse. It is in league with God, and the whole Universe; the whole Creation smiles upon it: there is something of God in it, and therefore it must needs be, a victorious and triumphant thing. Wickednesse is a weak, cowardly, and guilty thing, a fearfull and trembling Shadow.[82] It is the Child of Ignorance and Darknesse; it is afraid of Light, and cannot possibly withstand the power of it, nor endure the sight of its glittering Armour. It is allianced to none, but wretched forlorn and apostate Spirits, that do what they can, to support their own weak and tottering Kingdome of Darknesse: but are onely strong, in Weaknesse and Impotency. The whole Politie and Commonwealth of Devils, is not so powerfull, as one *Child of Light*, one *Babe in Christ*: they are not all able to *quench* the least *smoking flax*, to extinguish one spark of Grace. Darknesse is not able to make resistance against Light, but ever as it comes, flies before it. But if wickednesse, invite the Society of Devils to it, (as we learn by the sad experience of these present times in many examples of those that were possessed with Malice, Revengfulnesse, and Lust) so that those cursed Fiends do most readily apply themselves to it, and offer their service to feed it and encourage it; because it is their own Life and Nature, their own *kingdome of Darknesse*, which they strive to enlarge, and to spread the Dominions of: shall we then think that Holinesse, which is so nearly allied unto God, hath no good *Genius* at all in the World, to attend upon it, to help it and encourage it? Shall not the *Kingdome of Light*, be as true to its own Interest, and as vigilant for the enlarging of it self, as the *Kingdome of Darknesse*? Holinesse is never alone in the World, but God is always with it, and his loving *Spirit*, doth ever associate, and joyn it self to it. He then sent it into the World, is with it, as Christ speaketh of himself, *the Father hath not left me alone, because I do alwayes those things that please him.*[83] Holinesse is the Life of God, which he cannot but feed and maintain wheresoever it is; and as the Devils are always active to encourage evil, so we cannot imagine, but that the heavenly Host of blessed Angels above, are as busily employed, in the promoting of

[82] Cf. *Samson Agonistes*, 834 ('all wickedness is weakness'), and *Paradise Lost*, IV, 856.
[83] *John* 8. 29.

that which they love best, that which is dearest to God whom they serve, the *Life* and *Nature of God*. *There is joy in heaven at the conversion of one sinner*,[84] Heaven takes notice of it; there is a *Quire* of Angels that sweetly sings the *Epithalamium* of a Soul divorced from Sinne and Satan, and espoused unto Christ. What therefore the *Wiseman* speaks concerning *Wisdome*,[85] I shall apply to *Holinesse: Take fast hold of Holinesse, let her not go, keep her for she is thy Life: Keep thy heart with all diligence for out of it are the issues of Life*, & of Death too. Let nothing be esteemed, of greater consequence and concernment to thee, then what thou doest and actest, how thou livest. Nothing *without* us can make us either happy, or miserable; nothing can either *defile us*, or hurt us, but what *goeth out from us*, what Springeth and Bubbleth up, out of our own hearts. We have dreadfull apprehensions, of the Flames of Hell without us; we tremble and are afraid, when we hear of *Fire and Brimstone*, whil'st in the meantime, we securely nourish within our own hearts, *a true and living Hell*,
—*Et cæco carpimur igni*.[86]
the dark fire of our Lusts, consumeth our bowels within, and miserably scorcheth our souls, and we are not troubled at it. We do not perceive, how Hell steales upon us, whilest we live here. And as for Heaven, we onely gaze abroad, expecting that it should come in to us from without, but never look for the beginnings of it to arise within, in our own hearts.

But lest there should yet happely remain any prejudice against that, which I have all this while heartily commended to you; *True Holinesse*, and the *Keeping of Christs commandment*; as if it were a *Legall* and *Servile* thing, that would subject us to a *State* of *Bondage*, I must here needs adde a Word or two, either for the Prevention or Removall of it. I do not therefore mean, by *Holinesse*, the mere performance of outward Duties of Religion, coldly acted over as a task, not our habituall Prayings, Hearings, Fastings, multiplied one upon another (though these be all good, as subservient to an higher end) but I mean an inward *Soul* and *Principle* of *Divine Life*, that spiriteth all these; that enliveneth and quickeneth, the dead carkasse, of all our outward Performances whatsoever. I do not here urge, the *dead Law of outward Works*, which indeed if it be alone, subjects us to a *State of Bondage*; but the *inward Law* of the Gospel, the *Law of the Spirit of Life*, then

---

[84] Cf. *Luke* 15. 7.   [85] *Proverbs* 4. 13, 23.
[86] An allusion to Dido 'wasting in a hidden fire' (*Aeneid*, IV, 2).

which nothing can be more free and ingenuous: for it doth not act us by Principles without us, but is an inward *Self-moving* Principle, living in our Hearts. I do not urge the Law written upon *Tables of stone* without us (though there is still a good use of that too) but the Law of Holinesse written within upon the *Fleshly Tables of our hearts.* The first, though it work us into some outward Conformity to Gods Commandments, and so hath a good effect upon the World; yet we are all this while, but like dead Instruments of Musick, that sound sweetly and harmoniously, when they are onely struck, and played upon from without, by the Musicians Hand, who hath the Theory and *Law* of Musick, *living* within himself. But the Second, the *living* Law of the Gospel, the *Law of the Spirit of Life* within us, is, as if the *Soul of Musick*, should incorporate it self with the Instrument, and live in the Strings, and make them of their own accord, without any touch, or impulse from without, daunce up and down, and warble out their Harmonies. They that are acted only by an outward Law, are but like Neurospasts; or those little Puppets that skip nimbly up and down, and seem to be full of quick and sprightly motion, whereas they are all the while moved artificially by certain Wiers and Strings from without, and not by any Principle of Motion, from themselves within: or else, like Clocks and Watches, that go pretty regularly for a while, but are moved by Weights and Plummets, or some other Artificiall Springs, that must be ever now and then wound up, or else they cease. But they that are acted by the *new Law of the Gospel*, by the *Law of the Spirit*, they have an inward principle of life in them, that from the Centre of it self, puts forth it self freely and constantly into all obedience to the will of Christ. This *New Law of the Gospel*, it is a kind of *Musicall Soul*, informing the dead *Organ* of our Hearts, that makes them of their own accord delight to act harmoniously according to the Rule of Gods word. The Law that I speak of, it is a *Law of Love*, which is the most powerfull Law in the World; and yet it freeth us in a manner from all Law without us, because it maketh us become a *Law unto our selves*. The more it prevaileth in us, the more it eateth up and devoureth, all other Laws without us; just as Aarons *Living Rod*, did swallow up those Rods of the Magicians, that were made onely to counterfeit a little Life:

> *Quis Legem det amantibus?*
> *Major lex Amor est sibi.*[87]

[87] Boethius, III, xii, 47–8: 'Who can for lovers laws indite? / Love hath no law but her own will.'

Love is at once a Freedome from all Law, a State of purest Liberty, and yet a Law too, of the most constraining and indispensable Necessity.[88] The worst *Law* in the world, is *the Law of Sinne, which is in our members;* which keeps us in a condition of most absolute slavery, when we are wholy under the Tyrannicall commands of our lusts: this is a cruell *Pharaoh* indeed, that sets his hard task-masters over us, and maketh us wretchedly drudge in Mire and Clay. The *Law of the Letter* without us, sets us in a condition of a little more Liberty, by restraining of us from many outward Acts of Sinne; but yet it doth not disenthrall us, from the power of sinne in our hearts. But the *Law of the Spirit of life, the Gospel-Law of Love*, it puts us into a condition of most pure and perfect Liberty; and whosoever really entertaines this Law, he hath *thrust out Hagar* quite, he hath *cast out the Bondwoman and her Children*; from henceforth, *Sarah the Free woman*, shall live forever with him, and she shall be to him, a Mother of many children; her seed shall be *as the sand of the seashoar for number*, and *as the starres of heaven*.[89] Here is Evangelicall liberty, here is Gospel-freedome, when *the Law of the Spirit of life in Christ Jesus, hath made us free, from the Law of sinne and death*: when we have a liberty from sinne, and not a liberty to sinne:[90] for our dear Lord and Master hath told us, that *Whosoever committeth sinne, he is the servant of it*.[91] He that lies under the power, and vassallage of his base lusts, and yet talks of Gospel-freedome; he is but like a poore condemned Prisoner, that in his sleep dreams of being set at liberty, and of walking up and down wheresoever he pleaseth; whilst his Legs are all the while lock't fast in fetters and Irons. To please our selves with a Notion of Gospel-liberty, whilest we have not a Gospel-principle of Holinesse within us, to free us from the power of sinne, it is nothing else, but to gild over our Bonds and Fetters, and to phancy our selves to be in a Golden Cage. There is a Straitnesse, Slavery, and Narrownesse in all Sinne: Sinne crowds and crumples up our souls, which if they were freely spread abroad, would be as wide, and as large as the whole Universe. No man is truly free, but he that hath his *will* enlarged to the

---

[88] Possibly the most categorical assertion in the seventeenth century of a traditional paradox, as I have argued in *Milton and the Christian Tradition* (Oxford, 1966), p. 163.

[89] Cf. *Genesis* 21. 12 ff., 22. 17.

[90] The distinction is Augustine's. See *Enchiridion*, CV, and esp. *De correptione et gratia*, XXXIII.

[91] *John* 8. 34.

extent of Gods own will, by loving whatsoever God loves, and nothing else. Such a one, doth not fondly hug this and that particular created good thing, and envassal himself into it, but he loveth every thing that is lovely, beginning at God, and descending down to all his Creatures, according to the severall degrees of perfection in them. He injoyes a boundlesse Liberty, and a boundlesse Sweetnesse, according to his boundlesse Love. He inclaspeth the whole World within his outstretched arms, his soul is as wide as the whole Universe, as big as *yesterday, to day, and forever*.[92] Whosoever is once acquainted with this Disposition of Spirit, he never desires any thing else: and he loves the *Life of God* in himself, dearer then his own Life. To conclude this therefore; If we love Christ, and *keep his commandments, his commandments will not be grievous to us: His yoke will be easie, and his burden light*[93]*:* it will not put us into a State of Bondage, but of perfect Liberty. For it is most true of Evangelicall Obedience, what the wise man speaketh of Wisdome; *Her wayes, are wayes of pleasantnesse, and all her paths are peace; She is a tree of Life to those that lay hold upon her, and happy are all they that retain her*.[94]

I will now shut up all with one or two *Considerations* to perswade you further, to the *keeping of Christs Commandments*.

First, from the desire which we all have of *Knowledge*; If we would indeed *know* Divine Truths, the onely way to come to this, is by *keeping of Christs Commandments*. The Grossenesse of our apprehensions in *Spirituall things*, and our many mistakes, that we have about them, proceed from nothing, but those dull and foggy *Stemes*, which rise up from our *foul hearts* and becloud our Understandings. If we did but heartily comply with Christs commandments, and purge our hearts, from all grosse and sensuall affections, we should not then look about for *Truth* wholly without our selves, and enslave our selves to the Dictates of this and that Teacher, and hang upon the *Lips of men*; but we should find the Great Eternall God, inwardly teaching our souls, and continually instructing us more and more, in the mysteries of his will: and *out of our bellies should flow rivers of living waters*.[95] Nothing puts a stop and hinderance to the passage of Truth in the World, but the Carnality of our hearts, the Corruption of our lives. 'Tis not wrangling Disputes and Syllogisticall Reasonings, that are the mighty Pillars, that underprop *Truth* in the World; if we would but

---

[92] *Hebrews* 13. 8.   [93] Cf. *Matthew* 11. 30.
[94] *Proverbs* 3. 17–18.   [95] *John* 7. 38.

underset it with the Holinesse of our Hearts and Lives, it should never fail. *Truth* is a prevailing and conquering thing, and would quickly overcome the World, did not the Earthinesse of our Dispositions, and the Darknesse of our false hearts hinder it. Our Saviour Christ, bids the *Blind man*, wash off the *Clay* that was upon his eyes, in the *Pool of Siloam*, and then he should see clearly;[96] intimating this to us, that it is the Earthinesse of mens Affections, that darkens the Eye of their understandings in Spirituall things. Truth is alwayes ready, and near at hand, if our eyes were not closed up with Mud, that we could but open them, to look upon it. Truth, alwayes waits upon our souls, and offers it self freely to us, as the Sun offers its beams, to every Eye, that will but open, and let them shine in upon it. If we could but purge our Hearts, from that filth, and defilement, which hangeth about them, there would be no doubt at all of *Truths* prevailing in the World. For, *Truth is great, and stronger then all things; all the Earth calleth upon Truth, and the heaven blesseth it, all works shake and tremble at it. The Truth endureth, and is alwayes strong, it liveth and conquereth for evermore. She is the Strength, Kingdome, Power and Majestie of all ages. Blessed be the God of Truth.*

Last of all, if we desire a true *Reformation*, as we seem to do; Let us begin here in reforming our *hearts* and *lives*; in *keeping of Christs Commandments*. All outward Formes and Models of Reformation, though they be never so good in their kind; yet they are of little worth to us, without this *inward Reformation* of the heart. Tinne, or Lead, or any other baser Metal, if it be cast into never so good a Mold, and made up into never so elegant a Figure; yet it is but Tin, or Lead still, it is the same Metal, that it was before. And if we be Molded into never so good a Form of outward Government, unless we *new mold our Hearts* within too; we are but a little better, then we were before. If adulterate Silver, that hath much Allay or Drosse in it, have never so current a Stamp put upon it, yet it will not passe notwithstanding, when the Touch-stone trieth it. We must be *reformed within*, with a *Spirit* of *Fire*, and a *Spirit of Burning*, to purge us from the Drosse, and Corruption of our hearts; and refine us as Gold and Silver; and then we shall be *reformed truly*, and not before. When this once comes to passe, then shall Christ be set *upon his Throne* indeed, then the Glory *of the Lord shall overflow the Land*; then we shall be a People acceptable unto him, and as *Mount Sion*, which he dearly loved.

[96] *John* 9. 1 ff.

JOHN SMITH

The True Way or Method of Attaining to Divine Knowledge*

It hath been long since well observed, That every Art & Science hath some certain Principles upon which the whole Frame and Body of it must depend; and he that will fully acquaint himself with the Mysteries thereof, must come furnisht with some *Præcognita* or προλήψεις, that I may speak in the language of the Stoicks.[1] Were I indeed to define *Divinity*, I should rather call it *a Divine life*, then *a Divine science*; it being something rather to be understood by a *Spiritual sensation*, then by any *Verbal description*, as all things of Sense & Life are best known by Sentient and Vital faculties; γνῶσις ἑκάστων δι' ὁμοιότητος γίνετα, as the Greek Philosopher hath well observed, Everything is best known by that which bears a just resemblance and analogie with it:[2] and therefore the Scripture is wont to set forth a *Good life* as the *Prolepsis* and Fundamental principle of *Divine Science*; *Wisdom hath built her an house, and hewen out her seven pillars*:[3] But *the fear of the Lord is* חׇכְמָה רֵאשִׁית *the beginning of wisdome*,[4] the Foundation of the whole fabrick.

We shall therefore, as a *Prolegomenon* or Preface to what we shall afterward discourse upon the Heads of Divinity, speake something of this *True Method of Knowing*, which is not so much by *Notions*[5] as *Actions*; as Religion it self consists not so much in *Words* as *Things*. They are not alwaies the best skill'd in Divinity, that are the most studied in those *Pandects* which it is sometimes digested into, or that

---

* From *Select Discourses*, ed. John Worthington (1660), Disc. I [pp. 1–21.] I have omitted Worthington's subdivision of this discourse into three sections as well as his summaries of their argument.

[1] 'By preconception (πρόληψις) they mean a sort of apprehension or a right opinion or notion, or universal idea stored in the mind' (Diogenes Laertius, X, 33).

[2] Plotinus, I, viii, 1.
[3] Proverbs 9. 1.
[4] *Proverbs* 1. 7.
[5] Cf. above, p. 66, and note.

The True Way of Attaining to Divine Knowledge 129

have erected the greatest Monopolies of Art and Science. He that is most *Practical* in Divine things, hath the purest and sincerest Knowledge of them, and not he that is most *Dogmatical*. Divinity indeed is a true Efflux from the Eternal light, which, like the Sun-beams, does not only enlighten, but heat and enliven; and therefore our Saviour hath in his *Beatitudes* connext Purity of heart with the Beatifical Vision. And as the Eye cannot behold the Sun, ἡλιοειδὴς μὴ γινόμενος, unless it be *Sunlike*, and hath the form and resemblance of the Sun drawn in it; so neither can the Soul of man behold God, θεοειδὴς μὴ γινομένη, unless it be *Godlike*,[6] hath God formed in it, and be made partaker of the Divine Nature. And the Apostle S. *Paul* when he would lay open the right way of attaining to Divine Truth, he saith that *Knowledge puffeth up*, but it is *Love that edifieth*.[7] The knowledge of Divinity that appears in *Systems* and *Models* is but a poor wan light, but the powerful energy of Divine knowledge displaies it self in purified Souls: here we shall finde the true πεδίον ἀληθείας, as the antient Philosophy speaks, *the land of Truth*.[8]

To seek our Divinity meerly in Books and Writings, is *to seek the living among the dead*: we doe but in vain seek God many times in these, where his Truth too often is not so much *enshrin'd*, as *entomb'd*: no; *intra te quære Deum*, seek for God within thine own soul;[9] he is best discern'd νοερᾷ ἐπαφῇ, as *Plotinus* phraseth it, by *an Intellectual touch* of him:[10] we must *see with our eyes, and hear with our ears, and our hands must handle the word of life*, that I may express it in S. *John's* words.[11] Ἔστι καὶ ψυχῆς αἴσθησίς τις, The Soul it self hath its sense, as well as the Body: and therefore *David*, when he would teach us how to know what the Divine Goodness is, calls not for *Speculation* but *Sensation*, *Tast and see how good the Lord is*.[12] That is not the best & truest knowledge of God which is wrought out by the labour and sweat of the Brain, but that which is kindled within us by an heavenly warmth in our Hearts. As in the natural Body it is the Heart that sends up good Blood and warm Spirits into the Head, whereby it is best enabled to its several

---

[6] Plotinus, I, vi, 9.   [7] 1 *Corinthians* 8. 1.

[8] Plotinus, VI, vii, 13; cf. I, iii, 4.

[9] This affirmation—a testimony of the 'ethical inwardness' of the Cambridge Platonists—reverberates across their writings. See the previous selections from Whichcote and Cudworth, *passim*, as well as Smith, below, p. 149.

[10] Cf. Plotinus, I, ii, 6.   [11] Cf. 1 *John* 1. 1.

[12] *Psalms* 34. 8.

functions; so that which enables us to know and understand aright in the things of God must be a living principle of Holiness within us. When *the Tree of Knowledge* is not planted by *the Tree of Life*, and sucks not up sap from thence, it may be as well fruitful with *evil* as with *good*, and bring forth *bitter* fruit as well as *sweet*. If we would indeed have our Knowledge thrive and flourish, we must water the tender plants of it with Holiness. When *Zoroaster's* Scholars asked him what they should doe to get *winged Souls*, such as might soar aloft in the bright beams of Divine Truth, he bids them bathe themselves in *the waters of Life*: they asking what they were; he tells them *the four Cardinal Vertues*, which are *the four Rivers of Paradise*.[13] It is but a thin, aiery knowledge that is got by meer Speculation, which is usher'd in by Syllogisms and Demonstrations; but that which springs forth from true Goodness, is θειότερόν τι πάσης ἀποδείξεως, as *Origen* speaks,[14] it brings such a Divine light into the Soul, as is more clear and convincing then any Demonstration. The reason why, notwithstanding all our acute reasons and subtile disputes, Truth prevails no more in the world, is, we so often disjoyn *Truth* and true *Goodness*, which in themselves can never be disunited; they grow both from the same Root, and live in one another. We may, like those in *Plato's* deep pit with their faces bended downwards, converse with *Sounds* and *Shadows*;[15] but not with the *Life* and *Substance* of Truth, while our Souls remain defiled with any vice or lusts. These are the black *Lethe*-lake which drench the Soules of men: he that wants true Vertue, in heavn's Logick *is blind, and cannot see afar off*.[16] Those filthy mists that arise from impure and terrene minds, like an *Atmospheare*, perpetually encompass them, that they cannot see that Sun of Divine Truth that shines *about* them, but never shines *into* any *unpurged* Souls; the darkness comprehends it not, the foolish man understands it not. All the Light and Knowledge that may seem sometimes to rise up in unhallowed mindes, is but like those fuliginous flames that arise up from our culinary fire, that are soon quench'd in

[13] Most of the legends surrounding Zoroaster's life are available in Joseph Bidez and Franz Cumont, *Les Mages hellénisés* (Paris, 1938), 2 vols. This particular legend is related at some length by Pico in *De hominis digitnate* (p. 16 in the translation cited above [p. xvii]).

[14] 'more sacred than any evidence'. The phrase may not be Origen's, but the sentiment certainly is.

[15] The reference is of course to the allegory of the cave (*Respublica*, 514–16).

[16] 2 *Peter* 1. 9.

The True Way of Attaining to Divine Knowledge 131

their own smoak; or like those foolish fires that fetch their birth from terrene exudations, that doe but hop up & down, and flit to and fro upon the surface of this earth where they were first brought forth; and serve not so much to enlighten, as to delude us; nor to direct the wandring traveller into his way, but to lead him farther out of it. While we lodge any filthy vice in us, this will be perpetually twisting up it self into the thread of our finest-spun Speculations; it will be continually climbing up into the τὸ ʽΗγεμονικὸν,[17] the *Hegemonicall* powers of the Soul, into the bed of Reason, and defile it: like the wanton Ivie twisting it self about the Oak, it will twine about our Judgments and Understandings, till it hath suck'd out the Life and Spirit of them. I cannot think such black oblivion should possess the Mindes of some as to make them question that Truth which to Good men shines as bright as the Sun at noon-day, had they not foully defil'd their own Souls with some hellish vice or other, how fairly soever it may be they may dissemble it. There is a benumming Spirit, a congealing Vapour that ariseth from Sin and Vice, that will stupifie the senses of the Soul; as the Naturalists say there is from the *Torpedo* that smites the senses of those that approach to it. This is that venemous *Solanum*,[18] that deadly *Nightshade*, that derives its cold poyson into the Understandings of men.

Such as Men themselves are, such will God himself seem to be. It is the Maxim of most wicked men, That the Deity is some way or other like themselves:[19] their Souls doe more then whisper it, though their lips speak it not; and though their tongues be silent, yet their lives cry it upon the house-tops, & in the publick streets. That *Idea* which men generally have of God is nothing else but the picture of their own

---

[17] 'τὸ ἡγεμονικὸν, the ruling, governing, commanding, determining principle in us' (Cudworth, *Freewill*, p. 32). The concept was upheld most persistently by the Stoics. Cf. Cicero, *De nat. deo.*, II, 11, and Aetius, in *SVF*, II, 227: 'the Stoics call the ruling part of the soul τὸ ἡγεμονικὸν'.

[18] 'a plant, called also *strychnos*, nightshade' (C. T. Lewis and Charles Short, *A Latin Dictionary*, rev. ed. [Oxford, 1958], p. 1718).

[19] Cf. Whichcote, *Aphorisms*, § 388: 'Those, who are *Crafty*, think; the Wisdom of God warrants Him to Deceive: Those, who are *Revengeful*, think; the Goodness of God permits Him to be Cruel: Those who are *Arbitrary*, think; the Sovereignty of God is the Account of his Actions. Every one attributes to *God*, what he finds in *Himself*: but that cannot be a Perfection in God, which is a Dishonesty in Man.' See further above, p. 100, and below, p. 160. Cf. Cassirer, p. 32. Poetically the idea has most brilliantly been set forth in Browning's *Caliban upon Setebos*.

Complexion: that Archetypall notion of him which hath the supremacie in their mindes, is none else but such an one as hath been shap'd out according to some pattern of themselves; though they may so cloathe and disguise this Idol of their own, when they carry it about in a pompous Procession to expose it to the view of the world, that it may seem very beautiful, and indeed any thing else rather then what it is. Most men (though it may be they themselves take no great notice of it) like that dissembling Monk, doe *aliter sentire in Scholis, aliter in Musæis*, are of a different judgment in the Schools from what they are in the retirements of their private closets. There is *a double head*, as well as *a double heart*.[20] Mens corrupt hearts will not suffer their notions and conceptions of divine things to be cast into that form that an higher Reason, which may sometime work within them, would put them into.

I would not be thought all this while to banish the belief of all *Innate notions*[21] of Divine Truth: but these are too often smothered, or tainted with a deep dye of mens filthy lusts. It is but *lux sepulta in opaci materia*, light buried and stifled in some dark body, from whence all those colour'd, or rather discolour'd, notions and apprehensions of divine things are begotten. Though these *Common notions* may be very busie sometimes in the *vegetation* of divine Knowledge; yet the corrupt vices of men may so clog, disturb and overrule them, (as the Naturalists say this unruly and masterless *matter* doth the natural *forms* in the formation of living creatures) that they may produce nothing but Monsters miserably distorted & misshapen. This kind of Science, as *Plotinus* speaks, τῷ ὑλικῷ πολλῷ συνοῦσα, καὶ εἰς αὐτὴν εἰσδεξαμένη, εἶδος ἕτερον ἠλλάξατο κράσει τῇ πρὸς τὸ χεῖρον, *companying too familiarly with Matter, and receiving and imbibing it into it selfe, changeth its shape by this incestuous mixture.*[22] At best, while any inward lust is harboured

---

[20] Cf. *Psalms* 12. 2.

[21] 'By *Common Notions*', explained Henry More, 'I understand what ever is Noëmatically true, that is to say, true at first sight to all men in their wits, upon a clear perception of the Terms, without any further discourse or reasoning' (*Immortality*, pp. 7–8). These 'notions'—the κοιναὶ ἔννοιαι or *notitiae communes* of tradition—were upheld by all the Cambridge Platonists (e.g., Whichcote, *Discourses*, III, 430; Smith, *Discourses*, pp. 49 f.; More, *Discourses*, p. 137; cf. George Rust, *A Discourse of Truth* [1682], §§ 5, 12). But see also below, p. 218, and esp. pp. 223 ff. On Locke's celebrated attack on this concept, consult Richard I. Aaron, *John Locke*, 2nd ed. (Oxford, 1955), Pt. II, Ch. II, and John W. Yolton, *John Locke and the Way of Ideas* (1956). [22] Plotinus, I, vi, 5.

The True Way of Attaining to Divine Knowledge 133

in the minds of men, it will so weaken them, that they can never bring forth any masculine or generous knowledge; as *Ælian* observes of the stork, that if the Night-owle chanceth to sit upon her eggs, they become presently as it were ὑπηνέμια, and all incubation rendred impotent and ineffectual.²³ Sin and lust are alway of an hungry nature, and suck up all those vital affections of mens Souls which should feed and nourish their Understandings.

What are all our most sublime Speculations of the Deity, that are *not impregnated* with *true Goodness*, but insipid things that have no tast nor life in them, that do but swell like empty froath in the souls of men? They doe not feed mens souls, but onely puffe them up & fill them with Pride, Arrogance and Contempt and Tyrannie towards those that cannot well ken their subtile Curiosities: as those Philosophers that *Tully* complains of in his times, *qui disciplinā suam ostentationē scientiæ, non legem vitæ, putabant,* which made their knowledge onely matter of ostentation, to venditate and set off themselves, but never caring to square and govern their lives by it.²⁴ Such as these doe but Spider-like take a great deal of pains to spin a worthless web out of their own bowels, which will not keep them warm. These indeed are those silly Souls that are *ever learning, but never come to the knowledge of the Truth.*²⁵ They may, with *Pharaoh's* lean kine, eat up and devour all Tongues and Sciences, and yet when they have done, still remain lean and ill-favour'd as they were at first. Jejune and barren Speculations may be hovering and fluttering up and down about Divinity, but they cannot settle or fix themselves upon it: they unfold the Plicatures of Truth's garment, but they cannot behold the lovely face of it. There are hidden Mysteries in Divine Truth, wrapt up one within another, which cannot be discern'd but onely by divine *Epoptists.*²⁶

We must not think we have then attained to the *right knowledge* of Truth, when we have broke through the *outward Shell* of *words* & *phrases* that house it up; or when by a *Logical Analysis* we have found out the dependencies and coherencies of them one with another; or when, like stout champions of it, having well guarded it with the invincible strength of our Demonstration, we dare stand out in the face of

---

[23] Thus Aelian, *De nat. an.*, I, 37, where the term is ἀνεμιαῖα rather than ὑπηνέμια (HGW).
[24] Cicero, *Disp.*, II, 4.   [25] 2 *Timothy* 3. 7.
[26] ἐπόπτης: 'one admitted to the third and highest grade of the mysteries' (H. G. Liddell and Robert Scott, *A Greek–English Lexicon*, rev. ed. [Oxford, 1966], p. 676).

the world, and challenge the field of all those that would pretend to be our Rivalls.

We have many Grave and Reverend Idolaters that worship Truth onely in the Image of their own Wits; that could never adore it so much as they may seem to doe, were it any thing else but such a Form of Belief as their own wandering speculations had at last met together in, were it not that they find their own image and superscription upon it.

There is a *knowing of the truth as it is in Jesus*, as it is in a *Christ-like nature*, as it is in that sweet, mild, humble, and loving Spirit of Jesus, which spreads itself like a Morning-Sun upon the Soules of good men, full of light and life. It profits litle to know Christ himself after the flesh; but he gives his Spirit to good men, that searcheth the deep things of God. There is an inward beauty, life and loveliness in Divine Truth, which cannot be known but onely then when it is digested into life and practice. The Greek Philosopher could tell those high-soaring *Gnosticks* that thought themselves no less then *Jovis alites*, that could (as he speaks in the Comedy) ἀεροβατεῖν καὶ περιφρονεῖν τὸν ἥλιον,[27] and cried out so much βλέπε πρὸς τὸν Θεὸν, *look upon God*, that ἄνευ ἀρετῆς Θεὸς ὄνομα μόνον, *Without Vertue and real Goodness God is but a name*,[28] a dry and empty Notion. The profane sort of men, like those old Gentile Greeks, may make many ruptures in the walls of God's Temple, and break into the holy ground but yet may finde God no more there then they did.

Divine Truth is better understood, as it unfolds itself in the purity of mens hearts and lives, then in all those subtil Niceties into which curious Wits may lay it forth. And therefore our Saviour, who is the great Master of it, would not, while he was here on earth, draw it up into any *System* or *Body*, nor would his Disciples after him; He would not lay it out to us in any *Canons* or *Articles* of *Belief*, not being indeed so careful to stock and enrich the World with Opinions and Notions, as with true Piety, and a Godlike pattern of purity, as the best way to thrive in all spiritual understanding. His main scope was to promote an *Holy life*, as the best and most compendious way to a *right Belief*. He hangs all true acquaintance with Divinity upon the doing Gods will, *If any man will doe his will, he shall know of the doctrine, whether it be of God.*[29]

[27] Thus Socrates, in Aristophanes, *Nubes*, 225: 'Tread the air, and look down on the sun.' The use of Aristophanes as a reliable witness to Socratic ideas renders any comment superfluous!

[28] Plotinus, II, ix, 15. Also quoted by Cudworth, above, p. 98.

[29] *John* 7. 17.

The True Way of Attaining to Divine Knowledge 135

This is that alone which will make us, as S. *Peter* tells us, that we shall not be *barren nor unfruitful in the knowledge of our Lord and Saviour*.³⁰ There is an inward sweetness and deliciousness in divine Truth, which no sensual minde can tast or rellish: this is that ψυχικός ἀνὴρ, that *natural man* that savours not the things of God.³¹ Corrupt passions and terrene affections are apt of their own nature to disturb all serene thoughts, to precipitate our Judgments, and warp our Understandings. It was a good Maxime of the old Jewish Writers, שרה בעצב ולא בכעס רוח הקדש לא³² the Holy Spirit dwells not in terrene and earthly passions. Divinity is not so well perceiv'd by a subtile wit, ὥσπερ αἰσθήσει κεκαθαρμένῃ *as by a purified sense*, as *Plotinus* phraseth it.³³

Neither was the antient Philosophy unacquainted with this Way and Method of attaining to the knowledge of Divine things; and therefore *Aristotle* himself thought a Young man unfit to meddle with the grave precepts of Morality, till the heat and violent precipitancy of his youthful affections was cool'd and moderated.³⁴ And it is observed of *Pythagoras*, that he had several waies to try the capacity of his Scholars, and to prove the *sedateness* and *Moral* temper of their minds, before he would entrust them with the sublimer Mysteries of his Philosophy.³⁵ The *Platonists* were herein so wary and solicitous, that they thought the Mindes of men could never be purg'd enough from those earthly dregs of Sense and Passion, in which they were so much steeped, before they could be capable of their divine *Metaphysicks*: and therefore they so much solicite a χωρισμὸς ἀπὸ τοῦ σώματος, as they are wont to phrase it, *a separation from the Body*, in all those that would καθαρῶς φιλοσοφεῖν, as *Socrates* speaks, that is indeed, sincerely understand Divine Truth; for that was the scope of their Philosophy.³⁶ This was also intimated by them in their defining Philosophy to be μελέτη θανάτου *a Meditation of Death*;³⁷ aiming herein at onely a *Moral* way of *dying*, by loosening

---

³⁰ 2 *Peter* 1. 8.   ³¹ Cf. 1 *Corinthians* 2. 14.
³² 'The Holy Spirit does not dwell [*literally*, sing] in sadness or in anger.' Probably adapted from *Talmud*: Shabbath, 30b.
³³ Plotinus, II, iv, 15.   ³⁴ *Ethica nicomachea*, I, 3.
³⁵ Cf. Iamblichus, *Vit. Pyth.*, esp. XVII.
³⁶ Cf. Plato, *Phaedo*, 67d: 'And this separation and release of the soul from the body is termed death?—To be sure, he said.—And the true philosophers, and they only, are ever seeking to release the soul. Is not the separation of the soul from the body their especial study?—That is true.' Cf. *Sophista*, 253e.
³⁷ Cf. Plato, *Phaedo*, 80e–81a.

the Soul from the Body and this Sensitive life; which they thought was necessary to a right Contemplation of Intelligible things: and therefore besides those ἀρεταὶ καθαρτικαί[38] by which the Souls of men were to be separated from sensuality and purged from fleshly filth, they devised a further way of *Separation* more accommodated to the condition of Philosophers, which was their *Mathemata*, or Mathematical Contemplations, whereby the Souls of men might farther shake off their dependency upon Sense, and learn to go as it were alone, without the crutch of any Sensible or Material thing to support them; and so be a little inur'd, being once got up above the Body, to converse freely with Immaterial natures, without looking down again and falling back into Sense. Besides many other waies they had, whereby to rise out of this dark Body; ἀναβάσεις ἐκ τοῦ σπηλαίου,[39] as they are wont to call them, several steps and accents out of this miry cave of mortality, before they could set any sure footing with their Intellectual part in the land of Light and Immortal Being.

And thus we should pass from this Topick of our Discourse, upon which we have dwelt too long already, but that before we quite let it goe, I hope we may fairly make this use of it farther (besides what we have openly driven at all this while) which is, to learn not to devote or give up our selves to any private Opinions or Dictates of men in matters of Religion, nor too zealously to propugne the *Dogmata* of any Sect. As we should not like rigid Censurers arraign & condemn the Creeds of other men which we comply not with, before a full & mature understanding of them, ripened not onely by the natural sagacity of our own Reasons, but by the benign influence of holy and mortified Affection: so neither should we over-hastily *credere in fidem alienam*, subscribe to the Symbols and Articles of other men. They are not alwaies the *Best* men that blot most paper; Truth is not, I fear, so Voluminous, nor swells into such a mighty bulk as our Books doe. Those mindes are not alwaies the most chast that are most parturient with these learned Discourses, which too often bear upon them a foule stain of their unlawfull propagation. A bitter juice of corrupt affections may sometimes be strained into the inke of our greatest Clerks, their Doctrines may tast too sowre of the cask they come through. We are not alwaies happy in meeting with that wholesome food (as some are wont to call the

---

[38] 'purifying virtues'.
[39] 'ascents from the cave'. Cf. Plato, *Respublica*, 514–15, and Plotinus, II, ix, 6. See also below, p. 181.

The True Way of Attaining to Divine Knowledge 137

Doctrinal-part of Religion) which hath been dress'd out by the cleanest hands. Some men have too *bad hearts* to have *good heads*: they cannot be good at Theorie who have been so bad at the practice, as we may justly fear too many of those from whom we are apt to take the Articles of our Belief have been. Whilst we plead so much our right to the patrimony of our Fathers, we may take too fast a possession of their Errors as well as of their sober opinions. There are *Idola specûs*,[40] Innate Prejudices, and deceitfull *Hypotheses*, that many times wander up and down in the Mindes of good men, that may flie out from them with their graver determinations. We can never be well assur'd what our *Traditional* Divinity is; nor can we securely enough addict our selves to any Sect of men. That which was the Philosopher's motto, Ἐλεύθερον εἶναι δεῖ τῇ γνώμῃ μέλλοντα φιλοσοφεῖν, we may a little enlarge, and so fit it for an ingenuous pursuer after divine Truth: He that will finde Truth, must seek it with a *free judgment*, and a *sanctified minde*:[41] he that thus seeks, shall finde; he shall live in Truth, and that shall live in him; it shall be like a stream of living waters issuing out of his own Soule; he shall drink of the waters of his own cistern, and be satisfied; he shall every morning finde this Heavenly *Manna* lying upon the top of his own Soule, and be fed with it to eternal life; he will finde satisfaction within, feeling himself in conjunction with Truth, though all the World should dispute against him.

And thus I should again leave this Argument, but that perhaps we may all this while have seemed to undermine what we intend to build up. For if Divine Truth spring onely up from the Root of true Goodness; how shall we ever endeavour to be good, before we know what it is to be so: or how shall we convince the gainsaying world of Truth, unless we could also inspire Vertue into it?

To both which we shall make this Reply, That there are some *Radical Principles* of Knowledge that are so deeply sunk into the Souls of men, as that the Impression cannot easily be obliterated, though it may be much darkened. Sensual baseness doth not so grosly sully and bemire the Souls of all Wicked men at first, as to make them with

---

[40] One of the rare references to Bacon (from his *Novum Organum*, in *Works*, IV, 53 ff.), but subordinated as always to the principles of Cambridge Platonism. Cf. Whichcote, *Aphorisms*, § 607 (below, p. 332). On the attitude of the Cambridge Platonists to Bacon, see below, p. 187, note.

[41] The dictum in Greek is probably adapted from several analogous statements by Philo, Origen, Diogenes Laertius and others (see *SVF*, III, 86, 89, 146, etc.).

Diagoras to deny the *Deity*, or with *Protagoras* to doubt of, or with *Diodorus* to question the *Immortality* of Rational Souls.[42] Neither are the *Common Principles* of Vertue so pull'd up by the roots in all, as to make them so dubious in stating the bounds of Vertue and Vice as *Epicurus* was, though he could not but sometime take notice of them.[43] Neither is the *Retentive power* of Truth so weak and loose in all *Scepticks* as it was in him, who being well scourg'd in the streets till the blood ran about him, question'd when he came home, whether he had been beaten or not. *Arrianus*[44] hath well observed, That the *Common Notions* of *God* and *Vertue* imprest upon the Souls of men, are more clear and perspicuous then any else; and that if they have not more *certainty*, yet have they more *evidence*, and display themselves with less difficulty to our *Reflexive* Faculty then any Geometrical Demonstrations: and these are both available to prescribe out waies of Vertue to mens own souls, and to force an acknowledgment of Truth from those that oppose, when they are well guided by a skilfull hand. Truth needs not any time flie from Reason, there being an Eternal amitie between them. They are onely some private *Dogmata*, that may well be suspected as spurious and adulterate, that dare not abide the tryall thereof. And this Reason is not every where so extinguish'd, as that we may not by that enter into the Souls of men. What the *Magnetical* virtue is in these earthly Bodies, that Reason is in mens Mindes, which when it is put forth, draws them one to another. Besides in wicked men there are sometimes Distasts of Vice, and Flashes of love to Vertue;[45] which are the Motions which spring from a true Intellect, and the faint struglings

---

[42] Cudworth's *Int. System* provides full exposition of the views of the Greek philosophers named here. The most famous of the three is certainly Protagoras (5th cent. B.C.), 'the first of the Sophists', best known for his affirmation that 'man is a measure of all things' (*apud* Plato, *Cratylus*, 386a), which Plato dismissed by the counter-affirmation quoted above (headnote, p. 1). Consult further: Eugène Dupréel, *Les Sophistes* (Neuchâtel, 1948), 'Protagoras', and Mario Untersteiner, *The Sophists*, tr. K. Freeman (Oxford, 1954), Ch. I–III.

[43] Cf. R. D. Hicks, *Stoic and Epicurean* (1910), Ch. V, 'Epicurus and Hedonism'.

[44] Arrian (c. 96–c. 180), the Greek historian and philosopher, is especially noted for his account of Alexander's military exploits. He was also responsible for the preservation of Epictetus' *Diatribai* and *Enchiridion*.

[45] A point firmly demonstrated by poets, as in *The Faerie Queene*, I, iii, 5–6, and *Paradise Lost*, IX, 463 ff.

The True Way of Attaining to Divine Knowledge 139

of an Higher life within them, which they crucifie again by their wicked Sensuality. As Truth doth not alwaies act in good men, so neither doth Sense alwaies act in wicked men: they may sometimes have their *lucida intervalla*, their sober fits; and a Divine spirit blowing and breathing upon them may then blow up some live sparks of true Understanding within them; though they may soon endeavour to quench them again, and to rake them up in the ashes of their own earthly thoughts.

All this, and more that might be said upon this Argument, may serve to point out the *Way of Vertue*. We want not so much *Means* of knowing what we ought to doe, as *Wills* to doe that which we may know. But yet all that Knowledge which is separated from an inward acquaintance with Vertue and Goodness, is of a far different nature from that which ariseth out of a true *living sense* of them, which is the *best discerner* thereof, and by which alone we know the true Perfection, Sweetness, Energie, and Loveliness of them, and all that which is οὔτε ῥητὸν, οὔτε γραπτὸν,[46] that which can no more be known by a naked Demonstration, then Colours can be perceived of a blinde man by any Definition or Description which he can hear of them.

And further, the clearest and most distinct Notions of Truth that shine in the Souls of the common sort of men, may be extremely clouded, if they be not accompanied with that answerable practice that might preserve their integrity: These tender Plants may soon be spoyl'd by the continual droppings of our corrupt affections upon them; they are but of a weak and feminine nature, and so may be sooner deceived by that wily Serpent of Sensuality that harbours within us.

While the Soul is πλήρης τοῦ σώματος, *full of the Body*, while we suffer those *Notions* and *Common Principles* of Religion to lie asleep within us; that γενεσιουργὸς δύναμις, *the power of an Animal life*, will be apt to incorporate and mingle it self with them; and that Reason that is within us, as *Plotinus* hath well express'd it, becomes more and more σύμφυτος κακαῖς ταῖς ἐπιγινομέναις δόξαις, it will be infected with those evil Opinions that arise from our Corporeal life.[47] The more deeply our Souls dive into our Bodies, the more will Reason and Sensuality run one into another, and make up a most dilute, unsavourie, and muddie kinde of Knowledge. We must therefore endeavour more and more to withdraw our selves from these Bodily things, to set our

---

[46] 'neither spoken nor written'.
[47] Cf. Plotinus, III, v, 7.

Souls as free as may be from its miserable slavery to this base Flesh:[48] we must shut the Eyes of Sense, and open that brighter Eye of our Understandings, that other Eye of the Soul, as the Philosopher calls our Intellectual Faculty, *ἥν ἔχει μὲν πᾶς, χρῶνται δὲ ὀλίγοι*, which indeed all have, but few make use of it.[49] This is the way to see clearly; the light of the Divine World will then begin to fall upon us, and those sacred *ἐλλάμψεις*, those pure *Coruscations* of Immortal and Ever-living Truth will shine out into us, and in Gods own light shall we behold him. The fruit of this Knowledge will be sweet to our tast, and pleasant to our palates, sweeter then the hony or the hony-comb.[50] The Priests of *Mercury*, as *Plutarch* tells us, in the eating of their holy things, were wont to cry out *γλυκὺ ἡ ἀλήθεια*, *Sweet is Truth*.[51] But how sweet and delicious that Truth is which holy and heaven-born Souls feed upon in their mysterious converses with the Deity, who can tell but they that tast it? When *Reason* once is raised by the mighty force of the Divine Spirit into a converse with God, it is turn'd into *Sense*: That which before was onely *Faith* well built upon sure Principles, (for such our *Science* may be) now becomes *Vision*. We shall then converse with God *τῷ νῷ*,[52] whereas before we convers'd with him onely *τῇ διανοίᾳ* with our *Discursive faculty*, as the *Platonists* were wont to distinguish. Before we laid hold on him onely *λόγῳ ἀποδεικτικῷ*, with a strugling, Agonistical, and contentious Reason, hotly combating with difficulties and sharp contests of divers opinions, & labouring in it self, in its deductions of one thing from another; we shall then fasten our minds upon him *λόγῳ ἀποφαντικῷ*, with such a *serene* Understanding, *γαλήνῃ νοερᾷ*, such an *Intellectual calmness* and serenity as will present us with a blissful, steady, and invariable sight of him.

And now if you please, setting aside the *Epicurean* herd of Brutish men, who have drowned all their own sober Reason in the deepest *Lethe* of Sensuality, we shall divide the rest of Men into these Four ranks, according to that Method which *Simplicius* upon *Epictetus* hath

---

[48] Cf. More, *Enth. Tr.*, p. 60: 'the souls of men while they are in these mortall bodies are as so many Prisoners immured in severall prisons'. Thus Plato, *Phaedo*, 81 ff. (cf. *Gorgias*, 493a, and *Phaedrus*, 250c), and Plotinus, IV, viii, 1 and 3.

[49] Plotinus, I, vi, 8.   [50] Cf. *Psalms* 19. 10.

[51] *De Iside et Osiride*, LXVIII.

[52] Thus elsewhere in Smith's *Discourses* (p. 265): 'not so much *προσώπῳ πρὸς πρόσωπον*, as *νῷ πρὸς νοῦν*, not so much *Face to Face* as *Mind to Mind*'.

The True Way of Attaining to Divine Knowledge 141

already laid out to us,⁵³ with a respect to a Fourfold kinde of Knowledge, which we have all this while glanced at.

The First whereof is Ἄνθρωπος συμπεφυρμένος τῇ γενέσει, or, if you will, ἄνθρωπος ὁ πολὺς, that *Complex and Multifarious man* that is made up of Soul & Body, as it were by a just equality and Arithmetical proportion of parts and Powers in each of them. The knowledge of these men I should call ἀμυδρὸν δόξαν in *Plutarch's* phrase; a Knowledge wherein Sense and Reason are so twisted up together, that it cannot easily be unravel'd, and laid out into its first principles. Their highest Reason is ὁμόδοξος ταῖς αἰσθήσεσι complying with their senses, and both conspire together in vulgar opinion. To these that Motto which the *Stoicks* have made for them may very well agree, βίος ὑπόληψις, their *life* being steer'd by nothing else but *Opinion* and *Imagination*. Their higher notions of God and Religion are so entangled with the Birdlime of fleshly Passions and mundane Vanity, that they cannot rise up above the surface of this dark earth, or easily entertain any but earthly conceptions of heavenly things. Such Souls as are here lodg'd, as *Plato* speaks, are ὀπισθοβαρεῖς *heavy behinde*,⁵⁴ and are continually pressing down to this world's centre: and though, like the Spider, they may appear sometime moving up and down aloft in the aire, yet they doe but sit in the loome, and move in that web of their own gross fansies, which they fasten and pin to some earthly thing or other.

The Second is Ἄνθρωπος κατὰ τὴν λογικὴν ζωὴν οὐσιωμένος, The man that looks at himself as being what he is rather by his Soul then by his Body; that thinks not fit to view his own face in any other Glass but that of Reason and Understanding; that reckons upon his *Soul* as that which was made *to rule*, his *Body* as that which was born *to obey*, and like an handmaid perpetually to wait upon his higher and nobler part. And in such an one the *Communes notitiæ*, or common Principles of Vertue and Goodness, are more clear and steady. To such an one we may allow τρανεστέραν καὶ ἐμφανεστέραν δόξαν, *more clear and distinct Opinions*, as being already ἐν καθάρσει, in a Method or course of *Purgation*, or at least fit to be initiated into the *Mysteria minora* the lesser

---

⁵³ Hereafter (to p. 143) Smith borrows freely from Simplicius, *In Epict.*, Præfatio.

⁵⁴ Plotinus, VI, ix, 4—not Plato—speaks of the soul as ὀπισθοβαρὴς, 'weighted from beneath' (HGW). Cf. Whichcote, *Discourses*, II, 35: 'We are as they say *heavy behind* [marginal note: ὀπισθοβαρεῖς]. In this Body, the very Reason of our Mind is materiated, and the very Sentiments of our Souls (to use the common phrase) do taste of the Cask ...'

Mysteries of Religion. For though these *Innate notions* of Truth may be but poor, empty, and hungry things of themselves, before they be fed and fill'd with the practice of true Vertue; yet they are capable of being impregnated, and exalted with the Rules and Precepts of it. And therefore the Stoick suppos'd ὅτι τοιούτῳ προσήκουσιν αἱ ἠθικαὶ καὶ πολιτικαὶ ἀρεταί, that the doctrine of Political and Moral vertues was fit to be delivered to such as these; and though they may not be so well prepared for Divine Vertue (which is of an higher Emanation) yet they are not immature for Humane, as having the Seeds of it already within themselves, which being water'd by answerable practice, may sprout up within them.

The Third is Ἄνθρωπος ἤδη κεκαθαρμένος, He whose Soule is *already purg'd* by this lower sort of Vertue, and so is continually flying off from the Body and Bodily passion, and returning into himself. Such in S. *Peter's* language are those *who have escaped the pollutions which are in the world through lust*.[55] To these we may attribute a νόθη ἐπιστήμη, a lower degree of Science, their inward sense of Vertue and moral Goodness being far transcendent to all meer Speculative opinions of it. But if this Knowledge settle here, it may be quickly apt to corrupt. Many of our most refined Moralists may be, in a worse sense then *Plotinus* means, πληρωθέντες τῇ ἑαυτῶν φύσει, full with their own pregnancy;[56] their Souls may too much heave and swell with the sense of their own Vertue and Knowledge: there may be an ill *Ferment of Self-love* lying at the bottome, which may puffe it up the more with Pride, Arrogance, and Self-conceit. These forces with which the Divine bounty supplies us to keep a stronger guard against the evil Spirit, may be abus'd by our own rebellious Pride, enticing of them from their allegiance to Heaven, to strengthen it self in our Souls, and fortifie them against Heaven: like that supercilious *Stoick*, who when he thought his Minde well arm'd and appointed with Wisdome and Vertue, cry'd out, *Sapiens contendet cum ipso Jove de felicitate*.[57] They may make an aiery heaven of these, and wall it about with their own Self-flattery, and then sit in it as Gods, as *Cosroes* the Persian king was sometime laughed at for enshrining himself in a Temple of his own. And therefore if this *Knowledge* be not attended with *Humility* and a deep sense of *Self-penury* and *Self-emptiness*, we may easily fall short of that True Knowledge of God

---

[55] 2 *Peter* 2. 20.   [56] Plotinus, III, v, 7.

[57] Cf. Seneca, *Ep.*, XXV: 'when a man has limited his desires ..., he can challenge the happiness of Jove himself (*cum ipso Iove de felicitate contendat*), as Epicurus says'.

The True Way of Attaining to Divine Knowledge 143

which we seem to aspire after. We may carry such an Image and *Species* of our Selves constantly before us, as will make us lose the clear sight of the Divinity, and be too apt to rest in a meer *Logical life* (it's *Simplicius* his expression)[58] without any true participation of the *Divine life*, if we doe not (as many doe, if not all, who rise no higher) relapse and slide back by vain-glory, popularity, or such like vices, into some mundane and externall Vanity or other.

The fourth is Ἄνθρωπος θεωρητικὸς, The true Metaphysical and Contemplative man, ὃς τὴν ἑαυτοῦ λογικὴν ζωὴν ὑπερτρέχων, ὅλως εἶναι βούλεται τῶν κρειττόνων, who running and shooting up above his own *Logical* or *Self-rational* life, pierceth into the *Highest life*: Such a one, who by *Universal Love* and *Holy affection* abstracting himself from himselfe, endeavours the nearest Union with the Divine Essence that may be, κέντρον κέντρῳ συνάψας, as *Plotinus* speaks; knitting his owne centre, if he have any, unto the centre of Divine Being.[59] To such an one the *Platonists* are wont to attribute θείαν ἐπιστήμην a true *Divine wisedome*, powerfully displaying it self ἐν νοερᾷ ζωῇ in an *Intellectual life*, as they phrase it. Such a Knowledge they say is alwaies pregnant with *Divine Vertue*, which ariseth out of an happy Union of Souls with God, and is nothing else but a living Imitation of a Godlike perfection drawn out by a strong fervent love of it. This Divine Knowledge καλοὺς καὶ ἐραστοὺς ποιεῖ &c. as *Plotinus* speaks, makes us amorous of Divine beauty, beautifull and lovely;[60] and this *Divine Love and Purity* reciprocally exalts *Divine Knowledge*; both of them growing up together like that Ἔρως and Ἀντέρως that *Pausanias* sometimes speaks of.[61] Though by the *Platonists* leave such a *Life* and *Knowledge* as this is, peculiarly belongs to the true and sober Christian who lives in Him who is *Life* itself, and is enlightened by Him who is the *Truth* it self, and is made partaker of the *Divine Unction, and knoweth all things*, as S. John speaks.[62] This Life is nothing else but God's own breath within him, and an *Infant-Christ* (if I may use the expression) formed in his Soul, who is in a sense ἀπαύγασμα τῆς δόξης, *the shining forth of the Father's glory*.[63] But yet we must not mistake, this Knowledge is but here in its Infancy; there is an higher knowledge

---

[58] *In Epict.*, Praefatio (as before, note 53).
[59] Plotinus, VI, ix, 10. Also quoted by More, in *Reply*, p. 43.
[60] Plotinus, I, vi, 7.
[61] Eros and Anteros; in Pausanias, I, xxx, 1, and VI, xxiii, 3, 5. Smith invokes the same legend elsewhere in the *Discourses* (p. 332).
[62] 1 *John* 3. 20.   [63] *Hebrews* 1. 3.

or an higher degree of this knowledge that doth not, that cannot, descend upon us in these earthly habitations. We cannot here see מאירה באספקלריא in *Speculo lucido*; here we can see *but in a glass*, and that *darkly* too.[64] Our own *Imaginative* Powers, which are perpetually attending the highest acts of our Souls, will be breathing a grosse dew upon the pure Glasse of our Understandings, and so sully and besmear it, that we cannot see the Image of the Divinity sincerely in it. But yet this Knowledge being a true heavenly fire kindled from God's own Altar, begets an undaunted Courage in the Souls of Good men, & enables them to cast a holy Scorn upon the poor petty trash of this Life in comparison with Divine things, and to pitty those poor brutish *Epicureans* that have nothing but the meer husks of fleshly pleasure to feed themselves with. This Sight of God makes pious Souls breath after that blessed time when Mortality shall be swallowed up of Life, when they shall no more behold the Divinity through those dark Mediums that eclipse the blessed Sight of it.

[64] 1 *Corinthians* 13. 12. Cf. Culverwell's sermon on this text, in *Spiritual Opticks* (Cambridge, 1651).

JOHN SMITH

The Excellency and Nobleness of True Religion*

Proverbs 15. 24

The Way of life is above to the wise, that he may depart from hell beneath.

THE INTRODUCTION

IN this whole *Book of the Proverbs* we find *Solomon*, one of the Eldest Sons of Wisdom, alwaies standing up and calling her blessed: his Heart was both enlarged and fill'd with the pure influence of her beams, and therefore was perpetually adoring that Sun which gave him light. *Wisdome is justified of all her Children*;[1] though the brats of darkness and children of folly see no beauty nor comeliness in her, that they should desire her, as they said of Christ, *Esay* 53.[2] Τίς σύνεσις γένοιτο τοῖς μὴ ἐφαπτομένοις; That Mind which is not touch'd with an inward sense of Divine Wisdom, cannot estimate the true Worth of it.[3] But when Wisdom once displays its own excellencies and glories in a purified Soul, it is entertained there with the greatest love and delight, and receives its own image reflected back to it self in sweetest returns of Love and Praise. We have a clear manifestation of this sacred Sympathy in *Solomon*, whom we may not unfitly call *Sapientia Organum*, an Instrument which Wisdom herself had tuned to play her divine Lessons upon: his words were דִּבְרֵי־חֵפֶץ, every where full of Divine

---

* From *Select Discourses*, ed. John Worthington (1660), Disc. IX [pp. 377–451]. Worthington's subdivision of this discourse into an introduction and eleven chapters has been retained but the summaries he prefixed to each chapter are omitted.

[1] *Luke* 7. 35. Solomon was traditionally regarded as the author of the *Book of Proverbs, Ecclesiastes*, and *The Song of Solomon*. Only the authorship of the apocryphal *Wisdom of Solomon* had been controverted by the Church Fathers and later theologians.

[2] *Isaiah* 53. 2: 'he [the Suffering Servant] hath no form nor comeliness'.

[3] Adapted from Plotinus, III, vi, 6.

sweetness matched with strength and beauty, πολὺν νοῦν ἔχοντες ἔνδον· or, as himself phraseth it, *like apples of gold in pictures of Silver*.[4] The mind of *a Proverb* is *to utter Wisdom in a Mystery*, as the Apostle sometime speaks,[5] and to wrap up Divine Truth in a kind of Ænigmatical way, though in vulgar expressions. Which method of delivering Divine doctrine (not to mention the Writings of the ancient Philosophers) we find frequently pursued in the Holy Scripture, thereby *both opening and hiding* at once the Truth which is offered to us. A *Proverb* or *Parable* being once unfolded, by reason of its *affinity* with the *Phancy*, the more sweetly insinuates it self into that, and is from thence with the greater advantage transmitted to the *Understanding*. In this state we are not able to behold *Truth* in its own Native beauty and lustre; but while we are *vail'd* with mortality, *Truth* must *vail* it self too, that it may the more freely converse with us. S. *Austin* hath well assign'd the reason why we are so much delighted with *Metaphors*, *Allegories*, &c. because they are so much proportioned to our *Senses*, with which our *Reason* hath contracted an intimacy and familiarity.[6] And therefore God to accommodate his *Truth* to our weak capacities, does as it were *embody* it in *Earthly* expressions; according to that ancient Maxim of the Cabbalists, *Lumen Supernum nunquam descendit sine indumento*; agreeable to which is that of *Dionysius Areop.* not seldom quoted by the School-men, *Impossibile est nobis aliter lucere radium Divinum, nisi varietate sacrorum velaminum circumvelatum*. His words in the Greek are these, οὐδὲ δυνατὸν ἑτέρως ἡμῖν ἐπιλάμψαι τὴν θεαρχικὴν ἀκτῖνα, μὴ τῇ ποικιλίᾳ τῶν ἱερῶν παραπετασμάτων ἀναγωγικῶς περικεκαλυμμένην.[7]

[4] *Proverbs* 25. 11. The quotation in Hebrew is from *Ecclesiastes* 12. 10: 'acceptable words' (i.e., 'words that he [Solomon] wanted').

[5] 1 *Corinthians* 2. 7.

[6] According to Augustine, 'anything which we are taught by allegory or emblem affects and pleases us more, and is more highly esteemed by us, than it would be if most clearly stated in plain terms. I believe that the emotions are less easily kindled while the soul is wholly involved in earthly things; but if it be brought to those corporeal things which are the emblems of spiritual things, and then taken from these to the spiritual realities which they represent, it gathers strength by the mere act of passing from the one to the other, and, like the flame of a lighted torch, is made by the motion to burn more brightly, and is carried away to rest by a more intensely glowing love' (*Epistulae*, LV, 21; in *Letters*, VI, 220).

[7] Pseudo-Dionysius, *De coelesti hierarchia*, I: 'it is not possible that the supremely Divine Ray should otherwise illuminate us, except so far as it is

The Excellency and Nobleness of True Religion 147

Thus much by way of Preface or Introduction to these words, being one of *Solomon*'s excellent *Proverbs*, viz. *The way of life is above to the wise*. Without any mincing or mangling of the Words, or running out into any Critical curiosities about them, I shall from these Words take occasion to set forth *The Nobleness and Generous Spirit of True Religion*, which I suppose to be meant here by [*The way of life*.] The word לְמַעְלָה here rendered [*above*] may signifie *that which is divine and heavenly, high and excellent*, as the word ἄνω does in the New Testament, τῆς ἄνω κλήσεως, Phil. 3. 14. τὰ ἄνω, φρονεῖτε, Col. 3. 2. S. *Austin* supposeth the things of Religion to be meant by the τὰ ἄνω, *superna*, for this reason, *quòd merito excellentiæ longè superant res terrenas*.[8] And in this sense I shall consider it, my purpose being from hence to discourse of *the Excellent and Noble spirit of true Religion* (whether it be taken *in abstracto*, as it is in it self; or *in concreto*, as it becomes an inward Form and Soul to the Minds and Spirits of Good men;) and this in opposition to that *low and base-born spirit of Irreligion*, which is perpetually sinking from God, till it couches to the very Centre of misery, שְׁאוֹל מַטָּה, *the lowermost Hell*.

In discoursing upon this Argument, I shall observe this Method; viz. I shall consider *the Excellency and Nobleness of True Religion*
  1. In its Rise and Original.
  2. In its Nature and Essence.
  3. In its Properties and Operations.
  4. In its Progress.
  5. In its Term and End.

CHAP. I

We begin with the First, viz. *True Religion is a Noble thing in its Rise and Original, and in regard of its Descent*. True Religion derives its pedigree from Heaven, is βλάστημα τοῦ οὐρανοῦ· it comes from Heaven, and constantly moves toward Heaven again: it's a Beam from God, *as every good and perfect gift is from above, and comes down from the*

---

enveloped, for the purpose of instruction, in variegated sacred veils'. On the traditional theory of accommodation propounded here, see the references I cited in an essay on Milton's espousal of it in *Paradise Lost* (*Texas Studies in Literature and Language*, V [1963], 58–63).

[8] 'St Augustine supposeth the things of Religion to be meant by the τὰ ἄνω, *the heavenly things*, for this reason, *because by virtue of their excellence they are far superior to earthly things*'. Cf. Augustine, *Epistulae*, CCXLIV (*PL*, XXXIII, 1059), etc.

Father of lights, with whom is no variableness nor shadow of turning, as S. *James* speaks.⁹ God is the *First Truth* and *Primitive Goodness*: True *Religion* is a vigorous *Efflux* and *Emanation* of *Both* upon the Spirits of men, and therefore is called *a participation of the divine Nature.*¹⁰ Indeed God hath copied out himself in all created Being, having no other Pattern to frame any thing by but his own Essence; so that all created Being is *umbratilis similitudo entis increati*,¹¹ and is, by some stamp or other of God upon it, at least remotely allied to him: But *True Religion* is such a Communication of the Divinity, as none but the Highest of created Beings are capable of. On the other side *Sin* and *Wickedness* is of the *basest and lowest original*, as being nothing else but a perfect degeneration from God and those *Eternal Rules of Goodness* which are derived from him. Religion is an *Heaven-born* thing, *the Seed of God* in the Spirits of men, whereby they are formed to a similitude & likeness of himself. A true Christian is every way of a most noble Extraction, of an heavenly and divine pedigree, being born ἄνωθεν *from above*, as it is express'd *Joh.* 3.¹² The line of all earthly Nobility, if it were followed to the beginning, would lead to *Adam*, where all the lines of descent meet in One; and the Root of all Extractions would be found planted in nothing else but *Adamah*, red Earth:¹³ But a Christian derives his line from Christ, who is the Only-begotten Son of God, *the shining forth of his glory, and the Character of his person*, as he is stiled *Heb.* 1.¹⁴ We may truly say of Christ and Christians, as *Zebah* and *Zalmunna* said of *Gideon*'s brethren. *As he is, so are they* (according to their capacity,) *each one resembling the children of a king.*¹⁵ Titles of Worldly honour in Heavens heraldry are but only *Tituli nominales*; but Titles of Divine dignity signify some Real thing, some Real and Divine Communications to the Spirits and Minds of men. All Perfections and Excellencies in any kind are to be measured by their approach to that Primitive Perfection of all, God himself; and therefore Participation of the Divine nature cannot but entitle a Christian to the highest degree of dignity: *Behold what manner*

---

⁹ *James* 1. 17.   ¹⁰ See further below, p. 149.
¹¹ 'the shadowy likeness of an uncreated being'—i.e. an outline as of an incomplete being.
¹² *John* 3. 7. Cf. Whichcote, above, p. 71.
¹³ Smith is appealing to one of several theories concerning the derivation of 'Adam'. Consult Darwell Stone, 'Lexicon of Patristic Greek: 'Ἀδάμ', *Journal of Theological Studies*, XXIV (1922–23), 473 f.
¹⁴ *Hebrews* 1. 3.   ¹⁵ *Judges* 8. 21.

of love the Father hath bestowed upon us; that we should be called the Sons of God, 1 Jo. 3. 1.

Thus much for a more *general* discovery of *the Nobleness of Religion* as to its Fountain and Original; We may further and more *particularly* take notice of this in reference to that *Twofold fountain* in God, from whence all true Religion flows and issues forth, viz. 1. *His Immutable Nature*. 2. *His Will*.

1. *The Immutable Nature of God.* From thence arise all those *Eternal Rules of Truth and Goodness* which are the Foundation of all Religion, and which God at the first Creation folded up in the Soul of man. These we may call the *Truths of Natural inscription*;[16] understanding hereby either those *Fundamental principles* of Truth which Reason by a naked intuition may behold in God, or those necessary *Corollaries* and *Deductions* that may be drawn from thence. I cannot think it so proper to say, That God ought infinitely to be loved because he *commands* it, as because he is indeed an *Infinite and Unchangeable Goodness*. God hath stamp'd a Copy of his own Archetypal Loveliness upon the Soul, that man by reflecting into himself might behold there the glory of God, *intra se videre Deum*, see within his Soul all those Ideas of Truth which concern the Nature and Essence of God, by reason of its own resemblance of God; and so beget within himself the most free and generous motions of Love to God. Reason in man being *Lumen de Lumine*, a Light flowing from the Fountain and Father of Lights, and being, as *Tully* phraseth it, *participata similitudo Rationis æternæ*[17] (as the Law of Nature, the νόμος γραπτός, the Law written in mans Heart,[18] is *participatio Legis æternæ in Rationali creatura*[19]) it

---

[16] The appeal here is to the tradition of the *logoi spermatikoi* or *rationes seminales*. See above, pp. 26 and 132.

[17] The phrase is adapted not from Cicero but from Thomas Aquinas. Cf. *S. th.*, I, lxxxiv, 5: 'the human soul knows all things in the eternal types, since by participation of these types we know all things. For the intellectual light itself which is in us, is nothing else than a participated likeness of the uncreated light, in which are contained the eternal types (*lumen intellectuale, quod est in nobis, nihil est aliud quàm quædam participata similitudo luminis increati, in quo continentur rationes æternæ*). Whence it is written (Ps. iv, 6, 7), *Many say: who showeth us good things?* which question the Psalmist answers, *The light of Thy countenance, O Lord, is signed upon us*, as though he were to say: By the seal of the Divine light in us, all things are made known to us.'

[18] *Romans* 2. 15—the *locus classicus* of all Christian expositions of the law of nature. On the development of the concept, see C. H. Dodd, *New*

was to enable Man to work out of himself all those Notions of God which are the true Ground-work of Love and Obedience to God, and conformity to him: and in molding the inward man into the greatest conformity to the Nature of God was the Perfection and Efficacy of the Religion of Nature. But since Mans fall from God, the inward virtue and vigour of Reason is much abated, the Soul having suffered a πτερορρύησις, as *Plato* speaks, a *defluvium pennarum*:[20] those Principles of Divine truth which were first engraven upon mans Heart with the finger of God are now, as the Characters of some ancient Monuments, less clear and legible then at first. And therefore besides the *Truth of Natural inscription*

2. God hath provided *the Truth of Divine Revelation*, which issues forth from his own free *Will*, and clearly discovers the way of our return to God, from whom we are fallen. And this Truth, with the Effects and Productions of it in the Minds of men, the Scripture is wont to set forth under the name of *Grace*, as proceeding merely from the free bounty and overflowings of the Divine Love. Of this Revealed *Will* is that of the Apostle to be understood, τὰ τοῦ Θεοῦ οὐδεὶς οἶδεν, *None hath known the things of God*;[21] οὐδεὶς, *None*, neither Angel nor Man, could know the Mind of God, could unlock the Breast of God, or search out the Counsels of his Will. But God out of the infinite riches of his Compassions toward mankind is pleas'd to unbosom his Secrets, and most clearly to manifest *the way in to the Holiest of all*, and *bring to light life and immortality*,[22] and in these last ages to send his Son, who lay in his bosom from all Eternity, to teach us his Will

---

Testament Guides (Manchester, 1953), Ch. VI; A. R. Vidler and W. A. Whitehouse, *Natural Law*, 2nd ed. (1946); Joseph Dalby, *The Catholic Conception of the Law of Nature* (1943); etc. In the light of these studies consult the detailed discussion by Culverwell, Ch. IV et seq. (abridged in Campagnac, pp. 227 ff.), but also More's statement in *Ench. Eth.*, pp. 113-15. The line of descent to the Cambridge Platonists is lucidly set out by Hoopes.

[19] Cf. Culverwell, p. 29: 'as *Aquinas* does very well tells us, the Law of *Nature* is nothing else but *participatio Legis æternæ in Rationali creatura*, the copying out of the eternal Law, and the imprinting of it upon the breast of a Rational being'. The Thomistic passage referred to is *S. th.*, II : I, xci, 2.

[20] Freely adapted from *Phaedrus*, 246c: 'the imperfect soul (ἡ δὲ πτερορρυήσασα), losing her wings and dropping in her flight settles on the solid ground' etc.

[21] 1 *Corinthians* 2. 11. [22] *Hebrews* 9. 8 and 2 *Timothy* 1. 10.

The Excellency and Nobleness of True Religion 151

and declare his Mind to us. When we *look unto the Earth, then behold darkness and dimness of anguish*, that I may use those words of the Prophet *Esay*:[23] But when we look towards Heaven, then behold light breaking forth upon us, like the Eye-lids of the Morning, and spreading its wings over the Horizon of mankind sitting in darkness and the shadow of death, *to guide our feet into the way of peace*.[24]

But besides this *Outward revelation of God's will to men*, there is also an *Inward impression* of it on their Minds and Spirits, which is in a more special manner attributed to God. We cannot see divine things but in a divine light: God only, who is the true light, and in whom there is no darkness at all, can so shine out of himself upon our glassy Understandings, as to beget in them a picture of himself, his own Will and Pleasure, and turn the Soul (as the phrase is in *Job* 38.) חוֹתָם כָּחֹמֶר like wax or *clay to the Seal*[25] of his own light and love. He that made our Souls in his own image and likeness, can easily find a way into them. The Word that God speaks having found a way into the Soul, imprints it self there as with the point of a diamond, and becomes λόγος ἐγγεγραμμένος ἐν τῇ τοῦ μανθάνοντος ψυχῇ, that I may borrow *Plato*'s expression.[26] Men may teach the *Grammar* and *Rhetorick*, but God teaches the *Divinity*. Thus it is God alone that acquaints the Soul with the *Truths of Revelation*: and he also it is that does strengthen and raise the Soul to better apprehensions even of *Natural Truth*: God being that in the *Intellectual* world which the Sun is in the Sensible, (ὅπερ ἐν τοῖς αἰσθητοῖς ὁ ἥλιος, τοῦτο ἐν τοῖς νοητοῖς ὁ Θεός)[27] as some of the ancient Fathers love to speak, and the ancient Philosophers too, who meant God by their *Intellectus Agens*,[28] whose proper work they supposed to be not so much to enlighten the *Object*, as the *Faculty*.

[23] *Isaiah* 8. 22.   [24] *Luke* 1. 79.   [25] *Job* 38. 14.

[26] *Phaedrus*, 276a: 'an intelligent word graven in the soul of the learner'.

[27] The analogy between God and the sun or the soul is a Platonic commonplace (cf. *Respublica*, VII, 509 ff.). Among numerous variations on this theme, cf. Philo, *Quis rerum divinarum heres*, LIII, 263: 'what the reasoning faculty is in us, the sun is in the world, since both of them are light-bringers, one sending forth to the whole world the light which our senses perceive, the other shedding mental rays upon ourselves through the medium of apprehension'.

[28] As Aristotle sometimes did—at least according to Cicero, *De nat. deo.*, I, 13. On the Aristotelian conception of *intellectus agens* (νοῦς, 'mind'), see C. J. de Vogel, *Greek Philosophy*, Vol. II: *Aristotle, the Early Peripatetic School and the Early Academy* (Leyden, 1953), pp. 22 ff., 33 f., 215 f.

CHAP. II

We have done with the first Head, and come now to discourse with the like brevity on another (our purpose being to insist most upon the third Particular, viz. *The Nobleness of Religion in its Properties*, after we have handled the Second) which is *The Excellency and Nobleness of Religion in regard of its Nature*, whether it be taken *in abstracto* or *in concreto*; which we shall treat of promiscuously, without any rigid tying of our selves to exact Rules of Art: and so we shall glance at it in these following Notions, rising as it were step by step.

1. *A Good man, that is actuated by Religion, lives above the World and all Mundane delights and excellencies.* The Soul is a more vigorous and puissant thing, when it is once restored to the possession of its own Being, then to be bounded within the narrow Sphere of Mortality, or to be streightned within the narrow prison of Sensual and Corporeal delights; but it will break forth with the greatest vehemency, and ascend upwards towards Immortality: and when it converses more intimately with Religion, it can scarce look back upon its own converses (though in a lawfull way) with Earthly things, without a being touch'd with an *holy Shamefac'dness* & a *modest Blushing*; and, as *Porphyry* speaks of *Plotinus*, ἐῴκει μὲν αἰσχυνομένῳ ὅτι ἐν σώματι εἴη, it seems to be shamed that it should be in the Body.[29] It is only True Religion that teaches and enables men to dye to this world and to all Earthly things, and to rise above that vaporous Sphere of Sensual and Earthly pleasures, which darken the Mind and hinder it from enjoying the brightness of Divine light; the proper motion of Religion is still upwards to its first Original. Whereas on the contrary the Souls of wicked men ὑποβρύχιαι συμπεριφέρονται, as *Plato* somewhere speaks,[30] being moistned with the Exudations of their Sensual parts become heavy and sink down into Earthly things, and couch as near as may be to the Centre. Wicked men bury their Souls in their Bodies:[31] all their projects and designes are bounded within the compass of this

---

[29] Porphyry, *Vit. Plot.*, I.

[30] *Phaedrus*, 248a: 'not being strong enough they are carried round below the surface, plunging (ἀδυνατοῦσαι δὲ ὑποβρύχιαι ξυμπεριφέρονται), treading on one another, each striving to be first'.

[31] Cf. Whichcote, *Aphorisms*, § 294: '*Good men*, under the Power of Reason and Religion, are *Free*; in the worst Condition: *Bad men*, under the Power of Lust and Vice, are *Slaves*; in the best Condition.' See further below, pp. 158, 164, 332, etc.

Earth which they tread upon. The fleshly mind never minds any thing but Flesh, and never rises above the Outward Matter, but alwaies creeps up and down like Shadows upon the Surface of the Earth: and if it begins at any time to make any faint assays upwards, it presently finds it self laden with a weight of Sensuality which draws it down again. It was the Opinion of the *Academicks* that the Souls of wicked men after their death could not of a long season depart from the Graves and Sepulchers where their Mates were buried; but there wandred up and down in a desolate manner, as not being able to leave those Bodies which they were so much wedded to in this life.[32]

2. *A Good man, one that is actuated by Religion, lives in converse with his own Reason;* he lives at the height of his own Being. This a great Philosopher makes the Property of a Good man, μόνος ὁ τὴν ἀρετὴν ἔχων ἑαυτῷ συγγίνεσθαι δύναται, καὶ στέργειν ἑαυτόν· He knows how to converse with himself, and truly to love and value himself:[33] he measures not himself, like the Epicure, by his inferior and Earthly part, but by an Immortal Essence and that of him which is from above; and so does ἐπὶ τὴν ἐν ἑαυτῷ ἀρχὴν ἀναβαίνειν, climbe up to the height of that Immortal principle which is within him.[34] The *Stoicks* thought no man a fit Auditor of their *Ethicks*, till he were dispossess'd of that Opinion, That Man was nothing but συμπλοκὴ ψυχῆς καὶ σώματος, as professing to teach men how to live only κατὰ λόγον,[35] as they speak. Perhaps their Divinity was in some things too rigid; but I am sure a Good man acts the best of this their doctrine in the best sense, and knows better how *to reverence himself*, without any Self-flattery or admiration, then ever any *Stoick* did. He principally looks upon himself as being what he is rather by *his Soul* then by *his Body*:[36] he values himself by *his Soul*, that Being which hath the greatest affinity with God; and so does not seek himself in the *fading Vanities* of this life, nor in those poor and *low delights* of his *Senses*, as wicked men doe; but as the Philosopher doth well express it, ὅση δύναμις φεύγειν ἀπὸ τοῦ σώματος βούλεται, καὶ ἀπὸ τῶν σωματικῶν

---

[32] Cf. Plato's report in *Phaedo*, 81c–d.
[33] Abbreviated from Proclus, *Tim.*, 173c: 'he alone among partial animals [such as we are] who possess virtue, is able to associate with, and love himself with a parental affection'.
[34] Cf. Plotinus, VI, ix, 3.
[35] 'according to reason' (Diogenes Laertius, VII, 86; *SVF*, III, 43).
[36] Cf. above, p. 143.

παθῶν εἰς ἑαυτὸν συννεύειν·[37] and when the Soul thus retires into it self, and views its own worth and Excellency, it presently finds a chast and Virgin-love stirr'd up within it self towards it self, and is from within the more excited and obliged εἰς τὴν φυλακὴν τοῦ οἰκείου ἀξιώματος, as *Simplicius* speaks, to mind the preserving of its own dignity and glory.[38] To conclude this Particular, A Good man endeavours to walk by Eternal and Unchangeable Rules of Reason; *Reason* in a Good man sits in the Throne, & governs all the Powers of his Soul in a sweet harmony and agreement with it self: whereas Wicked men live only ζωὴν δοξαστικὴν,[39] being led up and down by the foolish fires of their own Sensual apprehensions. In wicked men there is a *Democracy* of wild *Lusts* and *Passions*,[40] which violently hurry the Soul up and down with restless motions. All Sin and Wickedness is στάσις καὶ ὕβρις τῆς ψυχῆς, a Sedition stirred up in the Soul by the Sensitive Powers against Reason. It was one of the great Evils that *Solomon* saw under the Sun, *Servants on horseback, and Princes going as servants upon the ground*.[41] We may find the *Moral* of it in every wicked man, whose *Souls* are only as *Servants* to wait upon their *Senses*. In all such men the whole Course of Nature is turned upside down, and the Cardinal points of Motion in this little world[42] are changed to contrary positions: But the Motions of a Good man are Methodical, Regular and Concentrical to Reason. It's a fond imagination that Religion should extinguish Reason; whenas, Religion makes it more illustrious and vigorous; and they that live most in the exercise of *Religion*, shall find their *Reason* most enlarged. I might adde, that *Reason* in relation to the capacitating of Man for converse with God was thought by some to be the *Formal Difference* of Man. *Plutarch*

---

[37] Simplicius, *In Epict.*, Praefatio. The sense of the statement is given in the words following.

[38] *Ibid.*   [39] 'a life of opinions or mere conjectures'.

[40] The sentiment is based on the common Renaissance disapprobation of democracy. Cf. Whichcote, *Aphorisms*, § 479: 'The Government of Man *should be* the Monarchy of Reason; it *is* too often a Democracy of Passions, or Anarchy of Humours.' See also Whichcote, *Discourses*, I, 173, and More, *Psychozoia*, II, 128 ff.

[41] *Ecclesiastes* 10. 7.

[42] The standard designation of man and the sublunary world in general, implying a correspondence with the greater world of the universe. On the commonplace nature of this idea, see the writers I cited in *Notes and Queries*, n.s., VII (1960), 54–6, and X (1963), 282–6.

after a large debate whether *Brutes* had not *Reason* in them as well as *Man*, concludes it negatively upon this ground, Because they had no knowledge and sense of the Deity, οἷς οὐκ ἐγγίνεται Θεοῦ νόησις.⁴³ In *Tully*'s account *this Capableness of Religion* seem'd to be nothing different from *Rationality*, and therefore he doubts not to give this for the most proper Characterism of *Reason*, That it is *Vinculum Dei & Hominis*.⁴⁴ And so with them (not to name others of the same apprehensions) *animal Rationale* & *animal capax Religionis* seem'd to be of the like importance; *Reason* as enabling and fitting Man *to converse with God* by *knowing* him and *loving* him, being a character most unquestionably differencing *Man* from *Brute* creatures.

3. *A Good man, one that is informed by True Religion, lies above himself, and is raised to an intimate Converse with the Divinity*. He moves in a larger Sphere then his own Being, and cannot be content to enjoy himself, excepting he may enjoy God too, and himself in God.

This we shall consider two ways.

1. In the *Self-denial* of Good men; they are content and ready to deny themselves for God. I mean not that they should *deny* their own *Reason*, as some would have it; for that were to deny a Beam of Divine light, and so to deny God, in stead of denying our selves for him. It is better resolved by some Philosophers in this point, that ἕπεσθαι λόγῳ *to follow Reason* is ἕπεσθαι Θεῷ *to follow God*; and again, Λόγῳ δὲ ὀρθῷ πείθεσθαι καὶ Θεῷ, ταυτόν ἐστι.⁴⁵ But by *Self-denial* I mean, the Soul's quitting all its own interest in it self, and an entire Resignation of it self to him as to all points of service and duty: and thus the Soul loves it self in God, and lives in the possession not so much of its own Being as of the Divinity; desiring only to be great in God, to glory in his Light, and spread it self in his Fulness; to be fill'd alwaies by him, and to empty it self again into him; to receive all from him, and to expend all for him; and so to live not as its own, but as God's. The highest ambition of a Good man is to serve the Will

---

⁴³ A rather extreme report of the 'conclusion' in Plutarch's *Bruta animalia ratione uti* [*Gryllus*], X.

⁴⁴ 'the bond (which unites) God and Man'. The phrase is of course one of the great commonplaces of Western thought.

⁴⁵ Cf. Hierocles, *Aur. carm.*, XIV: 'to be obedient to right reason is the same thing as to obey God, because a rational being, when it enjoys its due clarity, wills the same things that the divine law itself wills; and a soul disposed as is the mind of God, is consentient with him . . .'

of God: he takes no pleasure in himself nor in any thing within himself further then he sees a stamp of God upon it. Whereas wicked men are imprisoned within the narrow circumference of their own Beings, and perpetually frozen into a cold *Self-love* which binds up all the Innate vigour of their Souls, that it cannot break forth or express it self in any noble way. The Soul in which Religion rules, saies as S. *Paul* did, *I live; and yet not I, but Christ liveth in me*.[46] On the contrary, a Wicked man swells in his own thoughts, and pleaseth himself more or less with the imagination of a *Self-sufficiency*. The *Stoicks*, seeing they could not raise themselves up to God, endeavour to bring down God to their own Model, imagining the Deity to be nothing else but some greater kind of *Animal*, and a Wise man to be almost one of his Peers.[47] And this is more or less the Genius of Wicked men, they will be something in themselves, they wrap up themselves in their own Being, move up and down in a Sphere of *Self-love*, live a professed Independency upon God, and maintain a *Meum & Tuum* between God and themselves. It's the Character only of a Good man to be able to deny and disown himself, and to make a full surrender of himself unto God; forgetting himself, and minding nothing but the Will of his Creator; triumphing in nothing more then in his own *Nothingness*, and in the *Allness* of the Divinity. But indeed this his being Nothing is the only way to be all things; this his having nothing the truest way of possessing all things.

2. As a Good man lives *above himself* in a way of *Self-denial*, so he lives also above himself as he lives in *the Enjoyment of God*: and this is the very Soul and Essence of True Religion, to unite the Soul in the nearest intimacy and conjunction with God, who is πηγὴ ζωῆς, πηγὴ νοῦ, ῥίζα ψυχῆς, as *Plotinus* speaks.[48] Then indeed the Soul lives *most nobly*, when it feels it self to live and move and have its Being in God;[49] which though the Law of Nature makes the Common condition of all created Being, yet it is only True Religion that can give us a more feeling and comfortable sense of it. God is not present to Wicked men, when his Almighty Essence supports them and maintains them in Being; ἀλλ' ἔστι τῷ δυναμένῳ θίγειν παρόν, *but he is present to him that can touch him*, hath an inward feeling knowledge of God

---

[46] *Galatians* 2. 20.   [47] Cf. Seneca, *Ep.*, XXXI and LII.
[48] In VI, ix, 9: 'the well-spring of Life, well-spring also of Intellect, ... root of Soul'. Cf. Cudworth, *Int. System*, p. 134 (I, iii, 29).
[49] *Acts* 17. 28. Cf. above, p. 57.

and is intimately united to him; τῷ δὲ ἀδυνατοῦντι οὐ πάρεστι, but to him that cannot thus touch him he is not present.⁵⁰

Religion is Life and Spirit, which flowing out from God who is that Αὐτοζωή⁵¹ that hath life in himself, returns to him again as into its own Original, carrying the Souls of Good men up with it. The Spirit of Religion is alwaies ascending upwards, and spreading it self through the whole Essence of the Soul, loosens it from a Self-confinement and narrowness, and so renders it more capacious of Divine Enjoyment. God envies not his people any good, but being infinitely bountifull is pleased to impart himself to them in this life, so far as they are capable of his Communications: they stay not for all their happiness till they come to heaven. Religion alwaies carries its reward along with it, and when it acts most vigorously upon the Mind and Spirit of man, it then most of all fills it with an inward sense of *Divine* sweetness. To conclude, *To walk with God* is in Scripture made the Character of a Good man, and it's the highest perfection and privilege of Created Nature to converse with the Divinity. Whereas on the contrary Wicked men converse with nothing but their *Lusts* and the *Vanities* of this fading life, which here flatter them for a while with unhallowed delights and a mere Shadow of Contentment; and when these are gone, they find both *Substance* and *Shadow* too to be lost Eternally. But true Goodness brings in a constant revenue of solid and substantial Satisfaction to the Spirit of a good man, delighting alwaies to sit by those Eternal Springs that feed and maintain it: the Spirit of a Good man (as it is well express'd by the Philosopher) ἀκινέτως ἐνίδρυται ἐν τῇ οὐσίᾳ τῆς θείας ἀγαθότητος,⁵² & is alwaies drinking in Fountain-Goodness, and fills it self more and more, till it be filled with the fulness of God.

CHAP. III

Having discoursed *the Nobleness of Religion* in its *Original* and *Nature*; we come now to consider the *Excellency of Religion in its Properties*, its *proper Effects* and vital *Operations*. In treating of this Third Particular we shall, (as formerly we have done) without tying our selves precisely to any strict Rules of Art and Method, confound the Notions

---

⁵⁰ Plotinus, VI, ix, 7.

⁵¹ An adaptation of Plotinus' adjective αὐτοζῶν, 'self-living' (III, viii, 8).

⁵² Simplicius, *In Epict.*, I, actually reads ἀκινήτως ἐνιθρῦσθαι ἐν τῇ ὑπάρξει τῆς θείας ἀγαθότητος ('fixed in God's essential goodness').

of Religion *in abstracto* and *in concreto* together, handling them promiscuously. As Religion is a *noble* thing, 1. in respect of its *Original*, 2. in respect of its *Nature*; so also 3. in respect of its *Properties* and *Effects*.

1. The First *Propertie* and *Effect* of True Religion whereby it expresseth its own *Nobleness* is this, *That it widens and enlarges all the Faculties of the Soul, and begets a true Ingenuity, Liberty and Amplitude, the most free and Generous Spirit, in the Minds of Good men*. Those in whom Religion rules are בני חורים,⁵³ there is a true Generous Spirit within them, which shews the Nobleness of their Extraction. The Jewes have a good Maxime to this purpose, בתלמוד תורה אין לך בן חורין אלא מי שעוסק, *None truly Noble, but he that applies himself to Religion and a faithfull observance of the Divine Law*.⁵⁴ *Tully* could see so much in his *Natural Philosophy* as made him say, *Scientia Naturæ ampliat animum, & ad divina attollit*:⁵⁵ But this is most true of Religion, that in an higher sense it does work the Soul into a true & divine *amplitude*. There is a living Soul of Religion in Good men which, spreading it self through all their Faculties, spirits all the Wheels of motion, and enables them to dilate and extend themselves more fully upon God and all Divine things, without being pinched or streightened within themselves. Whereas wicked men are of most *narrow* and *confined* Spirits, they are so contracted by the *pinching particularities* of Earthly and created things, so imprisoned in a dark dungeon of *Sensuality* and *Selfishness*, so streightned through their *Carnal* designs and *Ends*, that they cannot stretch themselves nor look beyond the Horizon of *Time* and *Sense*.

The nearer any Being comes to God, who is that Infinite fullness that fills all in all, the more *vast* and *large* and *unbounded* it is; as the further it slides from him, the more it is *streightned* & *confined*; as *Plato* hath long since concluded concerning the condition of Sensual men, that they live ὀστρέου δίκην, *like a Shel-fish*, and can never move up and down but in their own prison, which they ever carry about with them.⁵⁶ Were I to define *Sin*, I would call it *The sinking of a*

---

⁵³ 'sons of nobles' (from *Ecclesiastes* 10. 17). The Hebrew phrase is an integral part of the complete sentence. ⁵⁴ Cf. *Pirke Aboth*, VI, 2.

⁵⁵ 'The knowledge of nature broadens the mind, and brings it to divine things.' The statement merges several passages in Cicero, e.g., *De officiis*, II, 5; *De nat. deo., passim*; etc.

⁵⁶ Cf. *Phaedrus*, 250c: ὀστρέου τρόπον δεδεσμευμένοι ('imprisoned in the body, like an oyster in his shell').

Mans Soul from God into a Sensual Selfishness. All the *Freedom* that wicked men have, is but (like that of banished men) to wander up and down in the wilderness of this world from one den and cave to another.[57]

The more high and *Noble* any Being is, so much *the deeper radication* have all its *Innate vertues* and Properties within it, and are by so much the *more Universal* in their issues and actings upon other things: and such an inward living principle of virtue and activity further heightned and united and informed with *Light* and *Truth*, we may call *Liberty*. Of this truly-noble and divine Liberty Religion is the Mother and Nurse, leading the Soul to God, and so impregnating that inward vital principle of *activity* amd *vigour* that is embosom'd in it, that it is able without any inward disturbance and resistance from any controlling Lusts to exercise it self, and act with the greatest complacency in the most full and ample manner upon that *First, Universal* and *Unbounded* Essence which is God himself. The most generous Freedom can never be took in its full and just dimensions and proportion, but then when all the Powers of the Soul exercise and spend themselves in the most large and ample manner upon the Infinite and Essential Goodness, as upon their own most proper Object. If we should ask a Good man, when he finds himself best at ease, when he finds himself most free; his answer would be, When he is under the most powerfull constraints of divine Love.[58] There are a sort of *Mechanical* Christians in the world, that not finding *Religion* acting like *a living form* within them, satisfie themselves only to make an *Art* of it, and rather *inform* and actuate *it*, then are *informed by it*; and setting it such bounds and limits as may not exceed the short and scant measures of their own home-born Principles, then they endeavour to fit the Notions of their own Minds as so many *Examples* to it: and it being a Circle of their own making, they can either ampliate or contract it accordingly as they can force their own Minds and Dispositions to agree and suit with it. But true Religion indeed is no *Art*, but an *inward Nature* that conteins all the laws and measures of its motion within it self. A Good man finds not his Religion *without* him, but as a living Principle *within* him; and all his Faculties are still endeavouring to unite themselves

[57] Cf. Whichcote, *Sermons*, p. 71: 'The Mind diverted from God wanders in Darkness and Confusion . . .' Similarly, Milton's fallen angels 'found no end, in wandring mazes lost' (*Paradise Lost*, II, 561).

[58] On the paradox of the love that liberates even as it 'constraineth (2 *Corinthians* 5. 14), see Cudworth, above, p. 125.

more and more in the nearest intimacy with it as with their proper Perfection. There is that amiableness in Religion, that strong Sympathy between the Soul and it, that it needs carry no Testimonials or Commendations along with it. If it could be supposed that God should plant a Religion in the Soul that had no affinity or alliance with it, it would grow there but as a strange slip. But God when he gives his Laws to men, does not by virtue of his *Absolute dominion* dictate any thing at randome, and in such an arbitratious way as some imagine; but he measures all by his own Eternal Goodness. Had God himself been any thing else then the *First and Greatest Good* of man, then to have loved him with the full strength of all our Faculties should not have been *the First and Greatest Commandment*, as our Saviour tells us it is.[59] Some are apt to look upon God as some *Peevish* and *Self-will'd* thing, because themselves are such: and seeing that their own *Absolute* and naked *Wills* are for the most part the *Rules* of all their actions and the impositions which they lay upon others; they think that Heaven's Monarchy is such an *arbitrary* thing too, as being govern'd by nothing else but by an *Almighty Absolute Will*. But the Soul that is acquainted most intimately with the *Divine Will*, would more certainly resolve us, That God's *Unchangeable Goodness* (which makes the Divinity an Uniform thing and to settle together upon its own Centre, as I may speak with reverence) is also *the Unchangeable Rule of his Will*; neither can he any more swerve from it, then he can swerve from himself. Nor does he charge any Duty upon man without consulting first of all with his *Goodness*: which being the Original and adequate Object of a Good man's Will and affections, it must needs be that all the issues and effluxes of it be entertain'd with an answerable complacency & chearfulness. This is the hinge upon which all true Religion turns, the proper Centre about which it moves; which taking a fast & sure hold of an innate and correspondent Principle in the Soul of man, raiseth it up above the confines of Mortality, and in the day of its mighty power makes it become a free-will-Offering unto God.

CHAP. IV

2. The Second *Property* or *Effect of Religion*, whereby it discovers its own *Nobleness* (and it is somewhat a-kin to the former Particular,

[59] *Matthew* 26. 17.

The Excellency and Nobleness of True Religion

and will help further to illustrate and enforce it) is this, *That it restores a Good man to a just power and dominion over himself and his own Will, enables him to overcome himself, his own Self-will and Passions, and to command himself & all his Powers for God.* 'Tis only Religion that restores that αὐτεξούσιον⁶⁰ which the Stoical Philosophy so impotently pretended to; it is this only that enthrones man's deposed Reason, and establisheth within him a just Empire over all those blind Powers and Passions which so impetuously rend a man from the possession and enjoiment of himself. Those turbulent and unruly, uncertain and unconstant Motions of *Passion* and *Self-will* that dwell in degenerate Minds, *divide* them perpetually from themselves, and are alwaies molding several factions and tumulous combinations within them against the dominion of *Reason*. And the only way to *unite* man firmly to himself is by uniting him to God, and establishing in him a firm amity and agreement with the First and Primitive Being.

There is nothing in the World so boisterous as a man's own *Self-will*,⁶¹ which is never guided by any fixt or steddy Rules, but is perpetually hurried to and fro by a blind and furious *impetus* of *Pride* and *Passions* issuing from within it self. This is the true source and Spring of all that *Envy, Malice, Bitterness of Spirit, Malecontentedness* and *Impatiency*, of all those *black and dark Passions*, those *inordinate desires and lusts*, that reign in the hearts and lives of wicked men. A man's own *Self-will* throws him out of all true enjoyment of his own Being: therefore it was our Saviours counsell to his disciples, *In patience possess your Souls*.⁶² We may say that of that *Self-will* which is lodg'd in the heart of a wicked man, as the Jews speak of the יצר הרע *figmentum malum* so often mention'd in their Writings, that it is שר המות, the Prince of death and darkness which is at continua enmity with Heaven, and זוהם הנחש the filthiness and poison of the

---

⁶⁰ 'αὐτεξούσιον, *sui potestas*, self power, commonly called liberty of will' (Cudworth, *Freewill*, p. 63 and *passim*). It is related to τὸ ἡγεμονικὸν (above, p. 131 and note), as Cudworth in particular made repeatedly clear (see Gysi, pp. 16 ff. and *passim*).

⁶¹ Smith's concern to p. 164 (as also thereafter) is a variation on the frequent denunciations by the Cambridge Platonists of self-will as of 'that monstrous Fiend, that deeply-rooted Dragon of Hell, *Self-love*' (More, *Dialogues*, I, 274). See above, pp. 98 ff., and below, pp. 188 ff., but also: Whichcote, *Discourses*, III, 174; More, *Discourses*, V, and Ward, pp. 12–15, 256–88; Worthington, *Discourses*, Disc. I; etc.

⁶² *Luke* 21. 19.

Serpent.⁶³ This is the Seed of the Evil Spirit which is perpetually at enmity with the Seed of God and the Heaven-born Nature:⁶⁴ It's design and scope is with a Giant-like pride to climb up into the Throne of the Almighty, and to establish an unbounded Tyranny in contradiction to the Will of God, which is nothing else but the Issue and Efflux of his Eternal and Unbounded Goodness. This is the very Heart of the old *Adam* that is within men. This is the Hellish Spirit of *Self-will*: it would solely prescribe laws to all things; it would fain be the source and fountain of all affaires and events; it would judge all things at its own Tribunal. They in whose Spirits this Principle rules, would have their own Fancies and Opinions, their perverse and boisterous Wills to be the just Square and Measure of all *Good* and *Evil*; these are the Plumb-lines they applie to all things to find out their *Rectitude* or *Obliquity*. He that will not submit himself to nor comply with *the Eternal and Uncreated Will*, but in stead of it endeavours to set up his own will, makes himself the *most real Idol* in the world, and exalts himself against all that is called God and ought to be worshipp'd. To worship a graven Image, or to make cakes & burn incense to the Queen of heaven, is not a worse Idolatry then it is for a man to set up *Self-will*, to devote himself to the serving of it, and to give up himself to a complyance with his own will as contrary to the Divine and Eternal Will. When God made the World, he did not make it merely for the exercise of his Almighty power, and then throw it out of his hands, and leave it alone to subsist by it self as a thing that had no further relation to him: But he derived himself through the whole Creation, so gathering and knitting up all the several pieces of it again; that as the first production and the continued Subsistence of all things is from himself, so the ultimate resolution and tendency of all things might be to him. Now that which first endeavoured a Divorce between God and his Creation, and to make a Conquest of it, was that Diabolical *Arrogancy* and *Self-will* that crept up and wound it self Serpent-like into apostate Minds and Spirits. This is the true strain of that Hellish nature, to live independently of

---

⁶³ The Hebrew phrase said to correspond to the Latin *figmentum malum* means 'the evil impulse' (*vide* Joseph Jacobs, 'Yeẓer ha-Ra'', in *The Jewish Encyclopedia*, new ed. [1925], XII, 601 ff.). The other two phrases are accurately translated in the text. The entire statement appears to be based on the traditional identification of Satan with both 'the evil impulse' and 'the angel of death' (consult *Talmud*: Baba Bathra, 16a).

⁶⁴Cf. *Genesis* 3. 15—the *protevangelium* referred to above, p. 62 and note.

The Excellency and Nobleness of True Religion 163

God, and to derive the *Principles* from *another Beginning*, and carry on the line of all motions and operations to *another End*, then God himself, by whom and to whom and for whom all things subsist.

From what hath been said concerning this powerful and dangerous Enemy that wars against our Souls and against the Divine Will, may the Excellency and Noble Spirit of True Religion appear, in that it tames the impetuousness and turbulency of this *Self-will*. Then indeed does Religion perform the highest and bravest conquests, then does it display the greatness of its strength and the excellency of its power, when it overcomes this great *Arimanius*,[65] that hath so firmly seated himself in the very Centre of the Soul. איזהו גבור, *Who is the man of Courage and Valour?* הכובש את יצרו, *it is he that subdues his Concupiscence*, his own Will; it is a Jewish Maxime attributed to *Ben Zoma*,[66] and a most undoubted truth. This was the grand *Lesson* that our great Lord & Master came to teach us, viz. *To deny our own Wils*; neither was there any thing that he endeavor'd more to promote by his own *Example*, as he tells us of himself, *I came down from heaven, not to doe mine own will, but the will of him that sent me*;[67] and again, *Lo, I come (in the volume of the Book it is written of me) to do thy will, O God, yea thy Law is within my heart*:[68] and in his greatest agonies, with a clear and chearful submission to the Divine will, he often repeats it, *Not my will, but thy will be done*:[69] and so he hath taught us to pray and so to live. This indeed is the true life and spirit of Religion, this is Religion in its Meridian altitude, its just dimensions. A true Christian that hath power over his own Will, may live nobly and happily, and enjoy a perpetually-clear heaven within *the Serenity* of his own Mind. When the Sea of this World is most rough and tempestuous about him, then can he ride safely at Anchor within the haven, by a sweet complyance of his will with God's Will. He can look about him, and

---

[65] Ahriman (Angra Mainyu), who according to Zoroastrianism is the Destructive Spirit in eternal conflict with Ohrmazd (Ahura Mazdāh), the Good Principle. Cf. R. C. Zaehner, *The Dawn and Twilight of Zoroastrianism* (1961), Ch. XII and *passim*; but see also Cudworth, *Int. System*, pp. 213, 289 ff. (I, iv, 13 and 16).

[66] Cf. *Pirke Aboth*, IV, 1: 'Ben Zoma said: ... Who is strong? He who controls his passions, as it is said Proverbs xvi. 32: "Better is the long suffering than the mighty, and one that ruleth his spirit than one who taketh a city" '.

[67] *John* 6. 38.   [68] *Psalms* 40. 7–8 (cf. *Hebrews* 10.7).
[69] *Luke* 22. 42.

with an even and indifferent Mind behold the World either to smile or frown upon him; neither will he abate of the least of his *Contentment*, for all the ill and unkind usage he meets withall in this life. He that hath got the Mastery over his own Will, feels no violence from without, finds no contests within; and like a strong man, keeping his house, he preserves all his Goods in safety: and when God calls for him out of this state of Mortality, he finds in himself a power to lay down his own life; neither is it so much taken from him, as quietly and freely surrendered up by him. This is the highest piece of prowess, the noblest atchievement, by which a man becomes Lord over himself, and the Master of his own Thoughts, Motions and Purposes. This is the Royal prerogative, the high dignity conferred upon Good men by our Lord and Saviour, whereby they overcoming this both His and their Enemy, their *Self-will* and *Passions*, are enabled to sit down with him in his Throne, as he overcoming in another way, is set down with his Father in his Throne; as the phrase is *Revelat.* 3.[70]

Religion begets the most *Heroick, Free and Generous motions* in the Minds of Good men. There is no where so much of a truly Magnanimous and raised Spirit as in those who are best acquainted with the power of Religion. Other men are Slaves and Captives to one Vanity or other: but the truly Religious is above them all, and able to command himself and all his Powers for God. That *bravery* and *gallantness* which seems to be in the great *Nimrods* of this world[71] is nothing else but the *swelling* of their own unbounded *pride* and *vain-glory*. It hath been observed of the greatest Monarchs of the world, that in the midst of their *Triumphs* they themselves have been led *Captives* to one *Vice* or another. All the *Gallantry* and *Puissance* which the Bravest Spirits of the world boast of, is but a poor *confined* thing, and extends it self only to some *Particular* Cases and Circumstances: But the *Valour* and *Puissance* of a Soul impregnated by Religion hath in a sort an *Universal* Extent, as S. *Paul* speaks of himself, *I can doe all things through Christ which strengtheneth me*;[72] it is not determined to this or that Particular Object or Time or Place, but πάντα *all things* whatsoever belong to a Creature fall under the level thereof. Religion is by S. *Paul* described to be πνεῦμα δυνάμεως *the Spirit of power* in opposition to *the Spirit of fear*, 2 Tim. 1.[73] as all *Sin* is by *Simplicius* wel described to be ἀδυναμία *impotency & weakness*.[74] Sin by its deadly infusions into the

---

[70] *Revelation* 3. 21.
[71] Cf. above, p. 94, note.
[72] *Philippians* 4. 13.
[73] 2 *Timothy* 1. 7.
[74] *In Epict.*, I.

The Excellency and Nobleness of True Religion 165

Soul of man wasts and eats out the innate vigour of the Soul, and casts it into such a deep Lethargy, as that it is not able to recover it self: But Religion, like that *Balsamum vitæ*, being once conveighed into the Soul, awakens and enlivens it, and makes it renew its strength like an Eagle, and mount strongly upwards towards Heaven; and so uniting the Soul to God, the Centre of life and strength, it renders it undaunted and invincible. Who can tell the inward life and vigour that the Soul may be fill'd with, when once it is in conjunction with an Almighty Essence? There is a latent and hidden virtue in the Soul of man which then begins to discover it self when the Divine Spirit spreads forth its influences upon it. Every thing the more Spiritual it is, and the higher and nobler it is in its Being, the more active and vigorous it is; as the more any thing falls and sinks into *Matter*, the more dull and sluggish & unwieldy it is. The *Platonists* were wont to call all things that participated most of *Matter* ὄντως μὴ ὄντα·[75] Now nothing doth more purifie, more sublimate and exalt the Soul then Religion, when the Soul suffers God *to sit* within it *as a refiner and purifier of Silver*, and when it *abides the day of his coming; for he is like a refiner's fire and like fullers sope*, Mal. 3.[76] Thus the Soul being purified and spiritualliz'd, and changed more and more into the glorious Image of God, is *able to doe all* things, *out of weakness is made strong*, gives proof of its Divine vigour and activity, and shews it self to be a Noble and Puissant Spirit, such as God did at first create it.

CHAP. V

3. The Third *Property* or *Effect* whereby *Religion* discovers its own *Excellency*, is this, *That it directs and enables a man to propound to himself the Best End and Scope of life*, viz. *The Glory of God the Highest Being, and his own assimilation or becoming like unto God.*

That Christian in whom Religion rules powerfully, is not so low in his ambitions as to pursue any of the things of this world as his *Ultimate End*: his Soul is too big for earthly designes and interests; but understanding himself to come from God, he is continually returning to him again. It is not worth the while for the Mind of Man to pursue any Perfection lower then its own, or to aim at any *End* more

---

[75] 'not actually existing'. See above, p. 38, note.
[76] Cf. *Malachi* 3. 2.

ignoble then it self is. There is nothing that more *streightens* and *confines* the free-born Soul then the *particularity, indigency* and *penury* of that *End* which it pursues: when it complies most of all with this lower world, τότε μάλιστα τὸ αὐτεξούσιον ἀμφισβητήσιμον ἔχει, as is well observed by an excellent Philosopher, the true *Nobleness* and *Freedome* of it is then *most disputable*, and the Title it holds to true *Liberty* becomes most litigious.[77] It never more slides and degenerates from it self, then when it becomes enthrall'd to some *Particular interest*: as on the other side it never acts more *freely* or *fully*, then when it extends it self upon the most *Universal End*. Every thing is so much the more Noble, *quò longiores habet fines*,[78] as was well observ'd by *Tully*. As *low Ends debase* a mans spirit, supplant & rob it of its birth-right; so the *Highest* and *Last End* raises and *ennobles* it, and *enlarges* it into a more Universal and comprehensive Capacity of enjoying that one Unbounded Goodness which is God himself: it makes it spread and dilate it self in the Infinite Sphere of the Divine Being and Blessedness, it makes it live in the Fulness of Him that fills all in all.

Every thing is most properly such as the *End* is which is aim'd at: the Mind of man is alwaies shaping it self into a conformity as much as may be to that which is his *End*; and the nearer it draws to it in the atchievement thereof, the greater likeness it bears to it. There is a Plastick Virtue, a Secret Energy issuing forth from that which the Mind propounds to itself as its *End*, to mold and fashion it according to its own Model. The soul is alwaies stamp'd with the same Characters that are engraven upon the *End* it aims at; and while it converses with it, and sets it self before it, *it is turned as Wax to the Seal*, to use that phrase in *Job*.[79] Man's Soul conceives all its Thoughts and Imaginations before his *End*, as *Laban*'s Ewes did their young before the Rods in the wateringtroughs.[80] He that pursues any *worldly* interest or *earthly* thing as his *End*, becomes himself also γεώδης *Earthly*: & the more the Soul directs it self to God, the more it becomes θεοειδὴς *God-like*,[81] deriving a print of that glory and beauty upon it self which it converseth with, as it is excellently set forth by the Apostle, *But we all with open face, beholding as in a glass the glory of the Lord, are changed into the same image, from glory to glory*.[82] That Spirit of

---

[77] Adapted from Simplicius, *In Epict.*, I. On αὐτεξούσιον, see above, p. 161, note.
[78] 'the further away its boundaries are'.
[79] *Job* 38. 14.
[80] Cf. *Genesis* 30. 39.
[81] Cf. below, p. 187.
[82] 2 *Corinthians* 3. 18.

Ambition and *Popularity* that so violently transports the Minds of men into a pursuit of *vainglory*, makes them as *vain* as that *Popular air* they live upon: the Spirit of this world that draws forth a mans designes after worldly interests, makes him as unstable, unconstant, tumultuous and perplex'd a thing as the world is. On the contrary, the Spirit of true Religion steering and directing the Mind and Life to God, makes it an Uniform, Stable and quiet thing, as God himself is: it is only true Goodness in the Soul of man guiding it steddily and uniformly towards God, directing it and all its actions to the one Last End and Chief Good, that can give it a true consistency and composedness within it self.

All *Self-seeking* and *Self-love* do but *imprison* the Soul, and *confine* it to its own home: the Mind of a Good man is too Noble, too Big for such a *Particular* life; he hath learn'd to despise his own Being in comparison of that Uncreated Beauty and Goodness which is so infinitely transcendent to himself or any created thing; he reckons upon his choice and best affections and designes as too choice and precious a treasure to be spent upon such a poor sorry thing as himself, or upon any thing else but God himself.

This was the life of Christ, and is in some degree the life of every one that partakes of the Spirit of Christ. Such Christians seek not their own glory, but the glory of him that sent them into this world: they know they were brought forth into this world; not to set up or drive a trade for themselves, but to serve the will & pleasure of him that made them, & to finish that work he hath appointed them. It were not worth the while to have been born to live, had it been only for such *a penurious End* as our selves are: it is most God-like and best suits with the Spirit of Religion, for a Christian to live wholy to God, to live the life of God, *having his own life hid with Christ in God*;[83] and thus in a sober sense he becomes *Deified*. This indeed is such a Θέωσις *Deification*[84] as is not transacted merely upon the Stage of *Fancy* by Arrogance and Presumption, but in the highest Powers of the Soul by a living and quickning Spirit of true Religion there uniting God and the Soul together in *the Unity* of *Affections*, *Will* and *End*.

I should now pass from this to another Particular; but because many are apt to misapprehend the Notion of *God's glory*,[85] and flatter them-

---

[83] Cf. *Colossians* 3. 3.   [84] See the Introduction, above, pp. 19 ff.
[85] For an argument parallel to Smith's here, see Whichcote, *Discourses*, III, 303 ff. (reiterated in IV, 31).

selves with their pretended and imaginary *aiming at the Glory of God*, I think it may be of good use, a little further and more distinctly to unfold *the Designe* that a Religious mind drives on *in directing it self and all its actions to God*. We are therefore to consider, that this doth not consist in some *Transient* thoughts of God and his *Glory* as the *End* we propound to our selves in any Undertakings: a man does not direct all his actions to *the Glory of God* by forming a Conception in his Mind, or stirring up a strong Imagination upon any Action, That that must be *for the Glory of God*: it is not the thinking of God's glory that is *glorifying* of him. As all other parts of Religion may be *apishly* acted over by *Fancy and Imagination*, so also may the Internal parts of Religion many times be acted over with much seeming grace by our *Fancy and Passions*; these often love to be drawing the pictures of Religion, and use their best arts to render them more beautifull and pleasing. But though true Practical Religion derives its force and beauty through all *the Lower Powers* of a mans Soul, yet it hath not its rise nor throne there: as Religion consists not in a *Form of Words* which signifie nothing, so neither doth it consist in *a Set of Fancies* or *Internal apprehensions*. Our Saviour hath best taught what it is to live to God's glory, or to glorifie God, viz. to be fruitfull in all holiness, and to live so as that our lives may shine with his grace spreading it self through our whole man.[86]

We rather *glorifie* God by entertaining the Impressions of his Glory upon us, then by communicating any kind of Glory to him. Then does a Good man become the Tabernacle of God wherein the Divine *Shechinah* does rest, and which the Divine glory fills, when the frame of his Mind and Life is wholly according to that Idea and Pattern which he receives from the Mount.[87] We best glorifie him when we grow most like to him: and we then act most for his glory, when a true Spirit of *Sanctity, Justice, Meekness*, &c. runs through all our actions; when we so live in the World as becomes those that converse with the great Mind and Wisdom of the whole World, with that Almighty Spirit that made, supports and governs all things, with that Being from whence all good flows, and in which there is no Spot, Stain or Shadow of Evil; and so being captivated and overcome by the sense of the Divine loveliness and goodness, endeavour to be like him, and conform our selves as much as may be to him.

[86] Cf. *John* 15. 8.
[87] 'As it is said of the Material Tabernacle, *Exodus* 25 [.9].' (Marginal note in the original text.)

When God *seeks his own Glory*, he does not so much endeavour any thing *without himself*. He did not bring this stately fabrick of the Universe into Being, that he might for such a Monument of his mighty Power and Beneficence gain some *Panegyricks* or Applause from a little of that fading breath which he had made. Neither was that gracious contrivance of restoring lapsed men to himself *a Plot* to get himself some Eternal *Hallelujahs*, as if he had so ardently thirsted after the layes of glorified spirits, or desired a Quire of Souls to sing forth his praises. Neither was it to let the World see how *Magnificent* he was. No, it is his own *Internal Glory* that he most loves, and the Communication thereof which he seeks: as *Plato* sometimes speaks of the Divine love, it arises not out of *Indigency*, as created love does, but out of *Fulness* and Redundancy;[88] it is an overflowing fountain, and that love which descends upon created Being is a free Efflux from the Almighty Source of love: and it is well pleasing to him that those Creatures which he hath made should partake of it. Though God cannot *seek his own Glory* so as if he might acquire any addition to himself, yet he may *seek it* so as to communicate it out of himself. It was a good Maxime of *Plato*, τῷ Θεῷ οὐδεὶς φθόνος·[89] wch is better stated by S. *James, God giveth to all men liberally, and upbraideth not.*[90] And by that Glory of his which he loves to impart to his Creatures, I understand those stamps and impressions of *Wisdom, Justice, Patience, Mercy, Love, Peace, Joy,* and other Divine gifts which he bestowed freely upon the Minds of men. And thus God triumphs in his own Glory, and takes pleasure in the Communication of it.

---

[88] Cf. *Symposium*, 203a; *Timaeus*, 30. It is of course hardly true that Plato 'speaks of the Divine love'. As F. M. Cornford has rightly emphasised, there is not 'the slightest warrant in Greek thought of the pre-Christian centuries for the notion of "over-flowing love", or love of any kind, prompting a god to make a world' (*Plato's Cosmology* [repr. New York, 1957], p. 35).

[89] Possibly adapted from *Phaedrus*, 247a: φθόνος γὰρ ἔξω θείου χοροῦ ἴσταται ('jealousy has no place in the celestial choir'). But *Timaeus*, 29e, seems to be more relevant: 'Why did the Creator make the World? . . . He was good, and therefore not jealous, and being free from jealousy he desired that all things should be like himself.' See also Plotinus, II, ix, 17, and Smith's further comment elsewhere in the *Discourses* (p. 66) on 'that sober *Thesis* of *Plato* in his *Timæus*, who attributes the *Perpetuation* of all substances to the Benignity and Liberality of the Creatour'.

[90] *James* 1. 5.

As God's seeking his own Glory in respect of us, is most properly the flowing forth of his Goodness upon us: so our seeking the Glory of God is most properly our endeavouring a Participation of his Goodness, and an earnest uncessant pursuing after Divine perfection. When God becomes so great in our eyes, and all created things so little, that we reckon upon nothing as worthy of our aims or ambitions but a serious Participation of the Divine Nature, and the Exercise of divine Vertues, *Love, Joy, Peace, Long-suffering, Kindness, Goodness,* and the like; When the Soul beholding the Infinite beauty and loveliness of the Divinity, and then looking down and beholding all created Perfection mantled over with darkness, is ravish'd into love and admiration of that never-setting brightness, and endeavours after the greatest resemblance of God in *Justice, Love* and *Goodness*; When conversing with him ἐν ἡσύχῳ ἐπαφῇ, by a secret feeling of the virtue, sweetness and power of his *Goodness,* we endeavour to assimilate our selves to him: Then we may be said to *glorifie* him indeed.[91] God seeks no glory but his own; and we have none of our own to give him. God in all things seeks himself and his own glory, as finding nothing *Better* than himself; and when we love him above all things, and endeavour to be most like him, we *declare plainly* that we count nothing *Better* then He is.

I doubt we are too nice Logicians sometimes in distinguishing between *the Glory of God* and *our own Salvation.* We cannot in a true sense seek *our own Salvation* more then *the Glory of God,* which triumphs most and discovers it self most effectually in *the Salvation* of Souls; for indeed *this Salvation* is nothing else but a true Participation of the Divine Nature. *Heaven* is not a thing *without us,* nor is Happiness any thing distinct from a true Conjunction of the Mind with God in a secret feeling of his Goodness and reciprocation of affection to him, wherein the Divine Glory most unfolds it self. And there is nothing that a Soul touch'd with any serious sense of God can more earnestly thirst after or seek with more strength of affection then This. Then shall we be happy, when God comes to be all in all in us. To love God *above our selves* is not indeed so properly to love him *above the salvation of our Souls,* as if these were distinct things; but it is to love him *above*

---

[91] Here as elsewhere Smith is inspired by a phrase in Plotinus, but the thought is his own. Plotinus had written: 'Life in the Supreme is the native activity of Intellect; in virtue of that silent converse (ἡσύχῳ ... ἐπαφῇ) it brings forth gods, brings forth beauty, brings forth righteousness, brings forth all moral good' (VI, ix, 9).

all our own sinfull affections, & *above our particular Beings*, and to conform our selves to him. And as that which is *Good relatively, and in order to us*, is so much the Better, by how much the more it is commensurate and conformed to us: So on the other side, that which is *good absolutely and essentially*, requires that our minds and Affections should, as far as may be, be commensurate and conform'd to it: and herein is God most glorified, and we made Happy. As we cannot truly love the First and Highest Good while we serve a designe upon it, and subordinate it to our selves: so neither is our own Salvation consistent with any such sordid, pinching and particular love. We cannot be compleatly blessed, till the *Idea Boni*, or the *Ipsum Bonum*, which is God, exercise its Soveraignty over all the Faculties of our Souls, rending them as like to it self as may consist with their proper Capacity.

CHAP. VI

4. The Fourth *Property* & *Effect of True Religion* wherein it expresseth its own *Nobleness* is this, *That it begets the greatest Serenity, Constancy and Composedness of Mind, and brings the truest Contentment, the most satisfying Joy and Pleasure, the purest and most divine Sweetness and Pleasure to the Spirits of Good men.* Every Good man, in whom Religion rules, is at *peace and unity* with himself, is as a City compacted together. Grace doth more and more reduce all the Faculties of the Soul into a perfect Subjection and Subordination to it self. The Union and Conjunction of the Soul with God, that *Primitive Unity*, is that which is the alone Original and Fountain of all *Peace*, and the Centre of *Rest*: as the further any Being slides from God, the more it breaks into discords within it self, as not having any Centre within it self which might collect and unite all the Faculties thereof to it self, and so knit them up together in a sweet confederacy amongst themselves. God only is such an *Almighty Goodness* as can *attract* all the Powers in man's Soul to it self, as being an Object transcendently adequate to the largest capacities of any created Being, and so unite man perfectly to himself in the true enjoyment of *one Uniform and Simple Good.*

It must be *one Last End and Supreme Good* that can *fix* Man's Mind, which otherwise will be tossed up and down in perpetual uncertainties, and become as many several things as those poor *Particularities* are which it meets with. A wicked man's life is so distracted by *a Multiplicity of Ends* and *Objects*, that it never is nor can be consistent to it self, nor continue in any composed, settled frame: it is the most intricate, irregular and confused thing in the world, no one part of it agreeing with another, because the whole is not firmly knit together by the power of some *One Last End* running through all.[92] Whereas the life of a Good man is under the sweet command of *one Supreme Goodness and Last End*. This alone is that living Form and Soul, which running through all the Powers of the Mind and the Actions of Life, collects all together into one fair and beautiful System, making all that Variety conspire into perfect Unity; whereas else all would fall asunder like the Members of a dead Body when once the Soul is gone, every little particle flitting each from other. It was a good Maxim of *Pythagoras* quoted by *Clemens Alexandrinus, Δεῖ καὶ τὸν ἄνθρωπον ἕνα γενέσθαι, Oportet etiam hominem unum fieri*.[93] *A divided Mind* and a *Multiform Life* speaks the greatest disparagement that may be: it is only the intermediation of *One Last End* that can reconcile a man perfectly to himself and his own happiness. This is the best temper and composedness of the Soul, ὅταν εἰς ἓν καὶ εἰς μίαν ὁμολογίαν ἑνωθῇ, as *Plotinus* speaks, when by a Conjunction with *One Chief Good and Last End*[94] it is drawn up into an Unity and Consent with it self; when all the Faculties of the Soul with their several issues and motions, though never so many in themselves, like so many lines meet together in one and the same Centre. It is not one and the same Goodness that alwaies acts the Faculties of a Wicked man; but as many several images and pictures of Goodness as a quick and working Fancy can represent to him; which so divide his affections, that he is no *One thing* within himself, but tossed hither and thither by the most independent Principles & Imaginations that may be. But a Good man hath singled out the Supreme Goodness, which by an Omnipotent sweetness draws all his affections after it, and so makes them all with the greatest complacency conspire together in the pursuit and embraces of it. Were there not some *Infinite and Self-sufficient Goodness*, and that *perfectly One*, ἀρχικὴ μονὰς, (as *Simplicius* doth phrase it)[95] Man

[92] Thus also *More*, in the last verse of his *Psychozoia*: 'The Good is uniform, the Evil infinite.' Cf. Whichcote, *Discourses*, III, 318, and also below, p. 179 and note.
[93] Clement of Alexandria, *Stromata*, IV, 23: 'that Pythagorean saying was mystically uttered respecting us, "that man ought to become one"'.
[94] Plotinus, VI, ix, 1.
[95] The primal monad (cf. Simplicius, *In Epict.*, Praefatio). Explained More: '*Monad, Μονὰς*, is *Unitas*, the principle of all numbers, an emblem of

would be a most miserably-distracted creature. As the restless appetite within Man after some Infinite and Soveraign Good (without the enjoyment of which it could never be satisfied) does commend unto us the Notion of a Deity: so the perpetual distractions and divisions that would arise in the Soul upon a Plurality of Deities, may seem no less to evince *the Unity* of that Deity. Were not this Chief Good perfectly *One*, were there any other equal to it; man's Soul would hang *in æquilibrio*, equally poised, equally desiring the enjoyment of both, but moving to neither; like a piece of Iron between two Loadstones of equal virtue. But when Religion enters into the Soul, it charms all its restless rage and violent appetite, by discovering to it the Universal Fountain-fulness of One Supreme Almighty Goodness; and leading it out of it self into a conjunction therewith, it lulls it into the most undisturbed rest and quietness in the lap of Divine enjoyment; where it meets with full contentment, and rests adequately satisfied in the fruition of the Infinite, Uniform and Essential Goodness and Loveliness, the true Αὐτόκαλον,[96] that is not πῇ μὲν καλὸν, πῇ δὲ οὐ καλὸν, ἀλλ' ὅλον δι' ὅλου καλόν, as a noble Philosopher doth well express it.[97]

The Peace which a Religious Soul is possessed of is such *a Peace as*

---

the Deity; And so the Pythagoreans call it Θεὸς, *God*' (*Democritus platonissans* [Cambridge, 1646], sig. Q3ᵛ). Generally, all Neoplatonists tended to describe 'the sum and substance of reality ... as the *Monad* or the *One*. They thus began by identifying the creative principle, in the first instance, with *Unity* (τὸ ἕν) as the origin of numerical series, from whence all subsequent numbers were 'derived', while the beginning of division was found to lie in the *Dyad*, duality being thus envisaged as a "second", though dependent principle, and as such the source of such further differentiation as might in turn "generate" multiplicity' (C. N. Cochrane, *Christianity and Classical Culture* [1940; repr. New York, 1957], p. 426).

[96] Thus also Worthington, *Discourses*, p. 104: 'God ... is beauty itself, αὐτόκαλον, "the original beauty".' Cf. Plotinus, IX, viii, 13, and Simplicius (next note).

[97] Thus Simplicius, *In Epict.*, XXXVIII: 'Beauty in the soul is free from all these [deformities], and is, not only the image and representation of beauty, but pure, substantial, unblemished, original beauty [αὐτόκαλον]; not graceful in one place, and not in another, but perfectly and all over so [οὐ πῇ μὲν καλὸν, πῇ δέ οὐ καλὸν, ἀλλ' ὅλον δι' ὅλον καλόν]. From whence it comes to pass, that, when the soul contemplates its own or another soul's beauty, all bodily graces lose their charms, and appear despicable and deormed in comparison'.

passeth all understanding: the *Joy* that it meets with in the ways of Holiness is *unspeakable and full of Glory*.[98] The Delights and Sweetnesses that accompany a Religious life are of a purer and more excellent Nature than the Pleasures of Worldly men. The Spirit of a Good man is a more pure and refined thing then to delight it self in the thick mire of Earthly and Sensual pleasures, which Carnal men rowle and tumble themselves in with so much greediness: *Non admittit ad volatum Accipitrem suum in terra pulverulenta*, as the Arabick Proverb hath it.[99] It speaks the degeneration of any Soul whatsoever, that it should desire to incorporate it self with any of the gross, dreggy, sensual delights here below. But a Soul purified by Religion from all Earthly dreggs, delights to mingle it self only with things that are most Divine and Spiritual. There is nothing that can beget any pleasure or sweetness but in some harmonical Faculty which hath some kindred and acquaintance with it. As it is in the *Senses*, so in every other Faculty there is such *a Natural kind of Science* as whereby it can single out its own proper Object from everything else, and is better able to define it to it self then the exactest Artist in the world can; and when once it hath found it out, it presently feels it self so perfectly fitted and matched by it, that it dissolves into secret joy and pleasure in the entertainment of it. True *Delight* and *Joy* is begotten by the conjunction of some discerning Faculty with its proper Object. The proper Objects for a Mind and Spirit are *Divine* and *Immaterial* things, with which it hath the greatest affinity, and therefore triumphs most in its converse with them; as it is well observed by Seneca, *Hoc habet argumentum divinitatis suæ, quòd illum divina delectant; nec ut alienis interest, sed ut suis:*[100] and when it converseth most with these high and noble Objects, it behaves it self most gracefully and lives most becoming it self; and it lives also most deliciously, nor can it any where else be better provided for, or indeed fare so well. A good man disdains to be beholding to the Wit or Art or Industry of any Creature to find him out and bring him in a constant revenue and maintenance for his

---

[98] *Philippians* 4. 7 and 1 *Peter* 1. 8.

[99] 'He does not allow his blinkered falcon on the dusty ground'. HGW has traced a variant in Georg Wilhelm Freytag, *Arabum proverbia* (Bonn, 1839), II, 579: 'ne mittas falconem in lacertas!' ('do not put the falcon on [some one's] shoulder!').

[100] *Nat. quæst.*, I, Prologus: 'A proof of [the soul's] divine origin is furnished by the pleasure it derives from what is divine; here it feels itself at home, not in a strange land' etc.

Joy and Pleasure: the language of his Heart is that of the Psalmist, *Lord, lift thou up the light of thy countenance upon me.*[101] Religion alwaies carries a sufficient Provision of *Joy and Sweetness* along with it to maintain it self withal: *All the ways of Wisdom are ways of pleasantness, and all her paths are peace.*[102] Religion is no sullen *Stoicisme* or oppressing *Melancholie*, it is no enthralling tyranny exercised over those noble and vivacious affections of Love and Delight, as those men that were never acquainted with the life of it may imagine; but it is full of a vigorous and masculine delight and joy,[103] & such as advanceth and ennobles the Soul, and does not weaken or dispirit the life and power of it, as Sensual and Earthly joys doe, when the Soul, unacquainted with Religion, is enforc'd to give entertainment to these gross & earthly things, for the want of enjoyment of some better Good. The Spirit of a Good man may justly behave it self with a noble disdain to all Terrene pleasures, because it knows where to mend its fare; it is the same Almighty and Eternal Goodness which is the Happiness of God and of all Good men. The truly-religious Soul affects nothing primarily and fundamentally but God himself; his contentment even in the midst of his Worldly enployments is in the Sun of the Divine favour that shines upon him: this is as the *Manna* that lies upon the top of all outward blessings which his Spirit gathers up and feeds upon with delight. Religion consists not in a toilesome drudgery about some Bodily exercises and External performances; nor is it onely the spending of our selves in such attendances upon God and services to him as are onely accommodated to this life, (though every employment for God is both amiable and honourable:) But there is something of our Religion that interests us in a present possession of that *joy which is unspeakable and glorious*; which leads us into the Porch of heaven, and to the confines of Eternity. It sometimes carries up the Soul into a mount of Transfiguration, or to the top of *Pisgah*, where it may take a prospect of the promised land; and gives it a Map or Scheme of its future inheritance: it gives it sometimes some anticipations of Blessedness, some foretasts of those joys, those rivers of pleasure which run at God's right hand for evermore.

[101] *Psalms* 4. 6 (cf. *Numbers* 6. 26).
[102] *Proverbs* 3. 17.
[103] Thus elsewhere in Smith's *Discourses* (pp. 469 ff.): 'A true Christian spirit is masculine and generous; it is no such poor, sluggish, pusillanimous thing as some men fansie it to be, but *active and noble*.' See also Whichcote, *Discourses*, II, 135; Worthington, *Discourses*, p. 435; etc.

I might further add as a *Mantissa*[104] to this present Argument, *the Tranquillity* and *Composedness* of a Good man's spirit in reference to all *External* molestations. Religion having made a through-pacification of the Soul within it self, renders it impregnable to all outward assaults: So that it is at rest and lives securely in the midst of all those boysterous Storms and Tempests that make such violent impressions upon the spirits of wicked men. Here the *Stoicks* have stated the case aright, That all *Perturbations of the Mind* arise not properly from an *Outward* but an *Inward* cause: it is not any *outward* Evil, but an *inward imagination* bred in the womb of the Soul it self, that molests and grieves it.[105] The more that the Soul is restored to it self, and lives at the height of it's own Being, the more easily may it disdain and despise any design or combination against it by the most blustering Giants in the world. A Christian that enjoys himself in God, will not be beholding to the worlds fair and gentle usage for the *composedness* of his mind; No, he enjoys that *Peace and Tranquillity within himself* which no creature can bestow upon him, or take from him.

But the *Stoicks* were not so happy in their notions about *the way to true Rest and Composedness of Spirit*. It is not (by their leave) the Souls collecting and gathering up it self within the Circumference of it's own Essence, nor is it a rigid restraining and keeping in its own issues and motions within the confines of its own natural endowments, which is able to conferre upon it that $\dot{\alpha}\tau\alpha\varrho\alpha\xi\iota\alpha$[106] and *Composedness of mind* which they so much idolize as the supreme and onely bliss of man, and render it free from all kind of perturbations: (For by what we find in *Seneca* and others, it appears, that the *Stoicks* seeking an *Autarchy* within themselves, and being loth to be beholden to God for their Happiness, but that each of them might be as God, self-sufficient and happy in the enjoyment of himself, endeavoured by their sour doctrine and a rigid discipline over their Souls, their severities against Passions and all those restless motions in the Soul after some Higher Good, to attain a complete $\dot{\alpha}\tau\alpha\varrho\alpha\xi\iota\alpha$ and a full

[104] (Tuscan): 'a worthless addition, make-weight' (C. T. Lewis and Charles Short, *A Latin Dictionary*, rev. ed. [Oxford, 1958], p. 1110).
[105] Cf. E. Vernon Arnold, *Roman Stoicism* (Cambridge, 1911), Ch. XIV.
[106] Cf. Smith's own comment elsewhere in the *Discourses* (pp. 135 ff.): 'the most Quintessential *Stoicks* find an $\alpha\dot{\upsilon}\tau\dot{\alpha}\varrho\varkappa\varepsilon\iota\alpha$ and $\dot{\alpha}\tau\alpha\varrho\alpha\xi\iota\alpha$ a Self-sufficiency and Tranquillity within their own Souls, arising out of the pregnancy of their own Mind and Reason'.

The Excellency and Nobleness of True Religion

contentment within themselves.)[107] But herein they mist of the true method of finding Rest to themselves, it being the Union of the Soul with God, that Uniform, Simple and unbounded Good, which is the sole Original of all true inward Peace. Neither were it an Happiness worth the having, for a Mind, like an Hermite sequestred from all things else, by a recession into it self, to spend an Eternity in self-converse and the enjoyment of such a Diminutive superficial Nothing as it self is and must necessarily be to it self. It is onely peculiar to God to be happy in himself alone; and God who has been more liberal in his provisions for man, hath created in man such a spring of restless motion, that with the greatest impatiency forceth him out of himself, and violently tosseth him to and fro, till he come to fix himself upon some solid and Self-subsistent Goodness. Could a man find himself withdrawn from all terrene and Material things, and perfectly retired into himself; were the whole World so quiet and calme about him, as not to offer to make the least attempt upon the composedness and constancy of his Mind; might he be so well entertain'd at his own home, as to find no frowns, no sour looks from his own Conscience; might he have that security from Heaven, that God would not disquiet his fancied Tranquillity by embittering his thoughts with any dreadful apprehensions; yet he should find something within him that would not let him be at rest, but would rend him from himself, & toss him from his own foundation & consistency. There is an insatiable appetite in the Soul of man, like a greedy Lion hunting after his prey, that would render him impatient of his own pinching penury, & could never satisfy it self with such a thin and spare diet as he finds at home. There are two principall faculties in the Soul which, like the two daughters of the Horsleach, are always crying, *Give, Give*:[108] these are those hungry Vultures which, if they cannot find their prey abroad, return and gnaw the Soul it self: where the carkasse is, there will the Eagles be gathered together. By this we may see how unavailable to the attaining of true Rest and Peace that conceit of the *Stoicks* was, who supposed the onely way and method hereto was this, To confine the Soul thus Monastically to its own home. We read in the Gospel of such a Question of our Saviour's, *What went you out into the wilder-*

---

[107] Consult previous note.

[108] *Proverbs* 30. 15. As John Marbecke explained in *A Booke of Notes and Common-places* (1581), p. 503: 'The Horse-leach hath two daughters ... that is, two forks in her tongue which he [Solomon] here calleth her two daughters, wherby she sucketh the bloud, and is neuer saciate.'

ness to see?[109] we may invert it, What do you return within, to see? A Soul confined within the private and narrow cell of its own particular Being? Such a Soul deprives it self of all that Almighty and Essential Glory and Goodness which shines round about it, which spreads it self through the whole universe; I say it deprives it self of all this, for the enjoying of such a poor petty and diminutive thing as it self is, which yet it can never enjoy truly in such a retiredness.

We have seen the Peacefull and Happy state of the truly-religious: But it is otherwise with wicked and irreligious men. *There is no peace to the wicked; but they are like the troubled Sea, when it cannot rest, whole waters cast up mire and dirt*; as it is exprest by the Prophet *Esay.*[110] The mind of a wicked man is like the Sea when it roars and rages through the striving of severall contrary winds upon it. Furious lusts and wild passions within, as they warre against Heaven and the more noble and divine part of the Soul, so they warr amongst themselves, maintaining perpetuall contests, & contending which shall be the greatest: *Scelera dissident.*[111] These indeed are the *Cadmus*-brood rising out of the Serpent's teeth, ready arm'd one against another:[112] whence it is that the Soul of a wicked man becomes a very unhabitable and incommodious place to it self, full of disquietness and trouble through the many contests and civil commotions maintained within it. The minds of wicked men are like those disconsolate and desolate spirits which our Saviour speaks of *Matth.* 12.[113] which being cast out of their habitation, wander up and down through dry and desert places, seeking rest but finding none. The Soul that finds not some solid and self-sufficient Good to centre it self upon, is a boisterous and restless thing: and being without God, it wanders up and down the world, destitute, afflicted, tormented with vehement hunger and thirst after some satisfying Good: and as any one shall bring it tidings, *Lo here*, or *Lo there is Good*, it presently goes out towards it, and with a swift and speedy flight hastens after it. The sense of an *inward* indigency

---

[109] *Matthew* 11. 7.

[110] *Isaiah* 57. 20–1. By contrast, cf. above, p. 163: 'When the Sea of this World...' etc.

[111] 'Crimes war amongst themselves.'

[112] The legend of 'the Cadmean Offspring' who did 'immediate Execution upon themselves' (Cudworth, *Int. System*, p. 146) is recounted among others by Ovid, *Met.*, III, 101 ff.

[113] *Matthew* 12. 43.

doth stimulate and enforce it to seek its contentment *without* it self, and so it wanders up and down from one creature to another; and thus becomes distracted by *a multiplicity of Objects.* And while it cannot find some One and Onely object upon which, as being perfectly adequate to its capacities, it may wholly bestow it self; while it is tossed with restless and vehement motions of *Desire* and *Love* through a world of painted beauties, false glozing Excellencies; courting all, but matching nowhere; violently hurried every whither, but finding nowhere *objectum par amori;*[114] while it converseth onely with these *pinching Particularities* here below, and is not yet acquainted with *the Universal Goodness;* it is certainly far from true Rest and Satisfaction, from a fixt, composed temper of spirit: but being distracted by *multiplicity* of *Objects* and *Ends,* there can never be any firm and stable peace or friendship at home amongst all its Powers and Faculties: nor can there be a firm amity and friendship abroad betwixt wicked men themselves, as *Aristotle* in his Ethicks does conclude, because all *Vice* is so *Multiform* and inconsistent a thing, and so there can be no true concatenation of *Affections* and *Ends* between them.[115] Whereas in all Good men Vertue and Goodness is one Form and Soul to them all, that unites them together, and there is the One, Simple and Uniform Good, that guides and governs them all. They are not as a Ship tossed in the tumultuous Ocean of this world without any *Compass* at all to stear by; but they direct their course by the certain guidance of the *One Last End,* as the true *Pole-starr* of all their motion. But while the Soul lies benighted in a thick Ignorance (as it is with wicked men,) and behold not some *Stable* and *Eternal Good* to move toward; though it may, by the strength of that Principle of *Activeness* within it self, spend it self perpetually with swift and giddy motions; yet it will be always contesting with secret disturbances, and cannot act but with many reluctancies, as not finding an object equall to the force and strength of its vast affections to act upon.

By what hath been said may appear the vast difference between the ways of *Sin* and of *Holinesse.* Inward distractions and disturbances, *tribulation and anguish upon every Soul that doth evil: But to every man that worketh good, glory, honour and peace,*[116] inward composednesse

---

[114] 'an object equal to love'.
[115] Aristotle, *Magna moralia,* I, 24: 'evil is multiform, but good uniform'. See also Whichcote, *Aphorisms,* § 281 (below, p. 329). Cf. above, p. 172, note.
[116] *Romans* 2. 9–10.

and tranquillity of spirit, pure and divine joys farr excelling all sensual pleasures; in a word, true Contentment of spirit and full satisfaction in God, whom the pious Soul loves above all things, and longs still after a nearer enjoyment of him. I shall conclude this Particular with what *Plotinus* concludes his Book, That the life of holy and divine men is βίος ἀνήδονος τῶν τῇδε, φυγὴ μόνου πρὸς μόνον, a life not touch't with these vanishing delights of Time, but a flight of the Soul alone to God alone.[117]

CHAP. VII

5. The Fifth *Property* or *Effect* whereby *True Religion* discovers its own *Nobleness and Excellency* is this, *That it advanceth the Soul to an holy boldness and humble familiarity with God, as also to a well-grounded Hope and comfortable Confidence concerning the Love of God toward it, and its own Salvation.* The truly religious Soul maintains an humble and sweet *familiarity* with God; and with great alacrity of spirit, without any *Consternation* and *Servility* of spirit, is enabled to look upon the Glory and Majesty of the most High: But *Sin* and *Wickedness* is pregnant with *fearfulness* and horrour. That *Trembling* and *Consternation* of Mind which possesses wicked men, is nothing else but a brat of darkness, an *Empusa*[118] begotten in corrupt and irreligious Hearts. While men *walk in darkness*, and *are of the night*, (as the Apostle speaks,) then it is onely that they are vext with those ugly and gastly *Mormos*[119] that terrify and torment them. But when once the Day breaks, and true Religion opens her self upon the Soul like the Eye-lids of the Morning, then all those shadows and frightfull Apparitions flee away. As all *Light and Love and Joy* descend from above from the Father of lights: so all *Darkness and Fearfulness & Despair* are from below; they arise from corrupt and earthly minds, & are like those gross Vapors arising from this Earthly globe, that not being able to get up towards heaven, spread themselves about the circumference of that Body where they were first begotten, infesting it with darkness and generating into Thunder and Lightning, Clouds and Tempests. But the higher a

[117] Plotinus, VI, ix, 11 (the concluding sentence of the *Enneads*).

[118] Ἔμπουσα: 'a demonic apparition sent by Hecate and assuming various shapes' (D. Demetrakos, Μέγα λεξικὸν τῆς ἑλληνικῆς γλώσσης [Athens, 1936–50], III, 2488). Thus in Aristophanes, *Ranae*, 288 ff.; etc.

[119] Μορμώ: 'a hideous female monster, used to frighten children' (Demetrakos, *ibid.*, VI, 4759).

The Excellency and Nobleness of True Religion 181

Christian ascends ἐκ τοῦ σπηλαίου[120] above this dark dungeon of the Body, the more that Religion prevails within him, the more then shall he find himself as it were in a clear heaven, in a Region that is calm and serene; and the more will those black and dark affections of *Fear and Despair* vanish away, and those clear and bright affections of *Love and Joy and Hope* break forth in their strength and lustre.

The Devil, who is the Prince of darkness and the great Tyrant, delights to be served with gastly affections and the most dismal deportments of *trembling* and *astonishment*; as having nothing at all of amiableness or excellency in him to commend himself to his worshippers. Slavery and servility (that γλωττόκομον τῆς ψυχῆς, as *Longinus* truly calls it)[121] is the badge and livery of the Devil's religion: hence those φρικτὰ μυστήρια[122] of the Heathens perform'd with much trembling and horror. But God, who is the supreme *Goodness* and Essentiall both *Love and Loveliness*, takes most pleasure in those *sweet and delightfull affections* of the Soul, viz. *Love, Joy* and *Hope*, which are most correspondent to his own nature. The ancient superstition of the Heathens was always very nice and curious in honouring every one of their Gods with Sacrifices and Rites most agreeable to their natures: I am sure there is no Incense, no offering we can present God with, is so sweet, so acceptable to him as our *Love* and *Delight* and *Confidence in him*; and when he comes into the Souls of men, he makes these his Throne, his place of rest, as finding the greatest agreeableness therein to his own Essence. A Good man that finds himself made partaker of the Divine nature, and transform'd into the image of God, infinitely takes pleasure in God, as being altogether Lovely, according to that in *Cant.* 5. מַחֲמַדִּים כֻּלּוֹ *Totus ipse est desideria;*[123] and his *Meditation* of God is *sweet unto him, Ps.* 104.[124] S. *John* that lay in the bosome of Christ who came from the bosome of the Father, and perfectly understood his Eternal Essence, hath given us the fullest description that he could make of him, when he tells us that *God is Love,* and he that dwells in God, dwells in love;[125] and reposing himself in the bosome of an Almighty Goodness, where he finds nothing but Love and Loveliness, he now

---

[120] 'from the cave' (as above, p. 136). On the 'dark dungeon of the Body', cf. above, p. 140, and note.
[121] 'cage of the soul' (Longinus, XLIV, 5).
[122] 'horrible mysteries'—i.e., the Orphic and other sacred religious rites.
[123] Cf. *Song of Solomon* 5. 16: 'totus [est] desiderabilis' (Vulgate); 'he is altogether lovely' (AV).
[124] *Psalms* 104. 34.   [125] 1 *John* 4. 16.

displays all the strength and beauty of those his choicest and most precious affections of *Love and Joy and Confidence*; his Soul is now at ease, and rests in peace, neither is there any thing to make afraid: He is got beyond all those powers of darknesse which give such continual alarms in this lower world, and are always troubling the Earth: He is got above all fears and despairs; he is in a bright clear region, above Clouds and Tempests, *infra se despicit nubes.* There is no frightful terribleness in the supreme Majesty. That men apprehend God at any time in such a dismayed manner, it must not at all be made an argument of his nature, but of our *sinfulness and weakness.* The Sun in the heavens always was and will be a Globe of Light and brightness, howsoever a purblind Eye is rather dazled then enlightned by it. There is an Inward sense in Mans Soul, which, were it once awaken'd and excited with an inward tast and relish of the Divinity, could better define God to him then all the world else. It is the sincere Christian that so tasts and sees how good and sweet the Lord is, as none else does: *The God of hope fills him with all joy and peace in believing*, so that he *abounds in hope*, as the Apostle speaks *Rom.* 15.[126] He quietly reposes himself in God; *his heart is fixed, trusting in the Lord*; he is more for a solid peace and setled calme of spirit, then for high Raptures and feelings of Joy or Extraordinary Manifestations of God to him: he does not passionately desire nor importunately expect such things; he rather looks after the Manifestations of the Goodness and Power of God within him, in subduing all in his Soul that is unlike and contrary to God, and forming him into his image and likeness.

Though I think it worthy of a Christian to endeavour *the Assurance of his own Salvation*; yet perhaps it might be the safest way to moderate his curiosity of prying into God's *Book of life*, and to stay a while untill he sees himself within the confines of *Salvation* it self. Should a man hear *a Voice* from Heaven or see *a Vision* from the Almighty, to testify unto him the Love of God towards him; yet methinks it were more desireable to find a Revelation of all *from within*, arising up from the Bottome and Centre of a mans own Soul, in the Reall and Internal impressions of *a Godlike nature* upon his own spirit; and thus to find *the Foundation and Beginning of Heaven and Happiness within himself*.[127]

[126] *Romans* 15. 13.
[127] Smith, like the other Cambridge Platonists (see above, p. 46 and note), frequently dwells on the idea that 'the *Foundations* of *Heaven* and *Hell* are laid in mens own Souls' (*Discourses*, p. 149). See below, pp. 192 f., 196, 329 f., as elsewhere in his *Discourses* (esp. pp. 174 ff., 463–8).

The Excellency and Nobleness of True Religion 183

it were more desirable to see the crucifying of our own Will, the mortifying of the mere Animal life, and to see a Divine life rising up in the room of it, as a sure Pledge and Inchoation of Immortality and *Happiness*, the very Essence of which consists in a perfect conformity and chearfull complyance of all the Powers of our Souls with the Will of God.

The best way of gaining *a well-grounded assurance of the Divine love* is this; for a man *to overcome himself and his own Will*: To him that overcomes shall be given that white stone, and in it the new name written, which no man knoweth but he that receives it. He that beholds the Sun of righteousness arising upon the Horizon of his Soul with healing in its wings, and chasing away all that misty darkness of his own *Self-will* and *Passions*; such a one desires not now the Starr-light to know whether it be Day or not, nor cares he to pry into Heaven's secrets and to search into the hidden rolles of Eternity, there to see the whole plot of his Salvation; for he views it transacted upon the inward stage of his own Soul, and reflecting upon himself he may behold a Heaven opened from within, and a Throne set up in his Soul, and an Almighty Saviour sitting upon it, and reigning within him: he now finds the Kingdome of Heaven within him, and sees that it is not a thing merely reserved for him without him, being already made partaker of the sweetness and efficacy of it. What the Jewes say of *the Spirit of Prophesy*, may not unfitly be applyed to the Holy Ghost, the true Comforter dwelling in the minds of good men as a sure Earnest of their Eternal inheritance, אין הנבואה שורה אלא על גבור, *The Spirit resides not but upon a man of Fortitude*,¹²⁸ one that gives proof of this *Fortitude* in subduing his own Self-will and his Affections. We read of *Elisha*, that he was fain to call for a Musical instrument and one to play before him, to allay the heat of his Passions before he could converse with the Prophetical Spirit.¹²⁹ The Holy Spirit is too pure and gentle a thing to dwell in a Mind muddied and disturb'd by those impure dreggs, those thick fogs and mists that arise from our Self-will and Passions: our prevailing over these is the best way to cherish the Holy Spirit, by which we may be sealed unto the day of redemption.

To conclude this Particular: It is a venturous and rugged guess and conceit which some men have, That in a perfect resignation of our Wills to the Divine will a man should be content with his own Damnation, and to be the Subject of Eternal Wrath in Hell, if it should so please

---

¹²⁸ *Talmud*: Sanhedrin, 89.   ¹²⁹ 2 *Kings* 3. 15.

God. Which is as impossible as it is for him that infinitely thirsts after a true Participation of the Divine Nature, and most earnestly endeavours a most inward Union with God in Spirit, by a denial of himself and his own will, to swell up in Self-love, Pride and Arrogancy against God; the one whereof is the most *substantial Heaven*, the other the most *real Hell*: whereas indeed by conquering our selves we are translated from Death to Life, and the kingdom of God and Heaven is already come into us.

CHAP. VIII

6. The Sixth *Property* or *Effect* wherein *Religion* discovers its own *Excellency* is this, *That it Spiritualizes Material things, and so carries up the Souls of Good men from Earthly things to things Divine, from this Sensible World to the Intellectual.*

God made the Universe and all the Creatures contained therein as so many Glasses wherein he might reflect his own Glory: He hath copied forth himself in the Creation;[130] and in this Outward World we may read the lovely characters of the Divine Goodness, Power and Wisdom. In some Creatures there are darker representations of God, there are the Prints and Footsteps of God; but in others there are clearer and fuller representations of the Divinity, the Face and Image of God; according to that known saying of the Schoolmen, *Remotiores Similitudines Creaturæ ad Deum dicuntur Vestigium*; *propinquiores verò Imago*.[131] But how to find God here and feelingly to converse with him, and being affected with the sense of the Divine Glory shining out upon the Creation, how to pass out of the *Sensible World* into the *Intellectual*, is not so effectually taught by that Philosophy which profess'd it most, as by true Religion: that which knits and unites God and the Soul together, can best teach it how to ascend and descend upon those golden links that unite as it were the World to God. That Divine *Wisdome* that contrived and beautified this glorious Structure, can best explain her own Art, and carry up the Soul back again in these reflected Beams to him who is the Fountain of them. Though Good men, all of them, are not acquainted with all those

[130] Cf. More on the 'naturall *Hieroglyphicks*' imprinted on the created order (below, p. 263).

[131] 'Creatures more remotely resembling God are said to be a trace; those with clear resemblance are called his likeness.' The sentiment is common to all spokesmen for 'inner illumination'.

The Excellency and Nobleness of True Religion 185

Philosophical notions touching the relation between Created and the Uncreated Being; yet may they easily find every Creature pointing out to that Being whose image and superscription it bears, and climb up from those darker resemblances of the Divine Wisdome and Goodness shining out in different degrees upon several Creatures, ὥσπερ ἀναβάθμοις τισὶ, as the Antients speak, till they sweetly repose themselves in the bosom of the Divinity:[132] and while they are thus conversing with this lower World, and are viewing *the invisible things of God in the things that are made*,[133] in this visible and outward Creation, they find God many times secretly flowing into their Souls, and leading them silently out of the Court of the Temple into the Holy Place. But it is otherwise with Wicked men; they dwell perpetually upon the dark side of the Creatures, and converse with these things only in a gross, sensual, earthly and unspiritual manner; they are so encompass'd with the thick and foggy mist of their own Corruptions, that they cannot see God there where he is most visible: *the Light shineth in darkness, but darkness comprehends it not*:[134] their Souls are so deeply sunk into that House of Clay which they carry about with them, that were there nothing of *Body* or bulky *Matter* before them, they could find nothing to exercise themselves about.

But Religion, where it is in truth and in power, renews the very Spirit of our Minds, and doth in a manner *Spiritualize* this outward Creation to us, and doth in a more excellent way perform that which the *Peripateticks* are wont to affirm of their *Intellectus agens*, in purging Bodily and Material things from the feculency and dregs of *Matter*, and separating them from those circumstantiating and streightning conditions of *Time* and *Place*, and the like;[135] and teaches the Soul to look at those *Perfections* which it finds here below, not so much as the Perfections of *This* or *That* Body, as they adorn *This* or *That* particular Being, but as they are so many Rays issuing forth from that First and Essential Perfection, in which they all meet and embrace one another in the most close friendship. Every Particular Good is a Blossom of the First Goodness; every created Excellency is a Beam descending from the Father of lights: and should we separate all these *Particularities* from God, all affection spent upon them would be unchast, and their embraces adulterous. We should love all things in

[132] Plotinus, VI, vii, 36.
[133] Cf. *Romans* 1. 20, esp. as discussed by Whichcote, above, p. 53.
[134] *John* 1. 5.
[135] Cf. Aristotle, *De anima*, 430a. See also the note on νοῦς, above, p. 151.

God, and God in all things, because he is All in all, the Beginning and Original of Being, the perfect Idea of their Goodness, and the End of their Motion. It is nothing but a thick mist of Pride and Self-love that hinders mens eyes from beholding that Sun which both enlightens them and all things else: But when true Religion begins once to dawn upon mens Souls, and with its shining light chases away their black Night of Ignorance; then they behold themselves and all things else enlightned (though in a different way) by one and the same Sun, and all the Powers of their Souls fall down before God and ascribe all glory to him. Now it is that a Good man is no more solicitous whether *This* or *That* good thing be *Mine*, or whether *My* perfections exceed the measure of *This* or *That* particular Creature; for whatsoever *Good* he beholds any where, he enjoys and delights in it as much as if it were his own, and whatever he beholds in himself, he looks not upon it as his *Property* but as a *Common* good; for all these Beams come from one and the same Fountain and Ocean of light in whom he loves them all with an Universal love: when his affections run along the stream of any created excellencies, whether his own or any ones else, yet they stay not here, but run on till they fall into the Ocean; they do not settle into a fond love and admiration either of himself or any others Excellencies, but he owns them as so many Pure Effluxes and Emanations from God, and in *a Particular* Being loves *the Universal* Goodness. *Si sciretur à me Veritas, sciretur etiam me illud non esse, aut illud non esse meum, nec à me.*[136]

Thus may a Good man walk up and down the World as in a Garden of Spices, and suck a Divine Sweetness out of every flower. There is a Twofold meaning in every Creature, as the Jews speak of their Law, a *Literal*, and a *Mystical*, and the one is but the ground of the other: and as they say of divers pieces of their Law, דבר למטה ומז למעלה,[137] so a Good man sayes of every thing that his Senses offer to him, *it speaks to his lower part, but it points out something above to his Mind and Spirit.* It is the drowsie and muddy spirit of Superstition which, being lull'd asleep in the lap of worldly delights, is fain to set some Idol at its elbow, something that may jogg it and put it in mind of God. Whereas true Religion never finds it self out of the Infinite Sphere of the Divinity, and whereever it finds *Beauty, Harmony, Goodness, Love, Ingenuity,*

---

[136] 'If the truth were known to me, it would also be known that it is not mine, nor from me.'

[137] 'what is here below is a hint of what is above'. The idea is a cabbalistic commonplace.

Wisdome, Holiness, Justice, and the like, it is ready to say, *Here,* and *There is God*: wheresoever any such Perfections shine out, an holy Mind climbs up by these Sun-beams, and raises up it self to God.

And seeing God hath never thrown the World from himself, but runs through all created Essence, containing the Archetypal Ideas of all things in himself, and from thence deriving and imparting several prints of Beauty and Excellency all the world over; a Soul that is truly θεοειδής God-like,[138] a Mind that is enlightened from the same Fountain, and hath its inward Senses affected with the sweet relishes of Divine Goodness, cannot but every where behold it self in the midst of that Glorious Unbounded Being who is indivisibly every where. A Good man finds every place he treads upon *Holy ground*; to him the World is God's Temple; he is ready to say with *Jacob,* Gen. 28. *How dreadfull is this place! this is none other but the House of God.*[139]

To conclude, It was a degenerous and unworthy Spirit in that Philosophy which first separated and made such distances between *Metaphysical* Truths & the Truths of *Nature*;[140] whereas the First and most antient Wisdom amongst the Heathens was indeed a Philosophical Divinity, or a Divine Philosophy; which continued for divers ages, but as men grew worse, their queazy stomachs began to loath it: which made the truly-wise *Socrates* complain of the Sophisters of that Age which began now to corrupt and debase it;[141] whereas heretofore the Spirit of Philosophy was more generous and divine, and did more purifie and ennoble the Souls of men, commending Intellectual things to

---

[138] Cf. above, p. 166.   [139] *Genesis* 28. 17.

[140] The reference may well be to Bacon who had written that '*Naturall Theology,* is truly called *Divine Philosophy.* And this is defined to be a Knowledge ... such as may be had by the light of Nature; and the Contemplation of the Creature; which Knowledge may be truly termed *Divine* in respect of the Object; and *Naturall* in respect of the Light' (*Of the Advancement and Proficience of Learning* [Oxford, 1640], p. 137 [Bk. III, Ch. II]; in *Works,* IV, 341). The Cambridge Platonists were in any case opposed to Bacon, not only because of his refusal to ground his philosophy on religion (see Raven, pp. 107 ff.) but because of his espousal of materialism (cf. C. T. Harrison, 'Bacon, Hobbes, Boyle, and the Ancient Atomists', *Harvard Studies and Notes in Philosophy and Literature,* XV [1933], 191–218). Only Culverwell manifests any enthusiasm for Bacon (pp. 157, 159, etc.; cf. Richard F. Jones, *Ancients and Moderns,* 2nd ed. [Berkeley, 1965], pp. 138 ff.).

[141] See Plato, *Sophista, passim.*

them, and taking them off from settling upon Sensible and Material things here below, and still exciting them to endeavour after the nearest resemblance of God the Supreme Goodness and Loveliness, and an intimate Conjunction with him; which, according to the strain of that Philosophy, was the true Happiness of Immortal Souls.

CHAP. IX

7. The Seventh and last *Property* or *Effect* wherein True Religion expresseth its own *Nobleness and Excellency*, is this, *That it raiseth the Minds of Good men to a due observance of and attendance upon Divine Providence, and enables them to serve the Will of God, and to acquiesce in it.* Wheresoever God hath a Tongue to speak, there they have Eares to hear; and being attentive to God in the soft and still motions of *Providence*, they are ready to obey his call, and to say with *Esay, Behold, here am I, send me.*[142] They endeavour to copy forth that Lesson which Christ hath set Christians, seriously considering how that they came into this world by God's appointment, not to doe their own Wills but the Will of him that sent them.

As this Consideration quiets the Spirit of a Good man who is no idle Spectator of *Providence*, and keeps him in a calm and sober temper in the midst of all Storms and Tempests; so it makes him most freely to engage himself in the service of *Providence*, without any inward reluctancy or disturbance. He cannot be content that *Providence* should serve it self of him as it doth even of those things that understand it least; but it is his holy ambition to serve it. 'Tis nothing else but Hellish pride and Self-love that makes men serve themselves, and so set up themselves as Idols against God: But it is indeed an argument of true Nobleness of Spirit for a man to view himself (not in the narrow Point of his own Being, but) in the unbounded Essence of the First Cause, so as to be ὅλως τοῦ κρείττονος,[143] and to live only as an Instrument in the hands of God who worketh all things after the counsel of his own will. *Optarem id me esse Deo quod est mihi manus mea*, was the expression of an holy Soul.[144]

To a Good man *to serve the Will of God*, it is in the truest and best sense *to serve himself*, who knows himself to be nothing without or in

[142] *Isaiah* 6. 8.
[143] Already quoted by Smith from Simplicius, above, p. 143.
[144] 'I should wish to be to God what my hand is to me'. The 'holy soul' need not necessarily be any specific individual.

The Excellency and Nobleness of True Religion

opposition to God; *Quò minùs quid sibi arrogat homo, eò evadit nobilior, clarior, divinior.*[145] This is the most divine life that can be, for a man to act in the world upon Eternal designes, and to be so wholy devoted to the Will of God, as to serve it most faithfully and entirely. This indeed bestows a kind of *Immortality* upon these flitting and *Transient* acts of ours, which in themselves are but the Off-spring of a moment. A *Pillar* or *Verse* is a poor sorry Monument of any Exploit, which yet may well enough become the highest of the worlds bravery. But Good men, while they work with God and endeavour to bring-themselves and all their actions to a unity with God, his Ends and Designs, enroll themselves in Eternity. This is the proper Character of holy Souls; Their Wills are so fully resolv'd into the Divine Will, that they in all things subscribe to it without any murmurings or debates: they rest well satisfied with, and take complacency in, any passages of Divine dispensation, ὡς ὑπὸ τῆς ἀρίστης γνώμης ἐπιτελουμένοις, as being ordered and disposed by a Mind and Wisedome above according to the highest rules of *Goodness*.[146]

The best way for a man rightly to enjoy himself, is to maintain an universal, ready and chearfull complyance with the Divine and Uncreated Will in all things; as knowing that nothing can issue and flow forth from the fountain of *Goodness* but that which is good: and therefore a Good man is never offended with any piece of Divine dispensation, nor hath he any reluctancy against that Will that dictates and determines all things by an Eternal rule of *Goodness*; as knowing, That there is an unbounded and Almighty *Love*, that without any disdain or envy freely communicates it self to every thing he made; that feeds even the young Ravens that call upon him; that makes his Sun to shine, and his Rain to fall, both upon the just and unjust; that always enfolds those in his everlasting armes who are made partakers of his own Image, perpetually nourishing and cherishing them with the fresh and vital influences of his Grace; as knowing also, That there is an All-seeing Eye, an unbounded Mind and Understanding, that derives it self through

---

[145] 'The less a man arrogates to himself, the more noble, glorious and divine he becomes'.

[146] Cf. Epictetus, *Ench.*, XXXI: 'For piety towards the gods know that the most important thing is this: to have right opinions about them—that they exist, and that they govern the universe well and justly—and to have set yourself to obey them, and to give way to all that happens, following events with a free will, in the belief that they are fulfilled by the highest mind (ὑπὸ τῆς ἀρίστης γνώμης ἐπιτελουμένοις)'.

the whole Universe, and sitting in all the wheels of motion, guides them all and powerfully governs the most excentrical motions of Creatures, and carries them all most harmoniously in their several orbes to one Last End. Who then shall give Law to God? *Where is the wise? where is the scribe? where is the disputer of this world?*[147] Where is he that would climb up into that בית דין של המעלה, the great Consistory in heaven, and sitting in consultation with the Almighty, instruct the Infinite and Incomprehensible Wisedome? Shall vain man be wiser then his maker? This is the hellish temper of wicked men, they examine and judge of all things by the line and measure of their own Self-will, their own Opinions and Designes; and measuring all things by a crooked rule, they think nothing to be straight; and therefore they fall out with God, and with restless impatience fret and vex themselves: and this fretfulness and impatiency in wicked men argues a breach in the just and due constitution of their Minds and Spirits.

But a Good man, whose Soul is restored to that frame and constitution it should be in, has better apprehensions of the ways and works of God, and is better affected under the various disposals of *Providence*. Indeed to a superficial observer of *Divine Providence* many things there are that seem to be nothing else but *Digressions* from the main End of all, and to come to pass by a fortuitous concourse of Circumstances; that come in so abruptly and without any concatenation or dependance one upon another, as if they were without any Mind or Understanding to guide them. But a wise man that looks from the Beginning to the End of things, beholds them all in their due place and method acting that part which the Supreme Mind and Wisedome that governs all things hath appointed them, and to carry on one and the same Eternal designe, while they move according to their own proper inclinations and measures, and aime at their own particular Ends.[148] It were not worth the while to live in a world κενῷ Θεοῦ καὶ προνοίας *devoid of God and Providence*, as it was well observ'd by the Stoick:[149] And to be subservient unto Providence is the holy ambition and great endeavour of a Good man, who is so perfectly overpower'd with the love of the Universal and Infinite Goodness, that he would not serve any Particular Good whatsoever, no not himself, so as to set up in the

[147] 1 *Corinthians* 1. 20.

[148] Cf. Sterry, *Discourse*, p. 166: 'In this light of eternity alone, is the Work of God seen aright, in the entire piece, in the whole design, from the beginning to the end'.

[149] Marcus Aurelius, II, 11.

world and trade for himself, as the men of this world doe who are *lovers of their own selves, and lovers of pleasures more then lovers of God*.[150]

CHAP. X

We have consider'd *the Excellency* of True Religion 1. in regard of its *Descent and Original*; 2. in regard of its *Nature*; 3. in regard of its *Properties and Effects*. We proceed now to a Fourth Particular, and shall shew

That Religion is a generous and noble thing in regard of its Progresse; it is perpetually carrying on that Mind in which it is once seated toward *Perfection*. Though the First appearance of it upon the Souls of good men may be but as the Wings of the Morning spreading themselves upon the Mountains, yet it is still rising higher and higher upon them, chasing away all the filthy mists and vapours of Sin and Wickedness before it, till it arrives to its Meridian altitude.[151] There is the strength and force of the Divinity in it; and though when it first enters into the Minds of men, it may seem to be *sowen in weakness*, yet it will raise it self *in power*. As Christ was in his *Bodily appearance*, he was still increasing in wisedome and knowledge and favour with God and man, untill he was perfected in glory: so is he also in his *Spiritual appearance* in the Souls of men; and accordingly the New Testament does more then once distinguish of Christ in his several ages, and degrees of growth in the Souls of all true Christians. Good men are always walking on from strength to strength, till at last they see God in Zion. Religion though it hath its infancy, yet it hath no old age: while it is in its Minority, it is always *in motu*; but when it comes to its Maturity and full age, it will always be *in quiete*, it is then always the same, and its years fail not, but it shall endure for ever. Holy and religious Souls being once toucht with an inward sense of Divine Beauty and Goodness, by a strong impress upon them are moved swiftly after God, and (as the Apostle expresses himself) *forgetting those things which are behind, and reaching forth unto those things which are before, they presse toward the Mark, for the prize of the high calling of God in Christ Jesus*; that so they may *attain to the resurrection of the dead*.[152]

[150] 2 *Timothy* 3. 2, 4.
[151] A marginal note in the original text quotes *Proverbs* 4. 18: 'The path of the just is as the shining light, that shineth more and more unto the perfect day'.
[152] *Philippians* 3. 13–14, 11.

Where a Spirit of Religion is, there is *the Central force of Heaven* it self quickening and enlivening those that are informed by it in their motions toward Heaven. As on the other side all unhallowed and defiled minds are within *the attractive power of Hell*, & are continually hastening their course thither, being strongly pressed down by the weight of their Wickedness. Ἀεί τινας ἔχει κινήσεις ἡ φύσις, as *Plutarch* hath well observ'd, Every nature in this world hath some proper Centre which it is always hastening to.¹⁵³ *Sin* and Wickedness does not hover a little over *the bottomeless pit* of Hell, and onely flutter about it; but it's continually sinking lower and lower into it. Neither does true *Grace* make some feeble assaies toward Heaven, but by a mighty Energy within it self it's always soaring up higher and higher into heaven. A good Christian does not onely court his Happiness, and cast now and then a smile upon it, or satisfy himself merely to be contracted to it; but with the greatest ardours of Love and Desire he pursues the solemnity of the just Nuptialls, that he may be wedded to it and made one with it. It is not an aiery speculation of *Heaven* as a thing (though never so undoubtedly) *to come*, that can satisfy his hungry desires, but the reall possession of it even in this life.¹⁵⁴ Such an Happiness would be less in the esteem of Good men, that were onely good to be enjoyed at the end of this life when all other enjoyments fail him.

I wish there be not among some such a light and poor esteem of *Heaven*, as makes them more to seek after *Assurance of Heaven* onely in the *Idea* of it as *a thing to come*, then after *Heaven it self*; which indeed we can never well be assured of, untill we find it rising up within our selves and glorifying our own Souls. When true *Assurance* comes, *Heaven* it self will appear upon the Horizon of our Souls, like a morning light chasing away all our dark and gloomy doubtings before it. We shall not need then to light up our Candles to seek for it in corners; no, it will display its own lustre and brightness so before us, that we may see it in its own light, and our selves the true possessours of it. We may be too nice and vain in seeking for *signes and tokens* of Christ's *Spiritual appearances* in the Souls of men, as well as the Scribes and Pharisees were in seeking for them at his *First appearance* in the World. When he comes into us, let us expect till the works that he shall doe within us may testify of him; and be not over-credulous, till we find that he doth

---

¹⁵³ The idea is not merely Plutarch's; it is a commonplace.

¹⁵⁴ A marginal note in the original text invokes *John 6.* 54 and 1 *John* 5. 11, 13.

those works there which none other could doe. As for a true well-grounded *Assurance,* say not so much, *Who shall ascend up into heaven, to fetch it down from thence?* or *who shall descend into the deep,* to fetch it up from beneath?[155] for in *the Growth* of true internal Goodness and in *the Progress* of true Religion it will freely unfold it self within us. Stay till the grain of Mustard-seed it self breaks forth from among the clods that buried it, till through the descent of the heavenly dew it sprouts up and discovers it self openly.[156] This holy *Assurance* is indeed the budding and blossoming of Felicity in our own Souls; it is the inward sense and feeling of the true life, spirit, sweetness and beauty of Grace powerfully expressing its own Energy within us.

Briefly, True Religion in *the Progresse* of it transforms those Minds in which it reigns from glory to glory: it goes on and prospers in bringing all enemies in subjection under their feet, in reconciling the Minds of men fully to God; and it instates them in a firm possession of the Supreme Good. This is *the Seed of God* within holy Souls, which is always warring against *the Seed of the Serpent,* till it prevail over it through the Divine strength and influence.[157] Though *Hell* may open her mouth wide and without measure, yet a true Christian in whom the seed of God remaineth, is in a good and safe condition; he finds himself born up by an Almighty arm, and carried upwards as upon Eagles wings; and the Evil one hath no power over him, or, as S. *John* expresseth it, ὁ Πονηρὸς οὐχ ἅπτεται αὐτοῦ, *the Evil one toucheth him not,* 1 Ep. chap. 5. v. 18.

CHAP. XI

We come now to the Fifth and Last Particular, viz. The Excellency of Religion in *the Terme and End of it,* which is nothing else but *Blessedness it self in its full maturity.* Which yet I may not here undertake to explain, for it is altogether ἄρρητόν τι,[158] nor can it descend so low as to accommodate it self to any humane style. Accordingly S. *John* tells us, *it does not yet appear what we shall be;* and yet that he may give us some glimpse of it, he points us out to God, and tells us, ὅμοιοι αὐτῷ ἐσόμεθα, *we shall be like him, for we shall see him as he is.*[159] Indeed the best way to get a discovery of it, is to endeavour as much as may be to be *Godlike,* to live in a feeling converse with God and in a powerful

---

[155] Cf. *Romans* 10. 6–7.
[156] Cf. *Mark* 4. 30 ff.
[157] Cf. above, p. 20 and note.
[158] 'something inexpressible'.
[159] 1 *John* 3. 2.

exercise and expression of all Godlike dispositions: So shall our inner man be best enabled *to know the breadth and length, the depth and height of that Love and Goodness which* yet *passeth all knowledg.*[160] There is a *State of Perfection* in the life to come so far transcendent to any in this life, as that we are not able from hence to take the just proportions of it, or to form a full and comprehensive notion of it. We are unable to comprehend the vastness and fullness of that Happiness which the most purified Souls may be raised to, or to apprehend how far the mighty power and strength of the Divinity deriving it self into created Being, may communicate a more Transcendent life and blessedness to it. We know not what latent powers our Souls may here contain within themselves, which then may begin to open and dilate themselves to let in the full streams of the Divine Goodness when they come nearly and intimately to converse with it; or how *Blessedness* may act upon those Faculties of our Minds which we now have. We know not what illapses and irradiations there may be from God upon Souls in Glory, that may raise them into a state of Perfection surpassing all our imaginations.

As for *Corporeal* Happiness, there cannot be any thing further added to the *Pleasure* of our *Bodies* or Animal part, then a restoring it from disturbing Passion and Pain to its just and natural constitution; and therefore some Philosophers have well disputed against the opinion of the *Epicureans* that make *Happiness* to conflict in *Bodily pleasure,* ὅτι πολλαπλάσιον ἔχει τὸ λυπηρὸν προηγούμενον·[161] and when *the molestation* is gone, and the just constitution of Nature recovered, *Pleasure* ceaseth. But the highest *Pleasure* of *Minds* and *Spirits* does not onely consist in the relieving of them from any antecedent pains or grief, or in a relaxation from some former molesting Passion: neither is their Happiness a mere Stoical ἀταραξία·[162] as the Happiness of the

---

[160] *Ephesians* 3. 18, 19.

[161] Cf. Simplicius, *In Epict.*, I: 'because this is most certain, that true Good is always attended with true pleasure (τῷ ἀληθινῷ ἀγαθῷ συνέστιν ἡ ἀληθινὴ ἡδονή); hence it is, that, wherever the soul discovers the least shadow of this, she catches at it greedily, without staying to consider of what kind the pleasure is; whether it be real, and agreeable to that Good which is truly so; or whether it be false, and only carries a counterfeit face of Good; never recollecting that it is necessarily attended with many troubles and uneasinesses, and would not be pleasure without these to introduce and recommend it to us (ὅτι πολλαπλάσιον ἔχει τό λυπηρὸν προηγούμενόν τε πάντως etc.)'.

[162] See above, p. 176 and note.

The Excellency and Nobleness of True Religion

Deity is not a mere *Negative* thing, rendring it free from all disturbance or molestation, so that it may eternally rest quiet within it self; it does not so much conflict *in Quiete*, as *in Actu & vigore*. A Mind and Spirit is too full of activity and energy, as too quick and potent a thing to enjoy a full and complete Happiness in *a mere Cessation*; this were to make *Happiness* an heavy Spiritless thing. The Philosopher hath well observ'd, that τῷ ἀληθινῷ ἀγαθῷ συνέστιν ἡ ἀληθινὴ ἡδονὴ,[163] there is infinite power and strength in Divine joy, pleasure and happiness commensurate to that Almighty Being and Goodness which is the Eternal source of it.

As Created Beings, that are capable of conversing with God, stand nearer to God or further off from him, and as they partake more or less of his *likeness*; so they partake more or less of that *Happiness* which flows forth from him, and God communicates himself in different degrees to them. There may be as many degrees of *Sanctity* and *Perfection*, as there are of States and Conditions of Creatures: and that is properly *Sanctity* which guides and orders all the Faculties and Actions of any Creature in a way suitable and correspondent to that rank and state which God hath placed it in: and while it doth so, it admits no sin or defilement to it self, though yet it may be elevated and advanced higher; and accordingly true Positive *Sanctity* comes to be advanced higher and higher, as any Creature comes more to partake of the life of God, and to be brought into a nearer conjunction with God: and so the *Sanctity* and *Happiness* of Innocency it self might have been perfected.

Thus we see how True Religion carries up the Souls of Good men above the black regions of *Hell* and Death. This indeed is the great ἀποκατάστασις[164] of Souls, it is *Religion* it self, or a reall participation of God and his Holiness, which is their true *restitution* and advancement. All that *Happiness* which Good men shall be made partakers of, as it cannot be born up upon any other foundation then *true Goodness and a Godlike nature* within them; so neither is it distinct from it. *Sin* and *Hell* are so twined and twisted up together, that if the power of *Sin* be once dissolv'd, the bonds of Death and Hell will also fall asunder. *Sin* and *Hell* are of the same kind, of the same linage and descent: as on the other side True *Holiness* or Religion and True *Happiness* are but two severall Notions of one thing, rather then distinct in themselves. *Religion* delivers us from *Hell* by instating us in a possession of True Life and

---

[163] See above, note 161.
[164] *Apocatastasis*: 'restoration'. Cf. the Introduction, above, p. 37.

Blisse. *Hell* is *rather a Nature* then *a place*: and *Heaven* cannot be so truly defined by any thing *without* us, as by something that is *within* us.

Thus have we done with those Particulars wherein we considered *the Excellency and Nobleness of Religion*, which is here exprest by חיים ארח *The way of life*, and elsewhere is stiled by *Solomon* עץ חיים *A tree of life*:[165] true Religion being an inward Principle of life, of a Divine life the best life, that which is *Life* most properly so called: accordingly in the Holy Scripture a life of Religion is stiled *Life*, as a life of Sin and Wickedness is stiled *Death*. In the ancient Academical Philosophy it was much disputed whether that *Corporeal and Animal life*, which was always drawing down the Soul into Terrene and Material things, was not more properly to be Stiled *Death* then *Life*. What sense hereof the *Pythagoreans* had may appear by this practise of theirs, They were wont to set up κενοτάφια Empty coffins in the places of those that had forsaken their School and degenerated from their Philosophy and good Precepts, as being Apostates from life it self, and dead to Vertue and a good life, which is *the true life*, & therefore fit only to be reckoned among *the dead*.[166]

For a Conclusion of this Discourse; The *Use* which we shall make of all shall be this, To awaken and exhort every one to a serious minding of Religion: as *Solomon* doth earnestly exhort every one to seek after true *Wisedome*, which is the same with *Religion* and Holiness, as *Sin* is with *Folly*; *Prov.* 4. 5. *Get Wisedome, get understanding*; and v. 7. *Get Wisedome, and with all thy getting get understanding. Wisedome is the principal thing*. This is the summe of all, *the Conclusion of the whole matter, Fear God, and keep his Commandements*; *for this is the whole* (duty, business and concernment) *of man*.[167] Let us not trifle away our time and opportunities which God hath given us, wherein we may lay hold upon Life and Immortality, in doing nothing, or else pursuing Hell and Death. Let us awake out of our vain dreams; Wisedome calls upon us, and offers us the hidden treasures of Life and Blessedness: Let us not perpetually deliver over our selves to laziness and slumbering. Say not, *There is a lion in the way*; say not, Though Religion be good, yet it is unattainable: No, but let us intend all our Powers in a serious resolv'd pursuance of it, and depend upon the assistance of Heaven

---

[165] Cf. *Proverbs* 3. 18; 15. 24.
[166] Thus Origen, *Cont. Cels.*, II, 12, and III, 51. Cf. Iamblichus, *Vit. Pyth.*, XVII.
[167] *Ecclesiastes* 12. 13.

The Excellence and Nobleness of True Religion 197

which never fails those that soberly seek for it. It is indeed the Levity of mens spirits, their heedlessness and regardlessness of their own lives, that betrays them to Sin and Death. It is the general practice of men αὐτοσχεδιάζειν τὸν βίον, *extempore vivere*,[168] as the Satyrist speaks; they ordinarily ponderate and deliberate upon every thing more then how it becomes them to live, they so live as if their Bodies had swallowed up their Souls: their lives are but a kind of Lottery: the Principles by which they are guided are nothing else but a confused multitude of Fancies rudely jumbled together. Such is the life of most men, it is but a meer *Casual* thing acted over at peradventure, without any fair and calm debates held either with Religion, or with Reason which in it self, as it is not distorted and depraved by corrupt men, is a true Friend to Religion, and directs men to God and to things good and just, pure, lovely and praise-worthy; and the directions of this Inward guide we are not to neglect. Unreasonableness or the smothering and extinguishing *the Candle of the Lord* within us[169] is no piece of Religion, nor advantageous to it: That certainly will not raise men up to God, which sinks them below men. There had never been such an *Apostasy from Religion*, nor had such a Mystery of iniquity (full of deceiveableness and imposture) been revealed and wrought so powerfully in the Souls of some men, had there not first come an *Apostasy from sober Reason*, had there not first been a falling away and departure from Natural Truth.

It is to be feared our nice speculations about a τὸ ἐφ' ἡμῖν[170] in Theology have tended more to exercise mens Wits then to reform their lives, and that they have too much descended into their practice, and have tended rather to take men off from minding Religion, then to quicken them up to a diligent seeking after it. Though the Powers of Nature may now be weakned, and though we cannot produce a living form of Religion in our own Souls; yet we are not surely resolved so into a sluggish *Passiveness*, as that we cannot, or were not in any kind

---

[168] 'to live according to the demands of the moment'. The idea need not necessarily be ascribed to any 'satyrist'; it is of course a commonplace.

[169] Cf. above, p. 50.

[170] 'In our own power', i.e., free will. Thus the third of Cudworth's '*Essentials* of *True Religion*' reads: 'That there is Something ἐφ' ἡμῖν, or, That we are so far forth *Principles* or *Masters* of our own *Actions*, as to be *Accountable* to *Justice* for them ...' (*Int. System*, 'Preface', sig. A3ᵛ). Similarly the phrase τὸ ἐφ' ἡμῖν links the opening lines of Cudworth, *Freewill*, with Epictetus, *Ench.*, I· Plotinus, VI, viii, 1; *et al.*

or manner of way to seek after it. Certainly a man may as well read *the Scriptures* as study a piece of *Aristotle*, or of Natural Philosophy or Mathematicks. He that can observe any thing comely and commendable, or unworthy and base, in another man, may also reflect upon himself, and see how *face answers to face*, as *Solomon* speaks *Proverbs* 27. 19. If men would seriously commune with their hearts, their own Consciences would tell them plainly, that they might avoid and omit more evil then they doe, and that they might doe more good then they doe: and that they doe not put forth that power which God hath given them, nor faithfully use those Talents[171] nor improve the advantages and means afforded them.

I fear the ground of most mens Misery will prove to be *a Second fall, and a Lapse upon a Lapse*. I doubt God will not allow that Proverb, *The Fathers have eaten sour grapes, and the childrens teeth are set on edge*,[172] as not in respect of *Temporal misery*, much less will he allow it in respect of *Eternal*. It will not be so much because our First parents incurred God's displeasure, as because we have neglected what might have been done by us afterwards in order to the seeking of God, his face and favour, while he might be found.

Up then and be doing; and the Lord will be with us. He will not leave us nor forsake us, if we seriously set our selves about the work. Let us endeavour to acquaint our selves with our own lives, and the true Rules of life, with this which *Solomon* here calls the *Way of Life*:[173] let us inform our Minds as much as may be in the Excellency and Loveliness of Practical Religion; that beholding it in its own beauty and amiableness, we may the more sincerely close with it. As there would need nothing else to deterr and affright men from *Sin* but its own ugliness and deformity, were it presented to a naked view and seen as it is: so nothing would more effectually commend Religion to the Minds of men, then the displaying and unfolding the Excellencies of its Nature, then the true Native beauty and inward lustre of Religion it self: οὔθ᾽ ἕσπερος, οὔθ᾽ ἑῶος οὕτω θαυμαστός· neither the Evening nor the Morning-Star could so sensibly commend themselves to our bodily Eyes,[174] and delight them with their shining beauties, as True Religion, which is an undefiled Beam of the uncreated light, would to a mind

---

[171] Cf. the parable of the talents (*Matthew* 25. 14 ff.).

[172] *Ezekiel* 18. 2.

[173] In the text of the present discourse, above, p. 145.

[174] The Greek phrase is taken from Aristotle (*Ethica nicomachea*, V, 5) who in turn quotes a fragment of Euripides.

capable of conversing with it. *Religion,* which is the true *Wisedome,* is (as the Author of the Book of Wisedome speaks of *Wisedome,*) *a pure influence flowing from the glory of the Almighty, the brightness of the Everlasting light, the unspotted mirrour of the power of God and the image of his Goodness: She is more beautiful then the Sun, & above all the order of Stars; being compared with the light, she is found before it.*[175]

Religion is no such austere, sour & rigid thing, as to affright men away from it: No, but those that are acquainted with the power of it, find it to be altogether sweet and amiable. An holy Soul sees so much of the glory of Religion in the lively impressions which it bears upon it self, as both wooes and winns it. We may truly say concerning Religion to such Souls as S. *Paul* spake to the Corinthians, *Needs it any Epistles of Commendation to you? Needs it any thing to court your affections? Ye are indeed its Epistle, written not with ink, but with the Spirit of the living God.*[176]

Religion is not like the Prophet's roll, sweet as honey when it was in his mouth, but as bitter as gall in his belly. Religion is no sullen *Stoicisme,* no sour *Pharisaisme*; it does not consist in a few Melancholy passions, in some dejected looks or depressions of Mind: but it consists in *Freedom, Love, Peace, Life* and *Power*; the more it comes to be digested into our lives, the more sweet and lovely we shall find it to be. Those spots and wrinkles which corrupt Minds think they see in the face of Religion, are indeed nowhere else but in their own deformed and misshapen apprehensions. It is no wonder when a defiled Fancy comes to be the Glass, if you have an unlovely reflection. Let us therefore labour to purge our own Souls from all worldly pollutions; let us breath after the aid and assistance of the Divine Spirit, that it may irradiate and inlighten our Minds, that we may be able to see Divine things in a Divine light: let us endeavour to live more in a real practice of those Rules of Religious and Holy living commended to us by our ever-Blessed Lord and Saviour: So shall we know Religion better, and knowing it love it, and loving it be still more and more ambitiously pursuing after it, till we come to a full attainment of it, and therein of our own Perfection and Everlasting Bliss.

[175] *Wisdom of Solomon* 7. 25–6, 29.
[176] 2 *Corinthians* 3. 1–3.

HENRY MORE

The Purification of a Christian Man's Soul*

I Peter i. 22, 23

Seeing ye have purified your souls in obeying the truth through the Spirit, unto unfeigned love of the brethren; see that ye love one another, with a pure heart, fervently: Being born again, not of corruptible seed, but of incorruptible, by the word of God which liveth and abideth for ever.

THE Text is an Exhortation to *Christian Love*, The Duty is enforced from a double Argument.

1. From the end of our Sanctification, in those words, *Seeing ye have purified your Souls in obeying the Truth through the Spirit*, εἰς φιλαδελφίαν ἀνυπόκριτον, unto (or *for*) *unfeigned brotherly love*. And this ushers in the Precept or Duty, *Love one another with a pure heart, fervently*.

2. The other Argument follows, of not less force than the former, which is drawn from the condition of our new Birth; *Being born again, not of corruptible seed, but of incorruptible by the word of God, which liveth and abideth for ever*.

THE several Truths or *Doctrines* contained in the First Argument are these, viz.

Doctrine I. *That the Christian mans Soul is Purified.*

Purified] 'Aγνίζειν is the word, synonymous to καθαρίζειν; both imply a purging or cleansing from filth. They are both used together, *James* 4. 8. in one signification: But yet there is a more special sense belonging to them both; they both signifie a Sacred and Ceremonial kind of cleansing and purification, and after, appropriation to God;

* From *Discourses on Several Texts of Scripture*, ed. John Worthington (1692), Disc. XIII [pp. 394–418]. A number of the Biblical references, originally inserted in the text, have been transferred to the notes. The title of the sermon is by the present editor.

as *Titus* 2. 14. where the word is καθαρίζω, with allusion to the Consecration of the *Levites*, *Numb.* 8. and their washing of their Cloths, and sprinkling the Water of Purification, is called ἁγνισμός.[1]

So that the *purifying* of the Soul (in the Text) implies *cleansing* and *appropriation*. But the Objects are not here express'd, yet very safely supposed; we cannot miss of them if we would. For from what should the Soul be purified, but from its filth? What is the filth of the Soul but Sin? To whom should the Soul thus purg'd be appropriated or consecrated? To it self? It is not purg'd, if not purg'd from it self. To the Creature? It is the height of Impiety, palpable Idolatry. To Sin? It is not Sense. To what then but to God its Creator and Redeemer, who gave himself, ἵνα καθαρίσῃ ἑαυτῷ λαὸν περιούσιον, *that he might purifie unto himself a peculiar people.*[2]

Thus is purified the Christians Soul; which is true not only in that narrower sense of taking the Soul, but also as it includes the Body, or the *Beast* as the *Platonists* call it;[3] even the very Passions, and more fiery motions which those Philosophers resemble to Horses drawing the Chariot of the Soul; these also shall be Sanctified: So that upon the reins of the Horses (if I may speak with *Zechary*) there is inscrib'd, *Holiness to the Lord.*[4] But certainly more properly and chiefly this Purification belongs to the Soul her self, and from thence will sink through all the powers and faculties of the Body, taking hold of them, wielding them and ruling them at its own pleasure, or at least not suffering it self to be over-ruled by them.

Now this *purifying* of a Christian implies, that he was unholy and foul before. And not only the whole man, but also whole mankind is in this sinful state till wash'd and purified. *Rom.* 3. 12. 1 *Joh.* 1. 8, 9, 10. where we have both these points confirm'd. 1. That we all have sinned, and stand obnoxious before God. 2. That by the worth and merit of Christ, and the effectual working of the Divine Spirit we have forgiveness, and that God doth cleanse us from all unrighteousness. And this is the true Christian Mystery: If we be Christians, we must be as certainly purified, as its certain we were once impure.

Doct. II. *That the Christians Soul is purified in obeying the Truth*

Here meets us the unwelcome visage of *Obedience*; but with its fac. turn'd upon a safe object the *Truth*. Where we may note, that it is not

---

[1] *Numbers* 8. 7 (LXX).   [2] *Titus* 2. 14.
[3] Cf. *Timaeus*, 69–70.   [4] *Zechariah* 14. 20.

any Obedience that purifies, but *the Obedience to the Truth*. A man may toil like a Mill-horse in a circuit of Ceremonies and outward performances, and yet but take his walk with the wicked, unless the Truth be obey'd.

Again it is such a Truth as Obedience belongs to, not an high aery speculative Truth; not a Truth only to be believed, but to be put in practice; for we cannot be said properly to obey speculative Truth, because the Soul there has no power to resist or disobey: For the Devil himself would gladly embrace and assent to all pure and inoffensive speculation, that doth not touch his own interest and present condition; and so would all his and Natures children, the most wicked men that are: And that the Devil is cast into a fit of trembling at this grand speculative Maxime, [*There is a God*]; is because his quick memory doth presently recollect that he is Just, and that himself stands obnoxious to his Justice; here is his interest toucht.

The *Truth* therefore here meant is not so much those general speculations of the Infinite Power and Wisdom of God, the Incomprehensible Trinity, *&c.* which both good and bad men do easily spend their time in, and promiscuously believe, and yet sit securely upon their lees, their hearts being untoucht, unbroken, unstir'd: But the Truths which we are said most properly to obey are the *Practical* Truths, such as *Matth.* 5. *Chap.* 16. 24. *Chap.* 11, *ult. Chap.* 7. 13 *&c.* The Purification of a Christian is in obedience to such Truths; and Christ admits none for his that be disobedient, *workers of iniquity*.[5]

Doct. III. *That the purified and obedient Soul is thus purged and obedient through the Spirit.*

This is he of whom *Malachi* 3. 2, 3. *But who may abide the day of his coming? and who shall stand when he appeareth? for he is like a refiners fire, and like fullers sope. And he shall sit as a refiner and purifier of silver, and he shall purifie the sons of Levi, and purge them as gold and silver; that they may offer unto the Lord an offering in righteousness.*

We having then so powerful a Purifier, what hinders but the Christian Soul may be purified? No doubt of this Refiners Art or Skill. Is his *Will* doubted of? It is one with the Will of God; and Gods Will is, that we be *purified*.[6] And Christ is no teacher of loosness, but of the height of Righteousness. 'Tis not the privilege of the Gospel

---

[5] Cf. *Matthew* 7. 23.   [6] Cf. 1 *Thessalonians* 4. 3.

that we may sin securely, because *Christus solvit*; but that we may live more exactly, because Christ requires it, and doth inwardly enable us to perform it.

See also *Rom.* 8. 1, 2, 3, 4. *There is therefore now no condemnation to them which are in Christ Jesus, who walk not after the flesh, but after the Spirit. For the law of the Spirit of life, in Christ Jesus, hath made me free from the law of sin and death. For what the law could not do, in that it was weak through the flesh, God sending his own Son, in the likeness of sinful flesh, and for sin condemned sin in the flesh: That the righteousness of the law might be fulfilled in us, who walk not after the flesh, but after the Spirit.*

Here we will acknowledge that God is able, his Spirit is willing, but we are uncapable of so great a good, by reason of the infirmity of the Flesh: But answer me, O vain man, what is this infirmity of the Flesh, is it not the strength of Sin? And is there any strength that can withstand the powerful operation of the Spirit of God? The weakness, or strength if you will, of the Body bears it towards the Earth; but the fire and activity of the Natural Spirits bears it above, and enables it to walk upright on the Earth, contrary to the bent of its own Essence and Nature. Shall not the Spirit of God then be as able to actuate and lead the Soul contrary to its accidental and ascititious[7] Principles, as the Natural Spirits to actuate the Body contrary to its innate and essential Principles? Certainly if it be not effectual in us, we our selves are in fault, who abuse our shuffling Phansie and Reason to fend off the stroke and power of Truth that at once would cleave our hearts, that's a tender place, the seat of Life it self; and any Religion but that which kills us and mortifies us. The Devil knew well enough what he said, and his Children make it good; *Skin for skin, and all that a man has will he give for his life.*[8] This is the shuffling hypocrisie of the Natural Spirit of man, and the root of infidelity.

But let us make better use of this precious Scripture. [*Seeing ye obeyed the Truth through the Spirit*]. 1*st.* For the encrease of Faith, and Confidence, and Courage in the wayes of *Obedience*, sith we have so strong assistance as the Spirit of our God, with true Christian Fortitude to conflict with all our Spiritual Enemies, wearing that Motto in our Minds Πάντα ἰσχύω ἐν τῷ ἐνδυναμοῦντι μὲ Χριστῷ.[9] 2*dly*,

---

[7] 'adscititious': supplemental.   [8] *Job* 2. 4.

[9] Adapted from 1 *Timothy* 1. 12: χάριν ἔχω τῷ ἐνδυναμώσαντί με Χριστῷ ('I thank Christ ... who hath enabled me').

For hearty Thankfulness to God when ever we find our selves successful in our Spiritual Warfare, as to the only giver of Victory. *3dly*, and *lastly*, For Humility, Æquanimity, and Christian Patience and expectancy towards our Neighbours that are not yet reclaim'd from their evil ways, being compassionate over them; not to insult in other mens weakness and miscarriages, sith we our selves stand not by our own power, but by the gracious assistance of our Saviour Jesus Christ: And certainly *Purification* arrived at its full end, will easily afford us this; for the end of Purification is *Brotherly Love*, which is the Fourth Doctrine.

> Doct. IV. *That this Purification of the Soul, and Obedience to the Truth through the Spirit, is for this end,* viz. *the eliciting of Brotherly Love and Sincerity in the Soul.*

Εἰς φιλαδελφίαν]. I know, sometimes ἀγάπη and φιλαδελφία are distinguished, as 2 *Pet.* 1. 7.[10] But that φιλαδελφία here may be as large as ἀγάπη, I know nothing considerable to the contrary. The word is capable of that Sense, ἀδελφὸς and אח being used in as great a latitude as *Proximus* and *Alter*, including all that descended from our Father *Adam*.

So that φιλαδελφία is *the love of our Neighbour*; and this Love is the end and height of our *Purification* and *Obedience*, the aim and scope of it, as much as concerns the Second Table.[11] Who is able to express so Divine an excellency? For certainly the unfeigned Love of men is the very Divine Love it self, whereby God loves himself and all things, and we also love God and all things in reference to him. This is that Love of whom the whole Universe was begotten, and that rock'd the cradle of the Infant World; the very Spirit of God, whose Splendour none can behold and live; for he must first be dead to himself, and extinguish the love of himself, before he can be touch'd and quickened by this Spirit of Life and Love.

THUS much for the Doctrines included in the *First* main Argument. In the *Second* are these; *viz.*

> Doctrine I. *That there is a Regeneration of the Soul.*

By understanding what *Generation* is, we may better know what is *Regeneration*.

1. The notion in general of *Generation* (according to *Aristotle*)

---

[10] *agape* ('love') and *philadelphia* ('brotherly love').
[11] *Romans* 13. 9–10, 1 *Timothy* 1. 5.

implies no more than a right and fit union of a form substantial with some capable subject, whether that form be elicited of the subject or matter, or be brought in from elsewhere, θύραθεν εἰσιοῦσα, as *Aristotle* speaks of the Rational Soul.[12]

2. There may be more Forms substantial than one in one subject; so they be but subordinate one to the other; and that a new Species doth not arise so much from the destruction of the pre-existent Form, as by addition of a new one, which might actuate the whole that doth pre-exist: As the *numerus ternarius* is not made by taking from the *numerus binarius*, but by adding an Unite therto. Thus *Aristotle* seems to speak, *Metaph.* 7. *Cap.* 3.[13]

3. Observe, That one Soul actuating a Body, if any part of that Body be cut off and lose the benefit of information, suppose an Hand or Foot, that is then said to be but equivocally what it was before; which implies it is then of another Nature or Species, as much of it as there is, though it be not an entire substance if compared with the whole; and consequently that the Soul actuating it, did then specificate it another way.

We have now a tolerable insight into *Generation*, and *Regeneration* is but this twice told. That which is this specifical substance now, by adding a new substantial Form thereto becomes something else: This is Regeneration. And to apply it to our selves. We are already once born according to Nature; our Bodies and Souls being fitly united together by him that is the Father of all Life, and the Lord of Nature: But though we be thus specificated, yet we are not thence perfected; but this *Binary* of Body and Soul the *Pythagoreans* would be bold to call but a miserable ἔλλειψις,[14] till that *Third* completing *Unite* be added, the θεία φύσις, that *Divine Nature*, or Spirit of God.

This Doctrine of *Regeneration* is inculcated often enough in Scripture, though not under this express name; but it is strongly enough implied in as many places as there is mention of *being born of God*: For what is that but *Regeneration*, or a Second Birth, and how oft is that repeated in S. *Johns* Writings? *John* 1. 12, 13. *But as many as received him, to them gave he power to become the sons of God, even to them that believe on his name: Which were born, not of blood, nor of the*

[12] *De anima*, III, 8.   [13] See further below, pp. 206 ff.
[14] *ellipsis*: 'defect'. More's understanding of Pythagorean number theory is inevitably sub-primitive, not to say partisan. An attempt to reconstruct the complex theory has been made by J. E. Raven, *Pythagoreans and Eleatics* (Cambridge, 1948), esp. Ch. IX–XI.

will of the flesh, nor of the will of man, but of God. Chap. 3. 5. *Jesus answered, Verily verily I say unto thee, Except a man be born of water and of the Spirit, he cannot enter into the kingdom of God.*

Regeneration is not a sleight tipping or colouring over with superficial qualities and habits, but is from a substantial principle of Life, that actuates the Soul as powerfully as the Soul doth the Body; is the Souls true form or ἐντελέχεια,[15] as the Soul is the Bodies ἐντελέχεια and form. For what doth ἐντελέχεια imply, but penetration and most intimate possession of the subject actuated or informed, and power, rule and command over the same to move it at pleasure? And doth not the Divine λόγος,[16] the Eternal *Word*, thus penetrate and possess the Souls of Godly men; even as the subtle Light doth the Air, of it self but a dark and forlorn body?

There is so perfect a correspondency between *Generation* and *Regeneration*, that unless prejudice and Sophistical curiosity keep it off, mans Reason would forwardly assent that the Christian *Regeneration* is no dry Metaphor, but full Truth: And that the *Regenerate* man is even as specifically distinct from the mere *Natural* man, as the Natural man from brute Beasts. We made it good even out of *Aristotle*, that the Species or Essences of things are as Numbers, *&c.* The *Ternarius* is not made by taking from the *Binarius*, but by adding another Unite thereunto: Therefore a man though he have one Form already, *viz. the Natural Soul*, it hinders not but he may have also another, *the quickening Spirit of God*. I will add a little more force to the Conclusion by taking notice of the grounds of our specificating things, and essentially distinguishing the one from the other; that we may discover the like grounds for our conclusion. What small and slight intimations from accidentary differences in Natural Bodies, have cast the Earth, Water and Air into so many distinct Species; and that they cannot put on one anothers outward qualities, without the generation of some inward substantial form! A little difference in weight and colour must imply a several Specification in Silver and Gold; and upon a little more occasion than colour and taste, must a Pigeon and a Partridge be distinct Species. Not that these things are false, but that there is as true grounds to find a real Specifical difference betwixt a Natural man and a man Regenerate. For if several colour, figure and weight,

---

[15] '*Entelechia,* Ἐντελέχεια: It is nothing else but *forma*, or *actus*, and belongs even to the most contemptible forms' (More, *Democritus platonissans* [Cambridge, 1646], sig. Q2ᵛ).

[16] *Logos* means both 'word' and 'reason'. Cf. below, p. 335, note.

though they be something near akin to one another, be a sufficient cause of surmisal that some inward essential form is within; surely then when we see the Soul of man figured and covered over with new Thoughts of Mind, new Knowledge, new Desires; it is as good an Argument that it is actuated by a new Principle of Life.

But here it will be replyed; Then any Chast man will Specifically differ from an Unchast man, Just men from Unjust, Philosophers from Idiots.

But it is not such an opposition as it seems at first sight. The improvement of Nature is no sign of a new Specification. A Horse that can go, may also trot, gallop, pace, swim and dance too, and yet not cease to be an Horse: But if I should see him flying in the Air, I should take him to be no Horse but a Devil. A Nightingal may vary with her voice into a multitude of interchangeable Notes, and various Musical falls and risings, and yet be but a Nightingal, no Chorister: But should she but sing one Hymn or *Hallelujah*, I should deem her no Bird but an Angel. So the highest improvement of Natural Knowledge, or mere Morality, will argue us no more than the Sons of Men: But to be of one will completely with God, will make us, or doth argue us to be the Sons of God. Stones, Dirt, Metals, Minerals, distinct enough one from another, agree in tending downwards to the Earth; and Fire is as much determinate to moving upward to the Natural Seat of that Element: But if that either of them, or Fiery or Earthy nature, move of its pleasure upward, downward, to the right, to the left, this way and the other way, even as it will; no man any longer will suppose it either Fire or Earth, but something else Specificated by a new internal principle. To be always bent down to the desire of the body and worldly delights, that motion is Bestial: To be always reaching at high things, that's Diabolical: To be disengag'd from a mans self, and stand indifferent to what ere the Will of God is, that's Angelical or Divine.

But it is again objected, If *Regeneration* imply a real new *Generation*, that then it must also imply a real Corruption; so that the Natural Soul shall be destroyed, or at least Natural Knowledge, Natural Principles of Reason.

Not a jot of this follows. Neither the Soul it self, nor its Natural Principles of Knowledge or Reason are destroyed or abated, but made up and perfected. Doth one Unite added to two pre-existent Unites destroy those Unites? Or rather, do they not all put together beget a new Number of another Species and Name? Or, to bring it more home, doth the Soul of man coming into the organiz'd Body, destroy the Body? Or doth it not rather perfect and compleat it? So doth also the Spirit of God coming into the Soul. But as for the pre-existent qualities, no more of those are destroy'd than are incompatible with the residence of that new Form, the Divine Spirit. Disobedience and wickedness be the only ἀσύστατα[17] with this new Birth. Reason is no more incompatible with this state, than phansie, memory, hearing, seeing, smelling, &c. Nor the improvement of Reason, or Arts and Sciences, then looking upon the Stars through a *Galilæos* Glass, or reading the Bible with an ordinary pair of Spectacles.

Doct. II. *That the Soul is Regenerated of no corruptible Seed, but incorruptible.*

There needs no Descant upon this, no Interpretation, the Words are so clear; no Proof, the Truth is so unquestionable.

Doct. III. *That this incorruptible Seed is the Word of God.*[18]

The Word of God has two or three Senses: It signifies *The written Word*, *The Word spoken*, and *Verbum mentis*, That which God conceives within himself. This last is chiefly *the Word*: The other but dead signs or shadows of it, differing as much from this, as a picture of a man from a living man; nay much more; as much at least as the shadow of the Garland hanging on a Signpost, and projected on the ground, differs from the best Wine in the Inne. The *Word spoken* perisheth with the speaking, *Vox audita perit*.[19] The *written Word* is indeed longer-liv'd, but Paper and Ink is not incorruptible and immortal: For *the heavens shall melt away with a noise, and the elements shall melt with fervent heat; the earth also, and the works that are therein, shall be burnt up.*[20] *The Word of God* then is safe no where but in his own bosom, cypher'd within himself in his own mind. This is his eternal Wisdom and incorruptible Word; the only incorruptible Seed.

Preaching and hearing, and reading and discoursing, they may be a kind of plowing or harrowing, or some such piece of Husbandry: But it is an hand out of the Clouds that sets his Seed of everlasting

[17] 'inconsistent (things)'.
[18] On the 'seed', cf. Whichcote's sermon, above, pp. 62 ff., and the Introduction, p. 20.
[19] From the proverb, 'Vox audita perit, litera scripta manet' ('The spoken word perishes, the written word abides').
[20] 2 *Peter* 3. 10.

Life in our hearts. Those are but some hungry talk of the best dishes, or spreading the table: This is the real food. Those but a note under the Physicians hand: This is the very Physick that restores to health.

> Doct. IV. *That this Word of God, which is the Seed of the Soul, is a living and everlasting Word.*

This *Word* is no other than the inward Word of God, which is his first-born Son, the everlasting Wisdom of the Father, which sat in Counsel with him when he made the World.[21] This Second *Hypostasis* is so acknowledged by the Heathen to be everlasting; they make it to be τῷ πρώτῳ ζῆν, *the first Life.* That it is a living Word, we have an ample testimony. *For the word of God is quick, and powerful, and sharper than any two-edged sword, piercing even to the dividing asunder of soul and spirit, and of the joynts and marrow, and is a discerner of the thoughts and intents of the heart. Neither is there any creature that is not manifest in his sight: but all things are naked, and opened unto the eyes of him with whom we have to do.*[22] Can these Attributes be given to any dead letter, or any transient hand? Can Words or Writings be so penetrating as to *divide asunder the Soul and Spirit?* &c.

'Tis true, Authors both Divine and Profane give very quick operations to the Words of the Tongue. *Prov.* 25. 15. *By long forbearing is a prince perswaded, and a soft tongue breaketh the bone.* Psal. 57. 4. *My soul is among lions, and I lie even among them that are set on fire, even the sons of men, whose teeth are spears and arrows, and their tongue a sharp sword.* Psal. 64. 3. *Who whet their tongue like a sword, and bend their bows to shoot their arrows, even bitter words.* And in *Homer,* κέρτομα βάζειν is *to speak words that cut to the heart.*[23] But for this, consider that it is not the words that do then so wound the mind, as the mind launceth it self, and plagues it self by those unruly phantasms she then occasionally creates in her self upon such speeches. One man being jear'd at a Comedy, bears himself so carelessly and jollily, that he walks cross the stage that all the people may take notice that he was the man that was so abused. Another so used, goes home and hangs himself; which is a sure experiment to prove that it is not words, but the Souls own thoughts that so wound and scorch her self. Words of themselves are but empty shells and husks, and can give no greater blow than the shadow of *Hercules*'s Club lifted up in the Sun; nor

---

[21] *Proverbs* 8. 27–9, *John* 1. 1–3.   [22] *Hebrews* 4. 12–13.
[23] The phrase is in fact Hesiod's (*Opera et dies*, 788).

can no more administer comfort than an Ivy-bush can quench our thirst. Wherefore it is plain that 'tis the Soul her self that creates these joys or disturbances in things Natural or Moral. But in real Conversion to God, in unfeigned Repentance, in the New Birth (as the Letter or outward Word is excluded, as has been cleared, so) the Soul her self is excluded, as being unable to regenerate her self; therefore what is left but God himself by his living Word? That's the immediate cause of Conversion and Regeneration, the other but occasions. If not, there is no supernatural act at all in Conversion and Regeneration.

Again, this Word of God is said *to be a discerner of the thoughts*, &c.[24] all which are manifest Properties of Life. Compareing therefore this place of the *Hebrews* with the Text, it is plain that there is a *living* and *everlasting Word*, and that that Word is meant in both these places: And if so, then its the same with S. *Johns* words, *In him was life, and the life was the light of men*.[25]

THUS much for the *Doctrines* or Truths, which are as so many enforcements to the great Duty, ἐκ καθαρᾶς καρδίας ἀλλήλους ἀγαπήσατε ἐκτενῶς.[26] The substance of the Duty is *mutual Love*; which is charged with a double modification, *viz*. of *quality*, ἐκ καθαρᾶς καρδίας, and of *quantity*, ἐκτενῶς; which implies extension, and is as much as ἐκτεταμένως, or intension, and is as much as ἐντενῶς.[27] Again, this ἔκτασις or extension, is either in reference to the object or else duration, and implies an universal Love, and continued. But no *English* word will fully answer to ἐκτενῶς: Therefore our Interpreters have been forc'd to make use but of one of these senses, *fervently*: And they have with more judgment, pitcht upon the sense of intention than extension, because that intention in some measure implies extension; but not *è contra*; for that which is (*ex. gr.*) very hot, has also a further extended sphear of calefaction, and doth last longer hot, than that which is at first but more remisly heated, as is manifested in heated Irons.

To make any subtle disquisition of the nature of *Love*, is not much to the purpose. Every one knows what it is to love himself, how he is affected towards himself: Let him but transfer that affection,

---

[24] *Hebrews* 4. 12.   [25] *John* 1. 4.
[26] 'Love one another with a pure heart fervently' (quoted from the text, above, p. 200).
[27] Not quite! While the adverbs ἐκτενῶς and ἐκτεταμένως alike have reference to ἔκτασις ('extension'), the adverb ἐντενῶς is properly related to ἔντασις ('tension' or—in More's word—'intension').

The Purification of a Christian Man's Soul

which he is so sensible of in himself, to his Neighbour, and the Duty is done more substantially and completely, than all Scholastical definitions and curious circumscriptions can be able to set it out. Be so affected to other men, as you would they should be to you, or as you are affected to your self: *This is the Law, and the Prophets.*

THE *Incitements* to this Duty are many: But I will confine my self to the Text, and cull out some three: As,

1. *From the Seed of the New Birth.*

For what is this Seed but the Son of God, by union with whom we also become the Sons of God, petty Deities? But sith that the Deity it self is nothing else but a sufficient and overflowing Goodness, creating all things, and sustaining them from no other principle than the Spirit of Goodness; though we cannot act as this absolute Deity, yet we may will according to that uncreated Will, which is nothing else but pure overspreading Love.

Again, this Seed, (as hath been shewed) which is the Word, is a living Seed. But where Life is, and Understanding or Sense, there must needs be Love, for it is the flower and sweet of all desire. What then can be the desire of the living Word but Love; and how can he want desire, sith he is Life; and what can he so much desire as the good and welfare of Mankind? What therefore should that part of Mankind that partake of this Divine Nature, desire more than the good of one another, and of those also, that as yet have not partaked of that Divine Nature: For God also loves those, or else how could ever any partake of it?

2. *From the Regeneration of the Soul.*

It is the Holy Ghosts own arguing, *Beloved, let us love one another: for love is of God; and every one that loveth, is born of God, and loveth God. And we have known and believed the love that God hath to us. God is love; and he that dwelleth in love, dwelleth in God, and God in him.*[28] By Righteousness and Unrighteousness, by Love and Hatred, are the Children of God and the Children of the Devil manifested. *In this the children of God are manifest, and the children of the devil: Whosoever doeth not righteousness, is not of God, neither he that loveth not his brother. We know that we have passed from death unto life, because we love the brethren: he that loveth not his brother, abideth in death.*[29] If Water or Earth be turn'd into Fire, we expect it should burn and be hot.

---

[28] 1 *John* 4. 7, 16.
[29] 1 *John* 3. 10, 14.

How shall then a Son of Satan, or the Earthly man, be turn'd by Regeneration into the Son of God, and not love?

3. *From the end of our Sanctification.*

Love is the very End of it. Shall Envy, shall Hatred, shall Lust, Ambition, Luxury, *&c.* shall all these enormous Desires and Affections be cast out of the Soul by Sanctity and Purity, that she may be but a transparent piece of Ice, or a spotless fleece of Snow? Shall she become so pure, so pellucid, so christalline, so devoid of all stains, that nothing but still shadows and night may possess that inward diaphanous Purity? Thus would she be no better than the nocturnal Air, no happier than a statue of Alabaster; it would be but a more cleanly sepulchre of a dead starved Soul. Nay, certainly all this cleansing and preparing is for something well worth that labour. The *Stoicks* themselves, that were such severe Sentencers of Passion, would retain φιλανθρωπία.[30] *Stoicism* it self brings in, upon that deadness and privation of other Passions, that divine motion of the Soul, which is Love or Goodwill to all Mankind. And shall Christianity be but a cold grave to the mortified Soul of man? No surely, there is a Resurrection to Life, Love and the Divinity, as well as a Death of the enormous Affections of this Mortal Body. Bitter Zeal, harsh Censure, busie Revenge, *&c.* are so far from being able to supply the place of Charity, that it's a manifest sign that we are as yet carnal and unsanctified.

[30] *philanthropia*: 'love of humanity'—also benevolence, humaneness, etc. (variously set forth in terms of clemency, courtesy, etc.).

HENRY MORE

An Antidote against Atheism*

BOOK ONE

I. *The seasonable usefulness of the present Discourse, or the Motives that put the Author upon these indeavours of demonstrating that there is a God.*

The grand truth which wee are now to bee imployed about, is the proving *that there is a God*; And I made choice of this subject as very seasonable for the times wee are in, and are coming on, wherein Divine Providence granting a more large release from Superstition, and permitting a freer perusall of matters of Religion, then in former Ages, the Tempter would take advantage where hee may, to carry men captive out of one darke prison into another, out of *Superstition* into *Atheisme* it self. Which is a thing feasible enough for him to bring about in such men as have adhered to Religion in a meere externall way, either for fashion sake, or in a blind obedience to the Authority of a Church. For when this externall frame of godlinesse shall breake about their eares, they being really at the bottome devoyd of the true feare and love of God, and destitute of a more free and unprejudic'd use of their facultyes, by reason of the sinfullnesse and corruption of their natures; it will bee an easy thing to allure them to an assent to that, which seemes so much for their present Interest; and so being imboldned by the tottering and falling of what they took for Religion before, they will gladly in their conceipt cast down also the very Object of that Religious Worship after it and conclude that there is as well no God as no Religion. That is, they have a mind there should be none, that they may be free from all wringings of conscience,

* From *An Antidote against Atheism* (1653). Book I is reprinted in its entirety; Book II, with some omissions; and Book III, with its chapter headings only. The work's 2nd edition (1655) carried a lengthy Appendix. There was a 3rd revised edition (1662) from which FM reprints Book I.

trouble of correcting their lives, and feare of being accountable before that great Tribunall.

Wherefore for the reclayming of these if it were possible, at least for the succouring and extricating of those in whom a greater measure of the love of God doth dwell (who may probably by some darkening cloud of Melancholy or some more than ordinary importunity of the Tempter be dissettled and intangled in their thoughts concerning this weighty matter) I held it fit to bestow mine indeavours upon this so usefull and seasonable an Enterprise, as to demonstrate *that there is a God.*

II. *What is meant by demonstrating there is a God, and that the mind of man, unlesse he do violence to his faculties, will fully assent or dissent from that which notwithstanding may have a bare possibility of being otherwise.*

But when I speak of demonstrating there is a God, I would not be suspected of so much vanity and ostentation as to be thought I mean to bring no Arguments, but such as are so convictive, that a mans understanding shall be forced to confesse that is is impossible to be otherwise then I have concluded. For for mine own part I am prone to believe, that there is nothing at all to be so demonstrated. For it is possible that *Mathematicall evidence* it self, may be but a constant undiscoverable delusion, which our nature is necessarily and perpetually obnoxious unto, and that either fatally or fortuitously there has been in the world time out of mind such a Being as we call *Man,* whose essential property is to be then most of all mistaken, when he conceives a thing most evidently true. And why may not this be as well as any thing else, if you will have all things fatall or casuall without a God? For there can be no curbe to this wild conceipt, but by the supposing that we our selves exist from some higher Principle that is absolutely *good* and *wise,* which is all one as to acknowledge *that there is a God.*

Wherefore when I say that I will demonstrate that there is a God, I do not promise that I will alwayes produce such arguments, that the Reader shall acknowledge so strong as he shall be forced to confesse that it is utterly unpossible that it should be otherwise. But they shall be such as shall deserve full assent and win full assent from any unprejudic'd mind.

For I conceive that we may give full assent to that which notwith-

An Antidote against Atheism 215

standing may possibly be otherwise: which I shall illustrate by severall examples. Suppose two men got to the top of mount *Athos*, and there viewing a stone in the form of an *Altar* with *ashes* on it, and the *footsteps of men* on those ashes, or some *words* if you will, as *Optimo Maximo*, or, τῷ ἀγνώστῳ θεῷ[1] or the like, written or scralled out upon the Ashes; and one of them should cry out, Assuredly here have been some men here that have done this: But the other more nice then wise should reply, Nay it may possibly be otherwise. For this stone may have naturally grown into this very shape, and the seeming ashes may be no ashes, that is no remainders of any fewell burnt there but some unexplicable and imperceptible Motions of the Aire, or other particles of this fluid Matter that is active every where, have wrought some parts of the Matter into the form and nature of ashes, and have fridg'd and plaid about so, that they have also figured those intelligible Characters in the same. But would not any body deem it a piece of weaknesse no lesse than dotage for the other man one whit to recede from his former apprehension, but as fully as ever to agree with what he pronounced first, notwithstanding this bare possibility of being otherwise?

So of *Anchors* that have been digged up, either in plaine fields or mountainous places, as also the Roman *Urnes* with ashes and inscriptions, as *Severianus*, *Ful:Linus* and the like, or Roman *Coynes*, with the *effigies* and *names* of the *Cæsars* on them; or that which is more ordinary, the *Sculls* of men in every Church-yard, with the right figure, and all those necessary perforations for the passing of the vessells, besides those conspicuous hollowes for the Eyes and rowes of teeth, the *Os Styloeides*, *Ethoeides*, and what not? if a man will say of them, that the Motion of the particles of the Matter, or some hidden Spermatick power has gendred these both *Anchors*, *Urnes*, *Coynes*, and *Sculls* in the ground, hee doth but pronounce that which humane reason must admit as possible: Nor can any man ever so demonstrate that those *Coynes*, *Anchors*, and *Urnes*, were once the Artifice of men, or that this or that *Scull* was once a part of a living man, that hee shall force an acknowledgment that it is impossible that it should be otherwise. But yet I doe not think that any man, without doing manifest violence to his facultyes, can at all suspend his assent, but freely and fully agree that this or that Scull was once part of a living man, and

---

[1] 'To the unknown god'—the inscription on an altar in Athens seen by St Paul (*Acts* 17. 23).

that these *Anchors*, *Urnes* and *Coynes*, were certainly once made by humane artifice, notwithstanding the possibility of being otherwise.

And what I have said of *Assent* is also true in *Dissent*. For the mind of man not craz'd nor prejudic'd will fully and unreconcileably disagree, by it's own natural sagacity, where notwithstanding the thing that it doth thus resolvedly and undoubtingly reject, no wit of man can prove impossible to bee true. As if wee should make such a fiction as this, that *Archimedes* with the same individuall body that hee had when the Souldiers slew him,[2] is now safely intent upon his Geometricall figures under ground, at the Center of the Earth, farre from the noise and din of this world that might disturb his Meditations, or distract him in his curious delineations he makes with his rod upon the dust; which no man living can prove impossible: Yet if any man does not as unreconcileably dissent from such a fable as this, as from any falshood imagineable, assuredly that man is next doore to madness or dotage, or does enormous violence to the free use of his Facultyes.

Wherefore it is manifest that there may bee a very firme and unwavering assent or dissent, when as yet the thing wee thus assent to may be possibly otherwise; or that which wee thus dissent from, cannot bee proved impossible to be true.

Which point I have thus long, and thus variously sported my self in, for making the better impression upon my Reader, it being of no small use and consequence, as well for the advertising of him, that the Arguments which I shall produce, though I doe not bestowe that ostentative term of *Demonstration* upon them, yet they may bee as effectuall for winning a firme and unshaken assent, as if they were in the strictest Notion such; as also to reminde him that if they bee so strong and so patly fitted and suteable with the facultyes of mans mind, that hee has nothing to reply, but only that for all this, it may possibly bee otherwise, that hee should give a free and full assent to the Conclusion. And if hee do not, that hee is to suspect himself rather of some distemper, prejudice, or weaknesse, then the Arguments of want of strength. But if the *Atheist* shall contrariwise pervert my candour and fair dealing, and phansy that he has got some advantage from my free confession, that the arguments that I shall use are not so convictive, but that they leave a possibility of the thing being

[2] During the Roman invasion of Syracuse (212 B.C.), Archimedes is said to have been slain by a soldier while intent upon figures he had traced in the dust. The tradition is related by Livy, *Ab urbe condita*, XXV, 31; Cicero, *De finibus bonorum et malorum*, V, 50; *et al.*

otherwise, let him but compute his supposed gains by adding the limitation of this possibility (*viz*. that it is no more possible, then that the clearest *Mathematicall evidence* may be false (which is impossible if our facultyes be true) or in the second place, then that the Roman *Urnes* and *Coins* above mentioned may prove to be the works of Nature, not the Artifice of man, which our facultyes admit to be so little probable, that it is impossible for them not fully to assent to the contrary) and when he has cast up his account, it will be evident that it can be nothing but his grosse ignorance in this kind of Arithmetick that shall embolden him to write himself down gainer and not me.

III. *An attempt towards the finding out the true Notion or Definition of God, and a cleare Conviction that there is an indelible* Idea *of a* Being absolutely perfect *in the Mind of Man.*

And now having premised thus much, I shall come on nearer to my present designe. In prosecution whereof it will bee requisite for mee, first to define *what God is*, before I proceed to demonstration *that he is*. For it is obvious for Mans reason to find arguments for the impossibility, probability, or necessity of the Existence of a thing, from the explication of the Essence thereof.

And now I am come hither, I demand of any *Atheist* that denies there is a God, or of any that doubts whether there be one or no, what *Idea* or *Notion* they frame of that they deny or doubt of. If they will prove nice & squeamish, and professe they can frame no notion of any such thing, I would gladly aske them, why they will then deny or doubt of they know not what. For it is necessary that he that would rationally doubt or deny a thing, should have some settled *Notion* of the thing hee doubts of or denies. But if they professe that this is the very ground of their denying or doubting whether there be a God, because they can frame no Notion of him, I shall forthwith take away that Allegation by offering them such a Notion as is as proper to God as any Notion is proper to any thing else in the world.

I define God therefore thus, *An Essence or Being fully and absolutely perfect.* I say *fully and absolutely perfect*, in counterdistinction to such perfection as is not full and absolute, but the perfection of this or that *Species* or *Kind* of finite *Beings*, suppose of a Lyon, Horse or Tree. But to be fully and absolutely perfect is to bee at least as perfect as the apprehension of a Man can conceive, without a Contradiction. But what is inconceivable or contradictious is nothing at all to us, for wee are not now to wagg one Atome beyond our facultyes. But what I have propounded is so farre from being beyond our facultyes, that I dare appeale to any *Atheist* that hath yet any command of Sense and Reason left in him, if it bee not very easie and intelligible at the first sight, and that if there bee a God, he is to be deemed of us, such as this *Idea* or *Notion* sets forth.

But if hee will sullingly deny that this is the proper Notion of God, let him enjoy his own humour; this yet remains undenyable that there is in Man, an *Idea* of a *Being absolutely and fully perfect*,[3] which wee frame out by attributing all conceivable perfection to it whatsoever, that implyes no Contradiction. And this Notion is Natural and Essentiall to the Soul of Man, and can not bee wash'd out, nor conveigh'd away by any force or trick of wit whatsoever, so long as the Mind of man is not crazed, but hath the ordinary use of her own facultyes.

Nor will that prove any thing to the purpose, when as it shall be alledg'd that this Notion is not so connaturall and Essentiall to the Soul, because she framed it from some occasions from without. For all those undenyable conclusions in Geometry which might be help'd and occasion'd from some thing without, are so Naturall notwithstanding and Essentiall to the Soul, that you may as soon un-soul the Soul, as divide her from perpetuall assent to those Mathematicall truths, supposing no distemper nor violence offered to her Facultyes. As for example, shee cannot but acknowledge in her self the *Several distinct Ideas of the five Regular Bodies*,[4] as also, *that it is impossible that there should bee any more than five*. And this Idea of a Being absolutely perfect is as distinct and indelible an Idea in the Soul, as the Idea of the five Regular Bodyes, or any other Idea whatsoever.

It remaines therefore undenyable, that there is an inseparable *Idea of a Being absolutely perfect* ever residing, though not alwayes acting, in the Soul of Man.[5]

---

[3] Cf. Smith on 'The *Common Notions* of a Deity, strongly rooted in Mens Souls' (*Discourses*, p. 31) (see also above, p. 132 and note).

[4] i.e., the tetrahedron, hexahedron, octahedron, dodecahedron, and icosahedron. On their Pythagorean and Platonic antecedents, consult Sir Thomas Heath, *A History of Greek Mathematics* (Oxford, 1921), I, 158 ff. More's emphasis on 'Mathematicall truths' is common to all the Cambridge Platonists (see the Introduction, above, pp. 12 ff.)

[5] More's argument is essentially that of Descartes, *Meditations*, III. See L. J. Beck, *The Metaphysics of Descartes* (Oxford, 1965), pp. 150 ff. For Cudworth's demonstrations of the existence of God, consult Gysi, pp. 86 ff.

IV. *What Notions are more particularly comprised in the* Idea *of a* Being absolutely perfect. *That the difficulty of framing the conception of a thing ought to bee no argument against the existence thereof: the nature of corporeall Matter being so perplex'd and intricate, which yet all men acknowledge to exist. That the* Idea *of a* Spirit *is as easy a Notion as of any other substance what ever. What powers and propertyes are contained in the Notion of a* Spirit. *That* Eternity *and* Infinity, *if God were not, would bee cast upon something else; so that* Atheisme *cannot free the mind from such Intricacyes.* Goodnesse, Knowledge, *and* Power, *Notions of highest perfection, and therefore necessarily included in the* Idea *of a* Being absolutely perfect.

But now to lay out more particularly the perfections comprehended in this Notion of a Being absolutely and fully perfect, I think I may securely nominate these; *Self-subsistency, Immateriality, Infinity as well of Duration as Essence, Immensity of Goodnesse, Omnisciency, Omnipotency,* and *Necessity of Existence.* Let this therefore bee the description of a being absolutely perfect, that it is a *Spirit, Eternall, Infinite in Essence and Goodnesse, Omniscient, Omnipotent, and of it self necessarily existent.* All which Attributes being Attributes of the highest *perfection* that falls under the apprehension of man, and having no discoverable imperfection interwoven with them, must of necessity be attributed to that which we conceive absolutely and fully *perfect.* And if any one will say that this is but to dresse up a Notion out of my own fancy, which I would afterwards slily insinuate to be the Notion of *a God*; I answer, that no man can discourse and reason of anything without recourse to settled notions decyphered in his own mind. And that such an exception as this implies the most contradictious absurdities imaginable, to wit, as if a man should reason from something that never entered into his mind, or that is utterly out of the ken of his own facultyes. But such groundlesse allegations as these discover nothing but an unwillingnesse to find themselves able to entertain any conception of God, and a heavy propension to sink down into an utter oblivion of him, and to become as stupid and senselesse in divine things as the very beasts.

But others it may be will not look on this notion as contemptible for the easie composure thereof out of familiar conceptions which the mind of man ordinarily figures it self into, but reject it rather for some unintelligible hard termes in it, such as *Spirit, Eternall,* and *Infinite,* for they do professe they can frame no Notion of *Spirit*, and that anything should be *Eternal* or *Infinite*, they do not know how to set their mind in a posture to apprehend, and therefore some would have no such thing as a *Spirit* in the world.

But if the difficulty of framing a conception of a thing must take away the existence of the thing it self, there will be no such thing as a *Body* left in the world, and then will all be *Spirit* or nothing. For who can frame so safe a notion of a *Body*, as to free himself from the intanglements that the extension therefore will bring along with it.[6] For this extended matter consists of either indivisible points, or of particles divisible *in infinitum*. Take which of these two you will, (and you can find no third) you will be wound into the most notorious absurdityes that may be. For if you say it consists of points, from this position I can necessarily demonstrate, that every *Speare* or *Spire-Steeple* or what long body you will is as thick as it is long; that the tallest *Cedar* is not so high as the lowest *Mushrome*; and that the *Moon* and the *Earth* are so neere one another, that the thicknesse of your hand will not go betwixt; that *Rounds* and *Squares* are all one figure; that *Even* and *Odde Numbers* are Equall one with another; and that the clearest *Day* is as dark as the blackest *Night*. And if you make choice of the other Member of the disjunction, your fancy will bee little better at ease. For nothing can be divisible into parts it has not: therefore if a body be divisible into infinite parts, it has infinite extended parts: and if it has an infinite number of extended parts, it cannot be but a hard mystery to the Imagination of Man, that infinite extended parts should not amount to one whole infinite extension. And thus *a grain* of *Mustard-seed* would be as well infinitely extended, as the whole Matter of the Universe; and a thousandth part of that grain as well as the grain it self. Which things are more unconceivable then any thing in the Notion of a *Spirit*. Therefore we are not scornfully and contemptuously to reject any Notion, for seeming at first to be clouded and obscur'd with some difficulties and intricacies of conception; sith that, of whose being we seem most assured, is the most intangled and perplex'd in the conceiving, of any thing that can be propounded to the apprehension of a Man. But here you will reply that our senses are struck by so manifest impressions from the Matter, that though the *nature* of it bee difficult to conceive, yet the

---

[6] On More's own 'intanglements' with the idea of 'extension', see the Introduction, above, pp. 31 f.

Existence is palpable to us, by what it acts upon us. Why, then all that I desire is this, that when you shall be reminded of some actions and operations that arrive to the notice of your sense or understanding, which unless we do violence to our faculties we can never attribute to *Matter* or *Body*, that then you would not be so nice and averse from the admitting of such a substance as is called a *Spirit*, though you fancy some difficulty in the conceiving thereof.

But for mine own part I think the *nature* of a *Spirit* is as conceivable, and easy to be defin'd as the nature of anything else. For as for the very *Essence* or bare *Substance* of any thing whatsoever, hee is a very Novice in speculation that does not acknowledge that utterly unknowable. But for the *Essentiall* and *Inseparable properties*, they are as intelligible and explicable in a *Spirit* as in any other subject whatever. As for example, I conceive the intire Idea of a *Spirit* in generall, or at least of all finite created and subordinate *Spirits*, to consist of these severall powers or properties, viz. *Self-penetration, Self-Motion, Self-contraction* and *Dilatation*, and *Indivisibility*; and these are those that I reckon more absolute; I will adde also what has relation to another, and that is the power of *Penetrating, Moving* and *Altering the Matter*. These properties and powers put together make up the *Notion* and *Idea* of a *Spirit*,[7] whereby it is plainly distinguished from a *Body*, whose parts cannot *penetrate* one another, is not *Self-moveable*, nor can *contract* nor *dilate* it self, is *divisible* and *separable* one part from another; But the parts of a *Spirit* can be no more separated, though they be dilated, then you can cut off the *Rayes* of the *Sunne* by a paire of Scissors made of pellucide Crystall. And this will serve for the settling of the *Notion* of a *Spirit*; the proofe of its *Existence* belongs not unto this place. And out of this description it is plain that a *Spirit* is a notion of more perfection then a *Body*, and therefore the more fit to be an Attribute of what is *absolutely perfect*, then a *Body is*.

But now for the other two hard terms of *Eternall* and *Infinite*, if any one would excuse himself from assenting to the Notion of a *God*, by reason of the Incomprehensiblenesse of those attributes, let him consider, that he shall whether he will or no be forced to acknowledge something *Eternal*, either *God* or the *World*, and the Intricacy is alike

---

[7] This summary is preparatory to More's full discussion in *Ench. Met.*, Ch. XXVII–XXVIII (translated—possibly by More himself—in Joseph Glanvill's *Saducismus triumphatus* [1681], pp. 99–179, under the title 'The Easie, True and Genuine Notion and Consistent Explication of the Nature of a Spirit' [reprinted in FM]).

in either. And though he would shuffle off the trouble of apprehending an *Infinite Deity*, yet he will never excricate himself out of the intanglements of an *Infinite Space*; which Notion will stick as closely to his Soul, as her power of *Imagination*.

Now that *Goodnesse*, *Knowledge* and *Power*, which are the three following Attributes, are Attributes of *perfection*, if a man consult his own Facultyes, it will be undoubtedly concluded, and I know nothing else he can consult with. At least this will be returned as infallibly true, that a *Being absolutely perfect* has these, or what supereminently containes these. And that *Knowledge* or something like it is in God, is manifest, because without animadversion in some sense or other, it is impossible to be *Happy*. But that a *Being* should bee *absolutely perfect*, & yet not happy, is as impossible. But *Knowledge* without *Goodnesse* is but dry Subtilty, or mischievous Craft; and *Goodnesse* with *Knowledge* devoyd of *Power* is but lame and ineffectuall: Wherefore what ever is *absolutely perfect*, is *Infinitely* both *Good*, *Wise* and *Powerfull*.

And lastly it is more *perfection* that all this be *Stable*, *Immutable* and *Necessary*, then *Contingent* or *but Possible*. Therefore the *Idea* of a *Being absolutely perfect* represents to our minds, that that of which it is the *Idea* is *necessarily* to exist. And that which of its own nature doth *necessarily* exist, must never fail to be. And whether the Atheist will call this *absolute perfect Being*, God or not, it is all one; I list not to contend about words. But I think any man else at the first sight will say that wee have found out the true *Idea* of *God*.

V. *That the soul of man is not* Abrasa Tabula, *and in what sense shee might be said ever to have had the actuall knowledge of eternal truths in her.*

And now we have found out this *Idea* of a *Being absolutely perfect*, that the use which wee shall hereafter make of it, may take the better effect, it will not be amisse by way of further preparation, briefly to touch upon that notable point in Philosophy, *whether the Soul of man be* Abrasa Tabula, *a Table book in which nothing is writ;*[8] or whether

---

[8] Cf. Cudworth, *Imm. Morality*, pp. 286–7 (IV, vi, 4): 'the Soul is not a meer *Rasa Tabula*, a Naked and Passive Thing, which has no innate Furniture or Activity of its own, nor anything at all in it but what was impressed upon it from without' (*apud* FM, p. 310).

shee have some innate Notions and Ideas in her self.[9] For so it is that shee having taken first occasion of thinking from externall objects, it hath so imposed upon some mens judgements, that they have conceited that the Soul has no Knowledge nor Notion, but what is in a *Passive* way impressed, or delineated upon her from the objects of *Sense*; They not warily enough distinguishing betwixt extrinsecall occasions and the adæquate or principal causes of things. But the mind of man more free and better exercised in the close observations of its own operations and nature, cannot but discover, that there is an active and *actuall Knowledge* in a man, of which these outward objects are rather the reminders then the first begetters or implanters. And when I say *actuall Knowledge*, I doe not mean that there is a certaine number of *Ideas* flaring and shining to the *Animadversive faculty* like so many *Torches* or *Starres* in the *Firmanent* to our outward sight, or that there are any *figures* that take their distinct places, & are legibly writ there like the *Red letters* or *Astronomical Characters* in an *Almanack*; but I understand thereby an active sagacity in the Soul, or quick recollection as it were, whereby some small businesse being hinted unto her, she runs out presently into a more clear and larger conception. And I cannot better describe her condition then thus; Suppose a skilful *Musician* fallen asleep in the field upon the grasse, during which time he shall not so much as dream any thing concerning his musical faculty, so that in one sense there is no *actuall skill* or Notion nor representation of any thing musicall in him, but his friend sitting by him that cannot sing at all himself, jogs him and awakes him, and desires him to sing this or the other song, telling him two or three words of the beginning of the song, he presently takes it out of his mouth, and sings the whole song upon so slight and slender intimation: So the *Mind* of *man* being jogg'd and awakened by the impulses of outward objects is stirred up into a more full and cleare conception of what was but imperfectly hinted to her from externall occasions; and this faculty I venture to call *actuall Knowledge* in such a sense as the sleeping Musicians skill might be called *actuall skill* when he thought nothing of it.

[9] More's affirmation here of the *notitiae communes* is the fullest formulation ventured by any Cambridge Platonist (see esp. above, p. 132 and note). Consult also FM, pp. 276–9, and More's further discussion in the Appendix of the *Antidote*, 2nd ed. (1655), pp. 296 ff. But it should be noted that endorsement of this tradition did not mean approval of its extreme use made by Lord Herbert of Cherbury in *De Veritate* (see below, p. 331, note).

VI. *That the Soul of Man has of her self* actuall Knowledge *in her made good by sundry Instances and Arguments.*

And that this is the condition of the Soul is discoverable by sundry observations. As for example, Exhibite to the Soul through the outward senses the figure of a *Circle,* she acknowledgeth presently this to be one kind of *figure,* and can adde forthwith that if it be perfect, all the lines from some one point of it drawn to the Perimeter, must be exactly *Equal.* In like manner shew her a *Triangle,* she will straightway pronounce that if that be the right figure it makes toward, the *Angles* must be closed in indivisible *points.* But this accuracy either in the *Circle* or the *Triangle* cannot be set out in any materiall subject, therefore it remains that she hath a more full & exquisite knowledge of things in her self, then the Matter can lay open before her. Let us cast in a third Instance, let some body now demonstrate this *Triangle* described in the Matter to have it's three Angles equall to two right ones; Why yes saith the Soul this is true, and not only in this particular *Triangle* but in all plain *Triangles* that can possibly be describ'd in the Matter. And thus you see the Soul sings out the whole song upon the first hint, as knowing it very well before.

Besides this, there are a multitude of *Relative Notions* or *Ideas* in the Mind of Man, as well *Mathematicall* as *Logicall,* which if we prove cannot be the impresses of any materiall object from without, it will necessarily follow, that they are from the Soul her self within, and are the naturall furniture of humane understanding. Such as are these, *Cause, Effect, Whole* and *Part, Like* and *Unlike,* and the rest. So *Equality* and *Inequality,* λόγος and ἀναλογία, *Proportion* & *Analogy, Symmetry* and *Asymmetry,* and such like: All which *Relative Ideas* I shall easily prove to be no materiall impresses from without upon the Soul, but her own active conception proceeding from her self whilst shee takes notice of *externall Objects.* For that these *Ideas* can make no Impresses upon the outward senses is plain from hence, because they are no *sensible* nor *Physicall affections* of the *Matter.* And how can that, that is no *Physicall affection* of the *Matter* affect our corporeall Organs of *Sense?* But now that these *Relative Ideas,* whether *Logical* or *Mathematicall* be no *Physicall, affections* of the *Matter* is manifest from these two arguments. First they may be produced when there has been no *Physicall Motion* nor alteration in the Subject to which they belong, nay indeed when there hath been nothing at all done to the Subject to which they doe accrue. As for example, suppose one side of a Room whitened the other not touch'd or medled with, this other has thus become unlike, and hath the Notion of *Dissimile* necessarily belonging to it, although there has nothing at all been done thereunto. So suppose two Pounds of *Lead*, which therefore are two *Equal* Pieces of that Metall; cut away half from one of them, the other Pound, nothing at all being done unto it, has lost it's Notion of *Equall*, and hath acquired a new one of *Double* unto the other. Nor is it to any purpose to answere, that though there was nothing done to this Pound of Lead, yet there was to the other; For that does not at all enervate the Reason, but shewes that the Notion of *Sub-double* which accrued to that Lead which had half cut away, is but our *Mode* of conceiving, as well as the other, and not any *Physicall affection* that strikes the corporeall Organs of the Body, as *Hot* and *Cold*, *Hard* and *Soft*, *White* and *Black*, and the like do. Wherefore the *Ideas* of *Equall* and *Unequall*, *Double* and *Sub-double*, *Like* and *Unlike*, with the rest, are no externall Impresses upon the Senses, but the Souls own active manner of conceiving those things which are discovered by the outward Senses.

The second argument is, that one and the same part of the Matter is capable at one and the same time, wholly and entirely of two contrary *Ideas* of this kind. As for Example, any piece of Matter that is a *Middle proportionall* betwixt two other pieces, is *Double*, suppose, and *Sub-double*, or *Tripple* and *Sub-tripple*, at once. Which is a manifest signe that these *Ideas* are no affections of the Matter, and therefore do not affect our senses, else they would affect the senses of *Beasts*, and they might also grow good Geometricians and Arithmeticians. And they not affecting our senses, it is plain that wee have some *Ideas* that we are not beholding to our senses for, but are the meer exertions of the Mind occasionally awakened, by the Appulses of the outward objects; Which the out-ward Senses doe no more teach us, then he that awakened the *Musician* to sing taught him his skill.

And now in the third and last place it is manifest, besides these single *Ideas* I have proved to be in the mind, that there are also severall complex Notions in the same, such as are these; *The whole is bigger then the part: If you take Equall from Equall, the Remainders are Equall: Every number is either Even or Odde*; which are true to the soul at the very first proposal; as any one that is in his wits does plainly perceive.

VII. *The mind of man being not unfurnish'd of* Innate Truth, *that wee are with confidence to attend to her naturall and unprejudic'd Dictates and Suggestions. That some Notions and Truths are at least naturally & unavoydably assented unto by the soul, whether shee have of her self Actuall Knowledge in her or not. And that the definition of a* Being absolutely perfect *is such. And that this* absolutely perfect Being *is God, the* Creatour *and* Contriver *of all things.*

And now we see so evidently the Soul is not unfurnished for the dictating of Truth unto us. I demand of any man, why under a pretence that shee having nothing of her own but may be moulded into an assent to any thing, or that shee does arbitrariously and fortuitously compose the severall Impresses shee receives from without, hee will be still so squeamish or timorous, as to be affraid to close with his own facultyes, and receive the Naturall Emanations of his owne mind, as faithfull Guides.

But if this seem, though it be not, too subtile which I contend for, viz; That the Soul hath *actuall knowledge in her self*, in that sense which I have explained, yet surely this at least will be confes'd to be true, that the nature of the Soul is such, that shee will certainly and fully assent to some conclusions, how ever shee came to the knowledge of them, unlesse shee doe manifest violence to her own Faculties. Which truths must therefore be concluded not fortuitous or arbitrarious, but Natural to the Soul: such as I have already named, as that *every Finite number is either even or odde. If you adde equal to equal, the wholes are equal*; and such as are not so simple as these, but yet stick as close to the Soul once apprehended, as that *The three angles in a Triangle are equal to two right ones: That there are just five regular Bodies neither more nor lesse*, and the like, which we will pronounce necessarily true according to the light of Nature.[10]

Wherefore now to reassume what we have for a while laid aside, the *Idea of a Being absolutely perfect* above proposed, it being in such sort let forth, that a man cannot rid his minde of it, but he must needs acknowledge it to be indeed the *Idea* of such a *Being*; it will follow that it is no arbitrarious nor fortuitous conceipt, but *necessary* and therefore natural to the Soul at least, if not ever actually there.

[10] On the multiple use made by More of *lumen naturale*, see FM, p. 310.

Wherefore it is manifest, that we consulting with our own natural light concerning the Notion of a *Being absolutely perfect*, that this Oracle tells us, that it is *A spiritual Substance, Eternal, Infinite in Essence and Goodness, Omnipotent, Omniscient, and of it self necessarily existent.*

For this answer is such, that if we understand the sense thereof, we cannot tell how to deny it, and therefore it is true according to the light of Nature. But it is manifest that that which is *Self-subsistent, infinitely Good, Omniscient* and *Omnipotent*, is the *Root* and *Original* of all things. For *Omnipotency* signifies a Power that can effect any thing that implies no contradiction to be effected; and *Creation* implyes no contradiction: Therefore this *perfect Being* can *create* all things. But if it found the Matter or other Substances existing aforehand of themselves, this *Omnipotency* and Power of *Creation* will be in vain, which the free and unprejudic'd Faculties of the Minde of man do not admit of. Therefore the natural notion of a *Being absolutely perfect*, implies that the same *Being* is *Lord and Maker of all things*. And according to Natural light that which is thus, is to be adored and worshipped of all that has the knowledge of it, with all humility and thankfullnesse; and what is this but to be acknowledged to be *God?*

Wherefore I conceive I have sufficiently demonstrated, that the *Notion* or *Idea* of *God* is as Naturall, Necessary and Essential to the Soul of Man, as any other *Notion* or *Idea* whatsoever, & is no more arbitrarious or fictitious then the Notion of a *Cube* or *Tetraedrum*, or any other of the *Regular Bodyes* in Geometry: Which are not devised at our own pleasure (for such figments and *Chimæras* are infinite,) but for these it is demonstrable that there can be no more than five of them. Which shews that their Notion is necessary, not an arbitrarious compilement of what we please.

And thus having fully made good the Notion of God, *What he is*, I proceed now to the next point, which is to prove, that *Hee is*.

VIII. *The first Argument for the Existence of God taken from the* Idea *of God as it is* representative of his Nature *and Perfection: From whence also it is undeniably demonstrated that there can be no more Gods then One.*

And now verily casting my eyes upon the true *Idea* of God which we have found out, I seem to my self to have struck further into this businesse then I was aware of. For if this *Idea* or *Notion* of God be true, as I have undenyably proved, it is also undeniably true that he doth exist; For this *Idea* of God being no arbitrarious Figment taken up at pleasure, but the necessary and naturall Emanation of the mind of Man, if it signifies to us that the Notion and Nature of God implyes in it *necessary existence* as we have shown it does, unlesse we will wink against our own naturall light, wee are without any further Scruple to acknowledge *that God does exist*. Nor is it sufficient grounds to diffide to the strength of this Argument, because our fancy can shuffle in this Abater, viz. That indeed this *Idea* of God, supposing God did exist, shews us that his Existence is necessary, but it does not shew us that he doth necessarily exist. For he that answers thus, does not observe out of what prejudice he is inabled to make this Answer, which is this: He being accustomed to fancy the Nature or Notion of every thing else without Existence, and so ever easily separating Essence and Existence in them, here unawares hee takes the same liberty, and divides Existence from that Essence to which Existence it self is essentiall. And that's the witty fallacy his unwarinesse has intangled him in.

Again when as we contend that the true *Idea* of God represents him as a *Being necessarily Existent*, and therefore that he does exist; and you to avoid the edge of the Argument reply, If he did at all exist; by this answer you involve your self in a manifest contradiction. For first you say with us, that the nature of God is such, that in its very Notion it implyes its *Necessary Existence*, and then again you unsay it by intimating that notwithstanding this true *Idea* and *Notion*, God may not exist, and so acknowledge that what is absolutely necessary according to the free Emanation of our Facultyes, yet may be otherwise: Which is a palpable Contradiction as much as respects us and our Facultyes, and we have nothing more inward and immediate then these to steer our selves by.

And to make this yet plainer at least if not stronger, when wee say that the *Existence* of God is *Necessary*, wee are to take notice that *Necessity* is a *Logicall Terme*, and signifies so firme a Connexion betwixt the *Subject* and *Prædicate* (as they call them) that it is impossible that they should bee dissevered, or should not hold together, and therefore if they bee affirm'd one of the other, that they make *Axioma Necessarium*, an Axiome that is necessary, or eternally true. Wherefore there being a *Necessary Connexion* betwixt *God* and *Existence;* this Axiome, *God does Exist*, is an Axiome Necessarily and Eternally true. Which we shall yet more clearly understand, if we compare *Necessity* and *Contingency* together; For as *Contingency* signifies not onely the *Manner of Existence* in that which is contingent according to its *Idea*, but does intimate also a *Possibility* of *Actual Existence*, (so to make up the true and easy Analogy) *Necessity* does not only signify the *Manner of Existence* in that which is *Necessary*, but also that it does *actually Exist*, and *could never possibly do otherwise*. For ἀναγκαῖον εἶναι and ἀδύνατον μὴ εἶναι, Necessity of Being and Impossibility of Not-being, are all one with *Aristotle*, & the rest of the *Logicians*. But the *Atheist* and the *Enthusiast*, are usually such profess'd Enemyes against *Logick*; the one meerly out of Dotage upon outward grosse sense, the other in a dear regard to his stiffe and untamed fancy, that shop of Mysteryes and fine things.[11]

Thirdly, wee may further add, that whereas wee must needs attribute to the *Idea* of God either *Contingency*, *Impossibility*, or *Necessity* of *Actuall Existence*, (some one of these belonging to every *Idea* imaginable) and that *Contingency* is incompetible to an *Idea of a Being absolutely perfect*, much more *Impossibility*, the *Idea* of God being compiled of no Notions but such as are *possible* according to the light of Nature, to which wee now appeal: It remains therefore that *Necessity of Actuall Existence* bee unavoidably cast upon the *Idea* of God, and that therefore God does *actually Exist*.

But fourthly and lastly, if this seem more subtile, though it bee no lesse true for it, I shall now propound that which is so palpable, that it is impossible for any one that has the use of his wits to deny it. I say therefore, that either God or this corporeall and sensible world must of it self *necessarily exist*. Or thus, Either *God* or *Matter* or *both* doe of themselves *necessarily exist*. If *both*, wee have what we would drive at, the *existency* of God.

But yet to acknowledge the necessary existence of the *Matter* of it self, is not so congruous and suteable to the light of Nature. For if any thing can exist *independently* of God, all things may; so that not onely the Omnipotency of God might be in vain, but besides there would be a letting in from hence of all confusion and disorder imaginable; Nay of some grand Devill of equall Power and of as large Command as God himself: Or if you will of six thousand Millions of such monstrous Gigantick Spirits, fraught with various and mischievous Passions, as well as armed with immense power, who in

[11] On More's constant attacks on 'enthusiasm', see the Introduction, above, pp. 9, 24 f.

anger or humour appearing in huge shapes, might take the Planets up in their prodigious Clutches, and pelt one another with them as boyes are wont to do with snowbals; And that this has not yet happened will bee resolved onely into this, that the humour has not yet taken them. But the frame of Nature and the generation of things would be still lyable to this ruine and disorder. So dangerous a thing it is to slight the naturall *dependencyes* and *correspondencyes* of our innate *Ideas* and *conceptions.*

Nor is there any Refuge in such a Reply as this, that the full and perfect Infinitude of the power of God, is able easily to overmaster these six thousand Millions of Monsters, and to stay their hands. For I say that six or fewer, may equallize the infinite power of God. For if any thing may be *self-essentiated* besides God, why may not a *Spirit* of just six times lesse power then God exist of it self? and then six such wil equallize him, a seventh will overpower him. But such a rabble of *self-essentiated* and *divided* Deities, does not only hazzard the pulling the world in pieces, but plainly takes away the Existence of the true God. For if there be any power or perfection whatsoever, which has its original from any other then God, it manifestly demonstrates that God is not God, that is, is not a *Being absolutely and fully perfect,* because we see some power in the world that is not his, that is, that is not from him. But what is fully and wholly from him, is very truly and properly his, as the *thought* of my minde is rather my mindes, then my thoughts.

And this is the only way that I know to demonstrate that it is impossible that there should be any more then *one* true God in the world; For if we did admit another beside him, this other must be also *self-originated*; and so neither of them would be God. For the *Idea* of God swallows up into it self all power and perfection conceivable, and therefore necessarily implies that whatever hath any Being, derives it from him.

But if you say the *Matter* does only exist and not *God,* then this *Matter* does *necessarily* exist of it self, and so we give that Attribute unto the *Matter* which our Natural Light taught us to be contain'd in the Essentiall conception of no other thing besides *God.* Wherefore to deny that of God, which is so necessarily comprehended in the true *Idea* of him, and to acknowledge it in that in whose *Idea* it is not at all contain'd (for *necessary Existence* is not contain'd in the *Idea* of any thing but of a *Being absolutely perfect*) is to pronounce contrary to our Natural light, and to do manifest violence to our Faculties.

An Antidote against Atheism

Nor can this be excused by saying that the Corporeall *Matter* is palpable and *sensible* unto us, but *God* is not, and therefore we pronounce confidently that it is, though God be not, and also that it is *necessary* of it self, sith that which is without the help of another must necessarily bee and eternally.

For I demand of you then sith you profess your selves to believe nothing but *sense*, how could *sense* ever help you to that truth you acknowledged last, *viz. That that which exists without the help of another, is necessary and eternal?* For *Necessity* and *Eternity* are no sensible Qualities, and therefore are not the objects of any *sense*; And I have already very plentifully proved, that there is other knowledge and perception in the Soul besides that of *Sense.* Wherefore it is very unreasonable, when as we have other faculties of knowledge besides the senses, that we should consult with the senses alone about matters of knowledge, and exclude those facultyes that penetrate beyond *Sense.* A thing that the profess'd *Atheists* themselves will not doe when they are in the humour of Philosophising, for their principle of *Atomes* is a business that does not fall under *Sense*, as *Lucretius* at large confesses.[12]

But now seeing it is so manifest that the Soul of man has other cognoscitive faculties besides that of *Sense* (which I have clearly above demonstrated) it is as incongruous to deny there is a *God*, because *God* is not an object fitted to the *Senses*, as it were to deny there is *Matter* or a *Body*, because that *Body* or *Matter*, in the imaginative Notion thereof, lies so unevenly and troublesomly in our *fancy* and *reason*.

In the contemplation whereof our understanding discovereth such contradictious incoherencies, that were it not that the notion is sustain'd by the confident dictates of *Sense, Reason* appealing to those more crasse Representations of *Fansy*, would by her shrewd *Dilemma's* be able to argue it quite out of the world. But our Reason being well aware that *corporeal* matter is the proper object of the sensitive faculty, she gives full belief to the information of Sense in her own sphear, slighting the puzzling objections of perplexed Fancy, and freely admits the existence of Matter, notwithstanding the intanglements of Imagination, as she does also the existence of God, from the contemplation of his *Idea* in our soul, not withstanding the silence of the senses therein. For indeed it were an unexcusable piece of folly and madnesse in a man, when as he has cognoscitive faculties reaching to

---

[12] *De rerum natura*, II, 312 ff., and IV, 111 ff.

the knowledge of God, and has a certain and unalterable *Idea* of God in his soule, which he can by no device wipe out, as well as he has the knowledge of *Sense* that reaches to the discovery of the Matter; to give necessary Self-existence to the *Matter*, no Faculty at all informing him so; and to take necessary Existence from *God*, though the natural notion of God in the Soul informe him to the contrary; and only upon this pretence, because God does not immediately fall under the Knowledge of the *Senses*; Thus partially siding with one kind of Faculty only of the Soul, and proscribing all the rest. Which is as humoursomely and foolishly done, as if a Man should make a faction amongst the Senses themselves, and resolve to believe nothing to be but what he could see with his Eyes, and so confidently pronounce that there is no such thing as the Element of *Aire* nor *Winds* nor *Musick* nor *Thunder*. And the reason forsooth must be because he can see none of these things with his Eyes, and that's the sole sense that he intends to believe.

IX. *The second Argument from the* Idea *of God as it is* Subjected in our Souls, *and is the fittest Naturall meanes imaginable to bring us to the knowledge of our Maker. That bare* possibility *ought to have no power upon the mind, to either hasten or hinder it's assent in any thing. We being delt with in all points as if there were a God, that naturally wee are to conclude there is one.*

And hitherto I have argued from the natural *Notion* or *Idea* of God as it respects that of which it is the *Idea* or *Notion*. I shall now try what advantage may be made of it, from the respect it bears unto our *Souls*, the *Subject* thereof, wherein it does reside.

I demand therefore who put this Indelible Character of God upon our Souls? why and to what purpose is it there? Nor do not think to shuffle me off by saying, We must take things as we find them, and not inquire of the finall Cause of any thing; for things are necessarily as they are of themselves, whose guidance and contrivance is from no principle of Wisdome or Counsell, but every substance is now and ever was of what nature and capacity it is found; having it's Originall from none other than it self; and all those changes and varieties we see in the World, are but the result of an Eternall Scuffle of coordinate Causes, bearing up as well as they can, to continue themselves in the present state they ever are, and acting and being acted upon by others, these varieties of things appear in the world, but every particular

Substance with the Essential Properties thereof is self-originated, and independent of any other.

For to this I answere, that the very best that can be made of all this is but thus much; that it is meerly and barely *possible*, nay if we consult our own faculties, and the Idea of God, utterly impossible: but admit it possible; this bare *possibility* is so laxe, so weak, and so undeterminate a consideration, that it ought to have no power to move the mind this way or that way that has any tolerable use of her own Reason, more then the faint breathings of the loose Aire have to shake a Mountaine of brasse. For if bare *possibility* may at all intangle our assent or dissent in things, we cannot fully mis-believe the absurdest Fable in *Æsop* or *Ovid*, or the most ridiculous figments that can be imagin'd; as suppose that *Eares of Corn in the field heare the whistling of the wind and chirping of the Birds; that the stones in the street are grinded with pain when the Carts go over them: that the Heliotrope eyes the Sun and really sees him as well as turns round about with him: that the Pulp of the Wall-nut, as bearing the signature of the brain, is indued with Imagination and Reason.* I say no man can fully mis-believe any of these fooleries, if bare *possibility* may have the least power of turning the Scales this way or that way. For none of these nor a thousand more such like as these imply a perfect and palpable Contradiction, and therefore will put in for their right of being deemed *possible*. But we are not to attend to what is simply *possible*, but to what our *naturall faculties* do direct and determine us to. As for Example, Suppose the Question were, *whether the Stones in the Street have sense or no*, we are not to leave the point as indifferent, or that may be held either way, because it is *possible* and implyes no palpable Contradiction, that they may have *sense* and that a *painfull sense* too. But we are to consult with our *naturall faculties*, and see whither they propend: and they do plainly determine the Controversy by telling us, that what has *sense* and is capable of *pain*, ought to have also progressive *Motion*, to bee able to avoyd what is hurtfull and painfull, and we see it is so in all Beings that have any considerable share of Sense. And *Aristotle* who was no doater on a *Deity*,[13] yet frequently does assume this principle ‛Η φύσις οὐδὲν μάτην ποιεῖ, That *Nature does nothing in vain*.[14] Which is either an acknowledgment of a *God*, or an appeale to our own *Rationall*

---

[13] A glance at one of the reasons why the Cambridge Platonists were less than fond of Aristotle. He was, as Smith wrote, 'not over-zealous of Religion' (quoted above, p. 6, note).

[14] *De caelo*, I, 4; cf. II, 5. See also Cudworth, below, p. 295.

Faculties. And I am indifferent which, for I have what I would out of either, for if we appeale to the naturall suggestions of our own faculties, they will assuredly tell us there is a God.

I therefore again demand and I desire to be answered without prejudice, or any restraint laid upon our naturall faculties, to what purpose is this indelible *Image* or *Idea* of God in us, if there be no such thing as *God* existent in the world? or who seal'd so deep an Impression of that Character upon our Minds?

If we were travailing in a desolate *wildernesse*, where we could discover neither Man nor house, and should meet with *Herds* of *Cattell* or *Flocks* of *Sheep* upon whose bodies there were branded certain *Markes* or *Letters*, we should without any hesitancy conclude that these have all been under the hand of some man or other that has set his name upon them. And verily when we see writ in our Souls in such legible Characters the *Name* or rather the *Nature* and *Idea* of God, why should we be so slow and backward from making the like reasonable inference? Assuredly he whose *Character* is signed upon our Souls, has been here, and has thus marked us that we and all may know to whom we belong. That *it is he that has made us, and not we our selves; that we are his people and the sheep of his Pasture.* And it is evidently plain from the *Idea* of God, which includes omnipotency in it, that we can be made from none other than he; as I have before demonstrated. And therefore there was no better way then by sealing us with this *Image* to make us acknowledge our selves to be his, and to do that worship and adoration to him that is due to our mighty *Maker* and *Creatour*, that is to our *God*.

Wherefore things complying thus naturally, and easily together, according to the free Suggestions of our *naturall Faculties*, it is as perverse and forced a buisinesse to suspend assent, as to doubt whether those Romane *Urnes* and *Coynes* I spoke of digg'd out of the Earth be the works of Nature or the Artifice of Men.

But if wee cannot yet for all this give free assent to this Position, that *God does Exist*, Let us at least have the Patience a while to suppose it. I demand therefore supposing God did *Exist*, what can the Mind of Man imagine that this God should do better or more effectuall for the making himself known to such a Creature as Man, indued with such and such faculties, then we find really already done? For God being a *Spirit* and *Infinite*, cannot ever make himself known Necessarily, and Adæquately by any appearance to our outward *Senses*. For if he should manifest himself in any outward figures or shapes, portending either love or wrath, terrour or protection, our faculties could not assure us that this were *God*, but some particular *Genius* good or bad: and besides such dazeling and affrightfull externall forces are neither becoming the divine Nature, nor suteable with the Condition of the Soul of Man, whose better faculties and more free God meddles with, does not force nor amaze us by a more course and oppressing power upon our weake and brutish senses. What remaines therefore but that he should manifest himself to our *Inward Man*? And what way imaginable is more fit, then the indelible Impression of the *Idea* of himself, which is (not divine life and sense, for that's an higher prise laid up for them that can win it, but) a naturall representation of the God-head and a Notion of his *Essence*, whereby the Soul of Man could no otherwise conceive of him, then an *Eternall Spirit, Infinite in goodnesse, Omnipotent, Omniscient, and Necessarily of himself Existent*. But this, as I have fully proved, we find *de facto* done in us, wherefore we being every way dealt with as if there were a God *Existing*, and no *faculty* discovering any thing to the contrary, what should hinder us from the concluding that he does really *exist*?

X. Naturall Conscience, *and* Religious Veneration, *arguments of the Existence of God.*

Hitherto we have argued for the Existency of the God-head from the naturall *Idea* of God, inseparably and immutably risiding in the Soul of Man. There are also other arguments may be drawn from what we may observe to stick very close to mans nature, and such is *Naturall remorse of Conscience*, and a feare and disturbance from the committing of such things as notwithstanding are not punishable by men: As also a *naturall hope* of being prosperous and successefull in doing those things which are conceived by us to be good & righteous; And lastly *Religious Veneration* or *Divine worship*; All which are fruits unforcedly and easily growing out of the nature of man; and if we rightly know the meaning of them, they all intimate that *there is a God*.

And first of *Naturall Conscience* it is plain that it is a fear and confusion of Mind arising from the presage of some mischief that may befall a man beside the ordinary course of Nature, or the usual occurrences of affaires, because he has done thus or thus. Not that what is supernatural or absolutely extraordinary must needs fall upon him, but that at least the ordinary calamityes and misfortunes, which are in the world, will be directed and levelled at him sometimes or other, because he hath done this or that Evill against his *Conscience*. And men doe naturally in some heavy *Adversity*, mighty *Tempest* on the Sea or dreadfull *Thunder* on the Land (though these be but from Naturall Causes) reflect upon themselves and their actions, and so are invaded with fear, or are unterrifide, accordingly as they condemne or acquit themselves in their own *Consciences*. And from this supposall is that magnificent Expression of the *Poet* concerning the just man

Nec fulminantis magna Jovis manus,

That he is not affrayd of the darting down of *Thunder* and *Lightening* from Heaven.[15] But this fear, that one should bee struck rather then the rest, or at this time rather then another time, because a man has done thus or thus, is a naturall acknowledgment that these things are guided and directed from some discerning principle, which is all one as to confesse that *there is a God*. Nor is it materiall that some alledge that *Mariners* curse and swear the lowdest when the storm is the greatest, for it is because the usualnesse of such dangers have made them loose the sense of the *danger*, not the sense of a *God*.

It is also very naturall for a man that follows honestly the dictates of his own *Conscience*, to be full of good hopes, and much at ease, and secure that all things at home and abroad will goe successfully with him, though his actions or sincere motions of his Mind act nothing upon Nature or the course of the world to change them any way: wherefore it implies that there is a *Superintendent Principle* over Nature, and the materiall frame of the world, that lookes to it so that nothing shall come to passe, but what is consistent with the good and welfare of honest and conscientious Men. And if it does not happen to them according to their expectations in this world, it does naturally bring in a belief of a world to come.

Nor does it at all enervate the strength of this Argument that some men have lost the sense and difference betwixt good and evill, if there be any so fully degenerate; but let us suppose it, this is a monster, and I suspect of his own making. But this is no more prejudice to what I ayme at, who argue from the *Naturall constitution* of a Man the *Existency of a God*; then if because *Democritus* put out his Eyes, some are born blind, others drink out their Eyes and cannot see, that therefore you should conclude that there is neither *Light* nor *Colours*: For if there were, then every one would see them, but *Democritus* and

---

[15] Cf. Horace, *Carmina*, III, iii, 6.

some others doe not see them. But the reason is plain, there hath been force done to their *Naturall Facultyes* and they have put out their sight.

Wherefore I conclude from *naturall Conscience* in a Man that puts him upon hope and fear of Good and Evill from what he does or omits, though those actions and omissions doe nothing to the change of the course of Nature or the affaires of the world, that there is an *Intelligent Principle* over universall Nature that takes notice of the Actions of Men, that is that *there is a God*; for else this *Naturall Faculty* would be false and vaine.

Now for *Adoration* or *Religious Worship* it is as universall as mankind, there being no Nation under the Cope of heaven that does not do divine worship to something or other, and in it to God as they conceive; wherefore according to the ordinary *naturall light* that is in all men, there is a God.

Nor can the force of this Argument be avoyded, by saying it is but an universall *Tradition* that has been time out of mind spread among the Nations of the world. For if it were so (which yet cannot at all be proved) in that it is universally received, it is manifest that it is according to the *light of Nature* to acknowledge there is a God. For that which all men admit as true, though upon the proposall of another, is undoubtedly to be termed true according to the *light of Nature*. As many hundreds of *Geometricall Demonstrations* that were first the inventions of some one man, have passed undenyable through all ages and places for true, according to the *light of Nature*, with them that were but Learners not Inventours of them. And it is sufficient to make a thing true according to the *light of Nature*, that no man upon a perception of what is propounded and the reasons of it (if it be not cleare at the first sight and need reasons to back it) will ever stick to acknowledge for a Truth. And therefore if there were any Nations that were destitute of the knowledge of a *God*, as they may be it is likely of the Rudiments of *Geometry*, so long as they will admit of the knowledge of one as well as of the other, upon due and fit proposall; the acknowledgment of a *God* is as well to be said to be according to the *light of Nature*, as the knowledge of *Geometry* which they thus receive.

But if it be here objected that a thing may be universally receiv'd of all Nations and yet be so farre from being true according to the *light of Nature*, that it is not true at all: As for example that the *Sun* moves about the *Earth*, and that the *Earth* stands still as the fix'd

Center of the world, which the best of Astronomers and the profoundest of Philosophers pronounce to be false:[16] I answere that in some sense it does stand still, if you understand by Motion the translation of a body out of the vicinity of other bodyes. But suppose it did not stand still, this comes not home to our Case; For this is but the just victory of Reason over the generall prejudice of Sense; and every one will acknowledge that Reason may correct the Impresses of Sense, otherwise we should admit the Sun and Moon to be no wider than a Sive, and the bodyes of the Starrs to be no bigger then the ordinary flame of a Candle. Therefore you see here is a clashing of the faculties one against another, and the strongest carryes it. But there is no faculty that can be pretended to clash with the judgement of Reason and natural Sagacity that so easily either concludes or presages that there is a God: wherefore that may well go for a Truth according to the *light of Nature* that is universally received of men, be it by what faculty it will they receive it, no other faculty appearing that can evidence to the contrary. And such is the *universall acknowledgment* that *there is a God*.

Nor is it much more materiall to reply, That though there be indeed a *Religious Worship* exercised in all Nations upon the face of the Earth, yet they worship many of them but *stocks* and *stones*, or some particular piece of Nature, as the *Sunne, Moon,* or *Starrs*; For I answer, That first it is very hard to prove that they worship any Image or Statue, without reference to some Spirit at least, if not to the omnipotent God. So that we shall hence at least win thus much, that there are in the Universe some more subtile and Immateriall Substances that take notice of the affairs of Men, and this is as ill to a slow Atheist, as to believe that *there is a God*.

And for that adoration some of them do the *Sunne* and *Moon*, I cannot believe they do it to them under the Notion of mere *Inanimate Bodies*, but they take them to be the habitation of some *Intellectuall Beings*, as that verse does plainly intimate to us, ʽΗέλιός θ᾽ ὅς πάντ᾽ ἐφορᾷ καὶ πάντ᾽ ἐπακούει. *The Sun that hears and sees all things*;[17] and this is very neer the true Notion of a *God*.

But be this *universall Religious Worship* what it will, as absurd as you please to fancy it, yet it will not faile to reach very farre for the

---

[16] More's acceptance of Copernicanism enrolls him among the enlightened thinkers of his age. As he once observed, 'He that would deal with a skilfull Philosopher, must not deny *the Motion of the Earth*, as being so solidly rational, not really repugnant to the Holy Scripture' (*Apology*, p. 483).

[17] *Iliad*, III, 277.

An Antidote against Atheism

proving of a *Deity*. For there is no naturall Faculties in things that have not their object in the world; as there is meat as well as mouths, sounds as well as hearing, colours as well as sight, dangers as well as feare, and the like. So there ought in like manner to be a *God* as well as a naturall propension in men to *Religious Worship*, *God* alone being the proper *Object* thereof.

Nor does it abate the strength of the Argument that this so deeply radicated property of *Religion* in Man, that cannot be lost, does so ineptly and ridiculously display it self in Mankind.

For as the plying of a *Dogges* feet in his sleep, as if there were some game before him, and the butting of a yong *lambe* before he has yet either hornes or Enemies to encounter, would not be in Nature, were there not such a thing as a *Hare* to be coursed, and an *horned Enemy* is be incountred with horns: So there would not be so universall an Exercise of *Religious Worship* in the world, though it be done never so ineptly and foolishly, were there not really a due *Object* of this worship, and a capacity in Man for the right performance thereof; which could not be unlesse there were a *God*.

But the Truth is, Mans Soul in this drunken drowsy condition she is in has fallen asleep in the body, and like one in a dreame talks to the bed-posts, embraces her pillow instead of her friend, falls down before statues in stead of adoring the Eternall and Invisible God, prayes to stocks and stones instead of speaking to him that by his word created all things.

I but you will reply that a young *Lambe* has at length both his weapon and an *Enemy* to encounter, and the dreaming *Dogge* did once and may again pursue some reall game; And so he that talks in his sleep did once conferre with men awake, and may do so again; But whole Nations for many successions of Ages have been very stupid Idolaters, and do so continue to this day. But I answere that this rather informes us of another great mystery, then at all enervates the present argument or obscures the grand truth we strive for. For this does plainly insinuate thus much, that Mankind is in a laps'd condition, like one fallen down in the fit of an Epilepsy, whose limbes by force of the convulsion are moved very incomposedly and illfavourdly; but we know that he that does for the present move the members of his Body so rudely and fortuitously, did before command the use of his Muscles in a decent exercise of his progressive faculty, and that when the fit is over he will doe so again.

This therefore rather implyes that these poore barbarous Souls had once the true knowledge of *God*, and of his *worship*, and by some hidden providence may be recover'd into it again; then that this propension to *Religious Worship*, that so conspicuously appears in them, should be utterly in vain: As it would be both in them and in all men else if there were no *God*.

XI. *Of the Nature of the* Soul *of Man, whether she be a meere* Modification *of the* Body, *or a* Substance *really* distinct, *and then whether* corporeall *or* incorporeall.

We have done with all those more obvious faculties in the Soul of Man, that naturally tend to the discovery of the Existence of a God. Let us briefly, before wee loose from our selves and lanch out into the vast Ocean of the Externall *Phænomena* of *Nature*, consider the Essence of the Soul her self, what it is, whether a meer *Modification* of the *Body* or *Substance distinct* therefrom; and then whether *corporeall* or *incorporeall*. For upon the clearing of this point wee may happily be convinced that there is a Spiritual Substance, really distinct from the Matter. Which who so does acknowledge will be easilier induced to beleeve there is a God.

First therefore if we say that the Soul is a meer *Modification* of the *Body*, the Soul then is but one universall Faculty of the Body or a many Facultyes put together, and those operations which are usually attributed unto the Soul, must of necessity be attributed unto the Body. I demand therefore to what in the body will you attribute *Spontaneous Motion?* I understand thereby a power in our selves of wagging or holding still most of the parts of our Body, as our hand suppose or little finger. If you will say that it is nothing but the *immission* of the *Spirits* into such and such Muscles, I would gladly know what does *immit* these *Spirits* and direct them so curiously. Is it *themselves*, or the *Braine*, or that particular piece of the Braine they call the *Conarion* or *Pine-kernell?*[18] whatever it be, that which does thus

---

[18] According to Descartes, 'the intervention of the soul in the affairs of the body (and, reciprocally, the intervention of the body in the affairs of the soul) is effected through the pineal gland, or the "gland Conarion", as Descartes himself describes it. It is, he says, "the principal seat of the soul, and the place where all its thoughts occur" ' (A. B. Gibson, *The Philosophy of Descartes* [1932], p. 223; see further Norman K. Smith, *New Studies in the Philosophy of Descartes* [1952], pp. 143 ff.). Descartes' own statements are esp. in *Passions de l'âme*, XXXIV, and in a letter to Mersenne (Œuvres, ed. C. Adam and P. Tannery [Paris, 1899], III, 263 ff.).

immit them and direct them must have *Animadversion,* and the same that has Animadversion has *Memory* also and *Reason.* Now I would know whether the Spirits *themselves* be capable of *Animadversion, Memory* and *Reason*: for it indeed seemes altogether impossible. For these animall Spirits are nothing else, but Matter very thin and liquid, whose nature consists in this, that all the particles of it be in Motion, and being loose from one another fridge and play up and down according to the measure and manner of agitation in them.

I therefore now demand which of the particles in these so many loosely moving one from another, has *Animadversion* in it? If you say that they all put together have, I appeal to him that thus answers how unlikely it is that that should have *Animadversion* that is so utterly uncapable of *Memory,* and consequently of *Reason.* For it is as impossible to conceive *Memory* competible to such a subject, as it is, how to write Characters in the water or in the wind.

If you say the *Brain* immits and directs these Spirits, how can that so freely and spontaneously move it self or another that has no Muscles? besides *Anatomists* tell us that though the Brain be the Instrument of sense, yet it has no sense at all of it self; how then can that that has no sense, direct thus spontaneously and arbitrariously the animall Spirits into any part of the Body? an act that plainly requires determinate sense and perception. But let the Anatomists conclude what they will, I think I shall little lesse then demonstrate that *the Brains have no Sense.* For the same thing in us that has *Sense* has likewise *Animadversion,* and that which has *Animadversion* in us has also a faculty of free and arbitrarious *Fansy* and of *Reason.*

Let us now consider the nature of the *Brain,* and see how competible those operations are to such a Subject. Verily if wee take a right view of this laxe pith or marrow in Mans head, neither our sense nor understanding can discover any thing more in this substance that can pretend to such noble operations as free Imagination and sagacious collections of Reason, then we can discern in a Cake of Sewet or a bowle of Curds. For this loose Pulp, that is thus wrapp'd up within our *Cranium* is but a spongy and porous body, and pervious not onely to the Animall Spirits but also to more grosse Juice and Liquor, else it could not well be nourished, at least it could not be so soft and moistened by drunkennesse and excesse as to make the understanding inept and sottish in its operations. Wherefore I now demand in this soft substance which we call the *Brain,* whose softnesse implyes that it is in some measure liquid, and liquidity implyes a severall

Motion of loosned parts; in what part or parcell thereof does *Fancy*, *Reason* and *Animadversion* lye? In this laxe consistence that lyes like a Net on heaps in the water, I demand in what knot, loop, or Intervall thereof does this faculty of the *Fancy* and active *Reason* reside? I believe you will be asham'd to assigne me any: and if you will say in all together, you must say that the whole brain is figured into this or that representation, which would cancell Memory and take away all capacity of there being any distinct Notes and places for the severall Species of things there represented. But if you will say there is in *Every part* of the brain this power of *Animadversion* and *Fansy*, you are to remember that the brain is in some measure a *liquid body*, and we must inquire how these loose parts vnderstand one anothers severall *Animadversions* and *Notions*: And if they could (which is yet very inconceivable) yet if they could from hence doe any thing toward the *immission* and *direction* of the *Animall Spirits* into this or that part of the Body, they must doe it by knowing one anothers minds, and by a joynt contention of strength, as when many men at once, the word being given, lift or tugge together for the moving of some so masly a body that the single strength of one could not deal with. But this is to make the severall particles of the brain so many *Individuall persons*; A fitter object for laughter then the least measure of beliefe.

Besides how come these many animadversions to seem but one to us, our mind being these, as is supposed? Or why if the figuration of one part of the brain be communicated to all the rest, does not the same object seem situated both behind us and before us, above and beneath, on the right hand and on the left, and every way as the Impresse of the object is reflected against all the parts of the braines? But there appearing to us but one animadversion and one site of things, it is a sufficient Argument that there is but one, or if there be many, that they are not mutually communicated from the parts one to another, and therefore there can be no such joynt endeavour toward one designe, whence it is manifest that the *Braines* cannot *immit* nor direct these *Animall Spirits* into what part of the Body they please.

Moreover that the *Braine* has *no Sense*, and therefore cannot impresse spontaneously any motion on the *Animall Spirits*, it is no slight Argument in that some being dissected have been found without Braines, and *Fontanus*[19] tells us of a boy at *Amsterdam* that had nothing

[19] Nicolaas Fonteyn, a seventeenth-century Dutch physician, author of several medical and pseudo-medical treatises.

but limpid water in his head in stead of Braines; and the Braines generally are easily dissolvable into a watry consistence, which agrees with what I intimated before. Now I appeale to any free Judge how likely these liquid particles are to approve themselves of that nature and power as to bee able by erecting and knitting themselves together for a moment of time, to beare themselves so as with one joynt contention of strength to cause an arbitrarious ablegation of the Spirits into this or that determinate part of the Body. But the absurdity of this I have sufficiently insinuated already.

Lastly the *Nerves*, I mean the Marrow of them which is of the self same substance with the Braine, have *no Sense* as is demonstrable from a *Catalepsis* or *Catochus*: but I will not accumulate Arguments in a Matter so palpable.

As for that little sprunt piece of the Braine which they call the *Conarion*, that this should be the very substance whose naturall faculty it is to move it self, and by it's Motions and Nods to determinate the course of the *Spirits* into this or that part of the Body, seems to me no lesse foolish and fabulous then the story of him that could change the wind as he pleased by setting his Cap on this or that side of his head.

If you heard but the magnificent stories that are told of this little lurking Mushrome, how it does not onely heare and see, but imagines, reasons, commands the whole fabrick of the Body more dextrously then an *Indian* boy does an *Elephant*, what an acute *Logician*, subtle *Geometrician*, prudent *Statesman*, skillfull *Physician* and profound *Philosopher* he is, and then afterward by dissection you discover this worker of Miracles to be nothing but a poor silly contemptible Knobb or Protuberancy consisting of a thin Membrane containing a little pulpous Matter much of the same nature with the rest of the Braine,

Spectatum admissi risum teneatis amici?

Would not you sooner laugh at it then goe about to confute it?[20] And truly I may the better laugh at it now, having already confuted it in what I have afore argued concerning the rest of the braine.

I shall therefore make bold to conclude that the Impresse of *Spontaneous Motion* is neither from the *Animall Spirits* nor from the *Braine*, and therefore that those operations that are usually attributed unto the

---

[20] Cf. Horace, *Ars poetica*, 5.

Soul are really incompetible to any part of the Body; and therefore that the *Soul* is not a meer *Modification* of the *Body*, but a *Substance distinct* therefrom.

Now we are to enquire whether this *Substance distinct* from what ordinarily we call the Body, be also it self a *Corporeall Substance*, or whether it be *Incorporeall*. If you say that it is a *Corporeall* Substance, you can understand no other then Matter more subtile and tenuous then the Animall Spirits themselves, mingled with them and dispersed through the vessels and Porosities of the Body, for there can be no Penetration of Dimensions. But I need no new Arguments to confute this fond conceipt, for what I said of the *Animall Spirits* before, is applicable with all ease and fitnesse to this present case. And let it be sufficient that I advertise you so much, and so be excus'd from the repeating of the same things over again.

It remains therefore that we conclude that that which impresses *Spontaneous Motion* upon the Body, or more immediately upon the Animall Spirits, that which *imagines*, *remembers*, and *reasons*, is an *Immateriall Substance distinct* from the *Body*, which uses the Animall Spirits and the Braines for Instruments in such and such Operations: and thus we have found a *Spirit* in a proper Notion and signification that has apparently these faculties in it; it can both *understand* and *move* Corporeall Matter.

And now this prize that we have wonne will prove for our designe of very great Consequence. For it is obvious here to observe, that the Soul of man is as it were ἄγαλμα θεοῦ a *Compendious Statue of the Deity*. Her substance is *a solid Effigies of God*. And therefore as with ease we consider the Substance and Motion of the vast *Heavens* on a little *Sphere* or *Globe*, so we may with like facility contemplate the nature of the *All-mighty* in this little *Meddall of God*, the Soul of Man, enlarging to Infinity what we observe in our selves when wee transferre it unto God; as we do imagine those *Circles* which we view on the *Globe*, to be vastly bigger while we fancy them as described in the *Heavens*.

Wherefore we being assur'd of this that there is a Spirituall Substance in our selves in which both these properties do reside, viz. of understanding and of moving Corporeall Matter, let us but enlarge our Minds so, as to conceive as well as we can of a Spirituall Substance that is able to move and actuate all Matter, whatsoever never so farre extended, and after what way and manner soever it please, and that it has not the knowledge onely of this or that particular thing, but a distinct and plenary Cognoscence of all things; and we have indeed a very competent apprehension of the Nature of the Eternall and Invisible God, who like the Soul of Man, does not indeed fall under sense, but does every where operate so, that his presence is easily to be gathered from what is discovered by our outward senses.

BOOK TWO

I. *The* Universall Matter *of the* World *be it homogeneall or heterogeneall, self-mov'd or resting of it self, that it can never be contriv'd into that* Order *it is without the Super-intendency of a God.*

The last thing I insisted upon was the Specifick nature of the Soul of Man, how it is an immateriall substance indued with these two eminent Properties, of Understanding and Power of moving corporeall Matter. Which truth I cleared, to the intent that when we shall discover such Motions and Contrivances in the largely extended Matter of the world as imply Wisdome and Providence we may the easilier come off to the acknowledgment of that Eternall Spirituall Essence that has fram'd Heaven and Earth, and is the Authour and Maker of all visible and invisible Beings.

Wherefore we being now so well furnish'd for the voiage, I would have my *Atheist* to take Shipping with me, and loosing from this particular Speculation of our own inward nature to lanch out into that vast Ocean, as I said, of the Externall *Phænomena* of *universall Nature*, or walke with me a while on the wide Theatre of this *Outward world*, and diligently to attend to those many and most manifest marks and signes that I shall point him to in this outward frame of things that naturally signify unto us that *there is a God*.[21]

And now first to begin with what is most generall, I say that the *Phænomena* of *Day* and *Night, Winter* and *Summer, Spring-time* and *Harvest*, that the manner of *rising* and *setting* of the *Sun, Moon* and *Starrs*, that all these are signes and tokens unto us that there is *a God*, that is, that things are so framed that they naturally imply a principle of *Wisdome* and *Counsell* in the *Authour* of them. And if there be such an *Authour* of externall Nature, there is a God.

But here it will be reply'd, that meere *Motion* of the *universall Matter* will at last necessarily grinde it self into those more rude and generall

---

[21] More was to return to this argument in *Discourses*, I, 20 ff.

Delineations of Nature that are observed in the Circuits of the Sunne, Moone and Starres, and the generall Consequences of them. But if the mind of man grow so bold as to conceipt any such thing, let him examine his Faculties what they naturally conceive of the *Notion of Matter*. And verily the great Master of this Mechanicall *Hypothesis*[22] does not suppose nor admitt of any *Specificall difference* in this universall Matter, out of which this outward frame of the World should arise. Neither do I think that any Man else will easily imagine but that all the Matter of the world is of one kind for its very Substance or Essence.

Now therefore I demand concerning this universall uniform Matter, whether naturally *Motion* or *Rest* belongs unto it. If *Motion*, it being acknowledg'd uniforme, it must be alike moved in *every part* or *particle* imaginable of it. For this Motion being naturall and essentiall to the Matter is alike every where in it, and therefore has loosened every Atome of it to the utmost capacity, so that every particle is alike, and moved alike. And therefore there being no prevalency at all in any one Atome above another in biggnesse or motion, it is manifest that this universall Matter to whom motion is so essential and intrinsecall, will be ineffectuall for the producing of any *variety of appearances* in Nature, and so no *Sunnes*, nor *Starres* nor *Earths*, nor *Vortices* can ever arise out of this infinitely thin and still Matter, which must thus eternally remain unperceptible to any of our Senses, were our Senses ten thousand Millions of times more subtile then they are. Indeed there could not be any such thing as either Man or Sense in the world. But we see this Matter shewes it self to us, in abundance of *varieties* of *appearance*; therefore there must be another principle besides the Matter to order the Motion of it so, as may make these *varieties* to *appear*: And what will that prove but *a God?*

But if you'l say that *Motion* is *not* of the *nature* of Matter (as indeed it is very hard to conceive it, the matter supposed homogeneall) but that it is inert and stupid of it self: then it must be moved from some other, and thus of necessity we shall be cast upon a God, or at least a Spiritual substance actuating the Matter, which the Atheists are as much affraid of, as children are of Spirits, or themselves of a God.

But men that are much degenerate know not the naturall Emanations of their own Minds, but think of all things confusedly, and therefore it may be will not stick to affirm, that either the parts of the Matter are *Specifically different*, or though they be not, yet some are *Moveable* of

---

[22] The culprit here (as elsewhere) is Descartes.

themselves, others inclinable to *Rest*, and was ever so; for it happened so to be, though there be no reason for it in the thing it self: which is to wound our Faculties with so wide a gap, that after this they will let in any thing, and take away all pretence to any principles of Knowledge.

But to scuffle and combat with them in their own dark Caverns, let the universall Matter be a heterogeneall *Chaos* of Confusion, variously moved and as it happens: I say there is no likelyhood that this mad *Motion* would ever amount to so wise a Contrivance as is discernable even in the generall Delineations of Nature. Nay it will not amount to a naturall appearance of what we see and is conceived most easy thus to come to passe, to wit, a round *Sunne, Moon,* and *Earth*. For it is shrewdly to be suspected that if there were no *Superintendent* over the Motions of those *Ætheriall Whirle-pooles,* which the French Philosophy[23] supposes that the form of the *Sun* and the rest of the *Starres* would be *oblong* not *round,* because the Matter recedes all along the *Axis* of a *Vortex,* as well as from the *Center,* and therefore naturally the Space that is left for the finest and subtilest Element of all, of which the *Sunne and Starres* are to consist, will be *Long* not *Round.* Wherefore this *Round* Figure we see them in, must proceed from some higher principle then the meere Agitation of the Matter:[24] But whether simply *Spermaticall,* or *Sensitive* also and *Intellectuall,* I'le leave to the disquisition of others who are more at leasure to meddle with such Curiosities.

The Businesse that lies me in hand to make good is this, that taking that for granted which these great Naturallists would have allowed, to wit, that *the Earth moves about the Sunne,* I say the laws of its Motion are such that, if they had been imposed on her by humane Reason and Counsell, they would have been no other then they are. So that appealing to our own faculties, we are to confesse that the Motions of the *Sunne* and *Starres,* or of the *Earth,* as our Naturallists would have it, is from a *knowing Principle,* or at least has pass'd the Approbation and Allowance of such a Principle.

For as Art takes what Nature will afford for her purpose, and makes up the rest her self; So the *Eternall Mind* (that put the universall Matter upon Motion, as I conceive most reasonable, or if the Matter be confusedly mov'd of its self, as the Atheist wilfully contends) this *Eternall Mind,* I say, takes the easy and naturall results of this general

---

[23] i.e., that of Descartes, in *Principia,* III, 34 ff.
[24] Implicit here is the traditional association of God with the circle. Cf. the Introduction, above, p. 36.

Impresse of *Motion*, where they are for his purpose, where they are not he rectifies and compleats them.

And verily it is farre more suteable to Reason that God making the *Matter* of that nature that it can by meere *Motion* produce something, that it should go on so farre as that single advantage could naturally carry it, that so the wit of Man, whom God has made to contemplate the *Phænomena* of Nature, may have a more fit object to exercise it self upon. For thus is the understanding of Man very highly gratifi'd, when the works of God and there manner of production are made intelligible unto him by a naturall deduction of one thing from another: which would not have been if God had on purpose avoided what the *Matter* upon *Motion* naturally afforded, and cancelled the laws thereof in every thing. Besides to have altered or added any thing further where there was no need, had been to *Multiply Entities* to no purpose.

Thus it is therefore with Divine Providence; what that one single Impresse of *Motion* upon the *universal Matter* will afford that is useful and good, it does allow and take in; what it might have miscarried in, or could not amount to, it directs or supplies. As in little pieces of wood naturally bow'd like a Mans Elbow, the Carver does not unbow it, but carves an hand at the one end of it, and shapes it into the compleat figure of a Mans Arme.

That therefore that I contend for is this, that be the *Matter moved* how it will, the *Appearances* of *things* are such as do manifestly intimate that they are either appointed all of them, or at least approved by an *universall Principle of Wisdome* and *Counsell*.

II. *The* perpetuall Parallelisme of the Axis of the Earth *and* its due proportion of Inclination, *as also the* course of the Moon crossing the Ecliptick, *evident arguments that the fluid Matter is guided by a divine Providence. The Atheists Sophisme of arguing from some petty inconsiderable Effects of the Motion of the Matter, that the said Motion is cause of all things, seasonably detected and deservedly derided.*

Now therefore to admit the Motion of the Earth, & to talk wth the Naturallists in their own Dialect, I demand whether it be better to have the *Axis* of the Earth *steddy*, and *perpetually parrallell* with its self, or to have it *carelesly tumble* this way and that way as it happens, or at least very variously and intricately. And you cannot but answer me that it is better to have it *steady* and *parallel*: For in this lyes the necessary

Foundation of the Art of *Navigation* and *Dialling*. For that steddy stream of Particles which is supposed to keep the *Axis* of the Earth parallel to it self, affords the Mariner both his *Cynosura* and his *Compass*. The *Load-stone* and the *Load-star* depend both on this. And *Dialling* could not be at all without it. But both of these *Arts* are pleasant, and the one especially of mighty importance to Mankind. For thus there is an orderly measuring of Time for our affaires at home, and an opportunity of Traffick abroad, with the most remote Nations of the world, and so there is a mutual supply of the severall commodities of all Countreys, besides the inlarging of our understanding by so ample Experience we get of both men and things. Wherefore if we were rationally to consult, whether the *Axis* of the Earth is to be held *steady* and *parallel* to it self, or to be left at *randome*, wee would conclude that it ought to be *steady*. And so we find it *de facto*, though the Earth move floating in the liquid Heavens. So that appealing to our own Facultyes, we are to affirm that the constant direction of the *Axis* of the Earth was established by a principle of *Wisdome* and *Counsell*, or at least approved of it.

Again, there being severall Postures of this steady direction of the *Axis* of the Earth, viz, either *Perpendicular* to a Plane going through the Center of the Sun, or *Coincident* or *Inclining*, I demand which of all these Reason and Knowledge would make choise of. Not of a *Perpendicular* posture, For both the pleasant variety and great conveniency of *Summer* and *Winter*, *Spring-time* and *Harvest* would be lost; and for want of accession of the Sun, these parts of the Earth that bring forth fruit now and are habitable, would be in an incapacity of ever bringing forth any, and consequently could entertain no Inhabitants; and those Parts that the full heat of the Sun could reach, he plying them allwayes alike without any annual recession or intermission, would at last grow tired and exhausted. And besides consulting with our own facultyes we observe, that an orderly *vicissitude* of things, is most pleasant unto us, and does much more gratifie the contemplative property in Man.

And now in the second place, nor would reason make choice of a *Coincident* position of the *Axis* of the Earth. For if the *Axis* thus lay in a Plane that goes through the Center of the Sun, the *Ecliptick* would like a *Colure* or one of the *Meridians* passe through the *Poles* of the Earth, which would put the Inhabitants of the World into a pittifull Condition. For they that scape best in the *Temperate Zone*, would be accloy'd with very tedious long Nights, no lesse then fourty dayes long, and they that now have their Night never above four and twenty houres, as *Friseland,*

Iseland, the further parts of *Russia* and *Norway*, would be deprived of the Sun above a hundred and thirty dayes together, our selves in *England* and the rest of the same *Clime* would be closed up in darknesse no lesse then an hundred or eighty continuall dayes, and so proportionably of the rest both in and out of the *Temperate Zones*. And as for *Summer* and *Winter*, though those vicissitudes would be, yet it could not but cause very raging diseases, to have the Sun stay so long describing his little Circles neer the Poles and lying so hot upon the Inhabitants that had been in so long extremity of Darknesse and Cold before.

It remaines therefore that the posture of the *Axis* of the Earth be *Inclining*, not *Coincident* nor *Perpendicular* to the forenamed Plane. And verily it is not onely *inclining*, but in so fit proportion, that can be no fitter excogitated, to make it to the utmost capacity as well pleasant as habitable. For though the course of the Sun be curbed within the compasse of the *Tropicks* and so makes those parts very hot, yet the constant gales of wind from the East (to say nothing of the nature and fit length of their nights) make the *Torrid Zone* not only habitable but pleasant.

Now this best posture which our Reason would make choise of, we see really established in Nature, and therefore, if we be not perverse and willful, we are to inferre that it was established by a *Principle* that has in it *Knowledge* and *Counsell*, not from a blind fortuitous jumbling of the parts of the Matter one against another, especially having found before in ourselves a *knowing Spiritual Substance* that is also able to move and alter the Matter. Wherefore I say we should more naturally conclude, that there is some such *universall knowing Principle*, that has power to move and direct the Matter; then to fancy that a confused justling of the Parts of the Matter should contrive themselves into such a condition, as if they had in them Reason and Counsell, and could direct themselves. But this directing Principle what could it be but *God*?

But to speake the same thing more briefly and yet more intelligibly, to those that are only acquainted with the *Ptolemaicall Hypothesis*: I say that being it might have happened that the annuall course of the *Sun* should have been through the *Poles* of the world, and that the *Axis* of the Heavens might have been very troublesomely and disorderly moveable, from whence all those inconveniencies would arise which I have above mentioned; and yet they are not but are so ordered as our own Reason must approve of as best; it is Naturall for a man to conceive, that they are really ordered by a *Principle* of *Reason* and *Counsell*, that is, that they are made by an all-wise and all-powerful *God*.

I will only adde one or two observables more, concerning the *Axis* of the Earth and the course of the *Moon*, and so I will passe to other things.

It cannot but be acknowledged that if the *Axis* of the Earth were *perpendicular* to the Plane of the Sun's *Ecliptick*, that her Motion would be more easy and naturall, and yet for the conveniencies afore mentioned we see it is made to stand in an *inclining* posture. So in all likelyhood it would be more easy and naturall for that hand-maid of the Earth the *Moon*, to finish her Monthly courses in the *Æquinoctiall Line*, but we see like the Sun she crosses it and expatiates some degrees further then the Sun him self, that her exalted light might be more comfortable to those that live very much North, in their long Nights.

Wherefore I conclude that though it were possible, that the confused agitation of the parts of the Matter might make a round hard heap like the *Earth*, and more thin and liquid bodies like the *Æther*, and *Sun*, and that the *Earth* may swimme in this liquid *Æther* like a rosted Apple in a great bowle of wine, and be carried about like straws or grasse cast upon a whirle-poole, yet that it's *Motion* and *Posture* should be so directed and attemper'd as we our selves that have Reason upon due consideration would have it to be; and yet not to be from that which is *Knowing* and in some sense *Reasonable*; is to our faculties, if they discerne any thing at all, as absonous and absurd as any thing can be. For when it had been easier to have been otherwise, why should it be thus, if some *Superintendent Cause* did not oversee and direct the Motions of the Matter, allowing nothing therein but what our Reason will confess to be to very good purpose?

But because so many *Bullets* joggled together in a Mans Hat will settle to such a determinate figure, or because the *Frost* and the *Wind* will draw upon dores and Glasse-windows pretty uncouth streaks like feathers, and other fooleries which are to no use or purpose, to inferre thence that *all the Contrivances* that are in *Nature*, even the frame of the *bodyes* both of *Men* and *Beasts*, are from no other principle but the jumbling together of the Matter, and so because that this does naturally effect something that it is the cause of all things, seems to me, to be a reasoning in the same *Mood* and *Figure* with that wise Market-mans, who going down a Hill, and carrying his *Cheeses* under his Armes, one of them falling and trundling down the Hill very fast, let the other go after it, appointing them all to meet him at his house at *Gotham*, not doubting but they beginning so hopefully would be able to make good the whole journey. Or like another of the same Town, who perceiving that his *Iron Trevet* he had bought had three feet, and could stand, expected also that it should walk too and save him the labour of the Carriage. So our profound *Atheists* and *Epicureans* according to the same pitch of Wisdom do not stick to inferre, because this confused *Motion* of the parts of the *Matter* may amount to a rude delineation of hard and soft, rigid and fluid, and the like, that therefore it will go on further and reach to the disposing of the Matter in such order as does naturally imply a *Principle*, that someway or other contains in it exact *Wisdome* and *Counsell*. A position more beseeming the Wise-men above mentioned, then any one that has the least command of his naturall wit and faculties.

Wherefore we having sufficiently detected the ridiculous folly of this present Sophisme, let us attending heedfully to the naturall emanations of unprejudic'd reason conclude, that *the Rising and Setting of the lights of Heaven, the vicissitude of Day and Night, Winter and Summer*, being so ordered and guided, as if they had been settled by exquisite consultation, and by clearest knowledge; that therefore that which did thus ordaine them is a *knowing Principle*, able to move, alter and guide the Matter according to his own will and providence, that is to say, that *there is a God*.

And verily I do not at all doubt but that I shall evidently trace the visible foot-steps of this *Divine Counsell* and *Providence*, even in all things discoverable in the world. But I will passe through them as lightly and briefly as I can.

III. *That* Rivers, Quarries of stone, Timber-Wood, Metalls, Mineralls, *and* the Magnet, *considering the nature of Man, what use he can make of them, are manifest signes that the rude Motion of the Matter is not left to it self, but is under the guidance and Superintendency of an all-wise* God.

Let us therefore swiftly course over the *Vallies* and *Mountains*, sound the depth of the *Sea*, range the *Woods* and *Forests*, dig into the Entrailes of the *Earth*, and let the *Atheist* tell me which of all these places are silent and say nothing of a *God*. Those that are most dumbe will at least compromize with the rest, that all things are by the guidance and determination (let the Matter move as it will) or at least by the allowance, and approbation of a *Knowing Principle*: as a Mason that makes a wall, sometimes meets with a *stone* that wants no cutting, and so only approving of it he places it in his work. And *a piece of Timber* may

An Antidote against Atheism

happen to be crack'd in the very place where the Carpenter would cleave it, and he need not close it first that he may cleave it asunder afterwards; wherefore if the meer Motion of the Matter can do any rude generall thing of good consequence, let it stand as allowable; but we shall find out also those things which do so manifestly savour of *Design* and *Counsell*, that we cannot naturally withhold our assent, but must say *there is a God.*

And now let us betake our selves to the search, and see if all things be not so as our Reason would desire them. And to begin at the Top first, even those rudely scattered *Mountains*, that seeme but so many Wens and unnaturall Protuberancies upon the face of the Earth,[25] if you consider but of what consequence they are, thus reconciled you may deeme them ornaments as well as usefull.

For these are Natures *Stillatories* in whose hollow Cavernes the ascending vapours are congealed to that universal *Aqua vitæ*, that good *fresh-water*, the liquor of life, that sustaines all the living Creatures in the world, being carried along in all parts of the Earth in the winging Channels of *Brookes* and *Rivers*. Geography would make it good by a large induction. I will onely instance in three or foure: *Ana* and *Tagus* run from *Sierra Molina* in *Spain*, *Rhenus*, *Padus* and *Rhodanus* from the *Alpes*, *Tanais* from the *Riphean*, *Garumna* from the *Pyrenean* Mountains, *Achelous* from *Pindus*, *Hebrus* from *Rhodope*, *Tigris* from *Niphates*, *Orontes* from *Libanus*, and *Euphrates* from the Mountains of *Armenia*, and so in the rest. But I will not insist upon this, I will now betake my self to what does more forcibly declare an Eye of Providence, directing and determining as well as approving of the results of the supposed agitation of the parts of the Matter.

And that you may the better feel the strength of my Argument, let us first briefly consider the nature of Man, what faculties he has, and in what order he is in respect of the rest of the Creatures. And indeed though his body be but weak and disarmed, yet his inward abilities of Reason and Artificial contrivance is admirable. He is much given to Contemplation, and the viewing of this Theatre of the world, to trafick and commerce with forrain Nations, to the building of Houses and Ships, to the making curious instruments of Silver, Brasse or Steele, and the like. In a word he is the flower and chief of all the products of

---

[25] This is not More's own perverse view but a summary of the usual attitude toward mountains. The fascinating story is related by Nicolson, *Aesthetics*.

Nature upon this Globe of the Earth. Now if I can shew that there are designes laid even in the lowest and vilest products of Nature that respect Man the highest of all, you cannot deny but that there is an *Eye* of *Providence* that respecteth all things, and passeth very swiftly from the Top to the Bottom, disposing all things wisely.

I therefore now demand, Man being of this nature that he is, whether these noble faculties of his would not be lost and frustrate were there not Materialls to excercise them on. And in the second place I desire to know, whether the rude confused *Agitation* of the *particles* of the Matter do certainly produce any such Materialls fit for Man to exercise his skill on or no; That is to say, whether there were any Necessity that could infallibly produce *Quarries* of *Stone* in the Earth which are the chief Materialls of the Magnificent Structures of building in the world; And the same of *Iron* and *Steel*, without which there had been no use of these stones; And then of *Sea-Coal* and other necessary *Fewel*, fit for the working or melting of these Metalls; and also of *Timber Trees*, for all might have been as well brush-wood and shrubs; And then assuredly there had been no such convenient shipping, what ever had become of other buildings; And so of the *Load-stone* that great help to Navigation, whether it might not have laine so low in the Earth as never to have been reached by the Industry of Man; and the same may be said also of other *Stones* and *Metalls*, that they being heaviest might have laine lowest. Assuredly the *Agitated* Matter, unlesse there were some speciall over-powering guidance over it, might as well have over-slipt these necessary useful things, as hit upon them: But if there had been such a Creature as Man, these very things themselves had been uselesse, for none of the bruit beasts make use of such commodities. Wherefore unlesse a man will doe enormous violence to his faculties, he must conclude that there is a contrivance of *Providence* and *Counsell* in all those things, which reacheth from the beginning to the end, and orders all things sweetly. And that *Providence* foreseeing what a kind of Creature she would make *Man*, provided him with materials from whence he might be able to adorne his present Age, and furnish History with the Records of egregious exploits, both of Art and Valour. But without the provision of the forenamed Materialls, the Glory and Pompe both of warre and Peace had been lost. For men instead of those magnificent buildings which are seen in the world, could have had no better kind of dwellings, then a bigger sort of Bee-hives or Birdsnests made of contemptible sticks and straws & durty morter. And instead of the usual pompe and bravery of warre, wherein is heard the solemne sound of the hoarse Trumpett, the couragious beating of the Drumm, the neighing and pransing of the Horses, clattering of Armour, and the terrible thunder of Cannons, to say nothing of the glittering of the Sword and Spear, the waving and fluttering of displayed Colours, the gallantry of Charges upon their well managed Steeds and the like: I say had it not been for the forenamed provision of *Iron*, *Steel* and *Brasse*, and such like necessary Materials, instead of all this glory and solemnity, there had been nothing but howlings and showtings of poor naked men belabouring one another with snag'd sticks, or dully falling together by the eares at Fisti-cuffs. Besides this, Beasts being naturally armed, and men naturally unarmed with any thing save their Reason, and Reason being ineffectuall having no materialls to work upon, it is plaine that that which made Men, Beasts and Metalls, knew what it did, and not forget it self in leaving Man destitute of naturall Armature, having provided Materialls, and giving him wit and abilityes to arme himself, and so to be able to make his party good against the most fierce and stoutest of all living Creatures whatsoever, nay indeed left him unarmed on purpose that he might arme himself and excercise his naturall wit and industry.

IV. *A further proof of divine Providence taken from the* Sea, *and the large train of Causes laid together in reference to* Navigation.

Having thus passed over the Hills and through the Woods and hollow Entrailes of the Earth, let us now view the wide *Sea* also, and see whether that do not informe us that there is a *God*, that is, whether things be not there in such sort as a rationall Principle would either order or approve, when as yet notwithstanding they might have been otherwise. And now we are come to view those *Campos natantes* as *Lucretius* calls them,[26] that vast Champian of water the *Ocean*, I demand first whether it might not have been *wider* then it is, even so large as to overspread the face of the whole Earth, and so to have taken away the habitation of Men and Beasts. For the wet particles might have easily ever mingled with the dry, and so all had either been *Sea* or *Quag mire*. Secondly though this distinction of *Land* and *Sea* be made, whether this watry Element might not have fallen out to be of so *thin* a consistency as that it would not beare Shipping; For it is so farre from impossibility, as there be *de facto* in Nature such waters, as the river *Silas* for example in *India*. And

[26] 'floating plains' (*De rerum natura*, V, 488, and VI, 405).

the waters of *Boristhenes* are so *thin* and light, that they are said to swim upon the top of the Stream of the river *Hypanis*. And we know there is some kind of wood so heavy, that it will sink in any ordinary kind of water.

 Thirdly and lastly, I appeale to any mans reason, whether it be not better that there should be a distinction of *Land* and *Sea*, then that all should be mire and water; and whether it be not better that the Timber-trees afford wood so light that it swim on the water, or the water be so heavy that it will beare up the wood, then the Contrary. That therefore which might have been otherwise, and yet is settled according to our own hearts wish who are knowing and rationall Creatures, ought to be deemed by us as established by *Counsell* and *Reason*. And the closer we looke into the buisinesse we shall discerne more evident foot-steps of Providence in it. For the two maine properties of Man being contemplation and sociablenesse or love of converse, there could nothing so highly gratify his nature as power of *Navigation*, whereby he riding on the back of the waves of the *Sea*, views the wonders of the Deep, and by reason of the glibnesse of that Element, is able in a competent time to prove the truth of those sagacious suggestions of his own mind, that is, whether the *Earth* be every way *round*, and whether there be any *Antipodes*, and the like; and by cutting the *Æquinoctiall line* decides that controversy of the habitablenesse of the *Torrid Zone*, or rather wipes out that blot that lay upon divine Providence, as if so great a share of the world had been lost, by reason of unfitnesse for habitation.

 Besides the falling upon *strange Coasts* and *discovering* Men of so great a diversity of manners from our selves, cannot but be a thing of infinite *pleasure* and advantage to the enlargement of our thoughts from what we observe in their conversation, parts, and Polity. Adde unto this the sundry *rarities of Nature*, and *commodities* proper to severall Countries, which they that stay at home enjoy by the travailes of those that go abroad, and they that travaile grow rich for their adventure.

 Now therefore *Navigation* being of so great consequence, to the *delight* and *convenience* of humane life, and there being both wit and courage in Man to attempt the Seas, were he but fitted with right Materialls and other advantages requisite; when we see there is so pat a provision made for him to this purpose, in large *Timber* for the building of his Ship, in a *thick Sea-water* sufficient to beare the Ships burden, in the *Magnet* or *Load-stone* for his Compasse, in the steady and parallell *direction of the Axis* of the Earth for his *Cynosura*; and then observing his naturall *wit* and *courage* to make use of them, and how that ingenit desire of *knowledge* and *converse*, and of the *improving* of his own *parts* and *happinesse* stirre him up to so notable a designe; we cannot but conclude from such a traine of Causes so fittly and congruously complying together, that it was really the counsell of an *universall* and *eternal Mind* that has the overseeing and guidance of the whole frame of Nature, that laid these causes so carefully and wisely together, that is, we cannot but conclude that *there is a God*.

And if we have got so fast foot-hold already in this truth by the consideration of such *Phænomena* in the world that seeme more *rude* and *generall*, what will the contemplation of the more *particular* and more *polished* pieces of Nature afford in *Vegetables*, *Animalls* and the *Body of Man?*

V. *Though the meere motion of the Matter may do something, yet it will not amount to the production of* Plants *and* Animalls. *That it is no Botch in Nature that some* Phænomena *be the results of Motion, others of Substantiall Formes. That* Beauty *is not a meere Phancy; and that the* Beauty of Plants *is an argument that they are from an Intellectuall Principle.*

Hitherto we have only considered the more rude and carelesse strokes and delineaments of divine Providence in the world, set out in those more large *Phænomena* of Day and Night, Winter and Summer, Land and Sea, Rivers, Mountains, Metalls and the like; we now come to a closer view of God and Nature in V*egetables*, *Animalls*, and *Man*.

And first of *Vegetables*, where I shall touch only these foure heads, their *Forme* and *Beauty*, their *Seed*, their *Signatures* & their great *Use* as well for Medicine as Sustenance. And that we may the better understand the advantage we have in this closer Contemplation of the works of Nature, we are in the first place to take notice of the condition of that Substance which we call *Matter*, how fluid and slippery and undeterminate it is of it self: or if it be hard, how unfit it is to be chang'd into any thing else. And therefore all things rot into a moisture before any thing can be generated of them, as we soften the wax before we set on the Seal.

Now therefore, unlesse we will be so foolish, as because the uniforme motion of the Aire, or some more subtile corporeall Element, may so equally compresse or beare against the parts of a little vapourous moisture as to forme it into round drops (as we see in the Dew and other Experiments) and therefore because this more rude and generall

Motion can do something, to conclude that it does all things; we must in all Reason confesse that there is an *Eternall Mind*, in vertue whereof the *Matter* is thus usefully formed and changed.

But meere rude and undirected Motion, because naturally it will have some kind of Results, that therefore it will reach to such as plainly imply a wise contrivance of *Counsell*, is so ridiculous a Sophisme, as I have already intimated, that it is more fit to impose upon the inconsiderate Souls of Fooles and Children then upon men of mature Reason and well exercis'd in Philosophy. Admit that *Raine* and *Snow* and *Wind* and *Haile* and *Ice* and such like Meteors may be the products of *Heat* and *Cold*, or of the *Motion* and *Rest* of certaine small particles of the Matter; yet that the usefull and beautifull contrivance of the *branches*, *flowers* and *fruits* of *Plants* should be so too (to say nothing yet of the bodyes of Birds, Fishes, Beasts and Men) is as ridiculous and supine a Collection, as to inferre that because mere Heat and Cold does *soften* and *harden waxe* and puts it into some shape or other, that therefore this mere Heat and Cold or Motion and Rest, without any art or direction made the *Silver Seal* too, and graved upon it so curiously some *Coat of Armes*, or the shape of some *Birds* or *Beasts*, as an *Eagle*, a *Lyon* and the like. Nay indeed this inference is more tolerable farre then the other, these effects of *Art* being more easy and lesse noble then those others of *Nature*.

Nor is it any botch or gap at all in the works of Nature that some particular *Phænomena* be but the easy results of that *generall Motion* communicated unto the Matter from God, others the effects of more curious *contrivance* or of the *divine Art* or *Reason* (for such are the λόγοι σπερματικοί the *Rationes Seminales*)[27] incorporated in the Matter, especially the Matter it self being in some sort vitall, else it would not continue the Motion that it is put upon when it is occasionally this or the other way moved; & besides, the Nature of God being the most perfect fullnesse of life that is possibly conceivable, it is very congruous that this outmost and remotest shadow of himself be some way though but obscurely vitall. Wherefore things falling off by degrees from the highest perfection, it will be no uneven or unproportionable step, if descending from the Top of this outward Creation, *Man*, in whom there is a principle of more fine and reflexive Reason, which hangs on, though not in that manner in the more perfect kind of Brutes, as sense also, loth to be curb'd within too narrow a compasse, layes hold upon

[27] See the Introduction, above, p. 26.

some kinds of *Plants*, as in those sundry sorts of *Zoophyta*, but in the rest there are no further foot-steps discovered of an animadversive forme abiding in them, yet there be the effects of and inadvertent form (λόγος ἔνυλος)[28] of materiated or incorporated Art or Seminall Reason: I say it is no uneven jot, to passe from the more faint and obscure examples of *Spermaticall* life, to the more considerable effects of *generall Motion*, in *Mineralls, Metalls* & sundry *Meteors*, whose easy & rude shapes have no need of any particular principle of life or *Spermaticall forme* distinct from the Rest or Motion of the particles of the Matter.

But there is that Curiosity of *forme* and *beauty* in the more noble kind of *Plants* bearing such a sutablenesse and harmony with the more refined sense and sagacity of the Soul of Man, that he cannot chose (his Intellectuall Touch being so sweetly gratified by what it deprehends in such like Objects) but acknowledge that some hidden Cause much a kin to his own nature, that is intellectuall, is the contriver & perfecter of these so pleasant spectacles in the world.

Nor is it at all to the purpose to object, that this buisinesse of *Beauty* and *comelinesse* of *proportion* is but a conceit, because some men acknowledge no such thing, & all things are alike handsome to them, who yet not withstanding have the use of their Eyes as well as other folkes. For I say this rather makes for what we ayme at, that pulchritude is convey'd indeed by the outward Senses unto the Soul, but a more intellectuall faculty is that which relishes it; as a *Geometricall Scheme* is let in by the Eyes, but the demonstration is discern'd by Reason. And therefore it is more rationall to affirm that some *Intellectuall Principle* was the Authour of this *Pulchritude* of things, then that they should be thus fashion'd without the help of that Principle. And to say that there is no such thing as *Pulchritude*, because some mens Souls are so dull & stupid that they relish all objects alike in that respect, is as absurd and groundlesse as to conclude there is no such thing as *Reason* and *Demonstration* because a naturall Fool cannot reach unto it. But that there is such a thing as *Beauty*, & that it is acknowledged by the whole generations of Men to be in *Trees, Flowers* and *Fruits*; the adorning and beautifying of *Buildings* in all Ages is an ample & undenyable Testimony. For what is more ordinary with them then the taking in flowers and fruitage for the garnishing of their worke? Besides I appeal to any man that is not sunk into so forlorne a pitch of Degeneracy, that he is as stupid to these things as the basest of Beasts, whether for Example a

---

[28] Cf. Plotinus, II, iii, 17.

rightly cut *Tetraedrum*, *Cube* or *Icosaedrum* have no more pulchritude in them, then any rude *broken stone* lying in the field or high wayes; or to name other solid Figures which though they be not Regular properly so called, yet have a settled Idea and Nature, as a *Cone*, *Sphear* or *Cylinder*, whether the sight of these doe not gratifie the minds of men more, and pretend to more elegancy of shape, then those rude cuttings or chippings of *free stone* that fall from the Masons hands and serve for nothing but to fill up the middle of the Wall, and so to be hid from the Eyes of Man for their uglinesse. And it is observable that if Nature shape any thing near this Geometricall accuracy, that we take notice of it with much content and pleasure; As if it be but exactly *round* (as there are abundance of such stones found betwixt two hills in *Cuba* an Iland of *America*) or *ordinatly Quinquangular*, or have the sides but *Parallell*, though the Angles be unequall, as is seen in some little stones, and in a kind of *Alabaster* found here in England; these stones I say gratifie our sight, as having a neerer cognation with the Soul of man, that is rationall and intellectuall; and therefore is well pleased when it meets with any outward object that fits and agrees with those congenit Ideas her own nature is furnished with. For *Symmetry*, *Equality*, and *Correspondency of parts* is the discernment of *Reason*, not the object of *Sense*, as I have heretofore proved.

Now therefore it being evident that there is such a thing as *Beauty*, *Symmetry* and *Comelinesse of Proportion* (to say nothing of the delightfull mixture of colours) and that this is the proper Object of the Understanding and Reason (for these things be not taken notice of by the Beasts) I think I may safely inferre that whatever is the first and principall cause of changing the fluid and undeterminated Matter into shapes so comely and symmetricall, as wee see in *Flowers* and *Trees*, is an *understanding Principle*, and knows both the nature of man and of those objects he offers to his sight in this outward and visible world. For these things cannot come by chance or by a multifarious attempt of the parts of the matter upon themselves, for then it were likely that the *Species* of things (though some might hit right, yet most) would be maym'd and ridiculous; but now there is not any ineptitude in any thing which is a signe that the fluidnesse of the Matter is guided and determined by the overpowering counsell of an *Eternall Mind*, that is, of a God.

If it were not needlesse I might now instance in sundry kinds of flowers, herbes and trees: but these objects being so obvious and every mans Phansie being branched with the remembrance of *Roses*, *Mari-*

golds, Gillyflowers, Pionyes, Tulips, Pansies, Primroses, the leaves and clusters of the Vine, and a thousand such like, of all which they cannot but confesse, that there is in them *beauty* and *symmetry* and gratefull *proportion,* I hold it superfluous to weary you with any longer induction but shall passe on to the three considerations behind, of their *Seed, Signatures* and *Usefulnesse,* and shall passe through them very briefly, the Observables being very ordinary and easily intelligible.

VI. *The* Seeds *and* Signatures of Plants, *arguments of a divine Providence.*

I say therefore in that every Plant has its *Seed,* it is an evident signe of divine Providence. For it being no necessary Result of the Motion of the Matter, as the whole contrivance of the Plant indeed is not, and it being of so great consequence that they have *Seed* for the continuance and propagation of their own *Species,* and for the gratifying of mans Art also, industry and necessityes, (for much of husbandry and gardening lyes in this) it cannot but be an Act of *Counsell* to furnish the severall kinds of Plants with their *Seeds,* especially the Earth being of such a nature, that though at first for a while it might bring forth all manner of *Plants,* (as some will have it also to have brought forth all kinds of *Animalls*) yet as last it would grow so sluggish, that without the advantage of those small compendious Principles of generation, the graines of *Seed,* it would yield no such births; no more then a Pump grown dry will yield any water, unless you pour a little water into it first, & then for one Bason-full you may fetch up so many Soe-fulls.

Nor is it materiall to object that stinking *weeds,* and *poysonous Plants* bear *seed* too as well as the most *pleasant* and most *usefull.* For even those stinking *weeds* and *poysonous Plants* have their use. For first the Industry of Man is excercised by them to weed them out where they are hurtfull. Which reason if it seem slight, let us but consider that if humane Industry had nothing to conflict and struggle with, the fire of mans Spirit would be half extinguished in the flesh, and then wee shall acknowledge that that which I have alledged is not so contemptible nor invalid.

But secondly who knows but it is so with poysonous *Plants,* as vulgarly is phansied concerning *Toads* and other poysonous *Serpents,* that they lick the venome from off the Earth? so poysonous *plants* may well draw to them all the maligne juice and nourishment that the other may be more pure and defæcate, as there are Receptacles in the body of

Man and Emunctories[29] to draine them of superfluous Choler, Melancholy and the like.

But lastly it is very well known by them that know any thing in Nature and Physick, that those herbs that the rude and ignorant would call *weeds* are the Materialls of very soveraigne Medicines, that *Aconitum hyemale* or *Winter wolfes-bane*, that otherwise is ranck poyson, is reported to prevail mightily against the bitings of vipers and scorpions, which *Crollius*[30] assenteth unto. And that that plant that bears death in the very name of it, *Solanum Læthiferum*, prevents death by procuring sleep, if it be rightly apply'd in a feaver. Nor are those things to be deemed unprofitable whose use we know not yet, for all is not to be known at once, that succeeding Ages may ever have something left to gratifie themselves in their own discoveries.

We come now to the *Signatures* of Plants, which seems no lesse Argument that the highest originall of the works of Nature is some *understanding Principle*, then that so care full provision of their *seed*. Nay indeed this respects us more properly and adæquately then the other, and is a certaine Key to enter Man into the knowledge and use of the Treasures of Nature. I demand therefore whether it be not a very easie and genuine inference from the observing that severall herbs are marked with some *marke* or *signe* that intimates their vertue, what they are good for; and there being such a creature as Man in the world that can read and understand these *signes* and *characters*, hence to collect that the Authour both of Man and them knew the nature of them both; For it is like the inscriptions upon Apothecaries Boxes that the Master of the Shop sets on, that the Apprentise may read them; nay it is better, for here is in herbs inscribed the very *nature* and *use* of them, not the meere *name*. Nor is there any necessity that all should be thus signed, though some be; for the rarity of it is the delight; for other wise it had been dull and cloying, too much harping upon the same string. And besides divine Providence would onely initiate and enter mankind into the usefull knowledge of her Treasures, leaving the rest to imploy our industry that we might not live like idle Loyterers and Truants. For the Theatre of the world is an excercise of Mans wit, not a lazy *Polyanthea*

---

[29] 'certain kernelly places in the body, by which principal parts void their superfluities; as under the Arm-pits for the Heart, under the Ears for the Brain, and the Groin for the Liver' (Thomas Blount, *Glossographia* [1656], sig. o7).

[30] Oswald Crollius (1560–1609), a German alchemist, author of the frequently reprinted *Basilica chimica* (Frankfurt, 1609).

An Antidote against Atheism

or book of Common places. And therefore all things are in some measure obscure and intricate, that the sedulity of that divine Spark the Soul of Man, may have matter of conquest and triumph when he has done bravely by a superadvenient assistance of his God.

But that there be some Plants that bear a very evident *Signature* of their *nature* and *use*, I shall fully make good by these following instances . . . .

The leaf of *Balme* and of *Alleluia* or *Wood-Sorrell*, as also the Roots of *Anthora* represent the heart in figure and are *Cardiacall*.

Wall nuts beare the whole *signature* of the head. The outward green *Cortex* answers to the *Pericranium*, and a salt made of it is singularly good for wounds in that part, as the kernell is good for the brains which it resembles.

Umbilicus Veneris is powerfull to provoke lust as *Dioscorides* affirmes. As also your severall sorts of *Satyrions* which have the evident resemblance of the genitall parts upon them: *Aron* especially, and all your *Orchisses*, that they have given names unto from some beasts or other, as *Cynosorchis*, *Orchis Myodes*, *Tragorchis* and the like. The last whereof, notorious also for its goatish smell and tufts not unlike the beard of that lecherous Animall, is of all the rest the most powerful Incentive to Lust.

The leaves of *Hypericon*, are very thick prick'd, or pinck'd with little holes, and it is a singular good wound-herb, as usefull also for deobstructing the pores of the body.

Scorpioides, *Echium*, or *Scorpion-grasse* is like the crooked tayle of a Scorpion, and *Ophioglossum* or *Adders-tongue* has a very plain and perfect resemblance of the tongue of a Serpent, as also *Ophioscorodon* of the intire head and upper parts of the body, and these are all held very good against poyson and the biting of Serpents. And generally all such plants as are speckled with spots like the skins of vipers or other venemous creatures, are known to be good against the stings or bitings of them, and are powerfull Antidotes against Poyson.

Thus did divine Providence by naturall *Hieroglyphicks* read short Physick lectures to the rude wit of man, that being a little entered and engaged he might by his own industry and endeavours search out the rest himself, it being very reasonable that other herbs that had not such *signatures*, might be very good for Medicinall uses, as well as they that had.

But if any here object that some herbs have the resemblance of such things as cannot in any likelyhood referre to Physick, as *Geranium*,

Cruciata Bursa Pastoris, & the like; I say they answer themselves in the very proposall of their Objection: For this is a signe that they were intended onely for ludicrous ornaments of Nature, like the flourishes about a great letter that signify nothing but are made onely to delight the Eye. And 'tis so farre from being any inconvenience to our first progenitours if this intimation of *signatures* did faile, that it cast them with more courage upon attempting the vertue of those that had no such *signatures* at all; it being obvious for them to reason thus, Why may not those herbs have medicinall vertue in them that have no *signatures*, as well as they that have *signatures* have no vertue answerable to the *signes* they beare? which was a further confirmation to them of the former conclusion.

And it was sufficient that those that were of so present and great consequence as to be Antidotes against poyson that so quickly would have dispatched poore rude and naked Antiquity, or to help on the small beginnings of the world by quickning and actuating their phlegmatick Natures to more frequent and effectuall Venery (for their long lives shew they were not very fiery) I say it was sufficient that herbs of this kind were so legibly *sign'd* with *Characters* that so plainly bewrai'd their usefull vertues, as is manifest in your *Satyrions*, *Ophioglossum*, and the like. But I have dwelt too long upon this Theory, wee'l betake our selves to what followes.

VII. *Arguments of divine Providence drawn from the* Usefulness *of* Plants.

We are at length come to the fourth and last consideration of *Plants*, *viz.* their *Use & Profitablenesse*. And to say nothing now of those greater *Trees* that are fit for *Timber*, and are the requisite Materials for the *building* of Ships and magnificent Houses, to adorne the Earth, and make the life of Man more splendid and delectable; as also for the erecting of those *holy Structures* consecrated to divine Worship, amongst which we are not to forget that famous Ædifice, that glorious Temple at *Jerusalem* consecrated to the great God of Heaven and Earth: As indeed it was most fit that he whose Guidance & Providence permitted not the strength of the Earth to spend it self in base gravel and pebbles insteed of Quaries of Stones, nor in briars and brush-wood insteed of Pines, Cedars and Okes, that he should at some time or other have the most stately magnificent *Temples* erected to him, that the wit and industry of Man and the best of those materials could afford. It

An Antidote against Atheism

being the most suteable acknowledgment of thanks for that piece of Providence that can be invented. And it is the very consideration that moved that pious King *David* to designe the building of a Temple to the God of *Israel*; See now, sayes he, I dwell in a house of Cedar, but the Arke of God dwelleth within Curtains.[31] But as I sayd I will add nothing concerning these things being contented with what I have glanced upon heretofore.

We will now briefly take notice of the *profitablenesse* of Plants for *Physick* and *Food* and then passe on to the consideration of *Animalls*. And as for their *Medicinall* uses, the large Herballs that are every where to be had are so ample Testimonies thereof, that I have said enough in but reminding you of them. That which is most observable here is this, that brute *Beasts* have some share in their vertue as well as *Men*. For the *Toad* being overcharged with the poison of the *Spider*, as is ordinary believed, has recourse to the *Plantane leafe*. The *Weasel* when she is to encounter the *Serpent*, armes her self with eating of *Rue*. The *Dog* when he is sick at the stomach, knows his Cure, falls to his *Grasse*, vomits, and is well. The *Swallowes* make use of *Celandine*; the *Linnet* of *Euphragia* for the repairing of their *sight*. And the *Asse* when hee's oppress'd with Melancholy, eats of the herbe *Asplenium* or *Miltwaste*, and so eats himself of the swelling of the *Spleene*. And *Virgill* reports of the *Dictamnum Cretense* or *Cretian Dittany*, that the *wild Goats* eate it when they are *shot* with darts or arrowes, for that herb has the vertue to work them out of their body and to heale up the wound.

――――*non illa feris incognita Capris*
Gramina, cum tergo volucres hasere sagittæ.[32]

Which things I conceive no obscure indigitation of *Providence*; For they doing that by instinct and nature, which men who have free Reason cannot but acknowledge to be very pertinent and fitting, nay such that the skillfullest Physitian will approve and allow; and these Creatures having no such reason and skill themselves, as to turne Physitians; it must needs be concluded that they are inabled to do these things by vertue of that *Principle* that contrived them, and made them of that nature they are, and that that *Principle* therefore must have *skill* and *knowledge*, that is, that it must be *God*.

We come now to the consideration of Plants as they afford *Food* both to Man and Beasts. And here we may observe that as there was a

---

[31] 2 *Samuel* 7. 2.   [32] *Aeneid*, XII, 414–15.

generall provision of *water* by setting the Mountains and Hills a broche, from whence through the Spring-heads and continued Rivulets drawn together (that caused afterwards greater Rivers with the long winding distributions of them) all the Creatures of the Earth quench their thirst: So divine Providence has spread her *Table* every where, not with a juicelesse green Carpet, but with succulent *Herbage* and nourishing *Grasse*, upon which most of the beasts of the field doe feed. And they that feed not on it, feed on those that eate it, and so the generations of them all are continued.

But this seeming rather *necessary* then *of choice*, I will not insist upon it. For I grant that Counsell most properly is there implyde where we discerne a variety and possibility of being otherwise, and yet the best is made choise of. Therefore I will onely intimate thus much, that though it were necessary that some such thing as *grasse* should be, if there were such and such Creatures in the world, yet it was not at all necessary that grasse and herbs should have that *colour* which they have, for they might have been red or white, or some such colour which would have been very offensive and hurtfull to our sight. But I will not insist upon these things; let us now consider the *Fruits* of *Trees*, where I think it will appear very manifestly, that there was one and the same Authour both of Man and them, and that assuredly he knew what he did when he made them. For could *Apples*, and *Oranges*, and *Grapes*, and *Apricocks*, and such like fruit, be intended for *Beasts* that hold their heads downward and can scarce look up at them, much lesse know how to reach them? When we feed our dogs, we set the dish or trencher on the ground, not on the Table. But you'le say that at last these fruits will fall down, and then the beasts may come at them: But one thing is, there are not many that desire them, and so they would rot upon the ground before they be spent, or be squander'd away in a moment of time, as it might easily fare with the most precious of Plants the *Vine*. But *Man* who knowes the worth of the *Grape* knowes to preserve it a long season (for it is both eaten and drunk some yeares after the vintage) as he does also gather the rest of the fruits of the Earth, and layes up both for himself and his Cattel: Wherefore it is plainly discoverable that Mans coming into the world, is not a thing of *Chance* or *Necessity*, but *a Designe*, as the bringing of worthy Guests to a well furnish'd Table....

I might now reach out to *Exotick Plants*, such as the *Cinnamon*-tree the *Balsame*-tree, the Tree that beares the *Nutmegge* invelloped with the *Mace*, as also the famous *Indian Nut*-tree, which at once almost affords all the Necessaries of life. For if they cut but the twiggs at Evening, there is a plentifull and pleasant Juice comes out, which they receive into Bottles and drink instead of *Wine*, and out of which they extract such an *Aqua vitæ*, as is very soveraign against all manner of sicknesses. The branches and boughs they make their *Houses* of; and the body of the Tree being very spongy within, though hard without, they easily contrive into the frame and use of their *Canoes* or *boates*. The kernell of the Nut serves them for *Bread* and *Meat*, and the shells for *Cups* to drink in, and indeed they are not mere empty *Cups*, for there is found a delicious cooling Milk in them: Besides there is a kind of Hemp that incloses the Nut, of which they make *Ropes* and *Cables*, and of the finest of it *Sailes* for their ships; and the leaves are so hard and sharpe-pointed, that they easily make *needles* or *bodkins* of them, for stiching their Sailes and for other necessary purposes. And that Providence may shew her self benigne as well as wise, this so notable a Plant is not restrain'd to one Coast of the world, as suppose the *East-Indies*, but is found also in some parts of *Africa*, and in all the Islands of the *West-Indies*, as *Hispaniola*, *Cuba*, as also upon the Continent of *Carthagena*, in *Panama*, *Norombega*, and several others parts of the new-found world.

But I thought fit not to insist upon these things, but to containe my self within the compasse of such Objects as are familiarly and ordinarily before our eyes, that we may the better take occasion from thence to return thanks to him who is the bountiful Authour of all the supports of life.

VIII. *The* Usefullnesse *of* Animalls *an Argument of divine Providence.*

We are now come to take a view of the nature of *Animalls*: In the contemplation whereof we shall use much what the same Method we did in that of *Plants*, for we shall consider in them also, their *Beauty*, their *Birth*, their *Make* and *Fabric* of body, and *Usefulnesse* to Man-kind. And to dispatch this last first. It is wonderfull easy and naturall to conceive, that as almost all are made in some sort or other for humane uses, so some so notoriously and evidently, that without maine violence done to our faculties we can in no wise deny it. As to instance in those things that are most obvious and familiar; when we see in the solitary fields a *Shepheard*, his *Flock*, and his *Dog*, how well they are fitted together; when we knock at a Farmers door, and the first that answers shall be his vigilant *Mastiffe*, whom from his use and office he ordinarily names *Keeper*, and I remember *Theophrastus* in his Character περὶ ἀγροικίας³³ tells us, that his Master when he has let the stranger in, ἐπιλαβόμενος τοῦ ῥύγχους taking his *Dog* by the snout will relate long stories of his usefullnesse and his services he does to the house and them in it. Οὗτος φυλάττει τὸ χωρίον καὶ τὴν οἰκίαν καὶ τοὺς ἔνδον. *This is he that keepes the yard, the house and them within.* Lastly when we view in the open Champian a brace of swift *Greyhounds* coursing a good stout and well-breathed *Hare*, or a pack of well tuned *Hounds*, and Huntsmen on their horsebacks with pleasure and alacrity pursuing their game, or heare them winding their Hornes neere a wood side, so that the whole wood rings with the Echo of that Musick and chearefull yelping of the eager *Doggs*: to say nothing of *Duck-hunting*, of *Foxe-hunting*, of *Otter-hunting*, and a hundred more such like sports and pastimes, that are all performed by this one kind of *Animall*; I say when we consider this so multifarious congruity and fitnese of things in reference to our selves how can we withhold from inferring, that that which made both *Dogs* and *Ducks* and *Hares* and *Sheep*, made them with a reference to us, and knew what it did when it made them? And though it be possible to be otherwise, yet it is highly improbable that the flesh of *Sheep* should not be designed for food for men; and that *Dogs* that are such a familiar and domestick Creature to Man, amongst other pretty feats that they doe for him, should not be intended to supply the place of a servitour too, and to take away the bones and scraps that nothing might be lost. And unlesse we should expect that Nature should make Jerkins & Stockings grow out of the ground, what could she doe better then afford us so fit materialls for *clothing* as the *Wooll* of the sheep, there being in Man Wit and Art to make use of it? To say nothing of the *Silkworme* that seems to come into the world for no other purpose, then to furnish man with more costly clothing, and to spin away her very entrailes to make him fine without.

Again when we view those large Bodies of *Oxen*, what can we better conceit them to be, then so many living and walking powdring Tubbs, and that they have *animam pro Sale*, as *Philo* speaks of Fishes, that their life is but for Salt to keepe them sweet till we shall have need to eate them? Besides their *Hides* afford us *Leather* for *Shooes* and *Boots*, as the *skins* of other beasts also serve for other uses. And indeed Man seems to be brought into the world on purpose that the rest of the Creation might be improved to the utmost usefulnesse & advantage;

³³ 'Boorishness' (*Char.*, IV).

For were it not better that the *hides* of Beasts and their *flesh* should be made so considerable use of as to *feed* and *cloath* Men, then that they should rot and stink upon the ground, and fall short of so noble an improvement as to be matter for the exercise of the wit of Man, & to afford him the necessary conveniences of life? For if Man did not make use of them, they would either dye of Age, or be torne a pieces by more cruel Masters. Wherefore we plainly see that it is an Act of *Reason* & *Counsel* to have made Man that he might be a Lord over the rest of the Creation, & keep good quarter among them.

And being furnish'd with fit Materialls to make himself weapons, as well as with naturall wit and valour, he did bid battaile to the very fiercest of them, and either chased them away into Solitudes and Deserts or else brought them under his subjection and gave lawes unto them; Under which they live more peaceably, and are better provided for (or at least might be, if Men were good) then they could be when they were left to the mercy of the *Lyon Bear* or *Tiger*. And what if he doe occasionally and orderly kill some of them for food? their dispatch is quick and so lesse dolorous then the paw of the Bear or the teeth of the Lyon, or tedious Melancholy and sadnesse of old Age, which would first torture them, and then kill them and let them rot upon the ground stinking and uselesse.

Besides, all the wit and Philosophy in the world can never demonstrate, that the killing and slaughtering of a Beast is any more then the striking of a bush where a birds Nest is, where you fray away the Bird and then seize upon the empty Nest. So that if we could pierce to the utmost *Catastrophe* of things, all might prove but a *Tragick-Comedy*.

But as for those *Rebells* that have fled into the *Mountains* and *Deserts*, they are to us a very pleasant subject of natural History, besides we serve our selves of them as much as is to our purpose. And they are not onely for ornaments of the Universe, but a continuall Exercise of Mans Wit and Valour when he pleases to encounter. But to expect and wish that there were nothing but such dull *tame* things in the world, that will neither bite nor scratch, is as groundlesse and childish as to wish there were no *choler* in the body nor *fire* in the universall compasse of Nature.

I cannot insist upon the whole result of this warre, nor must forget how that generous Animall the *Horse*, had at last the wit to yield himself up, to his own great advantage and ours. And verily he is so fitly made for us, that we might justly claim a peculiar right in him above all other Creatures. When we observe his patient service he does us at the *Plough*, *Cart*, or under the *Pack-saddle*, his *speed* upon the high way in matters of importance, his *dociblenesse* and desire of *glory* and *praise*, and consequently his notable atchievements in *war*, where he will knap the Speares a pieces with his teeth, and pull his Riders Enemy out of the Saddle; and then that he might be able to performe all this labour with more Ease, that his *hoofs* are made so fit for the Art of the *Smith*, and that round armature of Iron he puts upon them; it is a very hard thing not to acknowledge, that this so congruous contrivance of things was really from a *Principle* of *Wisdome* and *Counsell*. There is also another consideration of *Animalls* and their *usefulnesse*, in removing those Evills we are pester'd with by reason of the abundance of some other hurtfull Animalls, such as are *Mice* and *Rats* and the like; and to this end the *Cat* is very serviceable. And there is in the *West-Indies* a *beast* in the form of a Beare which *Cardan*[34] calls *Ursus Formicarius*, whose very businesse it is to eate up all the *Ants* which some parts of that Quarter of the World are sometimes excessively plagued withall.

We might add also sundry Examples of living Creatures that not onely bear a singular good affection to Mankind, but are also fierce Enemies to those that are very hurtfull and cruell to Man; and such are the *Lizard*, an Enemy to the *Serpent*; the *Dolphin* to the *Crocodile*; the *Horse* to the *Bear*; the *Elephant* to the *Dragon*, &c. but I list not to insist upon these things.

IX. *Arguments of divine Providence fetched from the* Pulchritude *of* Animalls, *as also from the* manner *of their* Propagation.

I return now to what I proposed first, the *Beauty* of living Creatures; which though the coarse-spirited *Atheist* will not take notice of, as relishing nothing but what is subservient to his Tyranny or Lust: yet I think it undeniable, but that there is comely *Symmetry & Beautifulnesse* in sundry living Creatures, a tolerable usefull *Proportion of parts* in all. For neither are all men and women exquisitly handsome, indeed very few, that they that are may raise the greater admiration in the minds of Men, and quicken their natural abilities to brave adventures either of Valour or Poetry. But as for the brute Creatures though some of them be of an *hatefull* aspect, as the *Toad*, the *Swine* & the *Rat*; yet these are but like discords in Musick to make the succeeding chord goe off more

---

[34] Gerolamo Cardano (1501–76), the celebrated Italian philosopher and mathematician.

pleasantly, as indeed most of those momentary inconveniences that the life of Man ever and anon meets withall, they but put a greater edge and vigour upon his Enioyments.

But it is not hard to find very many Creatures, that are either καλὰ χρήματα or ἀστεῖα as the Philosopher distinguishes, that are either very *goodly* things and *beautifull*, or at least *elegant* and *pretty*;[35] as most of your *Birds* are. But for *Statelinesse* and *Majesty* what is comparable to a *Horse*? whether you looke upon him single, with his Mane and his Taile waving in the wind, and hear him coursing and neighing in the pastures; or whether you see him with some gallant *Heros* on his back, performing gracefully his usefull postures, and practising his exploits of warre; who can withhold from concluding that a providence brought these together, that are fitted so well to each other that they seem but one compleat Spectacle of Nature? which imposed upon the rude people neere *Thessaly*, and gave the occasion of the fabulous *Centaurs*, as if they had been one living Creature made up of *Horse* and *Man*.

That which I drive at is this, there being that *Goodlinesse* in the bodies of *Animalls*, as in the *Oxe*, *Grey-hound* and *Stagge*; or that *Majesty* and *Statelinesse*, as in the *Lyon*, the *Horse*, the *Eagle* and *Cock*; or that grave *Awfullnesse*, as in your best breed of *Mastives*; or *Elegancy* and *Prettinesse*, as in your lesser *Dogs*, and most sorts of *Birds*, all which are severall Modes of *Beauty*, and *Beauty* being an intellectuall Object, as *Symmetry* and *Proportion* is (which I proved sufficiently in what I spake concerning the beauty of *Plants*) that which naturally followes from all this is, that the *Authour* or *Originall* of these Creatures, which are deemed *beautifull*, must himself be *intellectuall*, he having contrived so gratefull objects to the Mind or Intellect of Man.

After their Beauty let us touch upon their *Birth* or *manner* of *Propagation*. And here I appeale to any man whether the contrivance of *Male* and *Female* in living Creatures be not a genuine effect of *Wisdome* and *Counsell*; for it is notoriously obvious that these are made one for the other, and both for the continuation of the *Species*. For though we should admit with *Cardan* and other Naturallists, that the Earth at first brought forth all manner of *Animalls* as well as Plants, and that they might be fastned by the Navell to their common Mother the Earth, as they are now to the *Female* in the Wombe; yet we see she is growne steril and barren, and her births of *Animalls* are now very inconsiderable. Wherefore what can it be but a *Providence*, that whiles she did beare

---

[35] Cf. Aristotle, *Ethica nicomachea*, IV, 3.

she sent out *Male* and *Female*, that when her own Prolifick vertue was wasted, yet she might be a dry-Nurse or an officious Grand-mother to thousands of generations? And I say it is *Providence*, not *Chance* nor *Necessity*, for what is there imaginable in the parts of the Matter that they should necessarily fall into the structure of so much as an *Animall*, much lesse into so carefull a provision of differences of Sexes for their continuall propagation?

Nor was it the frequent attempts of the moved Matter that first light on *Animalls*, which perpetually were suddainly extinct for want of the differences of Sexes, but afterward by *chance* differenced their Sexes also, from whence their kinds have continued. For what is perpetuall, is not by *chance*; and the births that now are by putrefaction shew that it is perpetuall. For the Earth still constantly brings forth *Male* and *Female*.

Nor is it any thing to the purpose to reply (if you will make so large a skip as to cast your self from the land into the water to dive for Objections) that the *Eele*, though it be ζῶον ἔναιμον, an *Animall so perfect as to have bloud in it*, yet that it has no distinction of *Sexe*:[36] For if it have not, there is good reason for it, that creature arising out of such kind of Matter as will never faile generation. For there will be such like mud as will serve this end so long as there be Rivers and longer too, and Rivers will not faile so long as there is a Sea. Wherefore this rather makes for discriminative Providence that knew afore the nature and course of all things, and made therefore her contrivances accordingly, doing nothing superfluously or in vain.

But in other *Generations* that are more hazardous, though they be sometimes by putrefaction, yet she makes them *Male* and *Female*, as 'tis plain in *Frogs* and *Mice*. Nor are we to be scandalized at it, that there is such carefull provision made for such contemptible *Vermine* as we conceive them: For this onely comes out of pride and ignorance, or a haughty presumption that because we are incouraged to believe that in some sense all things are made for Man, that therefore they are not made at all for themselves. But he that pronounces thus, is ignorant of the nature of God and the knowledge of things. For if a good man be mercifull to his beast, then surely a good God is bountifull and benigne, and takes pleasure that all his Creatures enjoy themselves that have life and sense and are capable of any enjoyment. So that the swarmes of little *Vermine*, and of *Flyes*, and innumerable such like

---

[36] Aristotle, *Historia animalium*, VI, 16; *De partibus animalium*, II, 5.

diminutive Creatures, we should rather congratulate their coming into Being, then murmure sullenly and scornfully against their Existence; for they find nourishment in the world, which would be lost if they were not, and are againe convenient nourishment themselves to others that prey upon them.

But besides, life being individuated into such infinite numbers that have their distinct sense and pleasure and are sufficiently fitted with contentments, those little Soules are in a manner as much considerable for the taking off or carrying away to themselves the over-flowing benignity of the first Original of all things, as the *Oxe* the *Elephant* or *Whale*. For it is *sense*, not *bulk* that makes things capable of enjoyments.

Wherefore it was fit that there should be a safe provision made for the propagation and continuance of all the *kinds* of living Creatures, not onely of those that are *good*, but those also that we rashly and inconsiderately call *evill*. For they are at least good to enjoy themselves and to partake of the bounty of their Creatour. But if they grow noysome and troublesome to us, we have both power and right to curb them: For there is no question but we are more worth then they or any of the brute Creatures. . . .

X. *The* Frame *or* Fabrick of the Bodies of Animalls *plainly argue that there is a God.*

I come now to the last consideration of Animalls, the outward *Shape* and *Fabrick* of their *Bodies*, which when I have shew'd you that they might have been otherwise, and yet are made according to the most exquisite pitch of Reason that the wit of Man can conceive of, it will naturally follow that they were really made by *Wisdome* and *Providence*, and consequently that *there is a God*. And I demand first in generall concerning all those Creatures that have *Eyes* and *Eares*, whether they might not have had onely *one Eye* and *one Eare* a piece; and to make the supposition more tolerable, had the Eye on one side the head, and the Eare on the other, or the Eare on the Crown of the head, the Eye in the Forehead for they might have lived and subsisted though they had been no better provided for then thus. But it is evident that their having *two Eyes* and *two Eeares*, so placed as they are, is more safe, more sightly, and more usefull. Therefore that being made so constantly choice of, which our own Reason deemeth best, we are to inferr that that choice proceeded from *Reason* and *Counsell*.

Again I desire to know why there be no *three-footed Beasts*, (when I speak thus, I doe not meane *Monsters*, but a constant *Species* or kind of Animalls) for such a Creature as that would make a limping shift to live as well as they that have *foure*. Or why have not some beasts more than foure-feet, suppose *sixe*, & the two middlemost shorter then the rest, hanging like the two legges of a Man a horse-back by the horse sides? For it is no harder a thing for Nature to make such frames of Bodies then others that are more elegant and usefull. But the works of Nature being neither uselesse nor inept, she must either be wise her self, or be guided by some higher Principle of *Knowledge*: As that Man that does nothing foolishly all the dayes of his life, is either wise himself, or consults with them that are so.

And then again for the *armature* of Beasts, who taught them the use of their *weapons*? The *Lyon* will not kick with his Feet, but he will strike such a stroke with his *Tayle*, that he will breake the back of his Encounterer with it. The *Horse* will not use his Tayle unlesse against the busy flyes, but kicks with his *Feet* with that force that he layes his Enemy on the ground. The *Bull* and *Ram* know the use of their *Hornes* as well as the *Horse* of his *Hoofes*. So the *Bee* and *Serpent* know their *Stings*, and the *Beare* the use of his *Paw*. Which things they know merely by naturall instinct, as the Male knowes the use of the Female. For they gather not this skill by observation and experience, but the frame of their nature carries them to it, as it is manifest in young *Lambes* that will *butt* before they have horns. Therefore it is some higher *Providence* that has made them of this nature they are. And this is evident also in *Birds* that will *flutter* with their wings, when there is but a little Down upon them, and they are as yet utterly unusefull for flying.

And now I have fallen upon the mention of this kind of Creature, let me make my advantage of that general structure observable in them. The forme of their *Heads* being *narrow* and *sharpe*, that they may the better cut the Aire in their swift flight, and the spreading of their *Tayles*, parallel to the *Horizon* for the better bearing up their Body; for they might have been perpendicular as the Tayles of Fishes in the water. Nor is it any thing that the *Owle* has so broad a face, for her flight was not to be so swift nor so frequent.

And as for *Fishes* and the bladder of wind found in their Bodies, who can say it is conveigh'd thither by *chance*, but is contriv'd for their more easy swimming, as also the manner of their *finnes*, which consist of a number of gristly bones long and slender like pinnes and needles, and a kind of a skin betwixt, which is for the more exactnesse and makes them thin and flat like Oares. Which perfect artifice and accuracy might have been omitted and yet they have made a shift to move up and down in the water.

But I have fallen upon a subject that is infinite and inexhaustible, therefore that I be not too tedious I will confine my self to some few observations in ordinary *Beasts* and *Birds* (that which is most known and obvious being most of all to our purpose), and then I shall come to the contemplation of Man.

And indeed what is more obvious and ordinary then a *Mole*, and yet what more palpable Argument of *Providence* then she? The members of her body are so exactly fitted to her nature and manner of life: For her dwelling being under ground where nothing is to be seene, Nature has so obscurely fitted her with *Eyes*, that Naturalists can scarce agree whither she have any sight at all or no. But for amends, what she is capable of for her defence and warning of danger, she has very eminently conferr'd upon her: for she is exceeding quick of *hearing*. And then her *short Tayle* and *short Leggs*, but broad *Fore-feet* armed with *sharpe Clawes*, we see by the event to what purpose they are, she so swiftly working her self under ground and making her way so fast in the Earth, as they that behold it cannot but admire it. Her *Leggs* therefore are *short* that she need dig no more than will serve the mere thicknesse of her Body. And her *Fore-feet* are *broad*, that she may scoup away much Earth at a time. And little or no *Tayle* she has, because she courses it not on the ground like the *Rat* or *Mouse* of whose kinred she is, but lives under the Earth and is fain to dig her self a dwelling there: And she making her way through so thick an Element, which will not yield easily as the Aire or the Water, it had been dangerous to have drawn so long a train behind her: for her Enemy might fall upon her Reare and fetch her out before she had compleated or had got full possession of her works....

But there are as manifest foot-steps of divine Providence in other Creatures as in the *Mole*. As for Example, the *Hare*, whose temper and frame of body are plainly fitted on purpose for her Condition.

For why is she made so full of *Feare* and *Vigilancy* ever rearing up and listning whiles she is feeding? and why is she so exceeding *swift of foot*, and has her *Eyes* so *prominent*, and placed so that she can see better behind her then before her? but that her flight is her onely safety, and it was needful for her perpetually to eye her pursuing enemy, against whom she durst never stand at the Bay, having nothing but her long soft limber *Eares* to defend her. Wherefore he that made the *Hare* made the *Dog* also, and guarded her with these Properties from her eager foe, that she might not be too easy a booty for him, and so never be able to save her self, or afford the Spectatour any considerable Pastime. And that the *Hare* might not always get away from the *Grey-hound*, see how exquisitely his shape is fitted for the Course: For the narrownesse and slendernesse of his parts are made for speed; and that seeming impertinent long *Appendix* of his body, his Taile, is made for more nimble turning.

There are other *Animalls* also whose particular Fabrick of Body does manifestly appeare the Effect of *Providence* and *Counsell*, though Naturalists cannot agree whether it be in the behalf of the *Beast* thus framed or of *Man*. And such is that Creature which though it be Exotick yet is ordinarily known by the name of a *Camell*: For why are those *bunches* on his backe, but that they may be instead of a *Pack-saddle* to receive the burden? And why has he four *knees* and all his *Legges bending inwards*, like the fore-feet of other beasts, and a *Protuberancy* under his *Breast* to lean on, but that being a tall Creature he might with ease *kneel* down and so might the more gainly be loaden? . . .

XI. *The particular* Frames *of the Bodies of* Fowls *or* Birds *palpable signes of Divine Providence.*

We passe on now to the consideration of *Fowls* or *Birds*: where omitting the more generall Properties of having two Ventricles, and picking up stones to conveigh them into their second Ventricle, the Gizzerne, (which provision and instinct is a supply for the want of teeth) as also their having no Paps as *Beasts* have, their young ones being nourished so long in the Shell, that they are presently fit to be fed by the mouths of the old ones (which Observations plainly signify that Nature does nothing ineptly and foolishly, and that therfore there is a *Providence*) I shall content my self in taking notice only of some few kinds of this Creature that familiarly come into our sight, such as the *Cock*, the *Duck*, the *Swan* and the like. I demand therefore concerning the *Cock*, why he has *Spurres* at all, or having them how they come to be so fittingly placed. For he might have had none, or so misplaced that they had been utterly uselesse, and so his courage and pleasure in fighting had been to no purpose. Nor are his *Combe* and his *Wattles* in vaine, for they are an *Ornament* becoming his

Martiall Spirit, yea an *Armature* too, for the tugging of those often excuses the more useful parts of his head from harm. Thus fittingly does Nature gratify all Creatures with accommodations sutable to their temper, and nothing is in vaine. Nor are we to cavill at the red pugger'd attire of the *Turkey* and the long *Excrescency* that hangs down over his Bill, when he swells with pride and anger; for it may be a Receptacle for his heated bloud, that has such free recourse to his head, or he may please himself in it as the rude *Indians*, whose Jewells hang dangling at their Noses. And if the bird be pleasur'd we are not to be displeased, being alwaies mindfull that Creatures are made to enjoy themselves, as well as to serve us, and it is a grosse piece of Ignorance and Rusticity to think otherwise.

Now for *Swannes* and *Ducks* and such like *Birds* of the *Water*, it is obvious to take notice how well they are fitted for that manner of life. For those that swim, their *Feet* are framed for it like a paire of Oares, their Clawes being connected with a pretty broad Membrane, and their *Necks* are long that they may dive deep enough into the water. As also the *Neck* of the *Herne* and such like Fowl who live of Fishes and are fain to frequent their Element, who walk on long stilts also like the people that dwell in the Marshes; but their Clawes have no such Membranes, for they had been but a hindrance to those kind of birds that onely wade in the water and do not swim. It is also observable how Nature has fitted other *Birds* of *Prey*, who spy their booty from aloft in the Aire, and see best at that distance, scarce see at all neere at hand. So they are both the Archer and shaft, taking aime afar off, and then shooting themselves directly upon the desired Mark, they seize upon the prey having hit it. The works of *Providence* are infinite, I will close all with the description of that strange bird of *Paradise*, for the strangenesse has made it notorious.

There is a *Bird* that falls down out of the Aire dead, and is found sometimes in the *Molucco* Islands, that has no Feet at all no more then an ordinary Fish. The bignesse of her Body and Bill, as likewise the form of them, is much what as a Swallows; but the spreading out of her Wings and Tayle has no lesse compasse then an Eagles. She lives and breeds in the Aire, comes not near the Earth but for her buriall, for the largenesse and lightnesse of her Wings and Tayle sustain her without lassitude. And the laying of her Egges and brooding of her young is upon the back of the Male who is made hollow, as also the breast of the Female for the more easy incubation. Now that such contrivances as these should be without divine *Providence*, is as improbable to me as that the *Copper Ring* with the Greek inscription upon it found about the Neck of an overgrown *Pike*, should be the effect of unknowing Nature, not the Artifice and Skill of man.

XII. *Unavoydable Arguments for divine Providence taken from the* accurate Structure of Mans Body, *from the* Passions of his Mind, *and* fitnesse of the whole Man to be an Inhabiter of the Universe.

But we needed not to have rambled so farre out into the works of Nature, to seek out Arguments to prove a *God*, we being so plentifully furnish'd with that at home which we took the pains to seek for abroad. For there can be no more ample testimony of a *God* & a *Providence* then the *frame* and *structure* of our own *Bodyes*. The admirable *Artifice* whereof *Galen*, though a mere Naturalist, was so taken with, that he could not but adjudge the honour of a hymne to the wise Creatour of it.[37] The contrivance of the whole and every particular is so evident an argument of exquisite skill in the Maker, that if I should pursue all that suites to my purpose, it would amount to an entire Volume. I shall therefore only hint at some few things, leaving the rest to be supply'd by Anatomists. And I think there is no man that has any skill in that Art, but will confess the more diligently and accurately the frame of our *Body* is examined, it is found the more exquisitely conformable to our own Reason, Judgement, and Desire. So that supposing the same matter that our bodys are made of, if it had been in our own power to have made our selves, we should have fram'd our selves no otherwise then we are. To instance in some particular. As in our *Eyes*, the *number*, the *situation*, the *fabrick* of them is such that we can excogitate nothing to be added thereto, or to be altered either for their *beauty*, *safety*, or *usefulnesse*. But as for their *Beauty* I will leave it rather to the delicate wit and Pen of Poets and amorous persons, then venture upon so tender and nice a subject with my severer style. I will onely note how *safely* they are *guarded*, and *fitly framed* out for that *use* they are intended. The *Brow* and the *Nose* saves them from harder strokes: but such a curious part as the *Eye* being necessarily lyable to mischief from smaller matters, the *sweat* of the Forehead is fenced off by those two wreaths of haire which

---

[37] *De usu partium*, III, 15–16. Cudworth's citation of Galen (below, p. 289) is similarly partisan.

we call the *Eye brows*; and the *Eyelids* are fortify'd with little stiffe *bristles* as with *Palisadoes*, against the assault of Flyes and Gnats, and such like bold *Animalcula*. Besides the *upper-lid* presently claps down and is as good a fence, as a *Portcullis* against the importunity of the Enemy: Which is done also every night, whether there be any present assault or no, as if Nature kept garrison in this *Acropolis* of Mans body the *Head*, & look'd that such lawes should be duly observ'd, as were most for his safety.

And now for the *Use* of the *Eye* which is *Sight*, it is evident that this Organ is so exquisitely framed for that purpose, that not the least curiosity can be added. For first the *Humour* and *Tunicles* are purely *Transparent*, to let in light and colours unfoul'd and unsophisticated by any inward tincture. And then again the parts of the Eye are made *Convex*, that there might be a direction of many raies coming from one point of the Object unto one point answerable in the bottome of the *Eye*; to which purpose the *Crystalline Humour* is of great Moment, and without which the sight would be very obscure and weake. Thirdly the *Tunica Uvea* has a *Musculous power*, and can dilate & contract that round hole in it which is called the *Pupill* of the Eye, for the better moderating the transmission of light. Fourthly the inside of the *Uvea* is *black'd* like the wals of a Tennis-court, that the rayes falling upon the *Retina* may not, by being rebounded thence upon the *Uvea*, be returned from the *Uvea* upon the *Retina* again, for such a repercussion would make the sight more confused. Fifthly the *Tunica Arachnoides*, which invellops the *Crystalline Humour* by vertue of its *Processus Ciliares* can thrust forward or draw back that precious usefull part of the Eye, as the neernesse or distance of the Object shall require. Sixthly and lastly the *Tunica Retina* is *white*, for the better and more true reception of the *species* of things (as they ordinarily call them) as a white paper is fittest to receive those Images into a dark roome. If the wit of Man had been to contrive this *Organ* for himself, what could he have possibly excogitated more accurate? Therefore to think that meer Motion of the Matter, or any other blind Cause could have hit so punctually (for Creatures might have subsisted without this accurate provision) is to be either mad or sottish.

And the *Eye* is already so *perfect*, that I believe the Reason of Man would have easily rested here, & admir'd at it's own contrivance: for he being able to move his whole head upward and downward and on every side, might have unawares thought himself sufficiently well provided for. But Nature has added *Muscles* also to the *Eyes*, that no

Perfection might be wanting; For we have oft occasion to *move our Eyes*, our Head being unmoved, as in reading and viewing more particularly any Object set before us: and that this may be done with more ease and accuracy, she has furnish'd that Organ with no lesse than six severall *Muscles*. And indeed this framing of *Muscles* not only in the Eye but in the whole Body is admirable; For is it not a wonder that even all our flesh should be so handsomly contriv'd into distinct pieces, whose Rise and Insertions should be with such advantage that they do serve to move some part of the Body or other; and that the parts of our Body are not moved only so conveniently as wil serve us to walke and subsist by, but that they are able to move every way imaginable that will advantage us? For we can fling our *Leggs* and *Armes* upwards and downwards, backwards, forwards and round, as they that spin, or would spread a Molehill with their feet. To say nothing of *Respiration*, the constriction of the *Diaphragme* for the keeping down the *Guts* and so enlarging the *Thorax* that the *Lungs* may have play, and the assistance of the inward *Intercostall Muscles* in deep Suspirations, when we take more large gulps of Aire to coole our heart overcharged with Love or Sorrow. Nor of the curious fabrick of the *Larynx* so well fitted with muscles for the modulation of the *Voice*, tunable *Speech*, and delicious *Singing*. You may adde to these the notable contrivance of the *Heart*, it's two *Ventricles* and it's many *Valvulæ*, so fram'd and situated as is most fit for the reception and transmission of the bloud, which comes about through the *Heart*, and is sent thence away warm to comfort & cherish the rest of the Body: For which purpose also the *Valvulæ* in the *Veines* are made.

But I will rather insist upon such things as are easy and intelligible even to Idiots, who if they can but tell the *Joynts* of their *Hands* or know the use of their *Teeth*, they may easily discover it was *Counsel*, not *Chance*, that created them. For why have we *three Joynts* in our *Leggs* and *Armes* as also in our *Fingers*, but that it was much better than having but *two* or *four*? And why are our *fore-Teeth sharp* like cheesells to cut, but our *inward-Teeth broad* to grind, but that this is more exquisite then having them *all sharp* or *all broad*, or the *fore-Teeth broad* and the *other sharp*? But we might have made a hard shift to have lived though in that worser condition. Again why are the *Teeth* so luckily *placed*, or rather why are there not Teeth in *other bones* as well as in the *jaw-bones*? for they might have been as capable as these. But the reason is, Nothing is done foolishly nor in vaine, that is, there is a divine *Providence* that orders all things. Again to say nothing of the inward curiosity of the *Eare*, why is that outward frame of it, but that it is certainly known, that it is for the bettering of our Hearing?

I might adde to these that Nature has made the *hind-most parts* of our body which wee sit upon most fleshy, as providing for our Ease and making us a natural Cushion, as well as for instruments of Motion for our *Thighes* and *Legges*. She has made the *hinder-part* of the *Head* more strong, as being otherwise unfenced against falls and other casualties. She has made the *Back-bone* of several *Vertebræ*, as being more fit to bend, more tough & lesse in danger of breaking then if they were all one intire bone without those gristly Junctures. She has strengthened our *Fingers* and *Toes* with *Nailes*, wheras she might have sent out that substance at the end of the first or second joynt, wch had not been so handsome nor usefull, nay rather somewhat troublesome and hurtfull. And lastly she has made all the *Bones* devoid of *sense*, because they were to bear the weight of themselves and of the whole Body. And therefore if they had had *sense*, our life had been painfull continually and dolorous.

And what she has done for *us*, she has done proportionably in the contrivance of all *other Creatures*; so that it is manifest that a divine *Providence* strikes through all things.

And therefore things were contrived with such exquisite *Curiosity* as if the most watchfull wisdome imaginable did attend them, to say they are thus framed without the assistance of some Principle that has *Wisdome* in it, & that they come to passe from *Chance* or some other blind unknowing Originall, is sullenly and humorously to assert a thing, because we will assert it, and under pretense of avoyding Superstition, to fall into that which is the onely thing that makes Superstition it self hatefull or ridiculous, that is, a wilfull and groundlesse adhering to conceits without any support of Reason.

And now I have considered the fitnesse of the parts of Mans Body for the good of the whole, let me but consider briefly the fitnesse of the *Passions* of his *Minde*, whether *proper*, or *common* to him with the rest of Animalls, as also the fitness of the *whole Man* as he is *part of the Universe*, and then I shall conclude.

And it is manifest that *Anger* does so actuate the Spirits and heightens the Courage of men and beasts that it makes them with more ease break through the difficulties they incounter. *Feare* also is for the avoyding of danger, and *Hope* is a pleasant præmeditation of enjoyment, as when a Dog expects till his Master has done picking of the bone. But there is neither *Hope*, nor *Feare*, nor *Hate*, nor any peculiar Passion or Instinct in *Brutes* that is in vaine; why should we then think that Nature should miscarry more in *us* then in any other Creature, or should be so carefull in the Fabrick of our *Body*, and yet so forgetfull or unlucky in the framing of the faculties of our *Soules*; that that *Feare* that is so peculiarly naturall to us, *viz.* the *feare of a Deity*, should be in vaine, and that pleasant *Hope* and Heavenly Joyes of the mind which man is naturally capable of, with the earnest direction of his Spirit towards God, should have no reall Object in the world? And so Religious affection which Nature has so plainly implanted in the Soul of Man should be to no use, but either to make him ridiculous or miserable: Whenas we find no *Passion* or *Affection* in *Brutes* either common or peculiar but what is for their good and welfare.

For it is not for nothing that the *Hare* is so *fearfull* of the *Dog*, & the *Sheep* of the *Wolfe*; & if there be either *Fear* or *Enmity* in some Creatures for which we cannot easily discerne any reason in respect of themselves, yet we may well allow of it as reasonable in regard of us, and to be to good purpose. But I thinke it is manifest that *Sympathy* and *Antipathy*, *Love* and *Enmity*, *Aversation*, *Feare*, and the like, that they are notable whetters and quickners of the Spirit of life in all Animalls, and that their being obnoxious to dangers and encounters does more closely knit together the vitall Powers, and makes them more sensibly relish their present safety, and they are more pleased with an Escape then if they had never met with any Danger. Their greedy assaults also one upon another while there is *hope* of Victory highly gratifies them both. And if one be conquer'd and slaine, the Conqueror enjoyes a fresh improvement of the pleasure of life, the Triumph over his Enemy. Which things seeme to me to be contriv'd even in the behalf of these Creatures themselves, that their vitall heat and moysture may not always onely simber in one sluggish tenour, but some times boyle up higher and seeth over, the fire of life being more then ordinarily kindled upon some emergent occasion.

But it is without Controversy that these peculiar *Passions* of Animalls many of them are usefull to Men (as that of the *Lizards* enmity against the *Serpent*) all of them highly gratify his contemplative faculty, some seem on purpose contriv'd to make his Worship merry; For what could Nature intend else in that Antipathy betwixt the *Ape* and *Snayle*, that that Beast that seems so boldly to claime kinred of Man from the resemblance of his outward shape, should have so little Wit or Courage as to runne away from a *Snayl*, and very rufully and frightfully to look back, as being affraid she would follow him as *Erasmus* more largely and pleasantly tells the whole story?

But that Nature should implant in Man such a strong Propension to *Religion*, which is the *Reverence of a Deity*, there being neither *God* nor *Angell*, nor *Spirit* in the world, is such a Slurre committed by her as there can be in no wise excogitated any Excuse. For if there were a higher *Species* of things to laugh at us as wee doe at the *Ape*, it might seem more tolerable. But there can be no End neither ludicrous nor serious of this *Religious property* in Man, unlesse there be something of an higher Nature then himself in the world. Wherefore *Religion* being convenient to no other *Species* of things besides Man, it ought to be convenient at least for himself: But supposing there were no *God*, there can be nothing worse for Man then *Religion*.

For whether we look at the *Externall Effects* thereof, such as are bloudy *Massacres*, the *disturbance* and *subversion* of *Common weales*, *Kingdomes* and *Empires*, most salvage *Tortures* of particular persons, the *extirpating* and *dispossessing* of whole *Nations*, as it hath hapned in *America*, where the remorselesse *Spaniards* in pretence of being educated in a better *Religion* then the *Americans*, vilifyed the poor *Natives* so much, that they made nothing of knocking them on the head merely to feed their doggs with them, with many such unheard of crueltyes. Or whether we consider the great affliction that severe Governess of the life of Man brings upon those *Souls* she seizes on, by affrighting *horrours of Conscience*, by puzzeling and *befooling* them in the free use of their *Reason*, and putting a barre to more large searches into the pleasing *knowledge of Nature*, by anxious *cares* and disquieting *feares* concerning their *state* in the *life to come*, by *curbing* them in their naturall and kindly *injoyments* of the *life present*, and making *bitter* all the *pleasures* and contentments of it, by some *checks* of *Conscience* and suspicions that they do something now that they may rue eternally hereafter; Besides those ineffable *Agonies* of mind that they undergo that are more generously *Religious*, and contend after the participation of the divine Nature, they being willing, though with unspeakable paine, to be torn from themselves to become one with that Universall Spirit that ought to have the guidance of all things, and by an unfatiable desire after that just and decorous temper of mind (whereby all Arrogancy should utterly cease in us, and that which is due to God, that is, all that we have or can do, should be lively and sensibly attributed to him, and we fully and heartily acknowledge ourselves to be nothing, that is, be as little elated, or no more rellish the glory and praise of Men, then if we had done nothing or were not at all in being) doe plunge themselves into such *damps* and *deadnesse of Spirit*, that to be buried quick were lesse torture by farre, then such darke *privations* of all the *joyes* of *life*, then such sad and heart-sinking *Mortifications*: I say, whether we consider these *inward pangs* of the Soul, or the *externall outrages* caused by *Religion* (and Religious pretense will animate men to the committing such violences, as bare Reason and the single passions of the Mind unback'd with the fury of Superstition will never venture upon) it is manifest that if there were no *God*, no *Spirit*, no *Life to come*, it were farre better that there were no such *Religious propensions* in Man-kind, as we see universally there is.

For the feare of the Civill Magistrate, the convenience of mutuall ayde and support, and the naturall scourge and plague of diseases would contain men in such bounds of Justice, Humanity and Temperance, as would make them more clearly and undisturbedly happy, then they are now capable of being, from any advantage *Religion* does to either Publique State or private person, supposing there were *no God*.

Wherefore this *Religious affection* which Nature has implanted, and as strongly rooted in Man as the feare of death or the love of women, would be the most enormous slip or bungle she could commit, so that she would so shamefully faile in the last Act, in this contrivance of the nature of Man, that instead of a *Plaudite* she would deserve to be hissed off the Stage.

But she having done all things else so wisely, let us rather suspect our own ignorance then reproach her, and expect that which is allowed in well approved Comedies, θεὸς ἀπὸ μηχανῆς,[38] for nothing can unlose this knot but a *Deity*. And then we acknowledge Man to dwell as it were in the borders of the spirituall and materiall world (for he is *utriusque mundi nexus*, as *Scaliger* truly calls him)[39] we shall not wonder that there is such tugging and pulling this way and that way, upward and downward, and such broken disorder of things; those that dwell in the confines of two kingdomes, being most subject to disquiet and

---

[38] *Deus ex machina* (cf. Aristotle, *Poetica*, XV).

[39] Not only J. J. Scaliger, the eminent sixteenth-century French philosopher and scholar, but nearly every one else regarded man as the link between the visible and the invisible worlds. See, for instance, the authorities cited by Sir Walter Ralegh, *The History of the World* (1614), Bk. I, Pt. I, Ch. II, § 3. Cf. Smith, above, p. 154.

confusion. And hitherto of the *Passions* of the mind of Man, as well those that tye him down to the Body, as those that lift him up towards God. Now briefly of the *whole Man* as he is *part* of the *Universe*.

It is true if we had not been here in the world, we could not then have missed ourselves; but now we find our selves in being and able to examine the reasonableness of things, we cannot but conclude that our Creation was an Act of very exquisite *Reason & Counsel*. For there being so many notable Objects in the world, to entertaine such faculties as Reason and inquisitive Admiration, there ought to be such a member of this visible Creation as *Man*, that those things might not be in vaine: And if Man were out of the world, who were then left to view the face of *Heaven*, to wonder at the transcursion of *Comets*, to calculate Tables for the *Motions* of the *Planets* and *Fix'd Starres*, and to take their *Heights* and *Distances* with Mathematical Instruments, to invent convenient *Cycles* for the computation of time, and consider the severall *formes* of *Yeares*, to take notice of the *Directions*, *Stations* and *Repedations* of those Erratick lights, and from thence most convincingly to informe himself of that pleasant and true Paradox of the *Annuall Motion* of the *Earth*, to view the asperityes of the *Moon* through a *Dioptrick-glasse*, and venture at the Proportion of her *Hills* by their shadowes, to behold the beauty of the *Rain-bow*, the *Halo*, *Parelii* and other Meteors, to search out the causes of the *Flux* and *Reflux* of the *Sea*, and the hidden vertue of the *Magnet*, to inquire into the usefullnesse of *Plants*, and to observe the variety of the wisdome of the first Cause in framing their bodies, and giving sundry observable instincts to *Fishes*, *Birds* and *Beasts*? And lastly as there are particular Priests amongst Men, so the whole *Species* of *Man-kind* being indued with *Reason* and a power of finding out God, there is yet one singular end more discoverable of his Creation, *viz*. that he may be a *Priest* in this magnificent *Temple* of the *Universe*, and send up prayers and praises to the great Creatour of all things in behalf of the rest of the Creatures. Thus we see all filled up and fitted without any defect or uselesse superfluity.

Wherefore the *whole Creation* in generall and *every part* thereof being so ordered as if the most exquisite Reason and Knowledge had contrived them, it is as naturall to conclude that all this is the work of a *wise God*, as at the first sight to acknowledge that those inscribed *Urnes* and *Coynes* digg'd out of the Earth were not the Products of unknowing Nature, but the Artifice of Man.

BOOK THREE[40]

I. *That, good men not alwayes faring best in this world, the great examples of Divine Vengeance upon wicked and blasphemous Persons are not so convincing to the obstinate Atheist. The irreligious Feares and Sacrileges of* Dionysius *of* Syracuse. *Tha there have been true* Miracles *in the world as well as false, and what are the best and safest wayes to distinguish them that we may not be impos'd upon by History.*

II. *The Moving of a* Sieve *by a Charme.* Coskinomancy. *A Magicall cure of an Horse. The Charming of* Serpents. *A strange Example of one* Death-strucken *as he walked the Streets. A story of a suddain winde that had like to have thrown down the Gallows at the hanging of two Witches.*

III. *That* Winds *and* Tempests *are raised upon mere* Ceremonies *or forms of words, prov'd by sundry Examples.* Margaret Warine *discharg'd upon an Oake at a Thunder-Clap.* Amantius *and* Rotarius *cast headlong out of a Cloud upon a house top. The Witch of* Constance *seen by the Shepheards to ride through the Aire.*

IV. *Supernaturall Effects observ'd in them that are* Bewitch'd *and* Possess'd. *The famous Story of* Magdalena Crucia.

V. *Examples of Bewitch'd Persons that have had* Balls of Haire, Knives, Wood stuck with Pinns, pieces of Cloth, *and such like trash conveigh'd into their Bodies, with examples also of other Supernaturall Effects.*

VI. *The Apparition* Eckerken. *The Story of the* pyed Piper. *A* Triton *or* Sea-God *seen on the banks of* Rubicon. *Of the* Imps *of* Witches, *and whether those old women be guilty of so much dotage as the* Atheist *fancies them. That such things passe betwixt them and their* Imps *as are impossible to be imputed to* Melancholy. *The examination of* John Winnick *of* Molesworth. *The reason of* Sealing Covenants *with the* Divell.

VII. *The nocturnall* Conventicles *of* Witches; *that they have often dissolved & disappeared at the naming of the* Name *of* God *or*

---

[40] Only the chapter headings of this Book are given here, for the reasons stated above (pp. xxv and 32).

An Antidote against Atheism

Jesus Christ; *and that the party thus speaking has found himself alone in the fields many miles from home.* The Dancing *of Men, Women and cloven-footed* Satyres *at mid-day;* John Michaell *piping from the bough of an Oake, &c.*

VIII. *Of* Fairy Circles. *A larger discussion of those Controversies betwixt* Bodinus *and* Remigius, *viz. whether the Bodyes of Witches be really transformed into the shape of Wolves and other Creatures, whether the Souls of Witches be not sometimes at those nocturnall Conventicles, their bodies being left at home; as also whether they leave not their bodies in those Extasies they put themselves in when they promise to fetch certain newes from remote places in a very short time.*

IX. *The* Coldnesse *of those* bodyes *that* Spirits appear in *witnessed by the experience of* Cardan *and* Bourgotus. *The naturall Reason of this* Coldnesse. *That the Divell does really lye with Witches. That the very substance of Spirits is not* fire. *Spirits* skirmishing on the ground. *Field*-fights *and Sea*-fights *seen in the* Aire.

X. *A very memorable story of a certain pious man, who had the continuall Society of a* Guardian Genius.

XI. *Certain Enquiries upon the preceding Story; as, What these* Guardian Genii *may be. Whether* one or more *of them be allotted to every man, or to some* none. *What may be the reason of Spirits so* seldome appearing; *And whether they have any settled* Shape *or no. What their* manner *is* of assisting *men in either Devotion or Prophecy. Whether every mans Complexion is capable of the Society of a* good Genius. *And lastly whether it be lawfull to pray to God to send such a* Genius *or* Angel *to one or no.*

XII. *That whether the* Species *of things have been from all* Eternity, *or whether they rose out of the Earth by degrees* in Time, *the* Frame *of them is such, that against all the Evasions of the* Atheist *they naturally imply that there is a God.*

XIII. *That the Evasions of Atheists against* Apparitions *are so weak and silly, that it is an evident Argument that they are convinced in their own Judgements of the Truth of these kinds of Phænomena, which forces them to answer as well as they can, though they be so ill provided.*

RALPH CUDWORTH

The Digression concerning the Plastick Life of Nature, or an Artificial, Orderly and Methodical Nature*

2. ... Unless there be such a thing admitted as a Plastick Nature, that acts ἕνεκά του, *for the sake of something*,[1] and *in order to Ends*, Regularly, Artificially and Methodically, it seems that one or other of these Two Things must be concluded, That Either in the Efformation and Organization of the Bodies of Animals, as well as the other Phenomena, every thing comes to pass *Fortuitously*, and happens to be as it is, without the Guidance and Direction of any *Mind* or *Understanding*; Or else, that God himself doth all *Immediately*, and as it were with his own Hands, Form the Body of every Gnat and Fly, Insect and Mite, as of other Animals in Generations, all whose Members

---

* From *The True Intellectual System of the Universe* (1678), Book I, Ch. III, Sect. XXXVII, §§ 2–16, 19–26 [pp. 147–60, 162–74]. The term 'digression' is hardly accurate. As Cudworth pointed out in the Preface to the *Int. System* (sig. 1ᵛ), his concept of Plastic Nature is 'no *Wen*, or *Excrescency*, in the Body of this Book'. He explained that 'without such a *Nature*, either *God* must be supposed to Doe all things in the world Immediately, and to Form every *Gnat* and *Fly*, as it were with his own hands; which seemeth not so Becoming of him, and would render his *Providence*, to Humane Apprehensions, *Laborious* and *Distractious*; or else the whole *System* of this *Corporeal Universe*, must result onely from *Fortuitous Mechanism*, without the *Direction* of any *Mind*: which *Hypothesis* once admitted, would Vnquestionably, by degrees, *Supplant* and *Undermine* all *Theism*'.

[1] The phrase ἕνεκά του—elsewhere translated by Cudworth as 'for the sake of Ends', or as 'Final or Intending Causality'—is one of the major links in his argument. See below, pp. 301, 305, 309, 310, 313, etc.

have so much of Contrivance in them, that *Galen* professed he could never enough admire that Artifice which was in the Leg of a Fly, (and yet he would have admired the Wisdom of Nature more, had he been but acquainted with the Use of Microscopes.) I say, upon supposition of no *Plastick Nature*, one or other of these Two things must be concluded; because it is not conceived by any, that the things of Nature are all thus administred, with such exact Regularity and Constancy every where, merely by the Wisdom, Providence and Efficiency, of those Inferior Spirits, *Dæmons* or Angels. As also, though it be true that the Works of Nature are dispensed by a *Divine Law* and *Command*, yet this is not to be understood in a *Vulgar Sence*, as if they were all effected by the mere Force of a *Verbal Law* or *Outward Command*, because Inanimate things are not *Commandable* nor *Governable* by such a *Law*; and therefore besides the Divine Will and Pleasure, there must needs be some other Immediate *Agent* and *Executioner* provided, for the producing of every Effect; since not so much as a Stone or other Heavy Body, could at any time fall downward, merely by the Force of a *Verbal Law*, without any other *Efficient Cause*; but either God himself must immediately impel it, or else there must be some other subordinate Cause in Nature for that Motion. Wherefore the *Divine Law* and *Command*, by which the things of Nature are administred, must be conceived to be the Real Appointment of some *Energetick, Effectual* and *Operative Cause* for the Production of every Effect.

3. Now to assert the Former of these Two things, that all the Effects of Nature come to pass by *Material* and *Mechanical Necessity*, or the mere *Fortuitous Motion* of *Matter*, without any Guidance or Direction, is a thing no less Irrational than it is Impious and Atheistical. Not only because it is utterly Unconceivable and Impossible, that such Infinite Regularity and Artificialness, as is every where throughout the whole World, should constantly result out of the *Fortuitous Motion of Matter*, but also because there are many such Particular *Phænomena* in Nature, as do plainly transcend the *Powers of Mechanism*, of which therefore no Sufficient Mechanical Reasons can be devised, as the *Motion of Respiration* in Animals; as there are also other *Phænomena* that are perfectly Cross to the *Laws of Mechanism*; as for Example, that of the *Distant Poles* of the *Æquator* and *Ecliptick*, which we shall insist upon afterward. Of both which kinds, there have been other Instances proposed, by my Learned Friend Dr. *More* in his *Enchiridion Metaphysicum*, and very ingeniously improved by him to this very

purpose, namely to Evince that there is something in Nature besides Mechanism, and consequently Substance Incorporeal.[2]

Moreover those Theists, who Philosophize after this manner, by resolving all the Corporeal *Phænomena* into *Fortuitous Mechanism*, or the *Necessary and Unguided Motion of Matter*, make God to be nothing else in the World, but an *Idle Spectator* of the Various Results of the *Fortuitous* and *Necessary Motions* of Bodies; and render his Wisdom altogether Useless and Insignificant, as being a thing wholly Inclosed and shut up within his own breast, and not at all acting abroad upon any thing without him.

Furthermore all such *Mechanists* as these, whether *Theists* or *Atheists*, do, according to that Judicious Censure passed by *Aristotle* long since upon *Democritus*, but substitute as it were $\chi\varepsilon\tilde{\iota}\rho\alpha$ $\xi\upsilon\lambda\acute{\iota}\nu\eta\nu$ $\tau\acute{\varepsilon}\varkappa\tau o\nu o\varsigma$, a *Carpenters or Artificers Wooden Hand, moved by Strings and Wires, in stead of a Living Hand*.[3] They make a kind of Dead and Wooden World, as it were a Carved Statue, that hath nothing neither *Vital* nor *Magical* at all in it. Whereas to those who are Considerative, it will plainly appear, that there is a *Mixture* of *Life* or *Playstick Nature* together with *Mechanism*, which runs through the whole Corporeal Universe.

And whereas it is pretended, not only that all *Corporeal Phænomena* may be sufficiently salved *Mechanically*, without any *Final, Intending* and *Directive Causality*, but also that all other Reasons of things in Nature, besides the *Material* and *Mechanical*, are altogether *Unphilosophical*, the same *Aristotle* ingeniously exposes the Ridiculousness of this Pretence after this manner; telling us, That it is just as if a Carpenter, Joyner or Carver should give this accompt, as the only

---

[2] On More's work, see above, p. 31 and note. However, even more relevant are the affinities between Cudworth's 'Plastic Nature' and More's 'Spirit of Nature' (*Immortality*, Bk. III, Ch. XII–XIII [pp. 449–70]). According to More's 'rude Description', the Spirit of Nature is '*A substance incorporeal, but without Sense and Animadversion, pervading the whole Matter of the Universe, and exercising a plastical power therein according to the sundry predispositions and occasions in the parts it works upon, raising such Phænomena in the World, as cannot be resolved into meer Mechanical powers*' (*ibid.*, p. 450). More elsewhere defines the term 'plastical power'—$\delta\acute{\upsilon}\nu\alpha\mu\iota\varsigma$ $\pi\lambda\alpha\sigma\tau\iota\varkappa\acute{\eta}$—as 'that efformative might in the seed that shapes the body in its growth' (*The Interpretation Generall*, in *Poems*, p. 431). See also the Introduction, above, p. 26.

[3] *De partibus animalium*, I, 1,

Satisfactory, of any Artificial Fabrick or Piece of Carved Imagery, ὅτι ἐμπεσόντος τοῦ ὀργάνου τὸ μὲν κοῖλον ἐγένετο, τὸ δὲ ἐπίπεδον, that because the Instruments, Axes and Hatchets, Plains and Chissels, happened to fall so and so upon the Timber, cutting it here and there, that therefore it was hollow in one place, and plain in another, and the like, and by that means the whole came to be of such a Form.[4] For is it not altogether as Absurd and Ridiculous, for men to undertake to give an accompt of the Formation and Organization of the Bodies of Animals, by mere Fortuitous Mechanism, without any *Final* or *Intending Causality*,[5] as why there was an Heart here and Brains there, and why the Heart had so many and such different Valves in the Entrance and Outlet of its Ventricles, and why all the other Organick Parts, Veins and Arteries, Nerves and Muscles, Bones and Cartilages, with the Joints and Members, were of such a Form? Because forsooth, the Fluid Matter of the Seed happened to move so and so, in several places, and thereby to cause all those Differences, which are also divers in different Animals; all being the Necessary Result of a certain Quantity of Motion at first indifferently impressed, upon the small Particles of the Matter of this Universe turned round in a *Vortex*. But as the same *Aristotle* adds, no Carpenter or Artificer is so simple, as to give such an Accompt as this, and think it satisfactory, but he will rather declare, that himself directed the Motion of the Instruments, after such a manner, and in order to such Ends: Βέλτιον ὁ τέκτων, οὐ γὰρ ἱκανὸν ἔσται αὐτῷ, τὸ τοσοῦτον εἰπεῖν, ὅτι ἐμπεσόντος τοῦ ὀργάνου, &c. ἀλλὰ διότι τὴν πληγὴν ἐποιήσατο τοιαύτην, καὶ τίνος ἕνεκα, ἐρεῖ τὴν αἰτίαν, ὅπως τοιόνδε ἢ τοιόνδε, ποτὲ τὴν μορφὴν γένηται· *A Carpenter would give a better account than so, for he would not think it sufficient to say, that the Fabrick came to be of such a form, because the Instruments happened to fall so and so, but he will tell you that it was because himself made such strokes, and that he directed the Instruments and determined their motion after such a manner, to this End that he might make the Whole a Fabrick fit and useful for such purposes.*[6] And this is to assign the *Final Cause*. And certainly there is scarcely any man in his Wits, that will not acknowledge the Reason of the different *Valves* in the Heart, from the apparent Usefulness of them, according to those

---

[4] *Ibid.*
[5] Thus Descartes, in *Tractatus de homine et de formatione fœtus* (published posthumously, in 1664). See further D. B. Sailor, 'Cudworth and Descartes', *Journal of the History of Ideas*, XXIII (1962), 135 ff.
[6] *De partibus animalium*, I, 1.

particular Structures of theirs, to be more Satisfactory, than any which can be brought from mere Fortuitous Mechanism, or the Unguided Motion of the Seminal Matter.

4. And as for the Latter Part of the Disjunction, That every thing in Nature should be done Immediately by God himself; this, as according to Vulgar Apprehension, it would render Divine Providence Operose, Sollicitous and Distractious, and thereby make the Belief of it to be entertained with greater difficulty, and give advantage to Atheists; so in the Judgment of the Writer [of] *De Mundo*,[7] it is not so Decorous in respect of God neither, that he should αὐτουργεῖν ἅπαντα, set his own Hand, as it were, to every Work, and immediately do all the Meanest and Triflingest things himself Drudgingly, without making use of any Inferior and Subordinate Instruments. Εἴπερ ἄσεμνον ἦν [αὐτῷ] αὐτὸν δοκεῖν Ξέρξην αὐτουργεῖν ἅπαντα, καὶ διατελεῖν ἃ βούλοιτο, καὶ ἐφιστάμενον διοικεῖν, πολὺ μᾶλλον ἀπρεπὲς ἂν εἴη τῷ θεῷ. Σεμνότερον δὲ καὶ πρεπωδέστερον τὴν δύναμιν αὐτοῦ, διὰ τοῦ σύμπαντος κόσμου διηκοῦσαν, ἥλιον τε κινεῖν καὶ σελήνην, &c. *If it were not congruous in respect of the State & Majesty of* Xerxes *the Great King of* Persia *that he should condescend to do all the meanest Offices himself; much less can this be thought decorous in respect of God. But it seems far more August, and becoming of the Divine Majesty, that a certain Power and Vertue, derived from him, and passing through the Universe, should move the Sun and Moon, and be the Immediate Cause of those lower things done here upon Earth.*

Moreover it seems not so agreeable to Reason neither, that Nature as a Distinct thing from the Deity, should be quite Superseded or made to Signifie Nothing, God himself doing all things Immediately and Miraculously; from whence it would follow also, that they are all done either *Forcibly* and *Violently*, or else *Artificially* only, and none of them by any *Inward Principle* of their own.

Lastly: This Opinion is further Confuted, by that Slow and Gradual Process that is in the Generations of things, which would seem to be but a Vain and Idle Pomp, or a Trifling Formality, if the Agent were Omnipotent: as also by those ἁμαρτήματα (as *Aristotle* calls them)[8] those *Errors* and *Bungles* which are committed, when the Matter is Inept and Contumacious; which argue the Agent not to be Irresistible,

---

[7] Pseudo-Aristotle, *De mundo*, VII. This work, whose authenticity Cudworth rightly doubts, is now dated between 50 B.C. and A.D. 100.

[8] *Physica*, II, 8.

The Plastick Life of Nature

and that *Nature* is such a thing, as is not altogether uncapable (as well as *Humane Art*) of being sometimes frustrated and disappointed, by the Indisposition of Matter. Whereas an *Omnipotent Agent*, as it could dispatch its work in a Moment, so it would always do it *Infallibly* and *Irresistibly*; no *Ineptitude* or *Stubbornness* of Matter, being ever able to hinder such a one, or make him *Bungle* or *Fumble* in any thing.

5. Wherefore since neither all things are produced Fortuitously, or by the Unguided Mechanism of Matter, nor God himself may reasonably be thought to do all things Immediately and Miraculously; it may well be concluded, that there is a *Plastick Nature* under him, which as an Inferior and Subordinate Instrument, doth Drudgingly Execute that Part of his Providence, which consists in the Regular and Orderly Motion of Matter: yet so as that there is also besides this, a Higher Providence to be acknowledged, which presiding over it, doth often supply the Defects of it, and sometimes Overrule it; forasmuch as this *Plastick Nature* cannot act *Electively* nor with *Discretion*. And by this means the Wisdom of God will not be shut up nor concluded wholly within his own Breast, but will display it self abroad, and print its Stamps and Signatures every where throughout the World; so that God, as *Plato* (after *Orpheus*) speaks, will be not only the *Beginning* and *End*, but also the *Middle* of all things,[9] they being as much to be ascribed to his Causality, as if himself had done them all Immediately, without the concurrent Instrumentality of any Subordinate Natural Cause. Notwithstanding which, in this way it will appear also to Humane Reason, that all things are Disposed and Ordered by the Deity, without any Sollicitous Care or Distractious Providence.[10]

---

[9] Plato, *Leges*, IV, 716: 'God, as the old tradition declares, [holds] in his hand the beginning, middle, and end of all that is.' The 'old tradition' invoked by Plato (as by Pseudo-Aristotle, *De mundo*, VII) is probably the Orphic verses beginning, Ζεὺς πρῶτος γένετο, Ζεὺς ὕστατος κλπ.— 'Zeus is the first Zeus is the last etc.' (Orpheus, p. 91). Cf. Otto Kern, *De Orphei Epimenidis Pherecydis theogonis quaestiones criticae* (Berlin, 1888), p. 35.

[10] The basic flaw in Cudworth's theory of Plastic Nature is that 'it explained the unknown by asserting another quite hypothetical unknown' (Hunter, pp. 209 f.). As much was argued by Joseph Glanvill—the platonising friend of Henry More—when he wrote of similar assertions that 'The *Plastick* faculty is a fine word: But what it is, how it works, and whose it is, we cannot learn; no, not by a return into the *Womb*; neither

And indeed those Mechanick Theists, who rejecting a Plastick Nature, affect to concern the Deity as little as is possible in Mundane Affairs, either for fear of debasing him and bringing him down to too mean Offices, or else of subjecting him to Sollicitous Encumberment, and for that Cause would have God to contribute nothing more to the Mundane System and Oeconomy, than only the First Impressing of a certain Quantity of Motion, upon the Matter, and the After-conserving of it, according to some General Laws: These men (I say) seem not very well to understand themselves in this. Forasmuch as they must of necessity, either suppose these their *Laws* of *Motion* to execute themselves, or else be forced perpetually to concern the Deity in the Immediate Motion of every Atom of Matter throughout the Universe, in order to the Execution and Observation of them. The Former of which being a Thing plainly Absurd and Ridiculous, and the Latter that, which these Philosophers themselves are extremely abhorrent from, we cannot make any other Conclusion than this, That they do but unskilfully and unawares establish that very Thing which in words they oppose; and that their *Laws of Nature* concerning *Motion*, are Really nothing else, but a *Plastick Nature*, acting upon the Matter of the whole Corporeal Universe, both Maintaining the Same Quantity of Motion always in it, and also Dispensing it (by Transferring it out of one Body into another) according to such Laws, Fatally Imprest upon it. Now if there be a *Plastick Nature*, that governs the *Motion* of *Matter*, every where according to *Laws*, there can be no Reason given, why the same might not also extend further, to the Regular Disposal of that Matter, in the *Formation* of *Plants* and *Animals* and other things, in order to that Apt Coherent Frame and Harmony of the whole Universe.

6. And as this Plastick Nature is a thing which seems to be in it self most Reasonable, so hath it also had the Suffrage of the best Philosophers in all Ages. For First, it is well known, that *Aristotle* concerns himself in nothing more zealously than this, That Mundane things are not Effected, merely by the *Necessary* and *Unguided Motion* of *Matter*, or by *Fortuitous Mechanism*, but by such a *Nature* as acts *Regularly* and *Artificially* for *Ends*; yet so as that this *Nature* is not the Highest

---

will the *Platonick* Principles unriddle the doubt: For though the Soul be supposed to be the Bodies *Maker*, and the builder of its own house; yet by what kind of knowledge, Method, or Means, is as unknown' (*The Vanity of Dogmatizing* [1661], pp. 43–4; *apud* Hunter, as before).

Principle neither, or the Supreme *Numen*, but Subordinate to a Perfect *Mind* or *Intellect*, he affirming, that νοῦς αἴτιον καὶ φύσις τοῦδε τοῦ παντός, *That Mind together with Nature was the Cause of this Universe*; and that Heaven and Earth, Plants and Animals were framed by them both; that is, by *Mind* as the Principal and Directive Cause, but by *Nature* as a Subservient or Executive Instrument: and elsewhere joyning in like manner *God* and *Nature* both together, as when he concludes, *That God and Nature do nothing in vain*.[11]

Neither was *Aristotle* the First Broacher or Inventor of this Doctrine, *Plato* before him having plainly asserted the same. For in a Passage already cited, he affirms that *Nature together with Reason, and according to it, orders all things*; thereby making Nature, as a Distinct thing from the Deity, to be a Subordinate Cause under the Reason and Wisdom of it. And elsewhere he resolves, that there are ἔμφρονος φύσεως αἰτίαι, αἷς ὑπηρετούσαις ὁ θεὸς χρῆται, *Certain Causes of a Wise and Artificial Nature, which the Deity uses as Subservient to it self*; as also, that there are ξυναίτια οἷς ξυνεργοῖς θεὸς χρῆται, *Con-causes which God makes use of, as Subordinately Cooperative with himself*.[12]

Moreover before *Plato*, *Empedocles* Philosophized also in the same manner, when supposing Two Worlds, the one *Archetypal*, the other *Extypal*, he made φιλία and νεῖκος, *Friendship* & *Discord*, to be the ἀρχὴ δραστήριος, the *Active Principle and Immediate Operator* in this Lower World.[13] He not understanding thereby, as *Plutarch* and some others have conceited, Two Substantial Principles in the World, the one of *Good* the other of *Evil*,[14] but only a *Plastick Nature*, as *Aristotle* in sundry places intimates: which he called by that name, partly because he apprehended that the Result and Upshot of *Nature* in all *Generations* and *Corruptions*, amounted to nothing more than *Mixtures* and *Separations*, or *Concretion* and *Secretion* of *Preexistent things*, and partly because this *Plastick Nature* is that which doth reconcile the *Contrarieties* and *Enmities* of Particular things, and bring them into one *General Harmony* in the *Whole*. Which latter is a Notion that *Plotinus*, describing this very *Seminary Reason* or *Plastick Nature* of the World, (though taking it in something a larger sence, than we do

[11] *De caelo*, I, 4: ὁ δέ θεὸς καὶ ἡ φύσις οὐδὲν μάτην ποιοῦσιν. Cf. above, p. 233.
[12] Cf. *Timaeus*, 46d.
[13] Empedocles, XVI et seq. Cf. Simplicius, below, p. 296.
[14] In *De Iside et Osiride*, XLV et seq., Plutarch is largely concerned with Zoroastrian tenets.

in this place) doth ingeniously pursue after this manner; Ἀντιθεὶς δὲ ἀλλήλοις τὰ μέρη, καὶ ποιήσας ἐνδεᾶ, πολέμου καὶ μάχης σύστασιν καὶ γένεσιν εἰργάσατο· καὶ οὕτως ἐστὶν εἷς πᾶς, εἰ μὴ ἕν εἴη· γενόμενον γὰρ ἑαυτῷ τοῖς μέρεσι πολέμιον, οὕτως ἕν ἐστι καὶ φίλον, ὥσπερ ἂν εἰ δράματος λόγος εἷς, ὁ τοῦ δράματος, ἔχων ἐν αὐτῷ πολλὰς μάχας· τὸ μὲν οὖν δράματα μεμαχημένα, οἷον εἰς μίαν ἁρμονίαν, ἄγει σύμφωνον.— ὥς τε μᾶλλον ἄν τις τῇ ἁρμονίᾳ τῇ ἐκ μαχομένων εἰκάσειε. The Seminary Reason or Plastick Nature of the Universe opposing the Parts to one another and making them severally Indigent, produces by that means War and Contention. And therefore though it be One, yet notwithstanding it consists of Different and Contrary things. For there being Hostility in its Parts, it is nevertheless Friendly and Agreeable in the Whole; after the same manner as in a Dramatick Poem, Clashings and Contentions are reconciled into one Harmony. And therefore the Seminary and Plastick Nature of the World, may fitly be resembled to the Harmony of Disagreeing things.[15] Which Plotinick Doctrine, may well pass for a Commentary upon *Empedocles*, accordingly as *Simplicius* briefly represents his sence, Ἐμπεδοκλῆς δύο κόσμους συνίστησι, τόν μὲν ἡνωμένον καὶ νοητὸν, τὸν δὲ διακεκριμένον καὶ αἰσθητὸν, καὶ ἐν τούτῳ κόσμῳ τὴν ἕνωσιν ὁρᾷ καὶ τὴν διάκρισιν· Empedocles *makes Two Worlds, the one United and Intelligible, the other Divided and Sensible; and in this lower Sensible World, he takes notice both of Unity and Discord.*[16]

It was before observed, that *Heraclitus* likewise did assert a *Regular* and *Artificial Nature*, as the *Fate of things* in this Lower World; for his *Reason passing thorough the Substance of all things*, or *Ethereal Body, which was the Seed of the Generation of the Universe*, was nothing but that *Spermatick* or *Plastick Nature* which we now speak of. And whereas there is an odd Passage of this Philosophers recorded, κόσμον τόνδε οὔτε τις θεῶς οὔ τ' ἀνθρώπων ἐποίησε, *that neither any God nor Man made this World*, which as it is justly derided by *Plutarch* for its Simplicity,[17] so it looks very Atheistically at first sight; yet because *Heraclitus* hath not been accompted an Atheist, we therefore conceive the meaning of it to have been this, That the World was not made by any whatsoever, after such a manner as an Artificer makes an House, by Machins and Engins, acting from without upon the Matter, Cumbersomly and Moliminously, but by a certain *Inward Plastick Nature* of its own.

---

[15] Plotinus, III, ii, 16.   [16] Simplicius, *Arist. Cael.*, I.
[17] *De animae procreatione in Timæo Platonis*, IV.

The Plastick Life of Nature 297

And as *Hippocrates* followed *Heraclitus* in this (as was before declared) so did *Zeno* and the Stoicks also, they supposing besides an *Intellectual Nature*, as the *Supreme Architect* and Master-builder of the World, another *Plastick Nature* as the *Immediate Workman* and Operatour. Which *Plastick Nature* hath been already described in the words of *Balbus*, as a thing which acts not *Fortuitously* but *Regularly, Orderly* and *Artificially*;[18] and *Laertius* tells us, it was defined by *Zeno* himself after this manner, ἔστι δὲ φύσις ἕξις ἐξ αὐτῆς κινουμένη κατὰ σπερματικοὺς λόγους, ἀποτελοῦσά τε καὶ συνέχουσα τὰ ἐξ αὐτῆς ἐν ὡρισμένοις χρόνοις, καὶ τοαῦτα δρῶσα ἀφ᾽ οἵων ἀπεκρίθη· *Nature is a Habit moved from it self according to Spermatick Reasons or Seminal Principles, perfecting and containing those several things, which in determinate times are produced from it, and acting agreeably to that from which it was secreted.*[19]

Lastly, as the Latter *Platonists* and *Peripateticks* have unanimously followed their Masters herein, whose *Vegetative Soul* also is no other than a *Plastick Nature*; so the *Chymists* and *Paracelsians* insist much upon the same thing, and seem rather to have carried the Notion on further, in the Bodies of Animals, where they call it by a new name of their own, the *Archeus*.[20]

Moreover, we cannot but observe here, that as amongst the Ancients, They were generally condemned for down-right Atheists, who acknowledged no other Principle besides Body or Matter, Necessarily and Fortuitously moved, such as *Democritus* and the first Ionicks; so even *Anaxagoras* himself, notwithstanding that he was a professed Theist, and plainly asserted *Mind* to be a *Principle*, yet because he attributed too much to Material Necessity, admitting neither this *Plastick Nature* nor a *Mundane Soul*, was severely censured, not only by the Vulgar (who unjustly taxed him for an Atheist) but also by *Plato* and *Aristotle*, as a kind of spurious and imperfect Theist, and one

---

[18] Cudworth had earlier (in I, iii, 33) quoted 'the words of *Balbus* the Stoick, personated by Cicero [*De nat. deo.*, II, 32]: ... *when we say that the World is administered by Nature, we do not mean such a Nature as is in Clods of Earth and Pieces of Stone; but such as in a Tree or Animal, in whose Constitution there is no Temerity, but Order and Similitude of Art*'.

[19] Diogenes Laertius, VII, 148.

[20] 'the primeval power which assures life to every individual. Not only human beings, but animals and plants, even spirits, gnomes, metals, and stones each has its *Archeus*' (Henry M. Pachter, *Magic into Science: The Story of Paracelsus* [New York, 1951], pp. 137–8).

who had given great advantage to Atheism. *Aristotle* in his Metaphysicks thus represents his Philosophy, Ἀναξαγόρας τε γὰρ μηχανῇ χρῆται τῷ νῷ, πρὸς τὴν κοσμοποιΐαν, καὶ ὅταν ἀπορήσῃ διὰ τίν᾽ αἰτίαν, ἐξ ἀνάγκης ἐστί, τότε [παρ]έλκει αὐτὸν, ἐν δὲ τοῖς ἄλλοις πάντα μᾶλλον αἰτιᾶται τῶν γιγνομένων ἢ νοῦν· Anaxagoras *useth Mind and Intellect, that is, God, as a Machin in the* Cosmopœia, *and when he is at a loss to give an acccompt of things by Material Necessity, then and never but then, does he draw in Mind or God to help him out; but otherwise he will rather assign any thing else for a Cause than Mind.*[21] Now if *Aristotle* censure *Anaxagoras* in this manner, though a professed Theist, because he did but seldom make use of a *Mental Cause*, for the salving of the *Phænomena* of the World, and only then when he was at a loss for other *Material* and *Mechanical Causes* (which it seems he sometimes confessed himself to be) what would that Philosopher have thought of those our so confident *Mechanists* of later times, who will never vouchsafe so much as once to be beholding to God Almighty, for any thing in the Oeconomy of the Corporeal World, after the first Impression of Motion upon the Matter?

Plato likewise in his *Phædo* and elsewhere, condemns this *Anaxagoras* by name, for this very thing, that though he acknowledged *Mind* to be a *Cause*, yet he seldom made use of it, for salving the *Phænomena*; but in his twelfth *de Legibus*, he perstringeth him Unnamed, as one who though a professed Theist, had notwithstanding given great Encouragement to Atheism, after his manner; λέγοντες ὡς νοῦς εἴη ὁ διακεκοσμηκὼς πάνθ᾽ ὅσα κατ᾽ οὐρανὸν, αὐτοὶ δὲ πάλιν ἁμαρτάνοντες ψυχῆς φύσεως, ὅτι πρεσβίτερον εἴη σωμάτων, ἅπανθ᾽ ὡς εἰπεῖν ἔπος, ἀνέτρεψαν πάλιν, τὰ γὰρ δὲ πρὸ τῶν ὀμμάτων πάντα, αὐτοῖς ἐφάνη, τὰ κατ᾽ οὐρανὸν φερόμενα, μεστὰ εἶναι λίθων, καὶ γῆς, καὶ πολλῶν ἄλλων ἀψύχων σωμάτων, διανεμόντων τὰς αἰτίας παντὸς τοῦ κόσμου, ταῦτ᾽ ἦν τὰ τότε ἐξειργασμένα πολλὰς ἀθεότητας· *Some of them who had concluded, that it was Mind that ordered all things in the Heavens, themselves erring concerning the Nature of the Soul, and not making that Older than the Body, have overturned all again; for Heavenly Bodies being supposed by them, to be full of Stones, and Earth, and other Inanimate things (dispensing the Causes of the whole Universe), they did by this means occasion much Atheism and Impiety.*[22]

Furthermore the same *Plato* there tells us, that in those times of his, Astronomers and Physiologers commonly lay under the prejudice and

---

[21] *Metaphysica*, I, 4.   [22] *Leges*, XII, 967c.

The Plastick Life of Nature 299

suspicion of Atheism amongst the vulgar, merely for this reason, because they dealt so much in Material Causes, οἱ πολλοὶ διανοοῦνται τοὺς τὰ τοιαῦτα μεταχειρισάμενους, ἀστρονομία τε καὶ ταῖς μετὰ ταύτης ἀναγκαίαις ἄλλαις τέχναις, ἀθέους γίγνιθαι, καθεωρακότας ὡς οἱόντε γιγνόμενα ἀνάγκαις τὰ πράγματ᾽, ἀλλ᾽ οὐ διανοίαις βουλήσεως ἀγαθῶν πέρι τελουμένων· *The Vulgar think that they who addict themselves to Astronomy and Physiology, are made Atheists thereby, they seeing as much as is possible how things come to pass by Material Necessities, and being thereby disposed to think them not to be ordered by Mind and Will, for the sake of Good.*[23] From whence we may observe, that according to the Natural Apprehensions of Men in all Ages, they who resolve the *Phænomena of Nature*, into *Material Necessity*, allowing of no *Final* nor *Mental Causality* (disposing things in order to Ends) have been strongly suspected for Friends to Atheism.

7. But because some may pretend, that the *Plastick Nature* is all one with an *Occult Quality*, we shall here show how great a Difference there is betwixt these Two. For he that asserts an *Occult Quality*, for the Cause of any *Phænomenon*, does indeed assign no Cause at all of it, but only declare his own *Ignorance of the Cause*; but he that asserts a *Plastick Nature*, assigns a Determinate and proper Cause, nay the only Intelligible Cause, of that which is the greatest of all *Phænomena* in the World, namely the τὸ εὖ καὶ καλῶς,[24] the *Orderly, Regular and Artificial Frame* of things in the Universe, whereof the *Mechanick Philosophers*, however pretending to salve all *Phænomena* by *Matter* and *Motion*, assign no Cause at all. Mind and Understanding is the only true Cause of Orderly Regularity, and he that asserts a *Plastick Nature*, asserts *Mental Causality* in the World; but the *Fortuitous Mechanists*, who exploding *Final Causes*, will not allow *Mind* and *Understanding* to have any Influence at all upon the Frame of things, can never possibly assign any Cause of this Grand *Phænomenon*, unless *Confusion* may be said to be the Cause of *Order*, and *Fortune* or *Chance* of *Constant Regularity*; and therefore themselves must resolve it into an Occult Quality. Nor indeed does there appear any great reason why such men should assert an Infinite Mind in the World, since they do not allow it to act any where at all, and therefore must needs make it to be in Vain.

---

[23] *Ibid.*, 967a.
[24] 'of well and fit' (Cudworth's own translation [below, p. 312] of Aristotle, *Metaphysica*, I, 3).

8. Now this Plastick Nature being a thing which is not without some difficulty in the Conception of it, we shall here endeavour to do these Two things concerning it; First, to set down a right Representation thereof, and then afterwards to show how extremely the Notion of it hath been Mistaken, Perverted and Abused by those Atheists, who would make it to be the only *God Almighty*, or *First Principle* of all things.

How the Plastick Nature is in general to be conceiv'd, *Aristotle* instructs us in these words, εἰ ἐνῆν ἐν τῷ ξύλῳ ἡ ναυπηγικὴ ὁμοίως ἂν τῇ φύσει ἐποίει· *If the Naupegical Art, that is the Art of the Shipwright, were in the Timber itself, Operatively and Effectually, it would there act just as Nature doth.*[25] And the Case is the same for all other Arts; If the Oecodomical Art, which is in the Mind of the Architect, were supposed to be transfused into the Stones, Bricks and Mortar, there acting upon them in such a manner, as to make them come together of themselves and range themselves into the Form of a complete Edifice, as *Amphion* was said by his Harp, to have made the Stones move, and place themselves Orderly of their own accord, and so to have built the Walls of *Thebes*:[26] Or if the Musical Art were conceived to be immediately in the Instruments and Strings, animating them as a Living Soul, and making them to move exactly according to the Laws of Harmony, without any External Impulse. These and such like Instances in *Aristotle's* Judgment, would be fit Iconisms or Representations of *the Plastick Nature*, That *being Art it self acting Immediately upon the Matter as an inward Principle in it*; To which purpose the same Philosopher adds, that this thing might be further illustrated by another Instance or Resemblence, μάλιστα δὲ δῆλον, ὅταν τις ἰατρεύει αὐτὸς ἑαυτόν, τούτῳ γὰρ ἔοικεν ἡ φύσις· *Nature may be yet more clearly Resembled to the Medicinal Art, when it is imployed by the Physician, in curing himself.*[27] So that the meaning of this Philosopher is, that Nature is to be conceived as *Art* Acting not from without and at a Distance, but *Immediately* upon the thing it self which is Formed by it. And thus we have the first General Conception of the *Plastick Nature*, That *it is Art it self, acting immediately on the Matter, as an Inward Principle*.

9. In the next Place we are to observe, that though the *Plastick*

[25] *Physica*, II, 8.
[26] Thus Apollonius Rhodius, I, 736–41; Hyginus, LXIX; *et al.*
[27] *Physica*, II, 8. This view is criticised later (below, p. 302).

Nature be a kind of *Art*, yet there are some Considerable *Preeminences* which it hath above *Humane Art*, the First whereof is this; That whereas *Humane Art* cannot act upon the Matter otherwise than from without and at a distance, nor communicate it self to it, but with a great deal of *Tumult* and *Hurliburly*, *Noise* and *Clatter*, it using Hands and Axes, Saws and Hammers, and after this manner with much ado, by Knockings and Thrustings, slowly introducing its Form or *Idea* (as for Example of a Ship or House) into the Materials. Nature in the mean time is another kind of *Art*, which *Insinuating* it self *Immediately* into things themselves, and there acting more Commandingly upon the Matter as an Inward Principle, does its Work *Easily*, *Cleaverly* and *Silently*. Nature is *Art* as it were *Incorporated* and *Imbodied in matter*, which doth not act upon it from without *Mechanically*, but from within *Vitally* and *Magically*, οὔτε χεῖρες ἐνταῦθα, οὔτε πόδες, οὔτε τι ὄργανον ἐπακτὸν ἢ σύμφυτον, ὕλης δὲ δεῖ ἐφ' ἧς ποιήσει, καὶ ἣν ἐν εἴδει ποιεῖ, πάντιπον δῆλον. δεῖ δὲ καὶ τὸ μοχλεύειν ἀφελεῖν ἐκ τῆς φυσικῆς ποιήσεως. ποῖος γὰρ ὠθισμός, ἢ τὶς μοχλεία, &c. *Here are no Hands, nor Feet, nor any Instrument, Connate or Adventitious, there being only need of Matter to work upon and to be brought into a certain Form, and Nothing else. For it is manifest that the Operation of Nature is different from Mechanism, it doing not its Work by Trusion or Pulsion, by Knockings or Thrustings, as if it were without that which it wrought upon.*[28] But as *God* is *Inward* to every thing, so *Nature* Acts Immediately upon the Matter, as an *Inward* and *Living Soul* or *Law* in it.

10. Another Preeminence of *Nature* above *Humane Art* is this, That whereas *Humane Artists* are often to seek and at a loss, and therefore *Consult* and *Deliberate*, as also upon second thoughts mend their former Work; *Nature*, on the contrary, is never to seek what to do, nor at a stand; and for that Reason also (besides another that will be Suggested afterwards) it doth never Consult nor Deliberate. Indeed *Aristotle* Intimates, as if this had been the Grand Objection of the old Athestick Philosophers against the *Plastick Nature*, *That because we do not see Natural Bodies to Consult or Deliberate, therefore there could be Nothing of Art, Counsel or Contrivanee in them, but all came to pass Fortuitously.* But he confutes it after this manner: Ἄτοπον δὲ τὸ μὴ οἴεσθαι ἕνεκά του γίνεσθαι, ἐὰν μὴ ἴδωσι τὸ κινοῦν βουλευσάμενον, καίτοι καὶ ἡ τέχνη οὐ βουλεύεται· *It is absurd for Men to think nothing*

---

[28] Plotinus, III, viii, 2.

to be done for Ends, if they do not see that which moves to consult, although Art it self doth not Consult.²⁹ Whence he concludes that Nature may Act *Artificially*, *Orderly* and *Methodically*, for the *sake of Ends*, though it never *Consult* or *Deliberate*. Indeed *Humane Artists* themselves do not Consult properly as they are *Artists*, but when ever they do it, it is for want of *Art*, and because they are to seek, their Art being Imperfect and Adventitious: but *Art it self* or *Perfect Art*, is never to seek, and therefore doth never *Consult* or *Deliberate*. And *Nature* is this *Art*, which never hesitates nor studies, as unresolved what to do, but is always readily prompted; nor does it ever repent afterwards of what it hath formerly done, or go about, as it were upon second thoughts, to alter and mend its former Course, but it goes on in one Constant, Unrepenting Tenor, from Generation to Generation, because it is the Stamp or Impress of that Infallibly Omniscient Art, of the Divine Understanding, which is the very Law and Rule of what is simply the Best in every thing.

And thus we have seen the Difference between *Nature* and *Humane Art*; that the Latter is Imperfect Art, acting upon the Matter from without, and at a Distance; but the Former is *Art it self* or *Perfect Art*, acting as an *Inward Principle* in it. Wherefore when Art is said to imitate Nature, the meaning thereof is, that Imperfect *Humane Art* imitates that *Perfect Art of Nature*, which is really no other than the *Divine Art* it self, as before *Aristotle*, *Plato* had declared in his Sophist, in these words, τὰ φύσει λεγόμενα ποιεῖσθαι θείᾳ τέχνῃ· *Those things which are said to be done by Nature, are indeed done by Divine Art.*³⁰

11. Notwithstanding which, we are to take notice in the next place, that as *Nature* is not the *Deity* it self, but a Thing very remote from it and far below it, so neither is it the *Divine Art*, as it is in it self *Pure* and *Abstract*, but *Concrete* and *Embodied* only; for the *Divine Art* considered in it self, is nothing but *Knowledge*, *Understanding* or *Wisdom* in the Mind of God: Now Knowledge and Understanding, in its own Nature is κεχωρισμένον τι, *a certain separate and Abstract thing*, and of so Subtil and Refined a Nature, as that it is not Capable of being Incorporated with Matter, or Mingled and Blended with it as the *Soul* of it. And therefore *Aristotle's* Second Instance, which he propounds as most pertinent to Illustrate this business of Nature by, namely of the *Physicians Art curing himself*,³¹ is not so adequate

---

²⁹ *Physica*, II, 8.   ³⁰ *Sophista*, 265e.
³¹ Quoted more fully above, p. 300.

The Plastick Life of Nature 303

thereunto; because when the Medicinal Art Cures the Physician in whom it is, it doth not there Act as *Nature*, that is, as *Concrete* and *Embodied Art*, but as *Knowledge* and *Understanding* only, which is *Art Naked*, *Abstract* and *Unbodied*; as also it doth its Work, *Ambagiously*, by the Physician's Willing and Prescribing to himself, the use of such Medicaments, as do but conduce, by removing of Impediments, to help that which is *Nature* indeed, or the Inward *Archeus* to effect the Cure. Art is defined by *Aristotle*, to be λόγος τοῦ ἔργου ἄνευ ὕλης, *The Reason of the thing without Matter*;[32] and so the *Divine Art* or *Knowledge* in the Mind of God is *Unbodied Reason*; but *Nature* is *Ratio Mersa & Confusa, Reason Immersed and Plunged* into Matter, and as it were *Fuddled* in it, and *Confounded* with it. *Nature* is not the *Divine Art Archetypal*, but only *Ectypal*, it is a living Stamp or Signature of the Divine Wisdom, which though it act exactly according to its *Archetype*, yet it doth not at all Comprehend nor Understand the Reason of what it self doth. And the Difference between these two, may be resembled to that between the λόγος ἐνδιάθετος, *the Reason of the Mind and Conception*, called *Verbum Mentis*, and the λόγος προφορικὸς, *The Reason of External speech*;[33] the Latter of which though it bear a certain Stamp and Impress of the Former upon it, yet it self is nothing but *Articulate Sound*, devoid of all *Understanding* and *Sense*. Or else we may Illustrate this business by another Similitude, comparing the Divine *Art* and Wisdom to an *Architect*, but *Nature* to a *Manuary Opificer*; the Difference betwixt which two is thus set forth by *Aristotle* pertinently to our purpose; τοὺς ἀρχιτέκτονας περὶ ἕκαστον τιμιωτέρους καὶ μᾶλλον εἰδέναι νομίζομεν τῶν χειροτεχνῶν, καὶ σοφωτέρους, ὅτι τὰς αἰτίας τῶν ποιουμένων ἴσασιν. οἱ δ' ὥσπερ καὶ τῶν ἀψύχων ἔνια, ποιεῖ μὲν, οὐκ εἰδότα δὲ ποιεῖ, οἷον καίει τὸ πῦρ. τὰ μὲν οὖν ἄψυχα φύσει τινὶ ποιεῖν τούτων ἕκαστον· τοὺς δὲ χειροτέχνας δι' ἔθος. *We account the Architects in every thing more honourable than the Manuary Opificers, because they understand the Reason of the things done, whereas the other, as some Inanimate things, only Do, not knowing what they Do: the Difference between them being only this, that Inanimate Things Act by a certain Nature in them, but the Manuary Opificer by Habit.*[34] Thus Nature may be called the χειροτέχνης or *Manuary Opificer* that Acts subserviently under the

---

[32] *De partibus animalium*, I, 1.
[33] Cf. the *rationes seminales* referred to earlier, pp. 26 and 132.
[34] *Metaphysica*, I, 1.

Architectonical Art and Wisdom of the Divine Understanding, ἣ ποιεῖ μὲν οὐκ εἰδυῖα, *which does Do without Knowing the Reason of what it Doth.*[35]

12. Wherefore as we did before observe the *Preeminences* of Nature above Humane Art, so we must here take Notice also of the *Imperfections* and *Defects* of it, in which respect it falls short of *Humane Art,* which are likewise Two; and the First of them is this, That though it Act *Artificially* for the *sake of Ends*, yet it self doth neither *Intend those Ends,* nor *Understand the Reason of that it doth.* Nature is not *Master* of that *Consummate Art* and Wisdom according to which it acts, but only a *servant to it,* and a *Drudging Executioner* of the Dictates of it. This Difference betwixt *Nature* and *Abstract Art* or *Wisdom* is expressed by *Plotinus* in these words: τί διοίσει τῆς λεγομένης φύσεως φρόνησις; ὅτι ἡ μὲν φρόνησις πρῶτον, ἡ δὲ φύσις ἔσχατον, ἴνδαλμα γὰρ φρονήσεως ἡ φύσις, καὶ ψυχῆς ἔσχατον ὂν, ἔσχατον καὶ τὸν ἐν αὐτῇ ἐλλαμπόμενον λογὸν ἔχει. οἷον εἰ ἐν κηρῷ βαθεῖ, διικνεῖτο εἰς ἔσχατον ἐπὶ θάτερα ἐν τῇ ἐπιφανείᾳ τύπος· ἐναργοὺς μὸν ὄντος τοῦ ἄνω, ἰχνοῦς δὲ ἀσθενοῦς ὄντος τοῦ κάτω, ὅθεν οὐδὲ οἶδε φύσις, μόνον δὲ ποιεῖ. *How doth Wisdom differ from that which is called Nature? Verily in this Manner, That Wisdom is the First Thing, but Nature the Last and Lowest; for Nature is but an Image or Imitation of Wisdom, the Last thing of the Soul, which hath the lowest Impress of Reason shining upon it; as when a thick piece of Wax, is thoroughly impressed upon a Seal, that Impress which is clear and distinct in the superiour superfices of it, will in the lower side be weak and obscure; and such is the Stamp and Signature of Nature, compared with that of Wisdom and Understanding, Nature being a thing which doth only Do, but not Know.*[36] And elsewhere the same Writer declares the Difference between the Spermatick λόγοι, or *Reasons,* and *Knowledges* or Conceptions of the Mind in this manner; Πότερα δὲ οἱ λόγοι οὗτοι οἱ ἐν ψυχῇ νοήματα; ἀλλὰ πῶς κατὰ τὰ νοήματα ποιήσει; ὁ γὰρ λόγος ἐν ὕλῃ ποιεῖ, καὶ τὸ ποιοῦν φυσικῶς, οὐ νόησις, οὐδὲ ὅρασις, ἀλλὰ δύναμις τρεπτικὴ τῆς ὕλης, οὐκ ἐδυῖα, ἀλλὰ δρῶσα μόνον, οἷον τύπον καὶ σχῆμα ἐν ὕδατι. *Whether are these Plastick Reasons or Forms in the Soul Knowledges? But how shall it then Act according to those Knowledges? For the Plastick Reason or Form Acts or Works in Matter, and that which acts Nuturally is not Intellection nor Vision, but a certain Power of moving Matter, which doth not Know, but only Do, and makes as it were a Stamp or Figure in Water.*[37]

[35] Plotinus, II, iii, 17.   [36] *Ibid.*, IV, iv, 13.   [37] *Ibid.*, II, iii, 17.

And with this Doctrine of the Ancients, a Modern Judicious Writer and Sagacious Inquirer into Nature, seems fully to agree, that *Nature* is such a Thing as doth not *Know* but *only Do*: For after he had admired that *Wisdom* and *Art* by which the Bodies of Animals are framed, he concludes that one or other of these two things must needs be acknowledged, that either the *Vegetative* or *Plastick Power* of the Soul, by which it Fabricates and Organizes its own body, is more Excellent and Divine than the Rational; Or else, *In Naturæ Operibus neque Prudentiam nec Intellectum inesse, sed ita solùm videri Conceptui nostro, qui secundùm Artes nostras et Facultates, seu Exemplaria à nobismetipsis mutuata, de rebus Naturæ divinis judicamus; Quasi Principia Naturæ Activa, effectus suos eo modo producerent, quo nos opera nostra Artificialia solemus:* That in the *Works of Nature* there is neither *Prudence* nor *Understanding*, but only it seems so to our *Apprehensions*, who judge of these Divine things of Nature, according to our own *Arts* and *Faculties*, and *Patterns* borrowed from our selves; as if the *Active Principles of Nature* did produce their *Effects* in the same manner, as we do our *Artificial Works*.[38] Wherefore we conclude, agreeably to the Sence of the best Philosophers, both Ancient and Modern, That *Nature* is such a Thing, as though it act *Artificially* and for the *sake of Ends*, yet it doth but *Ape* and *Mimick* the *Divine Art* and *Wisdom*, it self not Understanding those Ends which it Acts for, nor the Reason of what it doth in order to them; for which Cause also it is not Capable of *Consultation* or *Deliberation*, nor can it *Act Electively* or with *Discretion*.

13. But because this may seem strange at the first fight, that Nature should be said to Act ἕνεκά τοῦ, *for the sake of Ends*, and *Regularly* or *Artificially*, and yet be it self devoid of *Knowledge* and *Understanding*, we shall therefore endeavour to perswade the *Possibility*, and facilitate the Belief of it, by some other Instances; and first by that of *Habits*, particularly those Musical ones, of Singing, Playing upon Instruments, and Dancing. Which *Habits* direct every Motion of the Hand, Voice, and Body, and prompt them readily, without any *Deliberation* or *Studied Consideration*, what the next following *Note* or *Motion* should be. If you jogg a sleeping Musician, and sing but the first Words of a Song to him, which he had either himself composed, or learnt before, he will presently take it from you, and that perhaps before he is

---

[38] William Harvey, *Exercitationes de generatione animalium* (1651), pp. 145–6 [Ex. 49]. The affinities between the views of Harvey and Cudworth are considerably qualified by the further quotations supplied by JLM (I, 240 ff.).

thoroughly awake, going on with it, and singing out the remainder of the whole Song to the End. Thus the Fingers of an exercised Lutonist, and the Legs and whole Body of a skilful Dancer, are directed to move Regularly and Orderly, in a long Train and Series of Motions, by those Artificial Habits in them, which do not themselves at all comprehend those *Laws and Rules of Musick* or *Harmony*, by which they are governed: So that the same thing may be said of these *Habits*, which was said before of Nature, That they do not *Know*, but *only Do*. And thus we see there is no Reason, why this *plastick Nature* (which is supposed to move Body *Regularly* and *Artificially*) should be thought to be an Absolute Impossibility, since *Habits* do in like manner, *Gradually Evolve* themselves, in a long Train or Series of *Regular* and *Artificial Motions*, readily prompting the doing of them, without comprehending that *Art* and *Reason* by which they are directed. The forementioned Philosopher illustrates the *seminary Reason* and *Plastick Nature* of the Universe, by this very Instance: ἡ τοίνυν ἐνέργεια αὐτῆς τεχνική· ὥσπερ ἂν ὁ ὀρχούμενος, κινούμενος εἴη. ὁ γὰρ ὀρχιστής, τῇ οὕτω τεχνικῇ ζωῇ ἔοικεν αὐτὸς, καὶ ἡ τέχνη αὐτόν κινεῖ, καὶ οὕτω κινεῖ, ὡς τῆς ζωῆς αὐτῆς τοιαύτης πῶς οὔσης. *The Energy of Nature is Artificial, as when a Dancer moves; for a Dancer resembles this Artificial Life of Nature, forasmuch as Art it self moves him, and so moves him as being such a Life in him.*[39] And Agreeably to this Conceit, the Ancient Mythologists represented the *Nature of the Universe*, by *Pan Playing upon a Pipe* or *Harp*, and being in love with the *Nymph Eccho*;[40] as if Nature did, by a kind of Silent Melody, make all the Parts of the Universe everywhere Daunce in measure & Proportion, it self being as it were in the mean time delighted and ravished with the Reecchoing of its own Harmony. *Habits* are said to be an *Adventitious* and *Acquired Nature*, and *Nature* was before defined by the Stoicks to be ἕξις, or a *Habit*:[41] so that

[39] Plotinus, III, ii, 16.
[40] Cf. Cudworth, *Imm. Morality*, pp. 183 ff. (IV, ii, 15): 'there is [an] Interiour Symmetry and Harmony in the Relations, Proportions, Aptitudes and Correspondencies of Things to one another in the Great *Mundane* System, or Vital Machine of the Universe, which is all Musically and Harmonically composed; for which Cause the Antients made *Pan*, that is, Nature to play upon an Harp'. Cudworth's interpretation of the myth, immediately following, corresponds to countless similar affirmations in Renaissance literature.
[41] Diogenes Laertius, VII, 148 (quoted more fully above, p. 297).

there seems to be no other Difference between these two, than this, that whereas the One is *Acquired* by *Teaching, Industry* and *Exercise;* the other, as was expressed by *Hippocrates*, is ἀπαίδευτος καὶ οὐκ μαθοῦσα, *Unlearned and Untaught*,⁴² and may in some sense also be said to be αὐτοδίδακτος, *Self-taught*,⁴³ though she be indeed always Inwardly Prompted, Secretly Whispered into, and *Inspired*, by the *Divine Art* and Wisdom.

14. Moreover, that something may Act *Artificially* and for *Ends*, without Comprehending the Reason of what it doth, may be further evinced from those *Natural Instincts* that are in Animals, which without Knowledge direct them to *Act Regularly*, in Order both to their own *Good* and the *Good* of the *Universe*. As for Example; the Bees in Mellification, and in framing their Combs and Hexagonial Cells, the Spiders in spinning their Webs, the Birds in building their Nests, and many other Animals in such like Actions of theirs, which would seem to argue a great Sagacity in them, whereas notwithstanding, as *Aristotle* observes, οὔτε τέχνῃ, οὔτε ζητήσαντα, οὔτε βουλευσάμενα ποιεῖ· They do these things, *neither by Art nor by Counsel nor by any Deliberation of their own*,⁴⁴ and therefore are not *Masters of that Wisdom* according to which they Act, but only *Passive* to the Instincts and Impresses thereof upon them. And indeed to affirm, that Brute Animals do all these things by a *Knowledge* of their own, and which themselves are Masters of, and that without Deliberation and Consultation, were to make them to be endued with a most *Perfect Intellect*, far transcending that of *Humane Reason*; whereas it is plain enough, that *Brutes* are not *above Consultation*, but *Below* it, and that these Instincts of Nature in them, are Nothing but a kind of *Fate* upon them.

15. There is in the next place another *Imperfection* to be observed in the *Plastick Nature*, that as it doth not comprehend the *Reason* of its own Action, so neither is it *clearly and Expressly Conscious of what it doth*; in which Respect, it doth not only fall short of *Humane Art*, but even of that very Manner of Acting which is in Brutes themselves, who though they do not Understand the Reason of those Actions, that their Natural Instincts lead them to, yet they are generally conceived to be Conscious of them, and to do them by *Phancy*; whereas the *Plastick Nature* in the *Formation* of Plants and Animals, seems to have

---

⁴² *Epid.*, VI, 5.
⁴³ As was said by Harvey, *Exercitationes* (1651), p. 146 (*apud* JLM, I, 243).
⁴⁴ *Physica*, II, 8.

no *Animal Fancie*, no Express συναίσθησις,⁴⁵ *Con-sense* or *Consciousness* of what it doth. Thus the often Commended Philosopher, ἡ φύσις οὐδὲ φαντασίαν ἔχει, ἡ δὲ νόησις φαντασίας κρείττων, φαντασία δὲ μεταξὺ φύσεως τύπον καὶ νοήσεως· ἡ μὲν γε οὐθενὸς ἀντίληψιν οὐδὲ σύνεσιν ἔχει. *Nature hath not so much as any Fancie in it; As Intellection and Knowledge is a thing Superiour to Fancie, so Fancie is Superiour to the Impress of Nature, for Nature hath no Apprehension nor Conscious Perception of any thing.*⁴⁶ In a Word, Nature is a thing that hath no such *Self-perception* or *Self-injoyment* in it, as Animals have.

16. Now we are well aware, that this is a Thing which the Narrow Principles of some late Philosophers⁴⁷ will not admit of, that there should be any *Action* distinct from *Local Motion* besides *Expressly Conscious Cogitation*. For they making the first General Heads of all Entity, to be *Extension* and *Cogitation*, or Extended *Being* and *Cogitative*, and then supposing that the Essence of Cogitation consists in *Express consciousness*, must needs by this means exclude such a *Plastick Life* of Nature, as we speak of, that is supposed to act without *Animal Fancie* or *Express Consciousness*. Wherefore we conceive that the first Heads of Being ought rather to be expressed thus; *Resisting* or *Antitypous Extension*, and *Life*, (*i.e.* Internal *Energy* and *Self-activity*:) and then again, that *Life* or *Internal Self-activity*, is to be subdivided into such as either acts with express Consciousness and *Synæsthesis*, or such as is without it; the Latter of which is this *Plastick Life* of Nature: So that there may be an *Action* distinct from *Local Motion*, or a *Vital Energy*, which is not accompanied with that *Fancie*, or *Consciousness*, *that is* in the *Energies* of the *Animal Life*; that is, there may be a simple *Internal Energy* or Vital Autokinesie, which is without that *Duplication*, that is included in the Nature of συναίσθησις, *Con-sense* and *Consciousness*, which makes a Being to be Present with it self, Attentive to its own Actions, or Animadversive of them, to perceive it self to Do or Suffer, and to have a *Fruition* or *Enjoyment* of it self. And indeed it must be granted, that what moves Matter or determines the Motion of it *Vitally*, must needs do it by some other *Energy* of its own, as it is Reasonable also to conceive, that it self hath some *Vital Sympathy* with that *Matter* which it Acts upon. But we apprehend, that Both these may be without Clear and *Express Consciousness*. Thus the Philo-

---

⁴⁵ 'Synæsthesis' is used in Aristotle's sense (*Ethica eudemia*, VII, 12). Cf. Plotinus, III, viii, 4.

⁴⁶ Plotinus, IV, iv, 13.

⁴⁷ Descartes and his disciples. See the Introduction, above, pp. 30 f.

The Plastick Life of Nature

sopher, πᾶσα ζωὴ ἐνέργεια, καὶ ἡ φαύλη, ἐνέργεια δὲ, οὐχ ὡς τὸ πῦρ ἐνεργεῖ, ἀλλ' ἡ ἐνέργεια αὐτῆς, κἂν μὴ αἴσθησίς τις παρῇ, κίνησίς τις οὐκ εἰκῇ. *Every Life is Energie, even the worst of Lives, and therefore that of Nature. Whose Energie is not like that of Fire, but such an Energie, as though there be no Sense belonging to it, yet is it not Temerarious or Fortuitous, but Orderly & Regular.*[48]

Wherefore this Controversie whether the Energy of the *Plastick Nature*, be *Cogitation*, or no, seems to be but a *Logomachy*, or Contention about Words. For if Clear and Express *Consciousness* be supposed to be included in *Cogitation*, then it must needs be granted that *Cogitation* doth not belong to the *Plastick Life* of *Nature*: but if the Notion of that Word be *enlarged* so as to comprehend all *Action* distinct from *Local Motion*, and to be of equal *Extent with Life*, then the *Energie of Nature is Cogitation*.

Nevertheless if any one think fit to attribute some Obscure and Imperfect *Sense* or *Perception*, different from that of *Animals*, to the *Energie* of *Nature*, and will therefore call it a kind of *Drowsie, Unawakened*, or *Astonish'd Cogitation*, the Philosopher, before mentioned, will not very much gainsay it: εἴτις βούληται σύνεσίν τινα ἢ αἴσθησιν αὐτῇ διδόναι, οὐχ οἵαν λέγομεν ἐπὶ τῶν ἄλλων τὴν αἴσθησιν ἢ τὴν σύνησιν, ἀλλ' οἷον εἴτις τὴν τοῦ ὕπνου τῇ τοῦ ἐγρηγορότος προσεικάσειε. *If any will needs attribute some kind of Apprehension or Sense to Nature, then it must not be such a Sense or Apprehension, as is in Animals, but something that differs as much from it, as the Sense or Cogitation of one in a profound sleep, differs from that of one who is awake.*[49] And since it cannot be denied but that the *Plastick Nature* hath a certain *Dull* and *Obscure Idea* of that which it Stamps and Prints upon Matter, the same Philosopher himself sticks not to call this *Idea* of *Nature*, θέαμα and θεώρημα, a *Spectacle* and *Contemplamen*, as likewise the Energy of *Nature* towards it, θεωρία ἄψοφος, a *Silent Contemplation*; nay he allows, that Nature may be said to be, in some Sence, φιλοθεάμων, a *Lover of Spectacles or Contemplation*. . . .[50]

19. From what hath been hitherto declared concerning the Plastick Nature, it may appear; That though it be a thing that acts for *Ends Artificially*, and which may be also called the *Divine Art*, and the *Fate*

---

[48] Plotinus, III, ii, 16. [49] *Ibid.*, III, viii, 4.
[50] The next two sections (§§ 17–18)—not reprinted here—attempt to demonstrate the reasonableness of the possibility that 'there may be some Vital Energy without Clear and Express συναίσθησις, *Con-sense* and *Consciousness*'.

of the *Corporeal World*; yet for all that it is neither *God* nor *Goddess*, but a Low and Imperfect Creature. Forasmuch as it is not *Master* of that *Reason* and *Wisdom* according to which it acts, nor does it properly *Intend* those *Ends* which it acts for, nor indeed is it Expresly Conscious of what it doth; it not *Knowing* but only *Doing*, according to *Commands* & *Laws* imprest upon it. Neither of which things ought to seem strange or incredible, since *Nature* may as well act *Regularly* and *Artificially*, without any Knowledge and Consciousness of its own, as Forms of Letters compounded together, may Print Coherent Philosophick Sence, though they understand nothing at all; and it may also act for the sake of those *Ends*, that are not intended by it self, but some Higher Being, as well as the *Saw* or *Hatchet* in the hand of the Architect or Mechanick doth, τὸ σκέπαρνον ἕνεκά του πελεκᾷ, ἀλλ' οὐ προλογιζόμενον, ἀλλὰ τῷ προλογιζομένῳ ὑπηρετοῦν, *the Ax cuts for the sake of something, though it self does not ratiocinate, nor intend or design any thing, but is only subservient to that which does so.*[51] It is true, that our *Humane Actions* are not governed by such exact Reason, Art, and Wisdom, nor carried on with such Constancy, Eavenness and Uniformity, as the Actions of *Nature* are; notwithstanding which, since we act according to a *Knowledge* of our *own*, and are *Masters* of that *Wisdom* by which our Actions are directed, since we do not act *Fatally* only, but *Electively* and *Intendingly*, with *Consciousness* and *Self-perception*; the Rational Life that is in us, ought to be accompted a much Higher and more Noble Perfection, than that *Plastick Life of Nature*. Nay, this *Plastick Nature*, is so far from being the *First* and *Highest Life*, that it is indeed the Last and Lowest of all *Lives*; it being really the same thing with the *Vegetative*, which is Inferiour to the *Sensitive*. The difference betwixt *Nature* and Wisdom was before observed, that *Wisdom* is the *First* and *Highest* thing, but *Nature* the *Last* and *Lowest*; this latter being but an Umbratile Imitation of the former. And to this purpose, this Plastick Nature is further described by the same Philosopher in these words, ἔστι τοίνυν οὗτος ὁ λόγος οὐκ ἄκρατος νοῦς, οὐδ' αὐτονοῦς, οὐδέγε ψυχῆς καθαρᾶς τὸ γένος. ἠρτημένος δὲ ἐκείνης, καὶ οἷον ἔκλαμψις ἐξ ἀμφοῖν νοῦ καὶ ψυχῆς, καὶ ψυχῆς κατὰ νοῦν διακειμένης γεννησάντων τὸν λόγον τοῦτον. *The Spermatick Reason or Plastick Nature, is no pure Mind or perfect Intellect, nor any kind of pure Soul neither; but something which depends upon it, being as it were an Effulgency or Eradiation, from both together,*

---

[51] Simplicius, *Arist. Phys.*, II.

The Plastick Life of Nature 311

*Mind and Soul, or Soul affected according to Mind, generating the same as a Lower kind of Life.*⁵²

And though this *Plastick Nature* contain no small part of *Divine Providence* in it, yet since it is a thing that cannot act Electively nor with Discretion, it must needs be granted that there is a *Higher and Diviner Providence* than this, which also presides over the Corporeal World it self, which was a thing likewise insisted upon by that Philosopher, γίνεται τὰ ἐν τῷ παντὶ οὐ κατὰ σπερματικοὺς, ἀλλὰ κατὰ λόγους περιληπτικοὺς, καὶ τῶν προτέρων, ἢ κατὰ τοὺς τῶν σπερμολόγων λόγους, οὐ γὰρ ἐν τοῖς σπερματικοῖς λόγοις ἔνι, καὶ τῶν γενομένων, παρὰ τοὺς σπερματικοὺς αὐτοὺς λόγους· *The things in the world are not administred merely by Spermatick Reasons, but by Perileptick (that is, Comprehensive Intellectual Reasons) which are in order of Nature before the other, because in the Spermatick Reasons cannot be contained that which is contrary to them,* &c.⁵³ Where though this Philosopher may extend his *Spermatick Reasons* further than we do our *Plastick Nature* in this place, (which is only confined to the Motions of Matter) yet he concludes, that there is a higher Principle presiding over the Universe than this. So that it is not *Ratio mersa & confusa, a Reason drowned in Matter, and confounded with it,* which is the Supreme Governour of the World, but a Providence perfectly Intellectual, *Abstract* and *Released.*

20. But though the Plastick Nature be the Lowest of all Lives, nevertheless since it is a *Life,* it must needs be *Incorporeal;* all Life being such. For Body being nothing but *Antitypous Extension,* or *Resisting Bulk,* nothing but mere *Outside, Aliud extra Aliúd,* together with *Passive Capability,* hath no *Internal Energy, Self-activity,* or *Life* belonging to it; it is not able so much as to *Move itself,* and therefore much less can it *Artificially direct* its own Motion. Moreover, in the Efformation of the Bodies of Animals, it is One and the self-same thing that directs the Whole; that which Contrives and Frames the Eye, cannot be a distinct thing from that which Frames the Ear; nor that which makes the Hand, from that which makes the Foot; the same thing which delineates the Veins, must also form the Arteries; and that which fabricates the Nerves, must also project the Muscles and Joynts; it must be the same thing that designs and Organizes the Heart and Brain, with such Communications betwixt them; One and the self-same thing must needs have in it, the entire Idea and the complete

---

⁵² Plotinus, III, ii, 16.   ⁵³ *Ibid.,* IV, iv, 39.

Model or Platform of the whole Organick Body. For the several parts of Matter distant from one another, acting alone by themselves, without any common *Directrix*, being not able to confer together, nor communicate with each other, could never possibly conspire to make up one such uniform and Orderly System or Compages, as the Body of every Animal is. The same is to be said likewise concerning the Plastick Nature of the whole Corporeal Universe, in which ἅπαντα πρὸς ἕν συντέτακται, *all things are ordered together conspiringly into One*. It must be one and the same thing, which formeth the whole, or else it could never have fallen into such an Uniform Order and Harmony. Now that which is One and the Same, acting upon several distant parts of Matter, cannot be Corporeal.

Indeed *Aristotle* is severely censured by some learned men for this, that though he talk every where of such a *Nature* as acts *Regularly*, *Artificially* and *Methodically*, in order to the Best, yet he does no where positively declare whether this Nature of his be *Corporeal* or *Incorporeal*, *Substantial* or *Accidental*, which yet is the less to be wondered at in him, because he does not clearly determine these same points concerning the Rational Soul neither, but seems to stagger uncertainly about them. In the mean time it cannot be denied, but that *Aristotle's* Followers do for the most part conclude this Nature of his to be *Corporeal*; whereas notwithstanding, according to the Principles of this Philosophy, it cannot possibly be such: For there is nothing else attributed to Body in it, besides these three, *Matter*, *Form* and *Accidents*; neither of which can be the *Aristotelick Nature*. First, it cannot be *Matter*; because *Nature*, according to *Aristotle*, is supposed to be the *Principle* of *Motion* and *Activity*, which Matter in it self is devoid of. Moreover *Aristotle* concludes, that they who assign only a Material Cause, assign no Cause at all τοῦ εὖ καὶ καλῶς, *of well and fit*,[54] of that *Regular and Artificial Frame of things which is ascribed to Nature*; upon both which accompts, it is determined by that Philosopher, that ἡ φύσις μᾶλλον ἀρχὴ καὶ αἰτία τῆς ὕλης, *Nature is more a Principle and Cause than Matter*,[55] and therefore it cannot be one and the same thing with it. Again, it is as plain, that *Aristotle's Nature* cannot be the *Forms* of particular *Bodies* neither, as Vulgar Peripateticks seem to conceive, these being all *Generated* and *Produced* by *Nature*, and as well *Corruptible* as *Generable*. Whereas Nature is such

---

[54] *Metaphysica*, I, 3 (as above, p. 299).
[55] *De partibus animalium*, I, 1.

a thing as is neither Generated nor Corrupted, it being the Principle and Cause of all Generation and Corruption. To make *Nature* and the *Material Forms* of Bodies to be one and the self-same thing, is all one as if one should make the *Seal* (with the Stamper too) to be one and the same thing, with the *Signature* upon the Wax. And Lastly, *Aristotle's* Nature can least of all be the *Accidents* or *Qualities of Bodies*; because these act only in Vertue of their Substance, neither can they exercise any *Active Power* over the Substance it self in which they are; whereas the *Plastick Nature* is a thing that *Domineers* over the Substance of the whole *Corporeal Universe*, and which Subordinately to the Deity, put both Heaven and Earth into this Frame in which now it is. Wherefore since *Aristotle's Nature* can be neither the *Matter*, nor the *Forms*, nor the *Accidents of Bodies*, it is plain, that according to his own Principles, it must be Incorporeal.[56]

21. Now if the Plastick Nature be Incorporeal, then it must of necessity, be either an Inferiour *Power* or *Faculty* of some *Soul*, which is also Conscious, Sensitive or Rational; or else a lower *substantial Life* by it self, devoid of Animal Consciousness. The Platonists seem to affirm both these together, namely that there is a *Plastick Nature* lodged in all particular Souls of Animals, Brutes and Men, and also that there is a General *Plastick* or *Spermatick Principle* of the whole *Universe* distinct from their Higher Mundane Soul, though subordinate to it, and dependent upon it, ἡ λεγομένη φύσις γέννημα ψυχῆς προτέρας δυνατώτερον ζώσης· *That which is called Nature, is the Off-spring of an higher Soul, which hath a more Powerful Life in it.*[57] And though *Aristotle* do not so clearly acknowledge the *Incorporeity* and *Substantiality* of Souls, yet he concurrs very much with this *Platonick* Doctrine, that *Nature* is either a *Lower Power* or Faculty of some Conscious Soul, or else an Inferiour kind of Life by it self, depending upon a *Superiour Soul.*

And this we shall make to appear from his Book *De Partibus Animalium*,[58] after we have taken notice of some considerable Preliminary Passages in it in order thereunto. For having first declared, that besides the *Material Cause*, there are other Causes also of Natural Generations, namely these two, ᾗτε οὗ ἕνεκα καὶ ὅθεν ἡ ἀρχὴ τῆς κινήσεως, *that for whose sake*, (or the Final Cause) *and that from which*

---

[56] For a sharp criticism of Cudworth's interpretation of Aristotle, see JLM, I, esp. 254 ff.
[57] Plotinus, III, viii, 4.
[58] Quotations hereafter (to p. 315) are from *De partibus animalium*, I, 1.

the Principle of Motion is, (or the Efficient Cause) he determines that the former of these Two, is the principal, φαίνεται δὲ πρώτη ἣν λέγομεν ἕνεκά τινος. λόγος γὰρ οὗτος, ἀρχὴ δὲ ὁ λόγος, ὁμοίως, ἔν τε τοῖς κατὰ τέχνην καὶ τοῖς φύσει συνεστηκόσιν. *The chiefest of these two Causes seems to be the Final or the Intending Cause; for this is Reason, and Reason is alike a Principle in Artificial and in Natural things*. Nay the Philosopher adds excellently, that there is more of *Reason* and *Art*, in the things of *Nature*, than there is in those things that are *Artificially* made by men, μᾶλλον δ' ἐστὶ τὸ οὗ ἕνεκα καὶ τὸ καλόν ἐν τοῖς φύσεως ἔργοις, ἢ ἐν τοῖς τῆς τέχνης· *There is more of Final or Intending Causality and of the reason of Good, in the works of Nature than in those of Humane Art*. After which he greatly complains of the first and most Ancient Physiologers, meaning thereby *Anaximander*, and those other Ionicks before *Anaxagoras*, that they considered only τὴν ὑλικὴν ἀρχὴν, *the Material Principle and Cause* of things, without attending to those Two other Causes, the *Principle of Motion*, and *that which aims at Ends*, they talking only, of Fire, Water, Air and Earth, and generating the whole World, from the Fortuitous Concourse of these Senseless Bodies. But at length *Aristotle* falls upon *Democritus*, who being Junior to those others before mentioned, Philosophised after the same Athestical manner, but in a new way of his own, by Atoms; acknowledging no other Nature, neither in the Universe, nor in the Bodies of Animals, than that of *Fortuitous Mechanism*, and supposing all things to arise from the different Compositions of Magnitudes, Figures, Sites, and Motions. Of which Democritick Philosophy, he gives his Censure in these following words, εἰ μὲν οὖν τῷ σχήματι καὶ τῷ χρώματι ἕκαστόν ἐστι, τῶν τε ζώων καὶ τῶν μορίων, ὀρθῶς ἄν Δημόκριτος λέγοι, &c. *If Animals and their several parts did consist of nothing but Figure and Colour, then indeed* Democritus *would be in the right: But a Dead man hath the same Form and Figure of Body, that he had before, and yet for all that he is not a Man; neither is a Brazen or Wooden Hand a Hand, but only Equivocally, as a Painted Physician, or Pipes made of Stone are so called. No member of a Dead Mans Body, is that which it was before, when he was alive, neither Eye, nor Hand, nor Foot. Wherefore this is but a rude way of Philosophizing, and just as if a Carpenter should talk of a Wooden Hand. For thus these Physiologers declare the Generations and Causes of Figures only, or the Matter out of which things are made, as Air and Earth. Whereas no Artificer would think it sufficient to render such a Cause of any Artificial Fabrick, because the Instrument happened to fall upon the Timber, that therefore it was*

The Plastick Life of Nature

Hollow here and Plane there; but rather because himself made such strokes, and for such Ends, &c.

Now in the close of all, this Philosopher at length declares, That there is another *Principle* of Corporeal things, besides the *Material*, and such as is not only the *Cause of Motion*, but also acts *Artificially* in order to *Ends*, ἔστι τι τοιοῦτον ὃ δὴ καὶ καλοῦμεν φύσιν, *there is such a thing as that which we call Nature*, that is, not the *Fortuitous Motion* of *Sensless* Matter, but a *Plastick Regular and Artificial Nature*, such as acts for *Ends* and *Good*; declaring in the same place, what this Nature is, namely that it is ψυχή, ἢ ψυχῆς μέρος, ἢ μὴ ἄνευ ψυχῆς, *Soul, or Part of Soul, or not without Soul*; and from thence inferring, that it properly belongs to a Physiologer, to treat concerning the Soul also. But he concludes afterwards οὐδὲ πᾶσα ψυχὴ φύσις, *that the whole Soul is not Nature*; whence it remains, that according to *Aristotle's* sence, Nature is ἢ ψυχῆς μέρος, ἢ μὴ ἄνευ ψυχῆς, *either part of a Soul or not without Soul*, that is, either a lower Part or Faculty of some Conscious Soul; or else an Inferiour kind of Life by it self, which is not without Soul, but Suborditate to it and dependent on it.

22. As for the Bodies of Animals *Aristotle* first resolves in General, that Nature in them is either the whole Soul, or else some part of it, φύσις ὡς ἡ κινοῦσα, καί ὡς τὸ τέλος τοῦ ζῴου, ἤτοι πᾶσα ἡ ψυχή, ἢ μέρος τι αὐτῆς, *Nature as the Moving Principle, or as that which acts Artificially for Ends*, (so far as concerns the Bodies of Animals) *is either the whole Soul, or else some Part of it*. But afterward he determines more particularly, that the Plastick Nature is not the whole Soul in Animals, but only some part of it; οὐ πᾶσα ψυχὴ φύσις, ἀλλά τι μόριον αὐτῆς, that is, *Nature in Animals*, properly so called, *is some Lower Power or Faculty* lodged in their respective Souls, whether Sensitive or Rational.

And that there is Plastick Nature in the Souls of Animals, the same *Aristotle* elsewhere affirms and proves after this manner: τί τό συνέχον εἰς τ' ἀναντία φερόμενα, τὸ πῦρ καὶ τὴν γῆν· διασπασθήσεται γὰρ εἰ μήτι ἔσται τὸ κωλύσον, εἰδ' ἐστὶ, τοῦτ' ἔστιν ἡ ψυχή, καὶ τὸ αἴτιον τοῦ αὐξάνεσθαι καὶ τρέφεσθαι· *What is that which in the Bodies of Animals holds together such things as of their own Nature would otherwise move contrary ways, and flie asunder, as Fire and Earth, which would be distracted and dissipated, the one tending upwards, the other downwards, were there not something to hinder them: now if there be any such thing, this must be the Soul, which is also the Cause of Nourishment and Augmentation.*[59] Where the Philosopher adds, that though some were of

[59] *De anima*, II, 4.

Opinion, that Fire was that which was the Cause of Nourishment and Augmentation in Animals, yet this was indeed but συναίτιον πῶς, οὐ μὴν ἁπλῶς γε αἴτιον, ἀλλὰ μᾶλλον ἡ ψυχὴ, *only the Concause or Instrument, and not simply the Cause, but rather the Soul.*[60] And to the same purpose he philosophizeth elsewhere, οὐδὲ γὰρ ἡ πέψις δι' ἧς ἡ τροφὴ γίνεται τοῖς ζώοις οὔτε ἄνευ ψυχῆς, οὔτε θερμότητός ἐστι, πυρὶ γὰρ ἐργάζεται πάντα· *Neither is Concoction by which Nourishment is made in Animals done without the Soul, nor without Heat, for all things are done by Fire.*[61]

And certainly it seems very agreeable to the *Phænomena*, to acknowledge something in the Bodies of Animals Superiour to Mechanism, as that may well be thought to be, which keeps the more fluid parts of them constantly in the same Form and Figure, so as not to be enormously altered in their Growth by disproportionate nourishment; that which restores Flesh that was lost, consolidates dissolved Continuities, Incorporates the newly received Nourishment, and joyns it Continuously with the preexistent parts of Flesh and Bone; which regenerates and repairs Veins consumed or cut off; which causes Dentition in so regular a manner, and that not only in Infants, but also Adult persons; that which casts off Excrements and dischargeth Superfluities; which makes things seem ungrateful to an Interiour Sense, that were notwithstanding pleasing to the Taste. That Nature of *Hippocrates*, that is the Curatrix of Diseases, αἱ φύσιες τῶν νουσέων ἰητροὶ,[62] and that *Archeus* of the Chymists or Paracelsians,[63] to which all Medicaments are but Subservient, as being able to effect nothing of themselves without it. I say, there seems to be such a Principle as this in the Bodies of Animals, which is not *Mechanical* but *Vital*; and therefore since Entities are not to be multiplied without necessity, we may with *Aristotle* conclude it to be μέρος or μόριον τῆς ψυχῆς, *a certain part of the Soul* of those Animals, or a Lower Inconscious Power lodged in them.

23. Besides this Plastick Nature which is in Animals, forming their several Bodies Artificially, as so many Microcosms or *Little Worlds*, there must be also a general Plastick Nature in the *Macrocosm* the whole Corporeal Universe, that which makes all things thus to conspire every where, and agree together into one Harmony. Concerning which *Plastick Nature* of the Universe, the Author [of] *de Mundo* writes after this manner, καὶ τὸν ὅλον κόσμον διεκόσμησε μία ἡ διὰ

---

[60] *De anima*, II, 4.
[62] Hippocrates, *Epid.*, VI. 5.

[61] *De respiratione*, VIII.
[63] See above, p. 297 and note.

πάντων διήκουσα δύναμις, *One Power passing thorough all things, ordered and formed the whole World.*[64] Again he calls the same πνεῦμα, καὶ ἔμψυχον, καὶ γόνιμον οὐσίαν, *a Spirit, and a Living and Generative Nature*,[65] and plainly declares it, to be a thing distinct from the *Deity*, but Subordinate to it and dependent on it. But *Aristotle* himself in that genuine Work of his before mentioned, speaks clearly and positively concerning this Plastick Nature of the Universe, as well as that of Animals, in these words, φαίνεται γὰρ ὥσπερ ἐν τοῖς τεχναστοῖς ἡ τέχνη, οὕτως ἐν αὐτοῖς τοῖς πράγμασιν ἄλλη τις ἀρχὴ καὶ αἰτία τοιαύτη ἦν ἔχομεν, καθάπερ τὸ θερμὸν καὶ τὸ ψυχρὸν ἐκ τοῦ παντός· διὸ μᾶλλον εἰκὸς τὸν οὐρανὸν γεγενῆσθαι ὑπὸ τοιαύτης αἰτίας, εἰ γέγονε, καὶ εἶναι διὰ τοιαύτην αἰτίαν μᾶλλον, ἢ τὰ ζῶα τὰ θνητά· τὸ γοῦν τεταγμένον καὶ ὡρισμένον πολὺ μᾶλλον φαίνεται ἐν τοῖς οὐρανίοις, ἢ περὶ ἡμᾶς· τὸ δὲ ἄλλοτε ἄλλως, καὶ ὡς ἔτυχε, περὶ τὰ θνητὰ μᾶλλον· οἱ δὲ τῶν μὲν ζώων ἕκαστον φύσει φασιν εἶναι καὶ γενέσθαι· τὸν δ' οὐρανὸν ἀπό τύχης καὶ τοῦ αὐτομάτου τοιοῦτον συστῆναι, ἐν ᾧ ἀπὸ τύχης καὶ ἀταξίας οὐδ' ὁτιοῦν φαίνεται· *It seemeth, that as there is Art in Artificial things, so in the things of Nature, there is another such like Principle or Cause, which we our selves partake of; in the same manner as we do of Heat and Cold, from the Universe. Wherefore it is more probable that the whole World was at first made by such a Cause as this (if at least it were made) and that it is still conserved by the same, than that Mortal Animals should be so: For there is much more of Order and determinate Regularity, in the Heavenly Bodies than in our selves; but more of Fortuitousness and inconstant Regularity among these Mortal things. Notwithstanding which, some there are, who, though they cannot but acknowledge that the Bodies of Animals were all framed by an Artificial Nature, yet they will needs contend that the system of the Heavens sprung merely from Fortune and Chance; although there be not the least appearance of Fortuitousness or Temerity in it.*[66] And then he sums up all into this Conclusion, ὥστε εἶναι φανερὸν ὅτι ἔστι τι τιοῦτον ὃ δὴ καὶ καλοῦμεν φύσιν. *Wherefore it is manifest, that there is some such thing as that which we call Nature,*[67] that is, that there is not only an *Artificial, Methodical* and *Plastick Nature in Animals*, by which their respective Bodies are framed and conserved; but also that there is such a *General Nature* likewise in the *Universe*, by which the Heavens and whole World are thus Artificially Ordered and Disposed.

[64] Pseudo-Aristotle, *De mundo*, V. On this work see above, Note 7.
[65] *Ibid*., IV.   [66] *De partibus animalium*, I, 1.   [67] *Ibid*.

24. Now whereas *Aristotle* in the forecited Words, tell us, that we partake of Life and Understanding, from that in the Universe, after the same manner as we partake of Heat and Cold, from that Heat and Cold that is in the Universe; It is observable, that this was a Notion borrowed from *Socrates*; (as we understand both from *Xenophon* and *Plato*) that Philosopher having used it as an Argumentation to prove a Deity. And the Sence of it is represented after this manner by the Latin Poet;

> *Principio Cœlum ac Terram, Camposque Liquentis,*
> *Lucentémque Globum Lunæ, Titaniáque Astra,*
> *Spiritus intus alit, totamque Infusa per Artus,*
> *Mens agitat Molem, & Magno se Corpore miscet.*
> *Inde Hominum Pecudúmque Genus, Vitæque Volantûm.*[68]

From whence it may be collected, that *Aristotle* did suppose, this *Plastick Nature* of the *Universe* to be, ἢ μέρος ψυχῆς, ἢ μὴ ἄνευ ψυχῆς, *Either Part of some Mundane Soul*, that was also Conscious and Intellectual, (as that Plastick Nature in Animals is) *or at least some Inferiour Principle, depending on such a Soul*. And indeed whatever the Doctrine of the modern Peripateticks be, we make no doubt at all, but that *Aristotle* himself held the Worlds Animation, or a Mundane Soul; Forasmuch as he plainly declares himself concerning it, elsewhere in his Book *De Cælo*, after this manner; ἀλλ' ἡμεῖς ὡς περὶ σωμάτων μόνον αὐτῶν, καὶ μονάδων, τάξιν μὲν ἐχόντων, ἀψύχων δὲ πάμπαν, διανοούμεθα· δεῖ δὲ ὡς μετεχόντων ὑπολαμβάνειν πράξεως καὶ ζωῆς· *But we commonly think of the Heavens, as nothing else but Bodies and Monads, having only a certain Order, but altogether inanimate; whereas we ought on the contrary to conceive of them, as partaking of Life, and Action:*[69] that is, as being endued with a Rational or Intellectual Life. For so *Simplicius* there rightly expounds the place, δεῖ δὲ ὡς περὶ ἐμψύχων αὐτῶν συλλογίζεσθαι, καὶ λογικὴν ἐχόντων ψυχὴν, ὡς καὶ πράξεως καὶ ζωῆς λογικῆς μετέχειν· τὸ μὲν γὰρ ποιεῖν, καὶ κατὰ τῶν ἀλόγων ψυχῶν κατηγοροῦμεν, καὶ κατὰ τῶν ἀψύχων σωμάτων, τὸ δὲ πράττειν κυρίως κατὰ τῶν λογικῶν ψυχῶν κατηγοροῦμεν· *But we ought*

---

[68] *Aeneid*, VI, 724–8: 'First of all, heaven and earth and the liquid fields, the shining part of the moon and the Titanian star, doth a spirit sustain inly, and a soul shed abroad in them sways all their members and mingles in the mighty frame. Thence is the generation of man and beast, the life of winged things...'

[69] *De caelo*, II, 12.

The Plastick Life of Nature 319

to think of the Heavens, as Animated with a Rational Soul, and thereby partaking of Action and Rational Life. For (saith he) though ποιεῖν be affirmed not only of Irrational Souls, but also of Inanimate Bodies, yet the word πράττειν does only denominate Rational Beings.[70] But further, to take away all manner of scruple or doubt, concerning this business; that Philosopher before in the same Book, ῥητῶς affirmeth ὅτι ὁ οὐρανὸς ἔμψυχος, καὶ ἀρχὴν κινήσεως ἔχει, That the Heaven is Animated, and hath a Principle of Motion within it self: Where by the Heaven as in many other places of Aristotle and Plato, is to be understood the Whole World.

There is indeed One Passage in the same Book De Cælo, which at first sight, and slightly considered, may seem to contradict this again, and therefore probably is that, which hath led many into a contrary Perswasion, that Aristotle denied the Worlds Animation, ἀλλὰ μὴν οὐδ᾽ ὑπὸ ψυχῆς εὔλογον ἀναγκαζούσης μένειν ἀΐδιον· οὐδὲ γὰρ τῆς ψυχῆς οἷόν τ᾽ εἶναι τὴν τοιαύτην ζωὴν ἄλυπον καὶ μακαρίαν· ἀνάγκη γὰρ καὶ τὴν κίνησιν μετὰ βίας οὖσαν, πεφυκότος τοῦ πρώτου σώματος ἄλλως κινεῖν συνεχῶς, ἄσχολον εἶναι, καὶ πάσης ἀπηλλαγμένην ῥαστώνης ἔμφρονος· εἴ γε μηδ᾽ ὥσπερ, τῇ ψυχῇ τῇ τῶν θνητῶν ζώων ἐστὶν ἀνάπαυσις ἡ περὶ τὸν ὕπνον γινομένη τοῦ σώματος ἄνεσις, ἀλλ᾽ ἀναγκαῖον Ἰξίονός τινος μοῖραν κατέχειν αὐτὴν ἀΐδιον καὶ ἄτρυτον. But it is not reasonable neither, to think that the Heavens continue to Eternity, moved by a Soul necessitating, or violently compelling them. Nor indeed is it possible, that the Life of such a Soul should be pleasurable or happy. Forasmuch as the continual Violent Motion of a Body (naturally inclining to move another way) must needs be a very unquiet thing, and void of all Mental Repose; especially when there is no such Relaxation, as the Souls of Mortal Animals have by sleep; and therefore such a Soul of the World as this, must of necessity be condemned to an Eternal Ixionian Fate.[71] But in these Words Aristotle does not deny the Heavens to be moved by a Soul of their own, (which is positively affirmed by him elsewhere) but only by such a Soul, as should Violently and Forcibly agitate, or drive them round, contrary to their own Natural Inclination, whereby in the mean time, they tended downwards of themselves towards the Centre. And his sence, concerning the Motion of the Heavens, is truly represented by Simplicius in this manner, τὸ δέ ὅλον φύσικον καὶ ἔμψυχον, ὑπὸ ψυχῆς κυρίως κινεῖται, διὰ μέσης τῆς φύσεως· The whole World or Heaven, being as well a natural, as an Animalish Body, is

---

[70] Arist. Cael., II.   [71] De caelo, II, 1.

*moved properly by Soul, but yet by means of Nature also, as an Instrument, so that the Motion of it is not Violent.*⁷² But whereas *Aristotle* there insinuates, as if *Plato* had held the Heavens to be moved, by a Soul violently, contrary to their Nature; *Simplicius*, though sufficiently addicted to *Aristotle*, ingenuously acknowledges his Error herein, and vindicating *Plato* from that Imputation, shews how he likewise held a Plastick Nature, as well as a Mundane Soul; but that amongst his Ten Instances of Motion,⁷³ the Ninth is that of Nature, τὴν ἕτερον ἀεὶ κινοῦσαν, καὶ μεταβαλλομένην ὑφ' ἑτέρου· *that which always moves another, being it self changed by something else;* as the Tenth, that of the Mundane Soul, τὴν ἑαυτὴν κινοῦσαν καὶ ἕτερα, *that which originally both moves it self and other things:* as if his Meaning in that place were, That though Nature be a Life and Internal Energy, yet it acts Subserviently to a Higher Soul, as the First Original Mover.

But the Grand Objection against *Aristotle's* holding the *Worlds Animation*, is still behind; namely from that in his *Metaphysicks*, where he determines the Highest Starry Heaven, to be moved by an *Immoveable Mover*, commonly supposed to be the Deity it self, and no Soul of the World; and all the other Spheres likewise to be moved by so many *Separate Intelligencies*, and not by *Souls*.⁷⁴ To which we reply, that indeed *Aristotle's First Immoveable Mover* is no *Mundane Soul*, but an *Abstract Intellect Separate from Matter*, and the very Deity it self; whose manner of moving the Heavens is thus described by him, κινεῖ δὲ ὡς ἐρώμενον, *It Moveth only as being Loved:*⁷⁵ wherefore besides this *Supreme Unmoved Mover*, that Philosopher supposed another Inferiour Moved Mover also, that is, a *Mundane Soul*, as the Proper and Immediate *Efficient Cause* of the Heavenly Motions; of which he speaks after this manner, κινούμενον δὲ τἄλλα κινεῖ, *that which it self being moved*, (objectively, or by Appetite and Desire of the First Good) *moveth other things*.⁷⁶ And thus that safe and sure-footed Interpreter, *Alex. Aphrodisius*, expounds his Masters Meaning; That the *Heaven* being *Animated*, and therefore indeed Moved by an *Internal Principle* of its own, is notwithstanding Originally moved by a certain Immoveable and Separate Nature, which is above Soul, τῷ νοεῖν τε αὐτό, καὶ ἔφεσιν καὶ ὄρεξιν ἔχειν τῆς ὁμοιώσεως αὐτοῦ, *both by its contemplating of it, and having an Appetite and Desire*, of

---

⁷² *Arist. Cael.*, II.
⁷⁴ Cf. *Metaphysica*, XII, 8.
⁷⁶ *Ibid.*
⁷³ Plato, *Leges*, X, 893 ff.
⁷⁵ *Ibid.*, XII, 7.

*assimilating it self thereunto.*⁷⁷ *Aristotle* seeming to have borrowed this Notion from *Plato*,⁷⁸ who makes the Constant Regular Circumgyration of the Heavens, to be an Imitation of the Motion or Energy of *Intellect*. So that *Aristotle's First Mover*, is not properly the *Efficient*, but only the *Final* and *Objective* Cause, of the Heavenly Motions, the Immediate Efficient Cause thereof being ψυχὴ καὶ φύσις, *Soul and Nature*.

Neither may this be Confuted from those other *Aristotelick Intelligences* of the Lesser Orbs; that Philosopher conceiving in like manner concerning them, that they were also the *Abstract Minds* or *Intellects* of certain other inferiour Souls, which moved their several Respective Bodies or Orbs, Circularly and Uniformly, in a kind of Imitation of them. For this plainly appears from hence, in that he affirms of these his *Inferiour Intelligences* likewise as well as of the *Supreme Mover*, that they do κινεῖν ὡς τέλος, *Move only as the end*.

Where it is Evident, that though *Aristotle* did plainly suppose a *Mundane Intellectual Soul*, such as also conteined, either in it, or under it, a *Plastick Nature*, yet he did not make either of these to be the *Supreme Deity*; but resolved the First Principle of things, to be *One Absolutely Perfect Mind* or *Intellect, Separate from Matter*, which was ἀκίνητος οὐσία, *an Immoveable Nature*,⁷⁹ whose *Essence was his Operation*, and which Moved only as being *Loved*, or as the *Final Cause*: of which he pronounces in this manner, ὅτι ἐκ τοιαύτης ἀρχῆς ἤρτηται ὁ οὐρανὸς καὶ ἡ φύσις, *That upon such a Principle as this, Heaven and Nature depends*;⁸⁰ that is, the *Animated Heaven*, or *Mundane Soul*, together with the *Plastick Nature* of the Universe, must of necessity depend upon such an Absolutely Perfect, and Immoveable *Mind* or *Intellect*.

Having now declared the *Aristotelick Doctrine* concerning the *Plastick Nature* of the Universe, with which the *Platonick* also agrees, that it is, ἢ μέρος ψυχῆς, ἢ μὴ ἄνευ ψυχῆς, *either Part of a Mundane Intellectual Soul*, (that is a Lower Power and Faculty of it) *or else not without it, but some inferior thing depending on it*; we think fit to add in this place, that though there were no such *Mundane Soul*, as both *Plato* and *Aristotle* supposed, distinct from the *Supreme Deity*, yet there might notwithstanding be a *Plastick Nature* of the Universe, depending immediately upon the *Deity it self*. For the *Plastick Nature*

---

⁷⁷ Alexander Aphrodisaeus, I, 1.
⁷⁸ *Leges*, X, 897 ff.
⁷⁹ Adapted from *Metaphysica*, XII, 6–7.
⁸⁰ *Metaphysica*, XII, 7.

essentially depends upon *Mind* or *Intellect*, and could not possibly be without it; according to those words before cited, ἐκ τοιαύτης ἀρχῆς ἤρτηται ἡ φύσις, *Nature depends upon such an Intellectual Principle*;[81] and for this Cause that Philosopher does elsewhere joyn νοῦς and φύσις, *Mind* and *Nature* both together.[82]

25. Besides this *General Plastick Nature* of the Universe, and those *Particular Plastick Powers* in the *Souls of Animals*, it is not impossible but that there may be other Plastick Natures also (as certain Lower Lives, or Vegetative Souls) in some Greater Parts of the Universe; all of them depending, if not upon some higher Conscious Soul, yet at least upon a Perfect Intellect, presiding over the whole. As for Example; Though it be not reasonable to think, that every Plant, Herb and Pile of Grass, hath a Particular Life, or Vegetative Soul of its own, distinct from the Mechanism of the Body; nor that the whole Earth is an Animal endued with a Conscious Soul: yet there may possibly be, for ought we know, one Plastick Nature or Life, belonging to the whole Terrestrial (or Terraqueous) Globe, by which all Plants and Vegetables, continuous with it, may be differently formed, according to their different Seeds, as also Minerals and other Bodies framed, and whatsoever else is above the Power of Fortuitous Mechanism effected, as by the Immediate Cause, though always Subordinate to other Causes, the chief whereof is the Deity. And this perhaps may ease the Minds of those, who cannot but think it too much, to impose all upon one Plastick Nature of the Universe.

26. And now we have finished, our First Task, which was to give an Accompt of the *Plastick Nature*, the Sum whereof briefly amounts to this; That it is a certain *Lower Life* than the *Animal*, which acts *Regularly* and *Artificially*, according to the Direction of *Mind* and *Understanding*, *Reason* and *Wisdom*, for *Ends*, or in Order to *Good*, though it self do not know the Reason of what it does, nor is *Master* of that Wisdom according to which it acts only a *Servant* to it, and *Drudging Executioner* of the same; it operating *Fatally* and *Sympathetically*, according to *Laws* and *Commands*, prescribed to it by a *Perfect Intellect*, and imprest upon it; and which is either a *Lower* Faculty of some *Conscious Soul*, or else an Inferiour kind of Life or *Soul* by it self; but essentially depending upon an *Higher Intellect*.

We procede to our *Second Undertaking*; which was to shew, how grossly those Two Sorts of *Atheists* before mentioned, the *Stoical* or

---

[81] Quoted more fully above, p. 321.
[82] As in the passage quoted above, p. 295.

The Plastick Life of Nature   323

Cosmo-plastick, and the *Stratonical* or *Hylozoick*,[83] both of them acknowledging this *Plastick Life of Nature*, do mistake the Notion of it, or Pervert it and Abuse it, to make a certain Spurious and Counterfeit God-Almighty of it, (or a *First Principle* of all things) thereby excluding the True Omnipotent Deity, which is a *Perfect Mind*, or *Consciously Understanding Nature*, presiding over the Universe; they substituting this Stupid *Plastick Nature* in the room of it.

Now the Chief Errors or Mistakes of these Atheists concerning the *Plastick Nature*, are there *Four* following. First, that they make that to be the *First Principle* of all, and the *Highest thing* in the Universe, which is the *Last* and *Lowest* of all *Lives*; a thing Essentially *Secondary*, *Derivative* and *Dependent*. For the *Plastick Life of Nature* is but the mere *Umbrage* of *Intellectuality*, a faint and shadowy *Imitation* of *Mind* and *Understanding*; upon which it doth as Essentially depend, as the Shadow doth upon the Body, the Image in the Glass upon the Face, or the Eccho upon the Original Voice. So that if there had been no *Perfect Mind* or *Intellect* in the World, there could no more have been any *Plastick Nature* in it, than there could be an *Image in the Glass* without a *Face*, or an *Eccho* without an *Original Voice*. If there be Φύσις, then there must be, Νοῦς, if there be a *Plastick Nature*, that acts *Regularly* and *Artificially* in Order to Ends, and according to the *Best Wisdom*, though it self not comprehending the reason of it, nor being clearly Conscious of what it doth; then there must of necessity be a *Perfect Mind* or *Intellect*, that is, a *Deity* upon which it depends. Wherefore *Aristotle* does like a Philosopher in joyning Φύσις and Νοῦς, *Nature* and *Mind* both together; but these *Atheists* do very Absurdly and Unphilosophically, that would make a *Sensless* and *Inconscious Plastick Nature*, and therefore without any *Mind* or *Intellect*, to be the *First Original* of all things.

Secondly, these Atheists augment the Former Error, in supposing those Higher *Lives* of *Sense* or *Animality*, and of *Reason* or *Understanding*, to rise both of them from that Lower Sensless *Life of Nature*,

---

[83] Two of the four principal forms of atheism distinguished by Cudworth earlier (*Int. System*, pp. 107 ff., 131 ff.). All four were said to involve, in one sense or another, a belief in Body, Matter, *Hyle* of some sort. Thus Cosmoplastic Atheism 'supposes one kind of *Plastick* and *Spermatick*, *Methodical* and *Artificial* Nature, but without any Sense or Conscious Understanding, to preside over the whole World'. Hylozoic Atheism acknowledges 'no other Deity than a certain Stupid and Plastic Life, in all the several parts of Matter, without Sense'.

as the only *Original Fundamental Life*. Which is a thing altogether as Irrational and Absurd, as if one should suppose the Light that is in the Air or *Æther*, to be the *Only Original* and *Fundamental Light*, and the Light of the Sun and Stars but a *Secondary* and *Derivative* thing from it, and nothing but the Light of the Air *Modificated* and *Improved* by *Condensation*. Or as if one should maintain that the Sun and Moon, and all the Stars, were really nothing else, but the mere *Reflections* of those *Images* that we see in Rivers and Ponds of Water. But this hath always been the Sottish Humour and Guise of *Atheists*, to invert the Order of the Universe, and hang the Picture of the World, as of a Man, with its Heels upwards. *Conscious Reason* and *Understanding*, being a far higher Degree of Life and Perfection, than that *Dull Plastick Nature*, which does only *Do*, but not *Know*, can never possibly emerge out of it; neither can the *Duplication* of *Corporeal Organs* be ever able to advance that *Simple* and *Stupid Life* of *Nature* into *Redoubled Consciousness* or *Self-perception*; nor any *Triplication* or indeed *Milleclupation*[84] of them, improve the same into *Rea[son* and] *Understanding*.

Thirdly; for the better Colouring of the Former Errors, the *Hylozoists* adulterate the *Notion* of the *Plastick Life of Nature*, confounding it with *Wisdom* and *Understanding*. And though themselves acknowledge, that no *Animal-sense*, *self-perception* and *Consciousness* belongs to it, yet they will have it to be a thing *Perfectly Wise*, and consequently every Atom of Sensless Matter that is in the whole World, to be *Infallibly Omniscient*, as to all its own *Capacities* and *Congruities*, or whatsoever it self can *Do* or *Suffer*; which is plainly Contradictious. For though there may be such a thing as the *Plastick Nature*, that according to the Former Description of it, can *Do* without *Knowing*, and is devoid of *Express Consciousness* or *Self-perception*, yet *Perfect Knowledge* and *Understanding* without *Consciousness*, is Non-sence and Impossibility. Wherefore this must needs be condemned for a great piece of Sottishness, in the *Hylozoick Atheists*, that they attribute *Perfect Wisdom* and *Understanding* to a *Stupid Inconscious Nature*, which is nothing but χειροτέχνης,[85] the mere *Drudging Instrument*, or *Manuary Opificer* of *Perfect Mind*.

Lastly, these Atheists err in this, that they make this *Plastick Life of Nature*, to be a mere *Material* or *Corporeal thing*; whereas Matter

---

[84] Actually, 'millecuplation': a thousand-fold increase.
[85] Cf. above, p. 303.

or Body cannot move it self, much less therefore can it *Artificially* order and dispose its own Motion. And though the *Plastick Nature* be indeed the Lowest of all *Lives*, yet notwithstanding since it is a *Life*, or *Internal Energy*, and *Self-activity*, distinct from *Local Motion*, it must needs be *Incorporeal*, all *Life* being Essentially such. But the Hylozoists conceive grossly both of *Life* and *Understanding*, spreading them all over upon Matter, just as Butter is spread upon Bread, or Plaster upon a Wall, and accordingly slicing them out, in different Quantities and Bulks, together with it; they contending that they are but *Inadequate Conceptions* of Body, as the only Substance; and consequently concluding, that the Vulgarly received *Notion of God*, is nothing else but such an *Inadequate Conception of the Matter* of the Whole Corporeal Universe, mistaken for a Complete and Entire Substance by it self, that is supposed to be the Cause of all things. Which fond Dream or Dotage of theirs, will be further confuted in due place. But it is now time to put a Period, to this long (but necessary) *Digression*, concerning the *Plastic Life of Nature*, or an *Artificial, Orderly* and *Methodical Nature*.

Appendix

BENJAMIN WHICHCOTE

Moral and Religious Aphorisms*

4. If there be no Knowledge, there is no *Beginning* of Religion; if there be no Goodness, there is no *Sincerity* of Religion; but a Contradiction to it; by *'holding the Truth in Unrighteousness'*.[1]

20. Where there is all Perfection in Conjunction, there is no place for any *Uncertainty*, or Unconstancy: Resolution and Performance, in Agents of any perfection, go *always* with the Reason of the thing.

24. There is a natural Propension in every thing, to *return* to its true state; if by violence it has been disturbed: should it not to be so in Grace, in the divine life? Virtue is the health, true state, natural complexion of the Soul: he, that is Vicious in his practice, is *diseased* in his mind.

28. When the Principles of our Religion become the *Temper* of our Spirits, then we are truly religious; and the only way to make them become so, is, to reason ourselves into an Approbation of them: for nothing, which is the Reason of Things, can be refused by the Reason of Man; when understood.

33. The *Rule* of Right is, the Reason of Things; the *Judgment* of Right is, the Reason of our Minds, *perceiving* the Reason of things.

36. Men have an itch; rather to *make* Religion, than to *use* it: but we are to *use* our Religion; not to make it.

39. Believe *Things*, rather than *Men*.

42. Man, *as Man*, is Averse to what is Evil and Wicked; for *Evil* is unnatural, and *Good* is connatural, to Man.

---

* From *Moral and Religious Aphorisms*, as revised by Samuel Salter (1753) from the edition by John Jeffery (1703).

[1] Cf. the text of the sermon above, pp. 42 ff., and see further below: §§ 169, 219, 281, etc.

48. There is no solid Satisfaction; but in a mental Reconciliation with the Nature of God, and the Law of righteousness.

53. He that never *changed* any of his opinions, never *corrected* any of his Mistakes: and He, who was never *wise* enough, to find out any mistakes in Himself; will not be *charitable* enough, to excuse what he reckons mistakes in Others.

62. The *Government* of our Spirits, is the greatest *Freedom.*

71. There is nothing proper and *peculiar* to Man; but the Use of Reason and Exercise of Virtue.

76. To go against *Reason*, is to go against *God*: it is the self same thing, to do that which the Reason of the Case doth require; and that which God Himself doth appoint: Reason is the *Divine* Governor of Man's Life; it is the very Voice of God.

84. The right of the case *is* the Law of heaven; and *should be* the law of the World.

87. *Religion* makes us live like Men: To do nothing, that will either sink us into Beasts; or transform us into Devils: An Intemperance and Sensuality make us Beasts; so Pride and Malice make us Devils.[2]

99. Reason *discovers*, what is Natural; and Reason *receives*, what is Supernatural.

100. Both *Heaven* and *Hell* have their Foundation *within Us.* *Heaven* primarily lies in a refined Temper; in an internal Reconciliation to the Nature of God, and to the Rule of Righteousness. The Guilt of Conscience, and Enmity to Righteousness, is the *inward* state of *Hell*. The Guilt of Conscience is the *Fewel of Hell*.[3]

109. God hath set up *Two Lights*; to enlighten us in our Way: the Light of *Reason*, which is the Light of his Creation; and the Light of *Scripture*, which is After-Revelation from him. Let us make use of these two Lights; and suffer neither to be put out.[4]

114. Nothing spoils human Nature more, than false Zeal. The *Good*

---

[2] Cf. Whichcote, *Sermons*, p. 430: 'By our *RELIGION*, we are preserved from those things that would sink us into the order of Beasts; by *Sensuality*, and *Carnal-Mindedness*: or that would transform us into the Likeness of Devils by *Pride, Presumption*, and *Self-conceit.*' The same note is sounded throughout, for instance above, p. 72, and below: §§ 87, 253.

[3] For Whichcote's other formulation of this basic tenet, see above, p. 46. Cf. below, §282.

[4] See Smith's exposition of this widespread idea, above, pp. 150 ff. But it is also implicit in two of Whichcote's sermons reprinted here (above, pp. 42 ff., 77 ff.).

Nature of an Heathen is more God-like, than the furious *Zeal* of a Christian.⁵

116. Good and Evil are not by *positive* Institution;⁶ are not things *arbitrary*; or during any Pleasure whatsoever: but Just Right and Holy, Wicked Impious and Profane, are so by their own nature and quality. If we understand this, as we ought; we abide in the Truth: if not, we are Self-flatterers; and live in a Lye. Things are, as they are; whether we *think* so or not: and we shall be judged by things as they be; not by our own presumptuous Imaginations.

129. For Contradiction to his *Reason*, a Man is challenged now; and will be condemned, at the great day of Judgment. It is the Reason of Things, and of our Minds, not the Power of God only, which condemns. *Fear thyself*; for thou art in more danger of being Condemned by the *Reason* of thy *Mind*, than of any Power whatsoever, of God or Man.

133. *Wickedness* doth as naturally make us miserable; as it makes us *unlike* to the most Happy Being. As *God* is Holy, and Happy; so *We* must be like him in *Holiness*, that we may be *Happy*. God's *infinite* Goodness makes him *completely* Happy: the degree of our Happiness holds *proportion* to the measure of our Goodness.

155. Had not *Infinite Goodness* been the Law of Heaven; there had never been any other Being, but God.

160. To be *Intemperate*, destroys the Individual; To be *Unrighteous*, dissolves the Community; To be *Impious*, denies God; cuts off from the Original, clips off the Sun beams. Would we neither *be* ourselves; nor have ought else to *be*?

169. Religion *begins* in Knowledge; *Procedes* in Practice; and *Ends* in Happiness.

172. To *Know* the Difference of Right and Wrong, speaks our *Wisdom*; to *Observe* that Difference, speaks our *Goodness*.

178. Govern thyself from *within*.

184. Man in this State *is not*, as he *should* be; because of Non-use, and Mis-use, and Abuse of Himself: of some one of which Every one is more or less Guilty.⁷

216. It is impossible for a Man to be made Happy, by putting him into a Happy *Place*; unless he be first in a Happy *State*.

⁵ See also above, p. 43 and note. Cf. Whichcote, *Discourses*, III, 51 ff.; and below: §§ 349, 499, 1182.

⁶ Cf. above, p. 50.

⁷ The statement also occurs *verbatim* in Whichcote, *Discourses*, II, 36.

219. The *first* act of Religion, is to *Know* what is True of God; the *second* act is to *Express* it in our Lives.[8]

221. The *Moral* part of Religion never alters. Moral Laws are Laws *of themselves*, without Sanction by Will; and the Necessity of them arises from the Things themselves.[9] All *other* things in Religion are *in Order to* These. The Moral Part of Religion does *sanctify* the Soul; and is *Final* both to what is Instrumental and Instituted.

232. The Unrighteous are condemned by *themselves*; before they are condemned of *God*.[10]

233. Complain not of *Nature*: for Nature (to them that use it *well*, possess it with it's *right* temper) is Sovereign to Man, Inclinable to Virtue, and Conservative thereof.

241. Virtue has *Reward*, and Vice has *Punishment*, arising out of itself.

246. If, through the Help of God, we do not Alienate our selves from the Things of the world; the Things of the world will certainly Alienate us from God.

248. We *Worship* God best; when we Resemble Him most.

253. Whosoever doth commit Sin, departeth from the *natural* Use of Himself, his Powers, and Faculties; He sinks below his own Nature: for there is no natural Action so mean; as every sinful Action is. Sin is below any man; Sin is every man's Dishonour.

272. Reason and Virtue are Things that have *Bounds* and Limits: but Vice and Passion have *none*.[11]

281. ... Sinners are made-up of Contradictions: contradictions to Truth and Reason, to God, to themselves, and to one another. *Virtue* is uniform, regular, constant and certain.

282. They, that are *Reconciled* unto God, in the Frame and Temper of their Minds; that Live according to the Law of Heaven (the everlasting and immutable Rule of Goodness, Righteousness and Truth;) may truly be said to have begun *Heaven*, while they are upon the earth: But They, who confound the Difference of good and evil; and who Care not to Approve themselves to God; but act without Difference

---

[8] Cf. Whichcote, *Sermons*, p. 70: 'The *first* Motion of Religion is to understand what is true of God: And the *second* is to express it in our Lives, and to copy it out in our Works. The *Former* is our Wisdom: And the Latter is our Goodness. In these Two consist the Health and Pulchritude of our Minds.'

[9] Cf. above, p. 61 and note.   [10] Cf. above, pp. 44 ff.

[11] The statement also occurs *verbatim* in Whichcote, *Sermons*, pp. 373–4.

or Distinction; *These* are Partakers of the *Devilish Nature*, and are in a Hellish State.

290. We must *now* Naturalize ourselves to the Employment of Eternity.[12]

298. In *Morality*, we are sure as in Mathematics.[13]

322. God doth all to his *own* Honour: He doth take care to Spread his own Nature, and Communicate his own Qualities and Perfections: and, in his Government of the World, Aims at *this*; that his Goodness, Righteousness, and Truth, may prevail every where; and have an *Universal* Empire and Sovereignty, in the Lives of Angels and Men.

338. Religion *in the Subject*, is not a Notion;[14] but the Frame and *Temper* of our Minds, and the *Rule* of our Lives: a man is not well *settled* in his Religion; until it is become the self-same with the *Reason* of his Mind.

341. In Morals it is most true; that every Man hath himself, as He useth Himself: for we work out of ourselves; and no man is *born* with Wisdom and Virtue.

349. Enthusiasm is the Confounder, both of Reason and Religion: therefore nothing is more necessary to the Interest of *Religion*, than the prevention of *Enthusiasm*.

367. Good men Study to *Spiritualize* their Bodies; Bad men do *Incarnate* their Souls.

369. Let all the strife of men be, who shall *Do Best*; who shall *Be Least*.[15]

375. Let not a man's *Self* be to him all in all.[16]

393. I have always found; that such *Preaching* of Others hath most commanded my *Heart*, which hath most illuminated my Head.

397. What is *Morally* Filthy, should be Equivalent to what is *Naturally* Impossible: we *should not*, is morally we *can not*.

401. The Law of Righteousness, is the Law of God's Nature, and the Law of His Actions.

457. There is nothing so intrinsically Rational, as *Religion* is;

---

[12] For a variant of this idea, see Whichcote, *Discourses*, I, 90 (quoted above, p. 41).

[13] See above, Introduction, p. 12 and note.

[14] On 'notions', good and bad, see above, p. 66 and note.

[15] Cf. below, §§ 925, 927.

[16] Cf. below, §§ 653, 675, 911, 987, and the censures of 'self-will' by Cudworth and Smith, above, .pp 98 ff. and 161 ff.

nothing, that can so Justify it self; nothing, that hath so pure Reason to recommend itself; as Religion hath.

460. Reason is not a shallow thing: it is the *first* Participation from God: therefore he, that observes Reason, observes God.

464. Heaven is *first* a Temper, and *then* a Place.

480. Better have no Confidence, than Self-Confidence.

499. The more *False* any one is in his Religion, the more *Fierce* and furious in Maintaining it; the more Mistaken, the more Imposing: The more any man's religion is *his own*, the more he is concerned for it; but cool and indifferent enough for that which is God's.

500. The longest Sword, the strongest Lungs, the most Voices, are false measures of Truth.[17]

509. If Evil be looked into, it will be Ashamed of itself.

530. We are no more than *Second* Causes; and our *Sufficiency* is only in *God*, who is the First. A Second Cause is no Cause, divided from the First.

541. Nothing is the *true Improvement* of our Rational Faculties; but the Exercise of the several *Virtues* of Sobriety, Modesty, Gentleness, Humility, Obedience to God, and Charity to Men.

559. As *Good*, doth *That*, in all cases; which is Just, Right and Good; so doth He require of *Us* nothing, but what is Just, Fit, Right, and Good.[18]

561. The *Law of Nature* is that, which is Reason; which is Right and Fit. *Will* stands for nothing, in disjunction from Reason, and Right: and our Apprehensions of Right are Regulated by the *Nature of Things*. To give *Will* or *Power* for Reason, is contrary to Reason. Will is no *Rule*, no *Justification* of any thing.

563. He is *Weak*; that cannot *Judge* what is the Right of the Case: and he is *Wicked*; that, for ends and purposes, will *vary* from it.

569. It is better for us, that there shou'd be *Difference* of Judgement; if we keep *Charity*: but it is most unmanly to *Quarrel*, because we differ.[19]

---

[17] A significant exception—also echoed by Smith (*Discourses*, p. 64)—to any attempt to seek truth in universally-held 'common ideas'. It neatly undercuts, for instance, the thesis of Lord Herbert of Cherbury in *De veritate* (Paris, 1624).

[18] The statement also occurs *verbatim* in Whichcote, *Discourses*, I, 381, but it is of course a commonplace of Cambridge Platonism.

[19] Cf. above, pp. 80 ff.

570. Let Him, that is assured, he Errs in *nothing*; take upon him to condemn *every* man, that Errs in *any* thing.

586. There are but *Two* things in Religion: Morals and Institutions: Morals may be known, by the *Reason* of the Thing; Morals are owned, as soon as spoken; and they are nineteen parts in twenty, of all Religion. Institutions depend upon *Scripture*; and no one Institution depends upon *one* Text of Scripture only: That Institution, which has *but one* Text for it, has *never a one*.

594. We are made-up of *two* parts, Soul and Body; and are under a twofold Obligation to ourselves: 1. to improve, refine, and settle our *Minds*, by moral Principles; 2. to preserve and subordinate our *Bodies*, as the habitation and instrument of the Mind, through Meditation and Temperance.

607. Lord *Verulam*.—Every one almost worships *Idolum Fori*, the Idol of general Imagination: Fools and conceited Persons worship *Idolum Specûs*, the Idol of particular Fancy. It is less to worship *Idolum Fori*; than *Idolum Specûs*; though *Best* to worship Neither.[20]

625. The *Spirit of God* in *us*, is a Living *Law*, Informing the Soul not Constrained by a Law, without, that enlivens not; but we act in the Power of an *inward Principle* of Life, which enables, inclines, facilitates, determines. Our *Nature* is reconciled to the Law of Heaven, the Rule of Everlasting Righteousness, Goodness, and Truth.

644. True *Reason* is so far from being an Enemy to any matter of Faith; that a man is disposed and qualified by Reason, for the entertaining those matters of Faith that are proposed by God.[21]

647. If the *Passions* be not under the government of Reason, the *Man* is under the government of his Passions; and lives as if he had *no* Reason. Passion ungoverned by Reason is *Madness*.

653. Self-will is the greatest *Idol* in the world: it is an Anti-Christ; it is an Anti-God.[22]

659. The *best* Discharge of *Government*, is Government of our selves; and there we *must* Begin.

---

[20] The reference is to Bacon's four classes of 'idols and false notions which are now in possession of the human understanding' (*Works*, IV, 53 ff.). Cf. above, p. 137. On the attitude of the Cambridge Platonists to Bacon, see above, p. 187, note.

[21] Cf. below, § 943.

[22] Cf. Whichcote, *Sermons*, p. 394: 'He that gives way to *Self-will*, is an Enemy of his own Peace, and is the greatest Disturber of the World: He is an *Anti-God*; imposeth upon God himself...' See also below, § 682.

Moral and Religious Aphorisms

675. He that is full of him-*self*, goes out of company as wise as he came in.

679. Universal Charity is a thing *Final* in Religion.[23]

682. *Sin* is an Attempt, to *controul* the immutable and unalterable Laws of everlasting Righteousness, Goodness, and Truth; upon which the Universe depends.

683. None can tell, *what* that man will do; who durst vary from Right: for, by the *same* Authority, that he varies from it in one Instance, he may in all.

712. Religion, which is a Bond of *Union*, ought not to be a Ground of Division: but is in an unnatural use, when it doth disunite. Men cannot *differ*, by *true* Religion; because it is true Religion to *agree*. The Spirit of Religion is a Reconciling Spirit.

713. *Sublime* Knowledge cannot dwell in an *unquiet* Spirit.[24]

747. Nothing more becomes us; than to *know*, what we **are**: *Ignorance* of one's *self* is the cause of *Pride*: and the strength of *Confidence* is the Weakness of *Judgment*.

748. They are the *only* Fools; who are self-conceited, confident. Ignorance and Folly are the *only* things, that *puff* men up.

750. Sin is, in it self, an *ill-natured* thing; a Sinner is an Incendiary, and sets the world on fire.[25]

755. If I have not a Friend, God send me an Enemy: that I may hear of my *Faults*. To be admonished of an Enemy, is *next* to having a Friend.

786. If I can shew a man Argument and Reason; I will convince his Judgment, against his Will.

798. Reverence God in *thyself*: for God is *more* in the *Mind* of Man, than in any part of this world besides; for we (and we *only* here) are made after the Image of God.

811. **Do not think**, God has done any thing concerning Thee; *before* thou camest into Being: whereby thou art determined, either to Sin or Misery. This is a Falsehood: and They, that entertain such thoughts, live in a Lie.

819. He, that takes himself out of God's hands into his own, by-and-by will not know what to do with himself.

---

[23] The occurrence of this statement *verbatim* in one of Whichcote's sermons is noted above, p. 39.

[24] The statement also occurs *verbatim* in Whichcote, *Sermons*, p. 372.

[25] Cf. Whichcote, *Sermons*, p. 145: 'The *Dictates of Reason* calmly guide us: But *Will, Humour, Lust*, and *Passion*, are Incendiary Principles.'

835. The *State* of Religion lies in a good Mind, and a good Life; all else is *about* Religion: and Men must not put the *Instrumental part* of Religion, for the *State* of Religion.

880. Nothing *without* Reason is to be *proposed*; nothing *against* Reason is to be *believed*: Scripture is to be taken in a rational sense.

889. Christian Religion *is not* Mystical, Symbolical, Ænigmatical, Emblematical; but uncloathed, unbodied, intellectual, rational, spiritual.

890. He that Acts *without* Judgment of Reason, will soon Act *contrary* to it.

903. God takes a large Compass, to bring about his *great* Works.

911. Where there is most of *God*, there is least of Self.

916. The *Spirit of a Man is the Candle of the Lord*; Lighted *by* God, and Lighting us *to* God. *Res illuminata, illuminans.*[26]

925. He knows most, who *Does* best.

926. We cannot be Undone, but by our Selves.

927. God expects, Man should *Do*; as He makes him capable.

929. *True* Religion hath done only good in the world: but *Superstition* which is the *Counterfeit* of Religion, hath done the worst and the greatest Mischiefs.

938. *God* is the Object, which does fully exhaust and draw-out, which does *perfectly* exercise and employ, the Faculties of Mind and Understanding.

942. The Reason of a man's Mind *must* be satisfied; no man *can* think against it.[27]

943. A man's *Reason* is no where so much satisfied; as in matters of Faith.

956. Religion doth possess and affect the *whole* man: in the Understanding, it is Knowledge; in the Life, it is Obedience; in the Affections, it is Delight in God; in our Carriage and Behaviour, it is Modesty, Calmness, Gentleness, Quietness, Candor, Ingenuity; in our Dealings, it is Uprightness, Integrity, Correspondence with the Rule of Righteousness: Religion makes men *Virtuous*, in all Instances.

957. Religion has different Denominations and *Names*, from different Actions, and Circumstances; but it is One *thing*, *viz*. Universal Righteousness: accordingly it had place, at *all* times; before the Law of *Moses*, under it, and since.

---

[26] Cf. above, pp. 12 and 50.
[27] Cf. above, §§ 393, 938; and below, § 997.

974. There is no *Fate*; but on our part Reason and Prudence; on God's part Providence: and this Providence, and all *necessary* Help, are as sure and certain; as the Existence and Perfections of God.

981. Determinations, *beyond* Scripture, have indeed *enlarged* Faith; but lessened *Charity*, and multiplied Divisions.[28]

987. None so Empty, as those; who are Full of *themselves*.

997. They have a Reason for it, which the Apostle had not; who *reject* the *Use* of *Reason* in matters of Religion: but we *must* be *Men*, before we *can* be *Christians*.

1004. We are not Men, so much by bodily Shape; as by Principles of Reason and Understanding: wherefore those, who discharge Reason from having any thing to do in matters of Religion, do not true Service to Religion: do rather pursue the Apostasy of the first *Adam*, and raze the foundations of God. For all the greater Rights, *majora jura, αἰώνια δίκαια*[29] are founded in Reason; are pre-supposed in Christianity, are acknowledged and reinforced.

1007. Religion *is not* a Hear-say, a Presumption, a Superstition; is not a customary Pretension and Profession; is not an Affectation of any Mode; is not a Piety of particular Fancy; consisting in some pathetic Devotions, vehement Expressions, bodily Severities, affected Anomalies and Aversions from the innocent Usages of others: *but* consisteth in a profound Humility, and an universal Charity.

1014. The more *Mysterious*, the more Imperfect: That, which is *mystically* spoken, is but *half* spoken: As Darkness is, in compare with Light; so Mystery, in comparison with Knowledge.

1023. As Sin is a Vitiating the Reason of Man; the Restauration must be by the Reason of God; by Christ, ὁ λόγος.[30]

1058. *Conscience* is God's Vice-gerent; Θεὸς ἔνοικος the God, dwelling within us.[31]

---

[28] Cf. above, p. 87, and see also Whichcote, *Discourses*, III, 449, and *Letters*, p. 118 (quoted above, p. 23).

[29] 'αἰώνια δίκαια, as *Justin Martyr* calls them, *Things Eternally Just*' (Cudworth, *Int. System*, p. 734).

[30] The reference to Christ as 'the Logos' is particularly meaningful to a platonising Christian since *logos* means both 'word' and 'reason'. More's comment is to the purpose: '*Logos, Λόγος*, The appellation of the Sonne of God. It is ordinarily translated, *the Word*, but hath an ample signification. It signifieth Reason, Proportion, Form, Essence, any inward single thought or apprehension' (*Democritus platonissans* [Cambridge, 1646], sig. Q3ᵛ).

[31] The closest precedent I could find is the reference of Hierocles to right reason as ἔνοικος θεὸς, 'an indwelling deity' (*Aur. carm.*, XI). Other terms

1069. The *Jewish* Church was not so under the Law, as not to be under Grace: and the *Christian* Church is not so under Grace, as not to be under the Law.

1104. The great Excellence of Christ's *Sacrifice* did consist in the Moral considerations belonging to it.

1118. We are *absent* from God; not by being *other-where*, than He is; who is everywhere; but by being *other-wise*, than He is; who is all Good: by a sensual Life, a worldly Mind, a wicked State....

1123. Take-away the *Self-conceited*; and there will be Elbow-room in the world. The Lesson given by Wisdom is Γνῶθι σεαυτόν;[32] and none have learned it, but the Wise.

1131. *Platonists'* principle of Creation, Ἔρως and Πενία· the Activity of divine Love; the Non-entity of all Creatures.[33] The grossest Errors are but Abuses of some noble Truths.

1181. To be *mischievous* to men, because of their Religion, will lie heavy upon men's Consciences; when they consider, How little Religion they had themselves; *when* they were not mischievous: And, if any die Martyrs; those, who put them to death, are Murtherers of the worst kind.

1182. Enthusiastic Doctrines—good things strained out of their Wits. Among Christians, those, that pretend to be *Inspired*, seem to be Mad: among the *Turks*, those, that are Mad, are thought to be Inspired.[34]

1188. Where the Doctrine is *necessary* and *important*; the Scripture is *clear* and *full*: but, where the Scripture is not clear and full; the Doctrine is not necessary or important.[35]

---

commonly deployed in connexion with conscience are noted in my *Milton and the Christian Tradition* (Oxford, 1966), p. 112.

[32] 'Know thyself.'

[33] Freely adapted from Plato's myth of the birth of Eros from Poros and Penia (*Symposium*, 203). Cf. Plotinus, III, v, 5 ff., and esp. Cudworth's interpretation in *Int. System*, pp. 122 ff. (I, iii, 18).

[34] See also the aphorism on 'enthusiasm', above, § 349 (cf. p. 330) and the Introduction, pp. 8 ff.

[35] Cf. above, p. 67.

Index

Aaron, Richard I., 132
Accommodation, theory of, 1, 146
Action, insistence on, 13*ff*., 108, 175, 198, etc
Aelian, xiv, 133
Aesop, 233
Aetius, 131
agape, 37, 204
Ahriman, 163
Alan of Lille, 36
Albinus, xiv, 3
Alexander the Great, 138
Alexander Aphrodisaeus, xiv, 321
Allen, Don C., 106
Ammonius Saccas, 3
Anaxagoras, 297, 298, 314
Anaximander, 314
Anderson, Paul R., xix, xxxii, 25, 30
Animal mechanism, 29
Anselm, St, 5, 10, 11
Apocalyptic thought, 40
Apocatastasis, 37, 195
Apollonius Rhodius, xiv, 300
Archeus, 26, 297, 303, 316
Archimedes, 216
Arianism, 33
Aristophanes, xiv, 134, 180
Aristotle, xiv, 3, 5, 6, 55, 57, 101, 135, 151, 179, 185, 198, 205, 229, 233, 271, 272, 284, 290, 291, 292, 295, 297, 298, 300, 301, 302, 307, 308, 312, 313, 314, 315, 316, 317, 318, 319, 320, 321
Arminianism, 22
Armstrong, A. H., 2, 37
Arnold, E. Vernon, 176
Arnold, Matthew, xix, xxxii, 32
Arnou, R., 1
Arrian, 138
Aspelin, Gunnar, xix, xxxii, 6, 27

Astrology, 22
ἀταραξία, 176, 194
Athanasius, St, xiv, 19, 38, 101
Atheism, 25*ff*., 35
   forms of, 323
   in Hobbes, 27*ff*.
   in Descartes, 29*ff*.
   More's 'antidote' against, 213*ff*.
Atonement, 5, 69*f*.
'Attic Moses' (Plato), 7
Augustine, St, xiv, 4, 5, 7, 19, 37, 38, 125, 146, 147
Austin, Eugene M., xxxi
αὐτάρκεια, 176
αὐτεξούσιον, 161, 166
   See also Free will

Bacon, Sir Francis, xiv, 137, 187, 332
Baeumker, Clemens, 36
Baker, Herschel, xix, xxxi
Baker, John Tull, xix, xxxii, 21
Baptism, 66
Barrow, Isaac, 39
Beach, Joseph W., 27
Beale, Mary, viii–ix, xxix
Beaumont, Joseph, 40
Beck, L. J., 218
Berkeley, George, 39
Bidez, Joseph, 130
Bigg, Charles, 1
Blount, Thomas, 83, 262
Boer, J. J. de, xxxi
Boethius, xiv, 124
Boyle, Robert, 30, 39
Brandt, Frithiof, 28
Bréhier, Émile, 2, 3, 18
Brett, R. L., 39
Browne, Sir Thomas, 32
Browning, Robert, 131
Bullough, Geoffrey, ix, xix, 4, 6, 9, 13

Bunyan, John, 8
Burnaby, John, 37
Burnet, Gilbert, 16, 39
Burtt, Edwin A., xix, xxxii, 12, 27, 31
Bush, Douglas, xx, xxxi

Cabbalism, 146, 186
Calvin, 4, 6, 19
Calvinism
  progress arrested, 40
Campagnac, E. T., xx, xxvi, 150
Candle of the Lord, 11*f.*, 18, 50, 197, 334
  See also Reason
Carbonara, Cleto, 2
Cardano, Gerolamo, 270, 271
Carré, M. H., xxxi, xxxii, 40
Cartesianism, *see* Descartes
Casaubon, Isaac, 7
Casey, R. P., 1
Cassirer, Ernst, xx, xxxi, 2, 17, 39, 40, 131
Catholic Church censured, 24*f.*, 86*f.*
Chadwick, Henry, 7
Chain of Being, 35
Chalcidius, xiv, 5
Charles II, xxix
Christ
  in history, 20*f.*
  as 'pattern', 15*f.*, 18
Cicero, xv, 5, 55, 96, 131, 133, 149, 151, 155, 158, 166, 216, 297
Circle, metaphor of, 36, 247
Clement of Alexandria, St, xv, 1, 7, 13, 41, 172
Cochrane, Charles N., 173
cogito ergo sum, 15
Cohen, Leonora D., xx, xxxii, 29
Coleridge, Samuel Taylor, xx, xxxii, 3
Colet, John, 2, 5, 19, 22
Colie, Rosalie L., xx, xxxi, xxxii, 22, 30
Common Notions, 26, 132, 138, 141, 149*f.*, 217*ff.*, 258, 304
Conarion, 240, 243
Conscience, 95, 235*f.*, 335
Conway, Lady, xxx
Cope, Jackson I., 32
Copernicanism, 39, 87, 238

Cornford, F. M., 3, 169
Corporealism, *see* Atheism
Cowley, Abraham, 28
Cragg, G. A., ix, xx, xxxi, 6, 13, 18, 33, 34
Crollius, Oswald, 262
Cromwell, xxix
Cudworth, Ralph, *biography*, xxx
  selections, 90*ff.*, 288*ff.*
  bibliography, xxxii
Culverwell, Nathanael, xi, xxvi, 11, 12, 144, 150, 187
Cumont, Franz, 130
Curry, Walter C., 26

Dalby, Joseph, 150
Damascius, xv
Daniélou, Jean, 1, 17
Dannenberg, Friedrich, 2
D'Arcy, M. C., 37
Degrees in nature, 35
Deification of man, 19*f.*, 70, 101, 167
Deiform, 18–19
Dell, William, 96
Demetrakos, D., ix, 180
Democritus, 27, 237, 314
Demos, Raphael, 3
Descartes, xv, xxx, xxxi, xxxii, 15, 29–31, 35, 218, 240, 246, 247, 291, 308
Diogenes Laertius, xv, 128, 137, 153, 297, 306
Dionysius the Areopagite, St, *see* Pseudo-Dionysius
Divine Sagacity, 13
  See also Reason
Dodd, C. H., 149
Dodds, E. R., 2
Dogmas, *see* 'Notions'
Donne, John, 3, 14, 22, 113
Dörrie, Heinrich, 3
Dryden, John, 27
Dualism, Cartesian, 30*f*
Dupréel, Eugène, 138

Empedocles, xv, 295, 296
Enthusiasm censured, 8*ff.*, 24*f.*, 43, 86, 89, 118, 229, 327*f.*, 330, 336
Epictetus, xv, 5, 109, 138, 140, 189, 197

Index

Epicureanism, 16, 27, 139, 140, 144
Epiphanius, 86
Erasmus, 2, 5, 22
eros, 37
Estienne, Henri, ix
Eucharist, 64*ff*.
Euripides, 198
Eusebius of Caesarea, xv, 4
Evil
    is multiform, 172, 179
    non-existent, 38, 113, 165, 328
Extension, 3, 220, 308

Faith and reason, 9*ff*., 140
Fall of Man, 22, 38*ff*.
Fate, 22, 335
Feibleman, James K., xx, 1, 3, 6
Feilchenfeld, Walter, 39
Ficino, Marsilio, xv, 2, 6, 15, 29
Finney, G. L., 36
Fonteyn, Nicolaas, 242
Forms, Platonic, 3, 26, 102, 187, 303
Fowler, Edward, xx, 8, 13, 14, 16, 39
Fox, Adam, 2
Free will, 20–3
Freytag, Georg W., 174

Gale, Theophilus, 7
Galen, xv, 278, 289
Galileo, 208
Gandillac, Maurice de, 2
George, Edward A., xx, xxxi, xxxii
Gibson, A. B., 31, 240
Gifford, George, 11
Gilson, Etienne, 3, 36
Glanvill, Joseph, xii, 31, 32, 293
Glover, W. B., 28
God
    αὐτόκαλον, 173
    'gaiety' of, 36
    glory of, 167*ff*.
    proofs of existence, 213*ff*.
    See also Goodness of Creation,
    Immensity of God
Golden Chain, 118
Good
    the Highest, 106, 171, etc.
    is uniform, 172, 179, 329

Goodness of creation, 36, 70, 106*f*., 169, 184, etc.
Grace, 150
    and Free will, 22*f*.
    and Nature, 10, 17, 21, 42
Greek Fathers, attitude to, 5, 22
Greene, Robert A., xx, xxxii, 9, 27, 31
Gregory, Joshua C., xxi, xxxii, 27, 30
Gregory of Nyssa, St, 17, 19
Gregory Palamas, 19
Grierson, Sir Herbert, xxxii
Gysi, Lydia, xxi, xxxii, 33, 161, 218

Hall, George, 11
Hall, Joseph, 11
Haller, William, 40
Harrison, A. W., xxxii
Harrison, C. T., 187
Harth, Philip, 2
Harvey, William, 305
Harward, Simon, 119
Heath, Sir Thomas, 218
Heaven and Hell, states of mind, 46, 50*f*., 113, 122, 170, 182*ff*., 192*ff*., 196, 327, 329*f*., 331
ἡγεμονικὸν, 131, 161
Hell, *see* Heaven and Hell
Henle, R. J., 5
Heraclitus, 296, 297
Herbert of Cherbury, Lord, 223, 331
'Hermes Trismegistus', xv, 6, 7, 36
Herndon, Sarah, xxxi
Hertling, G. F. von, 39
Hesiod, 209
Hicks, R. D., 138
Hierocles, xv, 5, 12, 19, 155, 335
Highest Good, 106, 171, etc.
Hippocrates, xvi, 297, 307, 316
History, Christian view of, 20
Hobbes, xvi, 27–28, 35, 38
Hollander, John, 36
Homer, xvi, 113, 116, 118, 209, 238
Hood, F. C., 28
Hooker, Richard, 2
Hoopes, Robert, xxi, xxxi, 13, 150
Horace, 5, 116, 236, 243
Hull, William, 22

Hunter, William B., xxi, xxxi, 26, 33, 293
Huntley, Frank L., 32
Hutin, Serge, xxi, 30
Hutton, James, 36
Hyginus, xvi, 300
hyle, 38, 323

Iamblichus, xvi, 1, 2, 4, 32, 135, 196
Ideas, Platonic, *see* Forms
Ignatius, 37
imitatio Christi, 15f., 18
Immensity of God, 34, 56, 158, 166
Immortality of soul, 29
Influence of Cambridge Platonists, 39f.
Inge, W. R., xxxi, 2, 19, 26, 38
Innate Ideas (Notions), *see* Common Notions
intellectus agens, 151, 185

Jacob, E. F., 12
Jacobs, Joseph, 162
Jammer, Max, xxi, xxxii, 31, 39
Jayne, Sears, 2
Jeffrey, John, xiii, 77, 326
Jerome, St, 5, 86
John Chrysostom, St, 86
John of the Cross, St, 17
John of Damascus, St, 38
John Scotus Erigena, 45
Johnson, Francis R., 115
Jones, Richard F., 187
Jones, Rufus M., xxi, xxxi, xxxii, 3, 9
Jordan, Wilbur K., xxi, xxxi, 40
Josephus, 8
Julian, The Emperor, xvi, 1–2
Justin Martyr, 335
Justinian, The Emperor, 1

Kant, 39
Kepler, 12
Kern, Otto, 293
Knowledge
 degrees of, 141ff.
 Divine, 128ff.
Kocher, Paul H., 12, 40
Koyré, Alexandre, xxi, xxxii, 12, 31, 39

Kristeller, Paul O., 6

Laird, John, xxi, 30, 33
Lamprecht, Sterling P., xxxi
Langerbeck, H., 3
Last Judgement
 imminence of, 90
Latitudinarianism, 39
Laud, William, 86
Law of Nature, *see* Natural Law
Lee, Umphrey, 24
Leibniz, 6, 39
Lichtenstein, Aharon, xxi, xxxii, 13, 17, 19, 40
Limborch, Philippus van, 22, 30
Literal sense, primacy of, 20, 186
Livy, 216
Locke, John, xxx, 16, 39, 132
Logoi spermatikoi, *see* Common Notions
Logos, 206, 335
Longinus, xvi, 181
Lord's Supper, 64ff.
Lot-Borodine, M., 19
Love
 God as, 36f., *passim*.
Lovejoy, Arthur O., xxii, 35, 39
Lowry, Charles E., xxii, xxxii
Lucretius, xvi, 231, 255
Luther, 4, 5, 17

McAdoo, H. R., xxii, xxxi, xxxii, 2, 13
Macarius, St, 19
Mackinnon, Flora I., ix, xx, 31, 212, 221, 222, 223, 226
Macrobius, 5
Marbecke, John, 177
Marcus Aurelius, xvi, 190
Marks, C. L., 39
Martineau, James, xxii, xxxii, 3, 15, 33, 39
Masham, Lady, xxx
Materialism, *see* Atheism
Mathematics, 12f., 136, 216f., 224f., 330
Matter, *see* Atheism
Melanchthon, Philipp, 79
Men, fourfold division, 141ff.
Mercy, 36f.
Microcosm, 154, 316

Index

Milton, John, 3, 33, 36, 62, 94, 122, 138, 147, 159
Mintz, Samuel I., xxii, xxxii, 13, 27, 28
Mitchell, W. Fraser, xxii, xxxi, 31, 34
μονάς, 172
More, Henry, *biography*, xxv
    poetry, xxv–xxvi
    selections, 200ff., 213ff.
    bibliography, xxxii
More, Sir Thomas, 2, 5, 22
Mosheim, J. L., ix, xxi, 305, 313
Mountains, 253
Muirhead, John H., xxii, xxxi, xxxii, 18, 28, 40
Mullinger, James B., xxii, xxxi
Munz, Peter, 2, 10
Music, metaphor of, 35f., 95, 117f., 124, 306, etc.
Mysticism, 16ff.

Nairne, A., xxxi
Napoli, Giovanni di, 29
Natural Law, 5, 46, 149f., 331
Nature
    and Grace, 10, 17, 21, 42
    Light of, 226
    Plastic, 26, 31, 288ff.
    Scale of, 35
    Spirit of, 26f., 290
Negative way, 17
Neoplatonism, 1ff.
Newton, xxx, 32, 39
Nicholas of Cusa, 12
Nicolson, Marjorie H., xxii, xxxii, 9, 25, 30, 31, 36, 39, 253
Norris, John, of Bremerton, xiii, 37, 46
Notions, censure of, 23, 66, 71, 96ff., 110, 128, 330
nous, 151, 185
Numenius of Apamea, 7
Nygren, Anders, 37

Occultism, 32, 286f.
Odingsells, Charles, 11
Ohrmazd, 163
Origen, xvi, 1, 3, 4–5, 19, 20, 32, 37, 38, 41, 130, 137, 196

Original Sin, 38
'Orpheus', xvii, 6, 293
Ovid, xvii, 178, 233

P., S., xxiii, 4, 6, 10, 13, 24, 39
Pachter, Henry M., 297
Panichas, G. A., xxxii, 17
Paracelsus, 297, 316
Pascal, 10, 30
Passmore, J. A., xxii, xxxii, 15, 25, 30, 38
Patrick, Simon, xxiii
Pauley, W. C. de, xxiii, xxxi, xxxii, 6, 13, 14, 15, 30, 38, 39
Pausanias, xvii, 143
Pawson, G. P. H., xxiii, xxxi, xxxii
Payne, Robert, 19
philadelphia, 204
Philo, xvii, 1, 3, 30, 137, 151, 268
Pico della Mirandola, Giovanni, xvii, 2, 4, 17, 19, 41, 130
Pinto, V. de S., xxiii, xxvi, 23, 36
Pistorius, P. V., 33
Plastic Nature, 26, 31, 288ff.
Plato, xvii; Intro., *passim*; 92, 102, 106, 130, 135, 136, 138, 140, 141, 150, 151, 152, 153, 158, 169, 181, 187, 201, 293, 295, 297, 298, 299, 302, 303, 318, 320, 321, 336
Platonic succession, 1ff.
Plotinus, xvii; Intro., *passim*; 98, 128, 129, 132, 134, 135, 136, 139, 140, 141, 142, 143, 145, 153, 156, 157, 169, 170, 172, 173, 180, 185, 197, 259, 295, 296, 301, 304, 306, 308, 309, 311, 313, 336
Plutarch, xvii, 140, 141, 155, 192, 295, 296
Porphyry, xvii, 1, 2, 3, 4, 35, 37, 152
Powicke, Frederick J., xxiii, xxxi, xxxii, 13, 22, 39, 43
Practice, insistence on, *see* Action
Preconception, 128
Predestination, 22
Prevenient Grace, 21
Pride, *see* Self-will
'Primitive theology of Gentiles', 6
Prior, Arthur N., xxxii
Proclus, xvii, xviii, 1, 2, 12, 20, 37, 153

Prophets, 15
Protagoras, 1, 138
Protevangelium, 20, 62f., 162
Pseudo-Aristotle, 292, 293, 317
Pseudo-Dionysius the Areopagite, xviii, 8, 13, 17, 34, 37, 146
Pythagoreanism, xviii, 6, 7, 135, 172, 173, 196, 205, 218

Quarles, Francis, 9, 12

Rahner, Hugo, 36
Ralegh, Sir Walter, 25, 284
Randall, J. H., 12
Rational mysticism, 17f.
rationes seminales, *see* Common Notions
Raven, Charles E., xxiii, xxxii, 27, 39, 187
Raven, J. E., 205
Ray, John, 27, 39
Reason
  defined, 12ff.
  and faith, 9ff., 16ff.
  in religion, *passim*. See also Candle of the Lord.
'Reason of things', 24, 43, 61, 326, 328, etc.
Religion
  defined, 72
  nature, properties, etc., 147ff.
  reason in, *passim*
Rich, A. N. M., 3
Right Reason, *see* Natural Law
Rist, J. M., 2
Robb, Nesca, 15
Roberts, Michael, xxxi
Robinson, John, 113
Rosenfield, Leonora C., 29
Ross, Alexander, 106
Ross, Sir David, 3
Royal Society, 34
Rufinus of Aquileia, 86
Rust, George, 3, 11, 36, 37, 132
Ryan, John K., xxxii

Sacraments, 64ff.
Sailor, Danton B., xxxii, 30, 291

Satan redeemed, *see* Apocatastasis
Saveson, J. E., xxxi, xxxii, 30
Scale of Nature, 35
Scaliger, J. J., 284
Schmitt, Charles B., 6
Schoedel, F. H., 8
Schroeder, Kurt, 2
Seaton, A. A., 40
Seed
  metaphor of, 20, 104, etc.
  Christ, 62ff.
  Word of God, 208ff.
Self-condemnation of sinners, 44ff., 329, etc
Self-love, *see* Self-will
Self-will denounced, 98ff., 156, 161ff., 183ff., 188ff., 330, 332, 333, etc.
Seneca, xviii, 142, 156, 174
Shaftesbury, Anthony, Third Earl of, xiii, 16, 39, 42, 62
Shorey, Paul, xxiii, 2, 6, 102
Sibbes, Richard, 9
Simplicius, xviii, 5, 18, 141, 143, 154, 157, 164, 166, 172, 173, 188, 194, 295, 296, 310, 318–19, 320
Sin, 38f., 44ff., 113
  'unnatural' to man, 49 326
  See also Evil
Smith, John, *biography*, xxix
  bibliography, xxxii
  selections, 128ff., 145ff.
Smith, Norman K., 31, 240
Snow, A. J., xxiii, xxxii, 31, 39
Socrates, 24, 134, 135, 187
Solitude of sage, 18
Sophists, 138, 187
Soul
  immortality of, 29
  pre-existence of, 32
Space
  and God, 31
  infinitisation of, 31f.
Spenser, Edmund, 138
Spirit
  and God, 32
  of Nature, 26f., 290
  and Space, 31
Spiritual and rational, 10, 21, 27, 41

Index

Spissitude, 31
Spitzer, Leo, 35
Sprat, Thomas, 34
Staudenbaur, C. A., xxxii
Steadman, John M., 106
Sterry, Peter, xiii, xxvi, 3, 11, 23, 35, 36, 38, 46, 118, 190
Steuco, Agostino, 6
Stewart, H. L., xxxi
Stewart, J. A., xxiii, xxxi
Stone, Darwell, 148
Strathmann, Ernest A., 25
Style of Cambridge Platonists, 33*ff.*
Subordinationism, 33
Superstition, attack on, 24*f.*, 61, 66*f.*, etc.
Swan, John, 119
Sweeney, L., 38
Synesius of Cyrene, xviii, 13, 35

Tatian, 7
Taylor, Jeremy, 15
Tertulian, 4, 11
Theiler, W., 2, 3
Themistius, xix
θεοδίδακτος, 59, 92
θεοειδής, 129, 166, 187
Theologia Germanica, 17
Theophrastus, xix, 268
θέωσις, *see* Deification
Theresa, St, 17
Theurgy, 4, 32
Thomas Aquinas, St, xix, 5, 149, 150
Tillotson, John, 16, 39
τὸ ἐφ' ἡμῖν, 197
   See also Free will
Toland, John, 16
Toleration, 40
Tollington, R. B., 1
Traherne, Thomas, 39
Trinity, Platonic and Christian, 33
Tuckney, Antony, xxvii, xxix, 9–12, 16, 20–1, 23
Tulloch, John, xxiii, xxxi, xxxii, 9, 33
Turner, John, 33
Tuveson, Ernest L., xxiii, xxxii, 15, 31, 39, 40, 90
Typology, 62

Underhill, Evelyn, 39
Untersteiner, Mario, 138

Vaughan, Thomas, 8–9
Vidler, A. R., 150
Virgil, xix, 5, 123, 265, 318
Virtues
   classical and Biblical, 14, 130
Vogel, C. J. de, 151

Wade, G. I., 39
Waith, Eugene M., 106
Walker, D. P., 6, 37
Warburton, William, 27
Ward, Richard, xxiii, 16, 22, 28, 161
Watkin, E. I., xxiii, xxxii, 25
Westcott, Brooke F., xxxi
Whichcote, Benjamin, *biography*, xxix
   selections, 42*ff.*, 62*ff.*, 77*ff.*, 326*ff.*
   bibliography, xxxi
Whitehead, Alfred North, 3
Whitehouse, W. A., 150
Whittaker, Thomas, 2, 12
Will, *see* Self-will
Willey, Basil, xxiv, xxxi, xxxii, 13, 31, 39
Williams, Henry G., ix, xxi, 133, 141, 174
Williamson, George, xxiv, xxxii, 24
Witchcraft, 32, 286*f.*
Wolfson, H. A., 1, 3
Worthington, John, xiii, 4, 16, 37, 46, 128, 144, 161, 173, 175, 200

Xenophon, 318

Yates, Frances A., xxiv, xxxii, 7
Yolton, John W., 132

Zaehner, R. C., 163
Zeal, *see* Enthusiasm
Zeller, E., 3
Zeno, 297
Zimmerman, Robert, 31
Zoroastrianism, 6, 130, 163, 295